Community
Mental Health

Loren R. Mosher, M.D., is Associate Director, Addiction, Victim, and Mental Health Services, Montgomery County, Rockville, Maryland, and Clinical Professor of Psychiatry, Uniformed Services University of the Health Sciences, Bethesda, Maryland.

Lorenzo Burti, M.D., is Associate Clinical Director, South Verona Community Mental Health Service, and Researcher, University of Verona Medical School, Verona, Italy

A NORTON PROFESSIONAL BOOK

Community
Mental Health

PRINCIPLES AND PRACTICE

Loren R. Mosher

Lorenzo Burti

W.W. NORTON & COMPANY · *NEW YORK* · *LONDON*

Published simultaneously in Canada by Penguin Books Canada Ltd.,
2801 John Street, Markham, Ontario L3R 1B4

Printed in the United States of America.

First Edition

41020 ◄

FEB 23 1989

Library of Congress Cataloging-in-Publication Data

Mosher, Loren R., 1933–
  Community mental health : principles and practice / Loren R.
  Mosher, Lorenzo Burti.—1st ed.
      p. cm.
  "A Norton professional book."
  Includes index.
  1. Community mental health services.   I. Burti, Lorenzo.
II. Title.
RA790.M62 1988
362.2′0422—dc19   88-19640
                                                           CIP

ISBN 0-393-70060-7

W. W. Norton & Company, Inc., 500 Fifth Avenue, New York, N.Y. 10110
W. W. Norton & Company Ltd., 37 Great Russell Street, London WC1B 3NU

1 2 3 4 5 6 7 8 9 0

To Dr. Piero Novelli and Professor Hrayr Terzian,
dear friends, esteemed colleagues, and sources of encouragement.

Foreword

PERSONALLY, I HATE FOREWORDS. I hardly ever read them (or only after having read the book), and I have never written one — until now. I hate forewords because in them somebody tells you how you should read and understand a book that somebody else, who certainly is more competent, has written. This is not fair. Let the author speak for himself! Listen to the author!

However, after having read Mosher and Burti's *Community Mental Health*, I accept the honor of writing a foreword for it with pleasure and grace. Because this is a wonderful book! It is exceptional, I think, in several ways. First of all, it clearly and understandably says so many things, grounded on elementary commonsense and humanity, which all of us who as psychiatrists or other professionals within the social field "know" or "feel" in some way, but without clear consciousness, so that we cannot fully use this knowledge in our everyday work with psychiatric patients. This book tells us, in great detail, how to translate our intuitions into clear, conscious, and operational understanding, and how to translate this new understanding into concrete day-to-day activities, into organizational structures, into precise therapeutic goals and approaches, and into adequate methods of evaluation.

Therefore, in my view, Mosher and Burti's work is not just a book on "community psychiatry" (or on "social psychiatry," as it is called elsewhere), but on "psychiatry tout court": It explains the context in which every kind of psychiatric intervention occurs, and it shows on this basis how this context should be utilized and structured to best meet the needs of our patients.

This book is also most welcome, because it presents a desperately needed complement — or rather counterpart — to the currently predominating technical, biological, and drug-oriented psychiatry. After a certainly too unilateral predomination of psychodynamic and sociodynamic concepts during the previous decades, contemporary psychiatry in the United States and elsewhere is, in fact, in danger of falling victim to another reductionistic "paradigm of understanding," namely the biological and medical one. Even though modern advances in understanding the biophysiological bases of brain functioning are certainly very impressive and promising, and even if it may be true, as Wilhelm Griesinger (mid-19th century German organic psychiatrist) said more than a century ago, that many illnesses or problems are essentially brain illnesses and brain problems, these brains and their disturbances still belong to a complete human being and take place within a global psychological, social, physical, and organizational context! The suffering individual, even when suffering from a "purely organic" disease, such as, for instance, Alzheimer's disease or brain injury, still needs to be perceived, understood, respected, and treated within this global situation. If not, he will be reduced to a mere disturbed brain function, to an anonymous "biological mechanism." In other words, his "psyche" — that is, the very thing the psychiatrist has to care for — will be neglected and destroyed.

This book tells us how to avoid such a danger by putting psychiatric patients and psychiatric problems into context. It is, therefore, a *"psycho-ecological book"* — and as such it is, I believe, a book of the psychiatry of the future.

Another fascinating aspect of this book is the fact that it represents an extraordinarily complete overview, as well as a synthesis, of the best and most interesting American and Italian experiences of the last 20 years in community psychiatry. In other words, this book is heavily grounded on experience. On the one hand, we have the personal experiences of the two authors, who for many years have worked within some of the most creative and successful projects of modern American and Italian community psychiatry. On the other hand, the book is firmly grounded on specific research; in fact, it probably represents the most complete and illuminating overview of the current body of Anglo-Saxon research and knowledge in relevant psychosocial issues available anywhere. And again, it not only provides a synthesis of the most important findings, but also translates and integrates these findings into down-to-earth measures and practical interventions.

Finally, the book is provocative: It challenges many deeply rooted beliefs and dogmas. Therefore, it will certainly provoke controversial discussions; many readers will (as I do) disagree with certain points or propositions, finding at times that the authors are too radical, that they go too far, or that they are in danger themselves of becoming reductionistic and unilateral on certain issues. Thus, this book certainly also has its limitations. After all, like any other treatise it reflects nothing but one aspect — even if it is a particularly interesting one — of the "current state of error" in our knowledge and understanding of psychiatric complexities and possible ways of dealing with them!

However, in my opinion this by no means prevents a very positive global evaluation of the contribution of the two authors: I hope and believe that Mosher and Burti's book will soon become a kind of "bible of the social worker," as Gerald Caplan's book on *Principles of Preventive Psychiatry** became more than 20 years ago. And I hope, too, that with its focus on practical issues and global psychosocial context, *Community Mental Health* will become an important element of perhaps the most important common task facing today's psychiatrists of all possible orientations: the task of constructing a truly realistic, multiconditional, biological-psychological-social model of the "psyche" and its disturbances, which will enable us to more adequately understand and treat our patients as real human beings!

Luc Ciompi, M.D.
Professor of Psychiatry and Medical Director,
Sociopsychiatric University Clinic,
Faculty of Medicine,
University of Berne, Switzerland

*Basic Books, 1964.

Contents

Acknowledgments

THIS BOOK WOULD NOT HAVE HAPPENED without a triumverate of wonderful women: Judy Schreiber, my best pal and helpmate; Arlene Frank, my indefatigable commenter/critic/editor; and Kiki Morton, magician of the word processor and "Can you find this?" I owe each of them deep, heartfelt thanks.

What are the origins of the concepts in this book? By now they're so interwoven that it's only possible to attribute certain domains to particular contexts and persons:

The influence of phenomenology and existentialism on my thinking began during my internship in San Francisco through discussions with Ludwig Lefebre (an existential analyst) and subsequently with Medard Boss (founder of Daseinanalysis) in Boston and Zurich, Leston Havens in Boston, R.D. Laing and Leon Redler in London.

Interest in an interpersonal understanding of very disturbed and disturbing persons and belief in the healing potential of psychosocial interventions I own primarily to experiences as a resident at the Massachusetts Mental Health Center (MMHC). Elvin Semrad, its late training director, imprinted me, as he did many others, with an abiding interest in trying to touch the seemingly untouchable patient. This book's interviewing chapter is an outgrowth of contact with this extraordinary teacher.

I was also introduced to research in a serious way at the MMHC. Milton Greenblatt, Gerald Klerman, Elliott Mishler, Martin Orne and Nancy Wax-

ler provided important role models. This early research experience was subsequently nurtured by Seymour Kety, William Pollin, David Rosenthal,
David Shakow, Margaret Singer, Jim Stabenau, and Lyman Wynne during
my two years at the NIMH intramural research program.

A year of study in London added to my research experience through
contacts with John Bowlby and Colin Parkes at the Tavistock Clinic, and Irv
Gottesman, James Shields, and Eliot Slater at the Maudsley Hospital. Clinical work at Anna Freud's Hampstead clinic, the Tavistock Clinic, and
Kingsley Hall (the Philadelphia Association's group living experiment in
East London) during that year broadened my horizons and introduced me to
the notion of nontreatment communal intervention—a notion that would
later be embodied in modified form in the Soteria project. Basically, that
year led me to decide that there were viable paradigms for understanding
and being with madness besides the medical disease one. As part of that
process I was also forced to examine, more critically than ever before, my
role as a mind policeman who involuntarily hospitalized and medicated
"mentally ill" persons. A number of the Philadelphia Association's members
(in addition to Laing and Redler) helped stimulate this process and provided
alternative conceptualizations from which I drew subsequently—Joe Berke,
Sid Briskin, Aaron Esterston, Morton Schatzman, and Anna Soldi.

Philip Epstein, Stanley Mayerson, Maurice Rappaport, and Julian Silverman, at that time all associated with Agnews State Hospital in San Jose,
California, offered important clinical and research experiences from their
"Blow Out" ward that helped guide the early development of the Soteria
project. A personal wisdom-enhancing long-term relationship with Con-
stance Hillis also evolved from that context. My NIMH pals, Sol Goldberg,
Martin Katz, Nina Schooler, and Sein Tuma, provided excellent research
design advice in the formative months of that project. Ann Reifman and
later Susan Matthews provided much needed data organization and analysis
skills. In the course of Soteria's 12-year life the project received so much
wanted and unwanted advice from research and clinical luminaries as to
make naming them all here impossible. However, Harrison Gough (U.C.
Berkeley), Jack Hilgard (Stanford), and David Rosenhan (Stanford) made
contributions for which I'd like to thank them. Of course, Voyce Hendrix
and Alma Menn made the whole project possible by routinely doing the
impossible—conducting logical positivist research in a phenomenological
setting! If only I'd had the wisdom to know in advance the incredible problems this paradox would cause. Manfred Blueler's unconditional support
over the years helped me weather the storms generated by the Soteria
project.

In 1977 I was fortunate in being able to help start Crossing Place, a
Washington DC version of Soteria House. Marilyn Kresky-Wolff and Edie

Maeda were instrumental in organizing and running this venture. Development of this new alternative to hospitalization came at a personally fortuitous time; a year before primary responsibility for the Soteria research data had been moved against my wishes from my NIMH office to the Mental Research Institute in Palo Alto, California. Crossing Place provided a new clinical and research facility in which I could continue to elaborate on the original Soteria model. It has continued to provide ongoing refinement and validation of my notions about the usefulness of residential alternatives to hospitalization. Pauline Bourgeois, Frank Kalibat, and the entire staff deserve special thanks for this.

It was in the early '70s, as chief of the NIMH's Center for Studies of Schizophrenia, that I first became aware of how abysmal most community care was for very disturbed and disturbing persons. The non-system dealing with them seemed more fragmented and disorganized than the persons for whom it was designed to care. Contacts with persons like Jerry Dincin of Chicago's Thresholds psychosocial rehabilitation center, Joe Fenton at the Federal Rehabilitation Agency, William TenHoor and Judith Turner-Crowson at the NIMH, and my involvement in the development and implementation of the NIMH's Community Support Program gave me the opportunity to begin to learn about, understand, and address community systems issues. Meanwhile, Washington based consulting to a psychiatric halfway house and apartment program provided useful experience with workable and effective pieces of a system. The entire Woodley House and apartment program staff provided me with excellent training. Later, the psychosocial rehabilitation piece was added to my armamentarium by the Green Door's dynamic matriarchy, mostly in the persons of Gail Marker, Ellen McPeak, and Judy Tolmach.

The family and systems orientation contained in this volume began in residency with Norman Paul's family intervention and Mishler and Waxler's innovative experimental approach. It continued at the NIMH intramural program through supervision and seminars with Irving Rykoff, Roger Shapiro, Helm Stierlin, and Lyman Wynne. Contacts and discussions with Gregory Bateson, Jay Haley, Cloe Madanes, Ross Speck, and many others have helped me formulate, define, and refine my views on families, networks and systems.

My co-author got me hooked on the Italian scene by translating the radical mental health reform Law, number 180, for me when the ink was barely dry. The Public Health Service and the NIMH deserve great credit for making possible my eight-month stay at the University of Verona Medical School to study Italy's new mental health system. Louis Wiencowski gets a special thanks for being so helpful in the process. Professor Antonio Balestieri was a most cordial host to me during my stay in Verona. Giavonni

Belanguer, Paolo Crepet, Bruno Orsini, Agostino Pirella, Antonio Slavich, Michelle Tansella, Hrayr Terzian, Giovanna Todini, Lorenzo Toresini, Paolo Tranchina, and Carlo Vetere provided me with invaluable opportunities to access the story of the Italian reform. In particular, Professor Terzian made it possible for me to meet the great Franco Basaglia shortly before his death. Franca Basaglia (his widow and senator from Venice) remains a dear friend, whose fingers seem always to be on the pulse of the reform.

The state of Virginia provided the finishing school for my notions of community mental health systems during five years of consultation. Two commissioners, Joseph Bevilacqua and Howard Cullum, placed this carpet-bagger in a whole array of community contexts. Karen Mallam and Leslie Tremain were extraordinarily helpful in briefing me for what I would face. Bob Vidaver, chair of psychiatry at Eastern Virginia Medical School in Norfolk, and Chris Mohring, formerly chief of Community Support in Richmond, provided excellent sounding boards and criticism of what I learned in their respective cities.

I owe a debt to the late Dick Price, Larry Telles, and the Esalen Institute for providing a wonderful setting for digesting, synthesizing, and reorganizing much of what's in this book through the annual "Alternative to Institutional Psychiatry" think weeks held in Big Sur, California. There isn't room to name everyone who contributed during these weeks but Dick Auerswald, Judi Chamberlain, Betty Dahlstrom, Steve Fields, Wade Hudson, Steven Mandiberg, Steve Rose, Ron Schraiber, Rae Unziker and Sally Zinman all made contributions that are woven into the fabric of this book.

Writing this book has been an interactive process; most chapters have been helpfully commented on, added to, and criticized by a variety of colleagues. Except for Richard Warner, medical director of the Boulder Mental Health Center and Richard Fragala, fellow U.S.U.H.S. psychiatry faculty member, they've already been mentioned in other contexts. Finally, I want to thank Harry Holloway, chairman of the department of psychiatry at the Uniformed Services University of the Health Sciences, for encouraging me to continue to pursue my interest in public community mental health — as part of my duties in the department.

It's particularly difficult to know how to thank all the patients who provided me with experiences I would translate into the clinical notions presented in this book. I look back with great humility on the state of ignorance with which I greeted my early psychiatric patients. I often wonder how they tolerated me. Nevertheless, to this day they remind me that each human being is unique. Whenever my eye begins to lose its freshness a patient will provide me with an awesome account of a life — one with twists and turns the like of which I've never heard before — and my eye is cleansed.

I only hope this volume is an accurate bottomup translation of their collective wisdom.

None of this would have been possible without my family — a mother who treasured and left me, a father who always expected I'd do well, brothers who tormented me into maturity, an uncle who was more than any nephew has the right to expect, a pediatrician who never labeled an almost dead measles encephalitis child as a vegetable-to-be, and a social network that had more holes than Swiss cheese — until it really mattered. My own children weathered foolish ambition, excessive travel, divorce, and too many moves. Despite all that they — and their mother Irene — can still tolerate their father's personal piccadillos without holding grudges. Thanks, and God bless you all.

— Loren R. Mosher

THE IDEAS EXPRESSED IN THIS BOOK primarily derive from practice in the exciting work setting of South Verona. Additional sources are the Italian deinstitutionalization movement and a number of fortunate encounters with exceptional people.

In particular, I owe much to Antonio Balestrieri, director of the Department of Psychiatry of the University of Verona, who first taught me clinical psychiatry, and continued to encourage my work and interests. His role in the passage of the Italian psychiatric reform is discussed in the book. I was introduced to research and inspired to go abroad for further training by Michele Tansella, director of the psychiatric register. His indefatigable drive in promoting community work and relevant research must also be mentioned. I am also indebted to him for the data on South Verona included in this volume and for reviewing the manuscript. Orazio Siciliani, clinical coordinator, has patiently supervised my clinical work and discretely corrected my mistakes. I learned much from his human qualities. I owe him my interest in phenomenology and in the humanistic approach. I am deeply grateful to Roberta Siani, who has been a peerless associate in all these years of professional, cultural and personal evolution, and an enthusiastic and inexhaustible coworker.

I owe team members I work with a thankful recognition for sharing practical work, expertise and human qualities. My professional and personal life would be gravely deprived without them. Thanks to Stefano Baratta, Paola Battistoni, Tina Bazzoli, Bruno Guerrini, Bruno Lorenzoni, Emma Nami, Luciana Perini, Sandro Ricci, Rinaldo Sassi, Cesare Turrina, Pietro Vantini. Many thanks go also to all the psychiatric residents who, over the years, have generously shared the clinical burden with unconditional enthusiasm. They have forced me to organize my ideas through the interactive process of teaching. I am also profoundly indebted to all my patients, who shaped the ideas presented in this book with their own life experience, suffering and courage. My professional work makes sense only because of them.

Concern about social aspects of mental health derive mostly from the Italian deinstitutionalization movement. It is impossible to mention all the contributors and I cite only a few: the personality of Franco Basaglia first captured me, as he did the rest of the audience, when I attended a conference in Padova in 1968. That impression returned on all the following encounters. I wish to remember also Franca Ongaro Basaglia, Giovanni Jervis, Agostino Pirella, and Paolo Tranchina. Lorenzo Toresini, a good friend since the times of medical school, has kept me always in touch with what was going on in Trieste and in Democratic Psychiatry. He made an important contribution to the ideas expressed in this book.

A year spent with the Soteria Project in Palo Alto, California shook my beliefs about madness and treatment and provided me with enduring professional and personal experience. The role of Alma Menn, the project director, was crucial in making it possible. She was an extraordinary guide, an unforgettable teacher and has been a dearest friend ever since. Kit Jepson, most dedicated clinical director of Emanon House, a replication of Soteria, was my sensible coach in the nuances of the healing milieu and kind of a big brother. All the members of the house, and project staff, shaped my experience and made me feel at home. I wish to thank them all. I am also indebted to the Mental Research Institute of Palo Alto, for its hospitality. In particular, Mary Ann Norfleet, Jules Riskin, Paul Watzlawick, and John Weakland added unique teaching opportunities in family and brief therapy. Vic Lovell and his psychodrama group, the late Dick Price, and the Esalen Institute substantially contributed to the experiential side of my sojourn in California. I am deeply grateful to the late Milton Erickson for arranging my visit to him in spite of a long waiting list. It was an encounter I will never forget. Meeting my co-author marked the beginning of an enduring and most fruitful cooperation and of a dear friendship. I am much obligated to him both professionally and personally. The University of Verona merits recognition for allowing and supporting my stay in the U.S. I wish to cite also Ira Glick for his valuable teachings and suggestions in the field of clinical psychiatry and outcome research.

The family and systems theory orientation referred to in this book derives mainly from almost a decade of training and supervision with Gianfranco Cecchin and Luigi Boscolo of the Centro Milanese di Terapia Familiare. I wish to thank also Giuliana Prata for her thoughtful professional help, and

Mara Selvini Palazzoli. Cristina Faccincani and Giancarlo Mignolli are invaluable family cotherapists. Interest in psychotherapy and introspective understanding was first aroused by a teacher in secondary school, Msgr. Aleardo Rodella, constantly revived by Roberto Pilla, long-time friend and sidekick in the search for a meaningful karma, and nourished by a number of the people already mentioned in other contexts.

Mark Spivak's unique approach to psychosocial rehabilitation has provided a framework that has guided my own views in this area. His influence in directing my interest to long-term patients and in shaping my clinical work with them was decisive. Jim Folsom also made a lasting impact on me for his rare skills and human qualities with difficult patients. I am indebted to Irving Blumberg, Robert Cancro, Carlo Lorenzo Cazzullo, and Ferdinando Pariante for involving me with different associations in the field of rehabilitation.

The writing of this book has been made possible by a number of people who provided information, data, comments and criticism. I wish to thank here those not already mentioned before: Domenico De Salvia for revising the data on the implementation of the Italian reform; Natale Calderaro, Luigi Ferrannini, Marco Lussetti, and Antonio Slavich for information and data on Genoa; Franco Domenici and Paolo Martini for Arezzo. Luc Ciompi, who agreed to write the foreword and was openhanded with encouragement, deserves a special thanks.

I wish finally to mention my family: my mother, who cared so much about me and sorrowfully left all too soon; my father, an internist, whose competent and compassionate approach to patients has always been an unattainable model to me; my stepmother, my brother and sisters, for their love and consideration.

— Lorenzo Burti

Preface: How This Book Came to Be

THE BIRTH OF COMMUNITY MENTAL HEALTH in Italy, and its rebirth in the USA, occurred in the early 1960s. One of us (LRM) received his psychiatric training (1962–66) contemporaneously with the passage of the CMHC act (1963) and its implementation two years later (1965 onwards). Although "social psychiatry" was part of residency training there were no community mental health centers in which to receive formal training. Hence, a fellowship year spent in London (1966–67) working part time at the Philadelphia Association's Kingsley Hall in East London was my first direct experience in this area. Before leaving for the year in London I had accepted a position in the Yale University department of psychiatry as a family studies apprentice researcher. Returning to New Haven from London in the summer of 1967 I found a department in transition from a traditional university research and training one to one that included a large, just completed, CMHC with the entire five-service array required by the federal legislation. At the same time the Viet Nam war was escalating. Doctors who had thought themselves immune from service were being called up by the still extant doctor draft. Several Yale junior faculty were so affected. Hence, upon my arrival in New Haven I was asked to run an inpatient ward in the CMHC whose chief was leaving to don a uniform.

During one of America's most socially tumultuous years (Viet Nam protests and King assassination riots, including ones in New Haven), I presided over a 20-bed inpatient service. Fresh from my London community experience I attempted to apply the principles I had learned there on this ward: No coercion (e.g. a voluntary, open setting); structure to evolve from the ground up rather than being imposed from above; presumption of personal responsibility; muting of roles and hierarchy; minimal numbers of rules; approaching patients from an interpersonal-phenomenologic stance, etc. Although located in a CMHC, before I took over, the ward had been organized like preexisting short-stay general hospital psychiatric wards in the New Haven complex. It was locked, had a highly structured milieu with a graded privilege system, and could select patients felt to be "appropriate." Most previously hospitalized psychotic patients were referred back to the large nearby state hospital. In fact, except for a brief stay (2–3 days) crisis residential service the CMHC was operated as an expansion of the existing university psychiatry department. Hence, this experience with "community mental health" did not, at that time (1967–68), represent much of a departure from practices I had learned while a psychiatric resident at the Massachusetts Mental Health Center (MMHC) in Boston. In fact, MMHC's 24-hour-a-day crisis walk-in service and its practice of holding individual trainees responsible for the ongoing care of all new patients they saw were more in keeping with modern community psychiatry concepts than most of what was done at the Connecticut Mental Health Center.

The open, destructured ward I created soon became a cause celebré within the CMHC and the rather traditional psychiatry department within which it was embedded. Some rather remarkable negative attributions were made to it, principally by psychoanalytically oriented senior department members. Old Eli was not ready to espouse a setting it viewed as a bastion of sex, drugs and rock and roll. From my 20-year later perspective it now seems that the ward, in addition to its deviance within the department, became a focus of, and a scapegoat for, many intergenerational concerns stimulated by that era of social protest.

That the attributions were largely unfounded became irrelevant. For example, one specific charge (the fight that evolved got legalistic as well as moralistic) was that the ward had "many more incidents" than similar ones located on the floors above and below it. Since incident reports were required to be written, and what constituted an incident was defined, it was possible to research this attribution. In fact, the ward had *fewer* incidents per patient day than the adjacent ones. As if the social attributions of deviance were not sufficient to marginalize the ward and its participants, medical treatment ones were added to the grievance list. Patients were "being encouraged to act out," staff were "not setting limits properly," and finally, it was suggested that the treatment patients received there "bordered on malpractice."

As a young relatively inexperienced person with little history in the department (hence few allies) it was difficult to have my views taken seriously or to deflect or confront meaningfully the scapegoating process that began to escalate. I decided to leave. Fortunately, I had won the respect of intramural researchers during my two-year tenure (1964–66) in the Section on Twin and Sibling studies (William Pollin, Chief) in the Adult Psychiatry Branch (Lyman Wynne, Chief) of the NIMH. Because of these contacts I was able to exercise a research option and joined the NIMH's rapidly expanding extramural research (grant review and funding) program. This provided a personal lesson in the usefulness of alternatives in times of difficulty. It is now reflected in the importance we accord to the availability of options within a community mental health service system.

I left Yale scarred, but convinced that the humanistic, flexible, consumer-oriented, empowering approach I had attempted there was correct — but had been applied in an inappropriate context. Clearly, attempting to do business in a very new way, within the bounds of an otherwise conservative company, could not work without the strong support of top management. Top management in this instance neither knew, nor trusted, this brash newcomer. I learned that either the hierarchy had to be strongly supportive or there should be no, or minimal, hierarchy associated with attempts at innovation. This lesson is reflected in this book by our commitment to small, relatively independent operational units with minimal hierarchies.

A year after my appointment as NIMH's Chief of the Center for Studies of Schizophrenia (1968) a fascinating grant proposal came across my desk. A group at Agnews State Hospital in San Jose, California proposed the creation of an experimental milieu that embodied many of the concepts I had attempted to implement on the ward at Yale. It was to be supervised by R. D. Laing (one of my London mentors), Fritz Perls (the well-known Gestalt therapist), and John Perry (a Jungian analyst interested in the treatment of schizophrenia). Intrigued, I went to California to discuss the project with its proposers. The original design contained no comparison setting and was turned down by the peer review process. The superstars lost interest. We (Julian Silverman, Maurice Rappaport and I) then developed a collaborative grant proposal that included a "usual" hospital treatment comparison group. Shortly after submission for review for funding the superintendent made clear that he could not support development of the experimental setting within the hospital.

That proposal was withdrawn and a new one, with a community-based setting outside any existing hierarchy, was proposed in its stead. What would become the Soteria project was born (1969–70). This collaborative grant eventually found an administrative home at the Mental Research Institute (MRI) in Palo Alto, California. MRI's innovative clinical track record (Bateson, Haley, Jackson, Watzlawick, Weakland, and others were associated with it at one time or another) provided a supportive context for the project. Soteria House was established in San Jose, California, in 1971. At last a proper administrative context, facility, and research and clinical staff had been assembled to test my controversial notions about the treatment of schizophrenia. A description of this community-based residential alternative to psychiatric hospitalization and its results are provided in Chapter 9. Although based at the NIMH in Rockville, Maryland, I initially had overall responsibility for the design and conduct of this research project in California. Unfortunately, after 1976 I was required to take a more peripheral role in the project. Absence of its NIMH "godfather" made the study more vulnerable to unwarranted criticism. A replication house (Emanon) closed in 1980 after six years of operation. The original house scraped by until 1983, when it too closed because of lack of funding.

After six years of work the project wanted to connect with other similar ones and present itself to a wider audience. My first direct contact with the Italian community mental health experience and Democratic Psychiatry (an alternative to Italy's equivalent of the American Psychiatric Association) occurred at the conference on Madness and Social Policy held in Palo Alto in the spring of 1977. Although I had heard of Basaglia's and Democratic Psychiatry's work for a number of years, I had never met any of the principals. While we shared a number of values and attitudes, the Italians were much more concerned with systemic issues and reform than was the Soteria Project. The conference provided an important opportunity for us to meet and exchange views. Partially as an outgrowth of this meeting a young Italian psychiatrist, Lorenzo Burti, came to spend a year working in the Soteria Project.

I (L. B.) first visited Soteria in 1976. Based on this experience I decided to spend a sabbatical year (November 1977–December 1978) with the project. I spent a great part of my stay participating as a volunteer in the everyday life of Soteria house and especially of its replication, Emanon house. This was an inspiring and unforgettable experience. I had the unique opportunity to both experience an unusual treatment setting and to temporarily give up my usual medical role and obligations and relate to the patients in a more immediate way. I was attracted by the phenomenological movement and had been looking for a humanistic approach to psychiatry. The Soteria Project embodied the ideas that had long fascinated me. I was particularly impressed by the high degree of freedom that a permissive, homelike milieu made possible, even with very disturbed patients off medication.

I was also intrigued by the degree of intimacy and caring and the real personal involvement of staff with patients. Life at Soteria showed that current ideas about the need for professional distance and neutrality in therapeutic relationships are questionable and context-related. Optimal distance, I concluded, is just a function of the therapist's ability to perform in human relationships at large and with psychotics in particular. It is largely determined by the surrounding milieu.

I was also struck by the idea that "being with," as opposed to "doing to," is the core of therapy. Life at Soteria made it clear that any technological add on, like an office-based psychotherapy, would be irrelevant. In fact, the whole context, the everyday routine, was the treatment. Traditional forms of psychotherapy seemed artificial and decontextualizing in that setting.

Before coming to the Soteria Project I had worked for five years as a psychiatrist at the Institute of Psychiatry of the University of Verona. In those days the Institute was composed of a 36-bed inpatient facility, an outpatient service, an emergency service and a liaison unit. Basically, it had the typical organization of a traditional university psychiatric department. However, faculty and staff had been influenced by the ideas and methods of the Italian reform movement and were evolving towards a psychosocial approach. Outpatient and community work were expanding. I was in regular contact with colleagues involved in the reform in Trieste. I was impressed by their ingenuity in finding down-to-earth solutions that allowed difficult mental hospital patients to live in the community. Their philosophical and political ideas were paired with a most effective pragmatism.

When I returned to Italy from California the new psychiatric law of 1978 (no. 180, see Chapter 12) had been passed. The Institute of Psychiatry of Verona had taken responsibility for a catchment area. This provided me with an excellent opportunity to put into practice what I had learned in the U.S. In addition, I had the opportunity to contextualize my personal interventions within a comprehensive network of services for a defined population. Home visits provided an ideal means of exploring the patient's environment. I had many occasions to experience the importance of basic needs on one side and environmental factors on the other (especially the family, neighbors, employer etc.) in precipitating and maintaining or ameliorating symptomatic behaviors. I came to understand better the therapeutic influence of social interventions in general and of welfare provisions in particular. More and more it became clear to me how important factors like long-term support to patients, a comprehensive approach to cases, teamwork, and attention to family dynamics were to achieving good outcomes. Family dynamics had interested me since the publication of *Paradox and Counterparadox* (Palazzoli et al., 1978). The book describes the systemic approach to schizophrenic families of the Milano school of family therapy (Boscolo, Cecchin, Prata, Selvini Palazzoli). My interest, and that of other Verona staff members, resulted in our obtaining training and clinical supervision from Dr. Cecchin for the past 10 years. A systems theory approach has proven as useful in community work as it was in a more traditional "one-way screen" setting. All these experiences, first collected and organized to teach medical students and psychiatric residents, became the raw material of my contribution to this book.

During his stay in California Lorenzo told me (LRM) of the law that had been passed by the Italian parliament in May of 1978. I could scarcely contain my excitement after I read his translation of the new law. Someone—an entire country—had finally bitten the institutional bullet; admissions to state hospitals were to be stopped! There soon began a series of negotiations that eventuated in my spending eight months in Verona (1980) studying the implementation and effects of this revolutionary law. As Chief of the Center for Studies of Schizophrenia I was involved in the development and implementation of NIMH's Community Support Program (1973–8). This experience gave me firsthand knowledge of the general lack of comprehensive community-based care *systems* for disturbed and disturbing persons in the USA. Hence, the authors' beginning collaboration in 1978 began at a propitious moment in a process of accretion that had begun more than a decade earlier for one of us (LRM).

The stay in Italy allowed me to devote my full attention to community care *systems*. Six months into my Italian stay I was invited to Scandinavia for a series of lectures. During my time there I collected information about their institution-oriented system and began to compare and contrast these (and those I had known in the US) with what I was seeing in Italy. The comprehensive care system described in Chapter 9 was first sketched out in a lecture given in Turku, Finland, in the fall of 1980. This was the nucleus around which this book was to take form some six years later. After my return to the U.S. I continued to follow personally the Italian situation. I relied on Dr. Burti and others for updated information. My Italian experience also began to serve as a dramatic contrast to the institution-dominated system I had been clinically involved within Washington, D.C., since 1972. I had helped found a Soteria House clone (Crossing Place) there in 1977. I had consulted with a supervised apartment program, halfway house, and a Fountain House model psychosocial rehabilitation program for a number of years. However, it was not until I began consultation with the Virginia Department of Mental Health in 1983 that the need for a comprehensive, systems and user oriented book on community mental health became apparent. While consulting with community-based programs around Virginia, it became obvious that a body of synthesized and summarized American and Italian experience relevant to their clinical needs would be extremely useful.

A symposium on training for community psychiatry at the 1984 APA meeting in Los Angeles (in which both authors participated) provided further confirmation that, in fact, there was a body of knowledge and experience in a new style of community mental health that needed synthesis and presentation. Although other commitments and initial concern about the viability of this project (mostly because of a general lack of interest in community mental health in the US) delayed our decision to go forward with it, this meeting was pivotal to the process. From the outset we believed it was necessary to provide readers with a method, a model of practice and extant program examples that embodied some or all of what we and others had found to be useful.

We were aware that community mental health workers were confronted daily with very difficult tasks and had often to draw upon an inconsistent set of knowledge and insufficient training to deal with them (Stern & Minkhoff, 1979). We thought that a book providing an up-to-date, consistent, and practical view of community mental health might rouse students' interest in community mental health and perhaps attract workers. The need for collecting and organizing existing material is also true in Italy where, in spite of a long tradition of deinstitutionalization and ten years of extensive clinical practice, a comprehensive model of what is currently done is lacking. A number of innovative patterns of intervention are well established, widely diffused and agreed upon, but hardly recognized as components of a comprehensive and consistent model. Paradoxically, traditional theoretical models tend to be referred to when trying to conceptualize these innovative practices.

In addressing these issues we were also intrigued by one specific aspect of community mental health: the basic *administrative* characteristics of community treatment. Accessibility of services and concern for the problems and *needs* of a given population provide an invaluable incentive for a more *humanistic* approach and for a more genuine encounter between the helper and the helpee, principally in the latter's natural environment. However, such a valuable opportunity may be lost if the system becomes too bureaucratic, uncoordinated, and/or fragmented. We decided therefore to address both dimensions, the administrative and the therapeutic one, convinced, as we are, that a more human *and* community-based psychiatry is not only long overdue, but also fashionable and *feasible*.

Our experience with, and commitment to, research on the efficacy of what we are proposing added the research focus that is apparent throughout this volume. We recognize that not all that we propose has been confirmed by research. We recognize that in some (many?) contexts our notions cannot be implemented without substantial modification. However, we ask that readers attempt to digest and integrate the gestalt of the volume before deciding on its applicability, or not, to their own settings.

Community
Mental Health

CHAPTER 1

What You Can Expect from This Book

THIS BOOK IS ABOUT THE HOW, not just the what, of community mental health. It is a practical, clinical book for community mental health practitioners, workers, clinicians, users, and families.

It is our intention to present an approach to community mental health that will bring together research and experience that have been shown to be both practical and effective. We believe that much more is known about effective community-based treatment than is currently acknowledged or implemented widely (see, for example Beiser, Shore, Peters, & Tatum, 1985, and Burti, Garzotto, Siciliani, Zimmerman-Tansella, & Tansella, 1986). Community mental health is not very fashionable in the U.S. at the moment. By way of contrast, it is mandatory in Italy. Its reputation in the U.S. suffers from attributions of having overpromised and not delivered, of being unscientific, of being dominated by nonphysicians, of being a major accomplice in the "failure" of deinstitutionalization, and most of all, of being ineffective in dealing with the most severely disturbed patients, except insofar as it fosters medication compliance.

These attributions, when seen contextually, become increasingly untenable. A movement that was funded in a way that achieved only one-third of its original aims (750 community mental health centers versus 2000 proposed) can hardly be held responsible for its "failure." Clearly, research into its effectiveness has not been highly regarded or funded. Hence, the question of whether it is "scientifically sound" remains, for a number of observ-

1

ers, largely unanswered. It is indeed currently dominated by nonphysicians who have come to power by default when psychiatrists left it wholesale for more lucrative hospital-based practices (Fenton, Leaf, Moran, & Tischler, 1984; Jerrell & Larsen, 1983; Knesper & Carlson, 1981). The present authors do not believe this nonmedical domination needs to be a problem. However, in practice, it tends to discourage M.D.'s from working in these programs because they don't have the power and control to which they are accustomed. As an accomplice in the "failure" of deinstitutionalization, community mental health's role must be seen in the context of the fact that money did not follow patients out of the hospital. As we will describe in subsequent chapters, there are a number of cost-effective community mental health programs in both the U.S. and Italy. The major difference between the two countries is that the numbers of good programs are increasing in Italy whereas this does not seem to be the case in the U.S.

Our experience, along with access to those of others, has engendered in us a much more positive view. We believe—and will set out "how to" principles to effect this belief—that the vast majority of disturbed and disturbing behavior can be effectively dealt with without the use of places called hospitals. We believe that the use of the person interacting with clients is a treatment that can be as powerful as, and have far fewer short- and long-term toxicities than, the drugs (principally neuroleptics) that are so overrelied upon currently. We will set out principles that will help maximize the usefulness of the person as a therapeutic instrument.

We believe that when madness is taken respectfully and seriously it is all too understandable. We will describe principles of interviewing and interaction that will facilitate the process of making madness meaningful. The degree to which an incomprehensibility zeitgeist exists about mad persons is mostly a reflection of the natural human and cultural tendency to wish not to have to deal with our own madness. Our willingness to incarcerate them in hospitals and our unwillingness to have them in our communities are concrete manifestations of this "out of mind, out of sight" attitude. We don't want to understand our own madness.

This zeitgeist is continuously reinforced by psychiatry's current "disease" orientation, which appears to be motivated by economics and its need for medical legitimacy. Thus, psychiatry's current energies are focused on a diagnostic system that lacks construct validity and that decontextualizes the person (Fenton, Mosher, & Matthews, 1981; Kendall, 1974; Kutchins & Kirk, 1986; McNair & Fisher, 1978; Mosher, 1978). The search for biologic causes and treatments related to this diagnostic system is the major focus of current psychiatric research. Psychiatry's power comes from the money it derives from treatment delivered in hospitals where, after all, "diseases" are traditionally treated. Roughly 16 billion dollars a year—70% of all mental health expenditures in the U.S. — is spent on inpatient care. These are places where, mostly because it is relatively cheap and effective in the short run, drug treatment is predominant. Therapeutic interpersonal interaction is given lip service but not frequently practiced. A pharmaceutical industry-psychiatry cabal has emerged. Drug 'em, slug 'em, easy does 'em. It is difficult to sustain and transmit a psychosocial treatment philosophy in places where a drug-oriented belief system is preeminent and patients stay only 10 to 15 days. This situation will likely be even more true as cost-containment pressures mount.

We believe that for too long theory has dictated practice rather than the other way around. Dogmatism rather than observation has prevailed. Until the mid '60s the most prevalent dictator was psychoanalytic theory. Today the dictator is reductionistic, antiquated, linear, cause-effect biologic theorizing. Excessive dedication to either results in major blind spots at best, and tunnel vision at worst, in the profession. The practices we espouse are ones that have been shown, pragmatically, to work. We have worked with what now, to us, seems to be a rather sophisticated but unarticulated theory. We hope this book will help articulate this theory for effective community mental health interventions.

This book is, in part, a response to our dissatisfaction with prevailing theories and practices. However, we view ourselves as responsible critics in that we offer viable alternatives to what we criticize. For example, psychiatry's current biologic orientation has strongly reinforced the practice of maintaining disturbed and disturbing people indefinitely on neuroleptic drugs. This has, in turn, created a new species, the tardive dyskinesic. Effective community treatment is made much more difficult when it is assured that most patients will eventually join this new species. They will, as a result of their psychopharmacologic treatment, be stigmatized by the impossible-to-hide, cosmetic disfigurement of tardive dyskinesia (T.D.).

It is especially painful to us that, in spite of a nearly 5% annual incidence in T.D. (i.e., in four years 20% of neuroleptic-maintained patients will have developed it) (Kane, Woerner, Weinhold, Wagner, Kinon, & Borenstein, 1984), it has become difficult to even raise the question of withdrawal or decreased neuroleptic dosage with psychiatrists presently in the public system. They have no experience with psychotic patients not on neuroleptics. For them not treating psychotics with neuroleptics constitutes malpractice. They fail to understand that more than two-thirds of schizophrenics recovered without drugs before they were available and that long-term outcome is no better today than it was before the introduction of neuroleptics (Bleuler, 1968; Ciompi, 1980; Harding, Brooks, Ashikaga, Strauss, & Breier, 1987a,b; Huber, Gross, Schuttler & Linz, 1980; Niskanen & Achte, 1972). We will describe programs that have successfully treated newly identified psychotic persons with little or no psychotropic medication. We will discuss how currently medicated, long-term clients can be weaned to either very low doses or no medication without substantially increasing the risk of relapse.

We are critical of psychoanalysts who provide important role models, instruction, and supervision to trainees who are treating psychotic individuals. They mostly fail to address in the supervisory process that which is most important to the trainee's patient – how, in the immediate situation, he has been failed by his family, his social network, and the social system. These concerns, as well as the practical, down-to-earth, questions of psychologic and physical survival, are treated as secondary or tertiary manifestations of an evolving psychopathologic process in the individual. Loss of ego boundaries, homosexual panic, overwhelming instinctual drives, symbiotic union, projective identifications, unconscious conflicts, transference distortions, etc., are discussed at length, despite reasonably compelling evidence that the application of these concepts in a psychotherapeutic process several hours a week with a person labeled schizophrenic offers no advantage over supportive reality-oriented psychotherapy (Gunderson, Frank, Katz, Vannicelli, Frosch & Knapp, 1984).

This exercise in therapeutic futility results in the trainee's feeling powerless and exploited. So, he reaches for what he knows he can do if he's a physician – labeling – and for what works – drugs – to restore his potency. Needless to say, if he becomes principally a psychotherapist after graduation he will assiduously avoid these helplessness-engendering disturbed and disturbing clients. This training failure has helped drive psychiatrists out of community psychiatry into hospital and private practice, where the real money and professional gratification are presumed to reside. We will spell out generic psychosocial therapeutic principles that we and others have found effective and that render their purveyors potent.

We are also critical of training programs whose major focus is biologic psychiatry. Although their students are well trained in the use of *DSM-III-R* and drugs, at the same time they learn to focus on the neurotransmitter level, leaving out the individual, his family, the community, and the wider sociocultural context. As a result, it is difficult for them to function in community-based programs. Not infrequently their training has produced in them an attitude that "you can't talk to disease." Ergo, patients with major psychotic disorders are seen only in terms of their medication status and responsiveness. Social factors in the production and course of disorder are given only token attention. As a consequence, they are therapeutically limited and, as is the case with psychoanalytic supervisees and psychotherapy, they feel powerless when medications don't result in an enduring remission. Since at least 40–50% of neuroleptic-maintained schizophrenic patients relapse over a two-year span without strong psychosocial programs, the likelihood of multiple failure experiences is substantial. It is not long before they become disillusioned with these relapsing patients and give them a "chronic mental illness" (i.e., hopeless) label.

This is not meant to eschew any possible role for biologic factors in disturbed and disturbing behavior. Rather, it is meant to highlight the fact that at the present time biologic factors are difficult to address therapeutically in individual patients. Unfortunately, training *in* the community for psychiatrists is not very available in either the U.S. or Italy. We described elsewhere a psychiatric program that does prepare psychiatrists for community-based work (Burti & Mosher, 1986).

As with psychiatrists, many psychologists are overcommitted to a particular theory (most often cognitive behaviorism) that dictates and confines, unnecessarily, what they can see in their clients and do in their work with them. With a few exceptions clinical psychologists have not dedicated themselves to the treatment of psychotic persons. They frequently head agencies that deal with this difficult clientele but don't deal with them directly. They too suffer from having few if any role models for this type of work. The excellent psychotherapeutic skills they've learned during their training are not made available to the most disturbed and disturbing patients. Our generic psychosocial intervention principles are largely derived from research in clinical psychology, in particular on various aspects of psychotherapy (e.g., Bordin, 1979; Frank, 1973; Gomes-Schwartz, 1978; Horowitz & Marmar, 1985; Luborsky, McLellan, Woody, O'Brien & Auerbach, 1985).

We recognize that, because they are not disease-oriented physicians and can't prescribe medications, psychologists tend to be deemed by the medical community as incapable of treating psychotic patients. They may also be prevented from doing so by insurance reimbursement practices and institutional rules. Hence, there are real barriers to their involvement with psychotic patients even if they would like to be.

We are critical of today's social workers. Oversimplified, their current training generally prepares them for one of two tracks—administration or office-based psychotherapy with the worried well. These are legitimate pursuits indeed, but where are the old-fashioned social workers who attended to the needs of whole persons? Mobilizing financial and other resources, environmental manipulation, and community follow-up used to be major foci of social casework. On the assumption that this work is less valuable, it is currently relegated to less talented or less well trained members of the profession. Thus, important potential helpers are kept away from the clientele that could well use their traditional skills. This is, of course, in part a response to social workers' facing the same problems described in the paragraph above for psychologists. This is an especially great loss, as it now appears that what is in fact *therapeutic* with this clientele is attention to their real life needs. In the context of a positive relationship, discussion of money, work, a place to live and friends is quite helpful. We believe our intervention principles will be highly relevant to the training of a new generation of social workers.

We are critical of nursing because, as a result of its ever growing need to learn new hospital-based procedures and techniques, it has lost much of its time-honored interpersonal caring focus. In fact, in the U.S.A. (in contrast to Italy), nurses are not well represented in community mental health programs. With the exception of public health nurses, they are usually not well prepared to work in the community. Their psychosocial skills have become much less valued and remunerated than their technical ones — as is the case with medicine in general. Again, our psychosocial principles can be profitably utilized by nurses. Unfortunately, they suffer, as do all the mental health professions, from a lack of role models and financial incentives for community mental health nursing.

The training process we have described (Burti & Mosher, 1986) provides the skills needed to address the particular psychologic, interpersonal, and social environmental needs of very disturbed and disturbing persons. It is basically an apprenticeship model with ongoing multidisciplinary supervision from experienced, dedicated role models. Although it refers specifically to the training of psychiatrists, we believe that with modifications to suit local circumstances and added special training for subgroups (e.g., in hypnotherapy for psychotherapy specialists) this type of training program is relevant to all the mental health professions that provide community mental health staff.

Thoughtful readers will by now recognize an emerging paradox: Having said we would present a new and more positive and hopeful view of community mental health, we have begun by calling the relevant professions and the contexts within which they work — especially hospitals (see Chapter 4) on the carpet — a not very positive act. The critique is necessary to provide us with a jumping-off point, as well as background and rationale for why we do things as we do. Although our theoretical stance, insofar as we have one, is an interpersonal phenomenologic one, our day-to-day practice has also been strongly influenced by the family therapy movement. We use, on a daily basis, a number of concepts and practices that are associated with this group. An open systems view; contextualization; reframing; use of analogy, metaphor and paradox; always thinking and acting, if possible, in family and social network terms; working with, and in, the social system as it is configured in the community — these are basic tenets that guide our work. Hence, the reader can expect that these concepts and practices will recur with some frequency.

Another basic principle underlying our work is a commitment to semantic simplicity. What we espouse is mostly commonplace and commonsense. We want our language to describe what we do in everyday, jargon-free terms. We do not want to be set apart from the people with whom we deal by our language; rather, we want this volume to be easily understandable to anyone who reads it. We do not have a new theory. We are not attempting to start a new "school" or "institute" or "center" that must define itself through its particular language or therapeutic approach. In fact, nothing in this book is really new. Rather, it is the result of re (again) search (looking). We believe that a great deal of mischief has been created in the lives of unsuspecting madpersons who have been set apart, and then stigmatized, by widespread jargonism—whether biologic, psychoanalytic, behavioristic, or what have you.

For us, a critical attribute of good community mental health workers is their ability to communicate in everyday, colloquially and contextually appropriate street language—that is, to tailor a very clear and relatively simple language to the interpersonal, cultural, ethnic, and religious circumstances in which they find themselves. To help trainees learn this skill we ask them to imagine themselves in a foreign country engaged in a very important conversation with someone who has only rudimentary skill in their language. To be understood they must communicate mostly in the present tense, with simple declarative sentences, using the simplest vocabulary possible. We also encourage them to listen carefully to how this foreigner consistently misuses English language construction and to try to change their own sentence structure to conform to the pattern of misuse and thereby improve their understandability to the other party. Mutual understanding is vitally important to what we do.

Another overarching principle guiding our work is that it is, insofar as possible, client/user/patient-centered. We use this complex slash phrase to indicate that what we espouse should be useful in whatever context the person seeks help; different contexts use different helpee designators. As will be seen in Chapter 3, our principal starting point is, whenever possible: What does the customer want? Lazare and colleagues have written eloquently on this approach (Lazare & Eisenthal, 1979; Lazare, Eisenthal & Frank, 1979). It is from this perspective that we have designed programs. Insofar as possible, program needs take a back seat to client needs. For example, we do not agree with the predetermined lengths of stay so commonly found in community-based transitional residential programs because they are determined by *program* and fiscal, rather than *client*, needs.

Having experience with and knowledge of needs that are at best peripheral to the needs of the help seekers, we acknowledge the validity of such needs. We know that people must be trained for community mental health work and that they must be trained in real life work places. However, this training need must not be met at the expense of the persons for whom the program is designed. In our experience valid needs like training too often become institutionalized. In extreme cases the program comes to exist to meet those needs, rather than the needs of the clients.

The institutionalization of organized ways of addressing nonclient programmatic needs is usually inevitable. This fact of institutional life can't be avoided, but it need not be counterproductive if it is explicitly acknowledged and its effects on client care carefully thought through and made explicit. This process must be addressed frequently, because it is very easy for nonclient-oriented needs to grow unwittingly until they consume a disproportionate amount of many people's time and energy—a price paid by the help seekers without knowing it. To reiterate: Both effective treatment and training can be done in the patients' own territory based on how they define their needs. Institutions like hospitals are not required for this process.

As the above comment suggests, a lot of what we have to say is simply common sense. As this fact became clear to us, we began to wonder: Why are we writing such a volume? Shouldn't most of what we have to say be obvious to any thoughtful person? Yes, it should be, but no, it has not been our experience that common sense is highly valued and reinforced in most community programs. It is even less so in large, institution-based programs. Somehow there is a prevailing ethos about dealing with madpersons that demands the suspension of common sense.

In addition to its client-centered focus, our approach is different from many in its emphasis on what's *right* rather than what's *wrong* with the client. Psychiatry's current obsession with how many Schneiderian symptoms can dance on the head of a schizophrenic is one that our experience has taught us is mostly antitherapeutic in its induction of a we/them separation. Preoccupation with psychopathology has a number of adverse effects: It parades clients' perceived failures in front of them continually. Demoralization, low self-esteem, being down on one's own case are usually the reasons people seek help. Given this, it does not seem very sensible to us to focus the potential helper's attention primarily on these basically negative attributions. The current practice of focusing on symptoms in the individual in order to arrive at a diagnosis is to decontextualize, dehistorify and depower the individual. The person's gestalt is lost. It also results, largely because it takes place in the zoo (office) instead of the jungle (the community), in a thrust toward separating persons from their worlds. This separation, as reinforced by the treatment system, is the source of stigmatization. This separation, when repeatedly experienced, gives a clear message: "We are not ready to attend to your whole person in the world in a serious way." Confirmation of part-human status is an experience reported to us by clients with an alarming frequency.

A psychopathologic focus also has an invidious effect on the diagnoser. The special technical language of diagnosis both separates the labeler from the labeled and provides an *illusion* of understanding. Unfortunately, our present diagnostic system has arbitrarily decided to act *as if* factors that are not directly related to personal psychopathology, such as where the person is seen, race, socioeconomic status, etc., do not influence the assessment of psychopathology. Hence, the knowledge we have that could mitigate some of the deleterious aspects of the diagnostic process by forcing it to include the assessment of context are *excluded* from the current diagnostic practice and from training for it. The pain that medical students experience from wrestling with *DSM-III* is something to behold. They seem to forever be trying to squeeze a round peg into a minutely defined square hole—with predictable confusion.

Although we are critical of the diagnostic process as currently practiced, we recognize that such categorizations may be helpful for recordkeeping, research and communication with other settings. Our perspective is that diagnosis is of limited utility (when trying to help a real patient) and, if overfocused on, a serious impediment to being helpful. Its most pernicious effects are on the relationship between helper and helpee. The distancing that the diagnostic process engenders can preclude the establishment of rapport—the sine qua non of being helpful. Today's psychiatry in particular seems bent on increasing its distance from its customers if the preoccupation it has with diagnosis is any guide—and we believe it is. To label is to pigeonhole and dispense with; unfortunately the labels don't say much about that which is most troubling and important to the person.

The principles and practices described in this volume are derived from our experiences with that large subgroup of mental health problems conventionally categorized as "functional mental illnesses." This includes persons for whom hospitalization or medications are not viewed as central to treatment, but who are still quite dysfunctional (e.g., personality disorders), those for whom rather effective drug treatment is available (e.g., schizophrenia, bipolar disorder), and children and adolescents. We do not consider ourselves qualified to apply these to the other subgroups among the "mental illnesses," e.g., primary substance abuse, organic mental disorders, and forensic problems. In each of these areas culturally specific, specialized approaches have been developed to deal with patients with these conditions. They will not be addressed here except to acknowledge they must be recognized so they can be referred appropriately. However, many of the principles we use are ones that are, or could be, used in these special situations.

We do not intend this book to be antipsychiatric. We do intend it to be critical of those psychiatrists who have become excessively enamoured of the "bio" part of a socio-psycho-biologic model. Labeling as "antipsychiatrists"

those of us who have retained a commitment to *the practice* of a psychosocially oriented brand of mental health care is a convenient form of invalida-
tion that allows for disregard for this perspective. We eschew this label.
What we espouse is what Manfred Bleuler called "the best type of psychiatry
I can think of" (Bleuler, personal communication, 1975) — humanistic, caring, thoughtful, empathic, and oriented to the care of the whole person.

We intend to provide readers with a readily understandable set of principles that will enable them to talk with, assess, understand, and develop
collaborative goals with disturbed and disturbing individuals. We hope to
provide nonconfining recipes to chefs who will use them innovatively rather
than prescriptively.

We acknowledge that a portion of what we propose will not fit well with
current conceptions and practices, especially in the U.S. However, we ask
that readers, before rejecting them, first try to understand and put our
principles into practice. Let their applicability, not their fashionability, be
their test.

Context

CHAPTER 2

The Ups and Downs of Community Mental Health in the United States

THE UNITED STATES HAS HAD TWO PERIODS of community psychiatry: the era of "moral treatment" (1740–1840) and 1963 to the present (see Barton & Sanborn, 1977; Beigel & Levinson, 1972; Bellak, 1964, 1974; Caplan & Caplan, 1967; Langsley, 1980, 1985; Langsley, Berlin & Yarvis, 1981; Serban, 1977; Zusman & Lamb, 1977).

The era of "moral treatment," based on transcendentalist philosophy, and its demise have been ably documented (Bockoven, 1963; Grob, 1973, 1983; Rothman, 1971, 1980). This kind and compassionate form of care, emphasizing mutual responsibility, worked well in the small, relatively homogeneous, New England protestant communities of that era. Unfortunately, massive immigration resulted in rapidly growing urban centers that were unable to apply these principles to the expanding, heterogenous, socially disorganized, communities of post-1840. Interestingly, the situation is much the same today as it was then; good community mental health systems are difficult to implement in rapidly growing megalopolises.

In contrast to Europe, where leprosaria could be converted into asylums (Galzigna & Terzian, 1980), beginning in the 1840s the U.S. built a totally new set of institutions for madpersons. These "new" institutions — ones that plague the U.S. mental health system to this day — began as Dorothea Dix's humanistic response to the misery she encountered in urban almshouses of that era (1840 onward). Madpersons, paupers, prostitutes, criminals and unintelligible foreigners were mixed together in these degrading settings.

13

However, it was not long before this "reform" had become principally a means of segregating the less attractive (mostly foreign immigrants) and the less competent (mostly the unemployed) from the rest of society. Large numbers of Mediterranean immigrants, exploitative roller-coaster capitalism, and the impact of the philosophy of social Darwinism provided reasons enough to justify disenfranchising and marginalizing so-called madpersons in custodial asylums. After all, they were clearly not the "fittest," hence their survival was of only marginal utility to the society. This attitude led to widespread neglect of public mental hospitals for more than 70 years (1880–1950) (Grob, 1983; Lamb, 1979).

Clifford Beers' *A Mind That Found Itself* (1939), recounting his experiences in Connecticut mental hospitals and his eventual successful self-help approach to his madness led to the development of mental health associations and child guidance clinics that were an early form of community mental health. At about the same time (1909), Adolph Meyer espoused a community-based approach to mental health problems. Unfortunately, neither of these events had any real impact on the state hospital system.

It was not until Deutsch's *Shame of the States* appeared, in 1948, with its exposé of the terrible conditions that existed in these institutions, that a true reform movement began. A number of powerful American Psychiatric Association members convinced the organization that it should spearhead a reform movement to correct the conditions Deutsch had described. The APA was in turn able to obtain the AMA's collaboration in this effort; hence the formation of the Joint Commission (APA and AMA) on Mental Health in 1956. In fact, there were ultimately 36 organizations represented on the Commission.

Interestingly, the Commission's recommendations (1961), were actually quite similar to those made a century earlier by Dr. John Galt (1819–62), the superintendent of Eastern State Hospital in Williamsburg, Virginia. He proposed in 1857 that the patients in his care be let out of the hospital to live and work and be cared for as necessary in a variety of community-based facilities! Galt believed his proposal would be the third revolution in psychiatry—the first being Pinel's unchaining of the insane and the second the development of humane care à la Tuke in England. More than a century later Bellak (1964, 1974) would call community mental health psychiatry's third revolution!

Galt, one of 12 founders of the Association of Medical Superintendents of American Institutions for the Insane, the forerunner of the American Psychiatric Association, correctly anticipated that his proposal would not find favor among his powerful hospital superintendent colleagues. Galt was working from the position of success; witness the ad (reproduced as Figure 2.1) he placed to attract middle- and upper-middle-class patients from other

To the friends of the Insane.

THE Directors of the Virginia Lunatic Asylum, at Williamsburg, would inform the public of the Southern States that, by a recent law of the Legislature, they are empowered to receive insane patients, paying board, from other States. This is the oldest Institution of the kind in the Union, having been founded by the Colonial Government in 1769; and is, from its location, best adapted for Southerners, being removed from the piercing cold of the North, and from the enervating heat of the South. Its curative capacity is of the highest order: nine out of ten cases recover, if received within the first six months of the disease. It is easy of access, as steamers daily stop at a wharf not far from the Asylum. The modern treatment, upon the non-restraint system, is in successful operation. The apartments admit of classification of patients according to their state of mind, and also a complete division of the classes of society. The fare is excellent, and the board $4 per week. We have neat bed-rooms, a parlor tastefully furnished with curtains, carpet, sofa, centre-table, ottomans, mirrors, books and a piano: airy verandahs for summer retreats; an extensive enclosure for evening rambles; a carriage for morning and evening rides; a reading room furnished with books and newspapers; and moreover various means of amusement.— A Chaplain resides in the building and preaches to the patients every Sabbath. Letters of inquiry should be directed to Dr. JOHN M. GALT, Physician and Superintendent of the Eastern Asylum, Williamsburg, Virginia.

March 14, 1846.

Zwelling, 1985, p. 49.

FIGURE 2.1
Newspaper Advertisement.
During the 1840s the hospital began a publicity campaign to attract middle-class, paying patients. This statement appeared in a Florida newspaper.

parts of the country: Wouldn't we like to be able to advertise a 90% cure rate of hospitalized cases with onsets within the previous six months? How many of today's inpatient units would guarantee nine of ten newly identified psychotic patients would be well and functioning without neuroleptic or lithium treatment after six months to one year of hospitalization? Unfortunately, the tides of history washed over Galt's radical proposal before he could implement it. At that time abolition of slavery was of much greater concern than emancipation of the insane. Galt, a confederate loyalist, killed himself following the Union's capture of Williamsburg in the spring of 1862. Although he was only 43, he had been its superintendent for 21 years. To this day Galt's then-radical proposal has received scant attention in the community mental health literature.

The Joint Commission's report is said to have been read cover to cover by President John Kennedy at the urging of his sister Eunice (Jack Ewalt, M.D., personal communication). His enthusiasm for change in the mental health system culminated in a special message to Congress on mental health in February 1963. The legislation authorizing a federally funded system of CMHC's was passed in October 1963 (PL 88-164).

The original bill, in circumventing states in the establishment of this federal program, represented a dramatic violation of traditional federal-state relationships. Basically, since President Pierce's 1854 veto, on constitutional grounds, of legislation that would have provided federal support for care of the indigent insane, the care of the mentally ill had been left the exclusive perogative of the states. This new federal support for the care of mentally disordered persons, rather than adding to state support, created a parallel and sometimes competitive care system organized by individual locales. In hindsight, this may have been a fatal error for a program with built-in phasedown of federal support. Why should states pick up the tab for a program in whose design and implementation they had had little or no role?

Passage of this legislation resulted in the transformation of the National Institute of Mental Health, one of the traditional research and training-focused institutes of the National Institutes of Health, into an organization with a third functional leg, i.e., service. The CMHC program put the NIMH in the position of directly underwriting payment for a form of "medical" treatment. It was not long, in terms of dollars, before the CMHC tail began to wag the NIMH research and training dog. In 1967, this new functional and fiscal reality led to the NIMH's being formally split off from the parent NIH and given a new administrative status. Many interested parties opposed this move as scientifically and bureaucratically unwise, believing the NIMH would be too exposed politically without the NIH's protective high-science umbrella. However, in times of prodigious growth and prosperity, the more-and-bigger-is-better philosophy is difficult to contain. In retrospect, the critics may have been correct, as the organization has often been politically buffeted. Even now, 20 years later, the National Alliance for the Mentally Ill has mounted a major campaign to move the NIMH back to being an NIH institute.

The CMHC program made the NIMH an administrator of a federally subsidized treatment system for a subset of the "ill." We presume the implication that this was a liberal venture into socialized medicine was either missed or muted by congressmen and bureaucrats alike as a consequence of the political context of that era. However, given this country's generally ambivalent attitude toward supporting the disenfranchised, it is not surprising that the legislation for this program would be repeatedly modified (see Foley & Sharfstein, 1983, for a complete account). Although Congress kept trying (the legislation was amended *seven* times in 12 years), no one is really sure whether it ever got it right.

The summary objectives of this series of legislative mandates were community mental health centers that would be:

1. Comprehensive; that is, provide inpatient, outpatient, emergency, partial hospitalization and consultation and education services;
2. Accessible and available (24 hours) to all residents of a limited geographical area regardless of ability to pay;
3. Coordinated with other relevant agencies;
4. Able to provide continuity of care; and
5. Emphasizing prevention through consultation and education with agencies and the public.

In a sense, this program obeyed a basic psychological law: the greater the ambivalence about something, the greater the number and types of unrealistic expectations and unsupportable attributions attached to it. The Nixon administration's wish to close out the CMHC program (by giving it to the states) because it was "successful" represents a particularly interesting example of this phenomenon.

The culmination of this program as a social movement was the passage of the Mental Health Systems Act of 1980—a law based in large part on what had been learned from the CMHC program and its spinoffs. This generally enlightened piece of legislation was repealed in the Omnibus Budget Reconciliation Act of 1981, as part of the Reagan administration's efforts to reduce domestic spending. It was replaced, in reduced dollar amounts, by block grants to the states. This change restored the traditional federal-state relationship the program had violated. Seven hundred and fifty or so of the 2000 CMHC's originally envisioned were in operation at that time.

As if it saw the handwriting on the wall for its control of the CMHC program, the NIMH began its Community Support Program (C.S.P.) in 1977. Its origins are best described as personal constructs of a few well placed individuals who then recruited support for them from the field at large (see Mosher, 1986). The Community Support Program did what the CMHC's never had; it moved the programmatic focus of interest from facilities and services in them (i.e., CMHC's) to support networks for individual clients. From the outset it worked directly with state mental health agencies (in contrast to the CMHC program). It is a program whose views promote decentralized, debureaucratized care and force a *systems view* on community mental health. C.S.P. continues to be under the direct control of the NIMH. The 10 elements of a community support system (Turner & Ten Hoor, 1978) (Table 2.1), despite a lack of theoretical cohesiveness and the fact that they mix treatment and nontreatment variables, have come to be widely accepted as the constituents of "good" community programs. The Community Support Program's conceptualizations serve as guidelines for community mental health program development throughout the U.S. CMHC block grant money may be used for their implementation. Because of its attention to political realities, the program has also generated a great deal of state support. Its philosophy has spread, despite the small amounts of federal money it has had to spend, because of frequently convened mega-meetings with representation of all interested parties—from clients to state mental health department heads. Interested readers are referred to *A Network for Caring* (1982) and Stroul (1986, 1987) for more detailed information about C.S.P.

The Community Support Program currently has a new carrot to offer states—money to develop state-wide plans for dealing with the long-term users of the system. The model plan the NIMH (1987) has put together is a good one; what will come of all this remains enigmatic. One major problem

TABLE 2.1
Community Support System Elements

1. Responsible *team*
2. Residential care
3. Emergency care
4. Medical care
5. Halfway house
6. Supervised (supported) apartments
7. Outpatient therapy
8. Vocational training and opportunities
9. Social and recreational opportunities
10. Family and network attention

From Turner & tenHoor, 1978.

with the legislation and the model plan is that both accept as inevitable the notion of large numbers of persons with prolonged mental disorders. For us, a properly organized and operating community system ought to produce fewer and fewer long-term clients by progressively decreasing its use of larger institutions in favor of small, home-like, community-based, normalizing ones.

A status report on the state of community mental health in the U.S. today is difficult. There are some relevant facts: About 750 of the 2000 CMHC's proposed are in operation. About one-quarter of the population of the U.S. has access to one. All 50 states have C.S.P. grants. In 1983 there were still about 130,000 patients in total institutions (Goldman, Adams, & Taube, 1983). It appears, overall, that the public mental health system has gotten the C.S.P. message. Psychosocial rehabilitation, supported (supervised) apartment programs, and case management are C.S.P. promulgated notions that have caught on and are growing in popularity and availability. Residential alternatives to hospitalization, neuroleptic-free treatment of psychosis, and the therapeutic importance of psychosocial interventions are notions that have not been as readily accepted. Medical domination, by siphoning off limited resources to support in-hospital care, continues to impede the development of the proper smorgasbord of psychosocially oriented community-based facilities. We believe that, although the medicalization of madness is clearly an excellent survival strategy for psychiatry, its disease-in-the-person orientation does not optimally serve the interests of users. A family and systems orientation seems a clearly more useful one for community mental health.

CHAPTER 3

The Context of Public Mental Health

THE SCOPE OF PSYCHIATRY

PSYCHOPATHOLOGY MAY BE CONSIDERED as one of many possible displays of human discomfort and suffering. By definition it is that kind of discomfort that comes to the attention of psychiatrists and other mental health workers. This tautological definition has the advantages of being operational and fits a basic characteristic of psychiatry—that of being a last resort specialty, i.e., if a case is not something else, it is psychiatric.

It is easy to demonstrate that, outside of a hard core, essentially formed by functional psychoses, neuroses, and a few other well-recognized syndromes, the boundaries of psychiatry are very blurred and change over time. New nosologic entities are added to both the I.C.D. and the D.S.M. at every revision, while others are dropped. It has been pointed out that when syndromes belonging to psychiatry have been identified in their etiopathogenesis, course, prognosis, etc., they have been taken away from psychiatry and given to other disciplines; for instance, cerebral syphilis and epilepsy, once within psychiatry's domain, have been assigned to syphilology and neurology, respectively.

As to clinical psychiatry, psychiatrists and other mental health professionals often deal with normal but "problematic" behaviors, such as marital crisis and any kind of violent behavior. This makes sense in that mental health professionals are expected to be experts in human dilemmas; however, it has an important consequence, since the intervention almost always implies the imposing of a psychiatric label, a diagnosis. It has been pointed out that it is difficult for a psychiatrist to avoid making a psychiatric diagnosis when the patient has been defined as a psychiatric case by others. A psychiatric diagnosis has been made *before* and independently of the psychiatrist; however, afterwards the psychiatric diagnosis is confirmed just because a psychiatrist is in charge—a self-fulfilling prophecy. When someone seeks treatment on his own, the psychiatrist has more latitude in how he adjudicates the case and whether or not the patient is given a psychiatric label (Goldberg & Huxley, 1980).

In many ways the relevance of psychiatric expertise is boundless. Therefore, the field of intervention tends to expand, to address more and more types of suffering. In part as a response to this boundlessness, efforts have been made to improve and standardize instruments of diagnosis and evaluation, with the expectation that a more clear-cut, scientific approach will provide clear boundaries and result in improved treatment for patients. Some of the limits and problems with this have been already discussed. It seems more reasonable that psychiatry be *aware* of its being the last resort, a shadowy territory exposed to a vast array of heterogeneous problems, and pay at least as much attention to the contextual components of a request for help as to individual ones.

In our work we do not discard the notions of clinical psychiatry. However, we are primarily concerned with *needs*; we prefer to consider symptoms as expressions of needs that may be recognized and possibly met, rather than as mere expressions of hypothetical, underlying, pathological processes, whose classification results in little advantage to the patient. Also, we envisage symptoms as relevant communications about unmet needs. We are interested in understanding the message in order to recognize the presenting needs; the psychological mechanisms of symptom formation are of little concern to us.

NEEDS AND REQUESTS

A *need* is the lack of something essential to the purposes of life. It expresses itself as suffering. If the person is *aware* of the existence of a good fit to stop the suffering, the need expresses itself as a desire. Therefore, a need may exist objectively, without a clear awareness of it, even if there is suffering. Or the desire may be absent, as in the case of a seriously depressed person. A desire may lead to action; if the subject is unable to reach the good he needs by himself, desire may be openly expressed as a *request* (Jervis, 1975).

Usually providers are not directly confronted with needs; they are confronted with requests for intervention. The problem is that between request and need there is a loose connection; they are on a continuum, with the request at the subjective edge, the need at the objective one. People can present an urgent request to have a minor need filled, as in the case of a demanding and plaintive neurotic; on the other side, a real, serious need may not be expressed at all, as in the case of a withdrawn, passive, long-term patient. Therefore, a request has to be carefully examined in order to recognize the need behind it.

The first step in the analysis of a request is to question who the customer is. The term *customer* is currently used to define the real purchaser of the intervention requested. In private practice the patient is generally also the customer: He goes to a professional and asks for help by himself. The patient is a client. In public mental health this may happen, but it is not the rule. Instead, in many cases the patient is brought to the attention of the agency *by others*. Often the patient is unwilling; the patient and the customer are not the same person. This topic will be discussed in detail in the interviewing section of Chapter 6.

In order to meet the patient's needs, one has to understand what they are. This is done first by interpreting what the patient presents metaphorically, principally through his symptoms. Traditional clinical psychiatry and especially psychodynamic psychotherapy seem to be most interested in the form of the request (i.e., type of psychopathology), in that the diagnosis is thought to give essential information on the person's mental processes, which are deemed to need a fix. The rationale behind this is that the person's mind *should be changed*; once this is accomplished the person will be able to meet his own needs (the content) by himself.

We are also interested in exploring and understanding the request. However, in sharp contrast to a traditional psychiatric approach, the content of the request, the underlying need, rather than the form, is critical because we believe that *meeting the patient's needs is therapeutic per se*. Doing so empowers the patient, establishes a bond, provides a channel for empathic and meaningful communication, and makes change possible. At times the improvement is prompt and dramatic.

In order to truly understand the meaning of requests, their context must be considered. The intervention made in response to a request is also inevitably part of, and denoted by, a context.* For example, antidepressants will likely be accepted more readily by a self-referred depressed person in a private office than by a depressed person brought to the public clinic against

---

*The context is not something objective, existing "out there," but depends on how the actors involved in the interaction perceive it. Nor is it stable: it changes over time and can even fluctuate in the course of the interaction.

his/her will. In many cases, once one knows the context, the patient's seemingly crazy behavior becomes understandable and appropriate and indicates a precise intervention. See, for instance, the example of Piero and Maria in the section on interviewing (Chapter 6).

In general psychotherapists are aware of the importance of the treatment context. For instance, they are careful with regard to the therapeutic setting, ritualizing the encounter in order to provide a definite "psychotherapeutic context." However, less attention is paid to the context surrounding the client and his problem.

When the encounter between client and treater takes place in a public psychiatric service, things are complicated by the fact that the context is ill defined and seldom therapeutic. This is a direct consequence of the characteristics of the participants, i.e., the public psychiatric service, the patient and the treater.

CHARACTERISTICS OF PUBLIC MENTAL HEALTH SERVICES

One might believe that a mental health service is a place where psychological disturbances are treated. This is an oversimplification and in many cases not true at all.

In fact, Paul (1978, p. 103) has pointed out that therapeutic effectiveness is *not* the principal goal of the psychiatric system and of its workers: "From top-level administrators, through program directors, to on-line staff, factors other than effective treatment considerations are primary determiners of action." A mental health service, especially a public one, has many attributed characteristics involving multiple goals. Such goals are vaguely stated and often conflict with one another. Besides therapeutic goals there are others related to giving welfare benefits, more or less explicitly stated goals involving social control of disturbing behaviors, consulting goals, legal and administrative ones, etc. There are also internal organizational goals and implicit or even secret ones, regarding career, profit, prestige, or allocation of money and equipment.

In addition to treatment, some common goals and related tasks of mental health agencies are the following:

1. *Control of disturbing behavior.* Mental health services are frequently asked to intervene with a patient, not on his behalf, but on behalf of the community. These are the cases when requests are made to remove a patient from the street or his apartment because he is perceived as an environmental threat or simply a nuisance to others. Treatment is meant as to "readjust him," which in turn means that he be not a nuisance anymore. Admission to the hospital and heavy

medication are the most welcome interventions. This has been defined as forcing conformity as opposed to treatment (see Chapter 4).

These patients might actually be in need of treatment (the most common justification alleged); however, what we wish to stress is that the reason for and the kind of intervention are *not* primarily in the interest of the patient. *This is practically never explicitly admitted*, as therapeutic rationales are always brought forth to justify the intervention.

Custodial care, not treatment, has long been recognized as the principal and "real" function of the mental hospital. Bachrach (1976, p. 19) has pointed out that "mental hospitals must not and cannot be eliminated until alternatives for the functions of asylum and custodial care have been provided."

2. *Dealing with legal medicine and welfare issues.* This has to do with counseling, diagnosing, writing certifications, insurance problems, welfare benefits, etc. In performing these tasks the professional is often rightfully concerned about not reinforcing the patient in his sick role. Sometimes the professional might resent being "used" as a mere bureaucrat, not as a therapist, by the patient or others. Explicitly acknowledging the ever growing bureaucratic components of careers in human services may help prevent disillusionment and frustration.

3. *Filling the gaps of the medical and welfare system.* Let us introduce this concept with an example:

A person is carried to the emergency room at night by the police because he is slightly drunk and acts a little bizarre; he is from out of town and has no money; he was treated by a mental health agency in the past, but presently is working and doing OK. In our system he is likely to be admitted, at least overnight (and we contend he *should be*, if the only alternatives are spending the night in jail or being abandoned), not because of a *specific* psychiatric condition — actually, is it always possible to find, or exclude, a *specific* psychiatric condition? — but because other social services are simply nonexistent. Community services should provide an array of options (see Chapter 9) to meet the different needs; otherwise improper use of existing options is the rule.

CHARACTERISTICS OF THE PATIENT

In Italy patients of public services are currently referred to as "users," not as "clients." We consider this wording correct; in fact, there is a profound difference between a private therapeutic relationship and a public one. The former, as a rule, is open to free, reciprocal negotiation between the two actors, i.e., provider and patient; the latter is predetermined to a large extent by health and welfare regulations. Therapeutic options for public patients are limited to what the service offers in terms of both programs and professionals. Often the patient cannot choose the therapist. Conversely, professionals working in a catchmented community service have to accept all requests brought to their attention. They can neither refuse to intervene nor select patients.

Welfare provisions greatly add to the secondary gain. The symptom may become a possession and a source of income, hence not to be given up; being a patient may be a career ending with a retirement on a pension.

Public mental health clients come from the most socially, economically, and educationally disadvantaged strata of society. Because they have little experience with or understanding of office-based psychotherapy, they should not be expected to be good psychotherapy candidates. They are rather like the new immigrant eating his first banana; he ate the peel and threw away the fruit! However, a properly designed program will be very therapeutic for them by decoding their requests so their needs can be met.

CHARACTERISTICS OF THE THERAPIST

The therapist has little more freedom than the patient. He cannot refuse an intervention and is often required to perform a mainly bureaucratic role. This leads to his being perceived by the patient as an officer rather than a professional. This may be frustrating for a professional, especially if he has psychotherapeutic training.

Mental health professionals should be aware that, once they play the role of "health officers," they no longer perform a purely professional role. Unfortunately, they have generally been trained for a traditional, purely professional career appropriate only to the private practice model. All this may lead to chronic frustration, burnout, role crisis, etc., and may account for American psychiatrists' disenchantment with CMHC work (Arce & Vergare, 1985; Clark & Vaccaro, 1987). When their skills, delivered with the best of intentions, do not "work" with these patients, professionals are faced with paradoxes: values seem inconsistent, expectations excessive with such difficult patients, and previous training and experience irrelevant for the task (Stern & Minkoff, 1979). The same thing is reported to happen to residents in training in community settings. In order to correct this situation, "good" supervisors should be available, but this is not the case — a final paradox (Minkoff & Stern, 1985). In short, with most "public" cases, the possibility of a free therapeutic contract is seriously hampered by limitations of both the patient and the therapist.

(RE)FRAMING THE CONTEXT

Once the context has been recognized, (1) it may just be discussed and defined, or (2) a more or less radical reframing may take place. In the first case, an explicit definition of the context is made by the worker, so that an agreement can be reached with the patient and other interested parties as to "where we are now" and what intervention can be made to suit the patient's needs. Given the vast array of intertwined and often contradictory goals and tasks of a public psychiatric service, this step is essential in order to ascertain if the mental health worker and the client(s) perceive the context in the same way. This also helps the patient to understand what he may expect from the intervention and to define and recognize his own needs.

Defining the context may also be used strategically in the therapeutic process. For example, explicitly defining the context as "custodial" in the case of an involuntary patient clears the air of hypocrisy and provides a honest foundation for the patient-therapist relationship.

In other cases the context needs to be *reframed* because it is strongly antitherapeutic, as happens, for example, in a typical institutional environment where efficiency and discipline prevail over understanding and caring. The patient is reinforced in the sick role and tends to become chronically dependent on the institution. All this goes against the therapeutic goal of encouraging the patient to maintain or resume a social role in the community. If the institution is antitherapeutic, the institution should be changed, instead of the patients and the workers who are forced into complementary procrustean beds. A radical change of the institution may be the *only real, therapeutic* intervention possible if the institution is antitherapeutic.

These principles characterized deinstitutionalization in Italy, where the primary target of intervention was the institution itself. Not only has there been a gradual discharge of patients into the community, but also the very existence of the "manicomio" has been criticized and resolution made to get rid of it. The term "institutional rehabilitation" was coined to describe this process, implying that change of the whole treatment environment was at stake.

REQUESTS CHANGE ALONG WITH CHANGE IN THE ORGANIZATION

In the process of designing a health service (in our case a psychiatric one) the major difficulty consists in finding concrete answers to the concrete demands coming from the surrounding reality. However, answers, while sticking to reality, should *surpass it as well, in order to transform it*. (Basaglia & Ongaro-Basaglia, 1975; italics added)

It has been suggested that in Italy the ongoing change in the organization of the delivery system is now producing a slow but detectable change in the characteristics of the requests made by patients and significant others. Requests tend to become more differentiated as a function of both the decentralization of services and, especially, the *quality* of interventions provided (De Salvia & Crepet, 1982). When a gamut of alternative interventions is provided, attitudes about mental health are changed both in the public (whose requests change) and in the professionals (with a change of beliefs and clinical practices).

For example, over the past 10 years Liliana, 52, has been in touch with the South Verona Mental Health Service for several episodes of severe depression. She used to go to the emergency room, or be brought by her relatives in critical condition, with the sole request of an admission to the hospital. Now she comes to the Mental Health Center when she feels dispirited and asks either to change medications, or to attend the day program, or to be helped at home with housework she is unable to accomplish. The same shift has been seen with general practitioners: They used to refer patients to the emergency room with a certificate for an admission; now their referrals are much more diversified. When a variety of alternatives is offered, the population is encouraged to present a broader array of requests; when only hospitalization is offered, there is a flattening of requests and eventually hospitalization is *the only* request presented when a psychiatric need is perceived. There is some evidence for this. A study (Pancheri, 1986) done in Portogruaro, a city northwest of Venice, showed that 28.2% of patients who had previous multiple hospitalizations asked to be hospitalized when seen in the emergency room. In contrast, no previously untreated patients and only 12.5% of those treated only by their G.P.'s sought hospitalization when seen in the emergency room.

There is also evidence that the existence of mental hospitals tends to *induce* requests for hospitalization. In research done by the Centro Studi del Ministero della Sanitá (Center for Studies of the Department of Health), on a sample of 34 Italian provinces in 1975, the rate of hospitalization was higher in those provinces having a mental hospital than in those without (3.09 vs. 1.59%; Centro Studi Ministero della Sanitá, 1977).

WHAT IS "TREATMENT"?

Besides the radical approach described above (reframing the context in a therapeutic direction), there are other possible options. A common (and certainly much easier) way is one of trying to replicate the private setting within a public institution. We define this as the "flower bed" alternative: A "therapeutic flower bed" is cultivated within the institution/service, whose organization at large, however, is *not* scrutinized. Typically, a therapist locks himself in a room with a patient and tries to make him into a "client," barricading the door against interferences from the institution and the community. This has the advantage of relying on the long experience of private professional practice, especially in the field of dynamic psychotherapy.

One limitation of the "flower bed" approach is that the work done in an hour of therapy is likely to be undone in the other 23 of institutional management. Further, it has the serious disadvantage of being appropriate only for patients who are fit for therapy; given the characteristics of patients referred to public services, the proportion of those meeting the criteria is relatively low. Most public patients are not very motivated for treatment of any kind, even though they might be in an extreme need of it. In the public sector, dealing with unmotivated or even resistant patients is the rule rather than the exception. Therefore, we believe that attitudes regarding motivation and therapeutic contract drawn from private practice are of little relevance in current public practice. Public therapists have to "seduce" patients into therapy all the time.

An important corollary of the "flower bed" perspective is that treatment and care are of a different breed, the latter being considered somehow "second class" with respect to treatment and a mere support to it. They are kept also separate, physically and professionally: Treatment takes place in the office, care in the ward; professionals are in charge of treatment, paraprofessionals provide care.

We believe that this distinction is arbitrary, since our patients, in their unique wholeness as individuals, have multiple needs, all important for their well-being. In particular, those patients who are typical of a community service are usually people with multiple needs: The community must provide for all the basic needs that were formerly met by the state hospital. In addition, there are "new" needs, derived from social evolution, such as being entitled to treatment, not just custody, being entitled to placement in the least restrictive environment, having the right not to be removed from one's own existential and social space, etc.

The modern evolution of community psychiatry, accelerated by reforms in the legislation and the catchmentation of psychiatric services, has changed the tasks of public psychiatry and the goals of intervention. A community service with global responsibility for a given population has to meet *all* that population's needs directly or indirectly related to mental health.

Treatment is not something that is "done"; rather, it is a functional characteristic of the approach to patients' needs. *The* therapeutic intervention does not exist; no intervention is by itself therapeutic or not. It is the sum of all interventions that has to be "therapeutic," and the service has to be organized in a way to make this possible. It may imply a profound structural rearrangement, so that consistency is obtained across the dimensions of goals, structure, and technology. Grafting an advanced service, either psychotherapeutic or community-oriented, onto a reactionary institution is nonsensical.

TOWARDS A MODEL OF TREATMENT
IN A COMMUNITY SERVICE

We believe that, in order to provide treatment, a service *has to* offer *prompt, adequate* and *consistent* answers to the needs of the population served:

- *has to:* The service has a responsibility towards the population.
- *prompt* and *adequate:* The service is often the first and the last resort. It cannot postpone interventions, have waiting lists, give evasive and partial answers.
- *consistent:* There must be consistency between values and goals, structure of the service, and therapeutic approach (including techniques).

In brief, treatment means meeting the needs of the population served. However, there is the risk of reinforcing the needs, instead of meeting them, thus making people chronically dependent upon the service, instead of promoting their independence. This is what happens, for example, when requests are taken literally and without adequate probing, and answers tend to become repetitious—in a word, "institutional." For example, the patient or the family requests multiple hospital admissions and these are granted without an evaluation of the overall scenario or a mid-to-long-term therapeutic strategy. This often happens if interventions are not integrated but are decided singly or independently. The best clinical judgment is not enough to protect against this risk, nor are good intentions. For instance, a common intervention, which is apparently indisputable but in our experience usually a mistake, is to hospitalize a patient to offer respite to the family. Putting aside a problem, for no matter how long, acts in the direction of inducing chronicity. In some cases admission might be inevitable, but a problem-solving *strategy*, at least minimal, must be present as well. Unfortunately, all too often the *limits of the service in providing alternatives* to hospitalization become a "clinical" need for admission.

Being therapeutic depends on *how* one meets needs and with what *goals*. To be therapeutic means to meet needs, but at the same time, ideally, to provide clients with the means and the motivation to work toward satisfying their needs on their own. The ultimate *goal* must be to free the patient from the service as he becomes capable of meeting his needs independently. At the organizational level, the various interventions have to be *integrated* among themselves and *consistently* aim at therapeutic goal. If the interventions that the service is able to offer are fragmentary and there is no therapeutic continuity, it is unlikely that the patient will become better integrated psychologically, no matter how sophisticated the psychotherapy he receives might be. Twenty-three hours of bad institutional care easily overcomes one hour of excellent psychotherapy.

Providing a therapeutic context is certainly more difficult and demanding in a public community setting; however, it may be more rewarding and effective. A public community service has some advantages over the private office or agency; in fact, it has more power and more resources. More power, because it is both the first filter and the last resort; the patient and the family have to contact the community service, sooner or later, for a number of reasons. Therefore, the therapist has more chances to engage the patient in a therapeutic work and a dropout does not mean end of contacts—the patient will eventually show up again. This may be used strategically. More resources, because a community service can rely on a vast array of different possible interventions, some of them very powerful and meaningful for the patient because they directly affect his real existence. We refer to admissions, discharges, allocation of welfare benefits, contacts with other social agencies, etc. The task of the worker is to use them in a goal-oriented (therapeutic) way, as defined before.

CHAPTER 4

A Dinosaur to Be:
A Proposal for Limiting Use
of Psychiatric Hospitals

OUR BASIC POSITION IS THAT *hospital*-based care is not necessary for most disturbed and disturbing persons if:

1. In-home family crisis intervention is available;
2. A properly organized intentional social environment (therapeutic community) (see Chapter 9) is available to those who cannot be maintained in the family environment or do not have a social network that can be organized to act as a temporary caregiver; and
3. The identified patient is not a *battle scarred veteran* of the mental health wars ("chronic") who is so attached to (the idea of) hospitals that he/she or the family is unwilling to accept treatment that does not include hospitalization.

These same three conditions must also be met if psychotropic drug treatment is to be avoided or minimized (see Chapter 5).

BACKGROUND

In the United States hospitals have for a century and a half been *the places* where serious mental illness is to be treated. While in European countries traditional psychiatric hospitals are frequently converted leprosaria (Galzigna & Terzian, 1980), in the United States a whole new set of

31

institutions were created, principally because of the crusading efforts of Dorothea Dix, to care for the insane.

The character of traditional psychiatric institutions changed on both sides of the Atlantic during the 1960s. Basically, they shifted from being custodial long-stay asylums to being places with an active treatment orientation. Initially this resulted in higher turnover rates, i.e., a rise in the number of admissions, shorter lengths of stay, and modest declines in total patients in residence. In the late '60s and early '70s state hospitals in the U.S. discharged large numbers of patients, mostly because of federal support through health insurance (Medicare/Medicaid) and disability pensions (SSI, SSDI). Deinstitutionalization was the order of the day. Simultaneously, psychiatric wards began to proliferate in general hospitals in the U.S. This shift in the site of care was propelled by a preferential availability of health insurance payment for treatment in general hospitals rather than in large psychiatric institutions. But the result was the same — an emphasis on institutional care.

Although Italy has had private freestanding psychiatric institutions in addition to the public mental hospitals (*manicomios*) since the beginning of the 20th century, there were essentially *no* psychiatric wards in general hospitals there (except for university hospitals) until after the reform of 1978. The reform mandated the development of small psychiatric wards in general hospitals throughout the country. As we approach the 1990s, the U.S. and Italian psychiatric hospital systems differ in one major way — in Italy it is no longer possible to be admitted to a large public mental hospital (*manicomio*). In both countries the bulk of hospital-based care for disturbed and disturbing behavior presently takes place on wards in general hospitals.

What, it may legitimately be asked, is so wrong with treating disturbed and disturbing persons in hospitals? Several things:

First, when the person is removed from his usual physical and interpersonal environment, a process of decontextualization is initiated.

Second, by enforcing regimentation and dependency, the hospital routine violates the person's senses of individuality, autonomy, and self-control. A process of dehistorification is begun.

Third, because the diagnostic process focuses on symptoms, pays little attention to the influence of context on behavior, and transforms "the problem" (something a person can feel responsible for) into a "disease" that becomes the doctor's responsibility, the patient becomes further decontextualized.

Fourth, the treatment process is based on a set of negative attributions that patients must *disprove* in order to show themselves to be getting better. Common sense tells us that operating in a field of negative attributions will likely have a negative effect on self-esteem and self-confidence and hence maintain or worsen, rather than alleviate, the problem (disease).

Although we single out hospitals in our criticism, we recognize that any setting in which the processes we describe above go on is open to the same criticism. Hospitals are extreme examples of the operation of these processes because of their size, hierarchy, medical authority, and very distressed clientele, who see themselves as being without options. We've seen many community residential programs that differed only in degree from hospitals on these variables.

AN EXAMPLE

Rather than rely only on our prose and experience to support our views of hospital wards, even "good" ones in general hospitals, we will present the findings of 120 hours of participant observation on a 30-bed public (county) community hospital psychiatric ward that served as the control treatment setting in the Soteria project (Mosher, 1977; Mosher & Menn, 1978; Wilson, 1975). The Soteria Project was a random assignment, two-year longitudinal follow-up study comparing outcomes of newly diagnosed schizophrenics treated without neuroleptic drugs in a small home-like facility in the community with the outcomes of similarly selected and studied patients who received "usual" treatment – short stays on a psychiatric ward in a general hospital and routine neuroleptic drug treatment.

The general hospital ward, affiliated with a university medical center's psychiatric training program, has 30 beds and an average length of stay of 15 days. The dispatching process is described by Wilson (1983) as follows:

1. Patching. Staff's initial contact with patients often revolves around the imposition of a variety of behavioral controls such as use of seclusion rooms, mechanical restraints, verbal instructions, and particularly heavy doses of psychotropic medications such as Haldol, Prolixin, or Thorazine. In essence, violent, out of control, or inappropriately bizarre patients are patched together by subduing their socially unacceptable symptoms as quickly as possible.

2. Medical screening. Because the psychiatric dispatching process (a term used to encompass the multiple, complex operations employed for "processing patients through" a clearing house model of care) takes place in a "medical" setting under the direction of physicians for the most part, a standardized routine of physical testing and diagnostic procedures is immediately initiated for all new admissions. These procedures include a physical exam, blood work, urinalysis, E.E.G., and a selected variety of others. Such screening also serves as an information gathering strategy in that on occasion a patient's psychiatric problem is discovered to be a consequence of a medical or physiological disorder. Properties of this process of screening are that it is extremely time-consuming for staff, that it requires accurate and proper completion of a multitude of requisitions and forms, and that it is rigidly imposed, even though a patient who is readmitted may have undergone the same screening process within the same week.

3. Piecing together a story. Proportionately speaking, the most staff time

and energy is devoted to this dimension of the dispatching process. In order to make subsequent decisions about distributing a patient to the appropriate aftercare placement, as well as the more immediate decision of which course of medications to begin, a diagnosis must be made. Thus, information gathering and intelligence operations consume staff's focus during the first 72 hours of a patient's confinement. The interaction of staff attempting to sleuth out and uncover information about a patient in order to engage in fate-making decisions, with patients who are attempting to cover up what they believe is damaging data about themselves, constitutes another key focus for staff/patient contact. The major modalities for this contact are the "Group Intake Interview" wherein a newly admitted patient is confronted by a group of staff in an interview room and questioned, and the "Second-hand Report" where bits and pieces of data are passed along from shift to shift verbally and on the patient's chart and then used to make generalizations about the patient. Properties of this process are its preconceived tendency, a reliance on speculations which easily become "truth," and the trickery involved in "finding things out."

4. Labeling and sorting. Once there is sufficient data to justify some decisions, patients are stamped with a psychiatric label. For the most part, patients in the study setting fell into the following diagnostic categories: schizophrenic, manic-depressive, alcohol or drug abuse, or violent character disorder of some type. Labeling acts as a key in deciding which medications to order and which aftercare placements to begin exploring. It also provides staff with an additional source of control in their dealings with patients, for with diagnosis comes an increased sense of being able to predict patient behavior and the ability to deal with patient communications and behaviors as typifications — "That's her hysterical personality coming out; those are just delusions, etc."

5. Distributing. The official goal of Community Mental Health legislation in California also includes a goal of moving mentally ill persons back into "the community" as rapidly as possible. Yet, psychiatric professionals in the study setting are constantly balancing this mandate against their perceived mandate to act as protectors of society and their patients. Consequently, staff act as fate-makers by distributing their "charges" to one of a variety of placement options for follow-up and aftercare. A property of the distributing stage of dispatching is its revolving door nature. Many of the setting's patients are "old familiars," who periodically rotate through the study setting and back out again. A number of patients are tracked by community liaison workers which contributes additional data taken into account when distributing decisions are made. Reports include that one aftercare facility or another "won't take her back again" so the options become limited by virtue of exhausting some of them over time.

The above conceptualization of "usual psychiatric care" in the study setting conveys, I hope, the complex nature of the psychiatric decision making and deposition process that goes on. Consequences of these operations include: (1) A very hectic and busy pace of work for staff while the hours "drift by" for patients. (2) A low accessibility of staff for patients — sitting and talking with patients has very low priority in view of all the tasks that must be accomplished. (3) A substitution of technology for potential face-to-face contacts (e.g., there's a mechanical cigarette lighter on the wall to discourage patients from bothering busy staff for lights, medications are announced over a loudspeaker instead of passed out by a nurse who seeks out patients around the ward, etc.). (4) Staff spend the majority of their time in interaction with other staff — in report, team meetings, intake interviews, and other meetings. (This observation differed on the two wards with more staff/patient contact on Ward I, in ritualized formats such as "anger group," "feelings group," etc., but these contacts were low on spontaneity, low on openness, and high on superficiality and control.) (5) Staff are the constants on the units with patients only passing through; thus a lot of energy is devoted to intrastaff conflict, problems, and the distribution of labor. (6) Most staff have a lot of integrity about their work — their value systems are relatively congruent with conventional psychiatric and medical model explanations of madness. (Wilson, 1975)

As Wilson notes, today's psychiatric hospital wards are used mostly for social control — removal of problem behavior from public view and containment of it through force and medication. Therefore, use of the word "treatment" with regard to what goes on in them is basically a mystification. The relative absence of a real psychosocial treatment orientation is in part the result of economic pressures. Patients are allowed to stay in these very expensive locked jail/hotels for only a short time. Time and bureaucratic constraints also make it difficult for the type hospital environment described here to be a therapeutic milieu. In particular, these wards offer little real support, socialization, validation, stimulus control, collaboration, or respite, six of the ten functions necessary for a milieu to be therapeutic (see Chapter 9, p. 116).

HOSPITALS AND ECONOMICS

Medicalization of ordinary human problems is driven by economic considerations. Health insurance will pay for care on psychiatric wards in general hospitals; consequently, that is where disturbed individuals find themselves. What began in the 1840s as humanitarian reform was first perverted into custodial segregation (1870–1960) and then into a dehumanizing, decontextualizing growth industry in the 1970s. In the '60s and '70s wards for adults proliferated; in the '80s it has been places for adolescents. The industry is thriving on its new adolescent fodder. Middle- and upper-middle-class family problems come to roost in the person of the defective individual adolescent. The psychiatric system has joined parents in reframing a difficult, problematic, or embarrassing behavior as "illness." However, the less palatable juvenile justice system is avoided; that system is left to deal with the basically similar problems of less economically powerful poor families.

Unfortunately, no one seems particularly concerned about the consequences of inducting a new group of adolescents into patienthood: (1) creation of a new generation of institutionalized persons who will filter down into the *public mental health system*, and (2) further erosion of the basic fabric of American family life. Psychiatry's message to the American family is clear: "We know how to raise your offspring better than you do. Send them to our just opened adolescent ward (if you're insured or wealthy) and we'll return them 'fixed'." It is more effective and cheaper to intervene with these families in their homes or the clinic. If an adolescent has to be removed, it should be either to a nearby family-like residential setting or to a boarding school in his or her own community (see the example in Boulder, Colorado, Chapter 17). Community programs should establish as the highest priority a policy of non-institutionalization of children and adolescents. They must be protected from the known adverse consequences of hospitalization.

REASONS TO AVOID USE OF HOSPITALS

Reducing our reliance on inpatient hospital care is justified on a number of grounds:

1. *Humanitarian.* Because these institutions treat persons as objects, basic human qualities like individuality, autonomy, independence, and sense of personal responsibility are undermined. Reducing their use will prevent this process of dehumanization.
2. *Moral.* Hospitals are known to cause the iatrogenic disease "institutionalism" (Barton, 1959; Wing & Brown, 1970) or social breakdown syndrome (Gruenberg & Huxley, 1970; Gruenberg, Snow, & Bennett, 1969; Kasius, 1966). Not using them will keep the prevalence of these syndromes to a minimum.
3. *Economic.* Because inpatient care consumes 70% of mental health dollars, reducing its use will allow support of badly needed, more effective, and more normalizing community programs.
4. *Scientific.* Nineteen of 20 studies comparing inpatient psychiatric hospitalization with a variety of alternative forms of care found the alternatives as effective, or more so, and less costly (when measured) (Straw, 1982). These studies also found hospitals to be habit-forming; hospital-treated patients tended to recycle through the hospital whereas alternatively treated clients did not.

Despite all the problems with hospital care, for a variety of historical, political, economic, cultural, and professional reasons it has not been possible to disrupt the intimate association of madness and hospitals. The mental health professions, especially their most powerful and prestigious members, psychiatrists, have entered into an agreement with society to help it rid itself of troublesome members. Even Italy's radical reform of a mental health system retained hospital-based treatment as a major (and sometimes, unfortunately, only) component of the new system. Its retention, the result of a political compromise, illustrates the power of the hospital/madness associative link.

INDICATIONS FOR INPATIENT HOSPITAL USE

While we abhor today's overreliance on inpatient care, we acknowledge a continuing need for about 10 hospital beds per 100,000 population (the U.S. has just over 300,000 psychiatric beds, or about 130 per 100,000!). This estimate assumes that an additional 10 beds will be available in residential alternatives to hospitalization. When would these expensive hospital beds be used? Basically, we believe they should be used only when those functions offered *only* in places called hospitals are required by a particular client. These include:

1. Complex, technologically sophisticated, diagnostic processes that require frequent observation by specially trained personnel available only in hospitals (e.g., special infusions, PET, CAT, or MRI scans). In fact, in most instances these can be done on an outpatient basis.
2. Initiation of a treatment process with risks that need to be monitored over a period of time by specially trained personnel (e.g., preplanned drug detoxification, beginning lithium or neuroleptic drugs in persons with complicating medical problems).
3. Medical treatment of a person sufficiently disturbed or suicidal or homicidal so as to render care elsewhere too difficult for the staff, other patients, families, or significant others.
4. Treatment of acute intoxicated states (alcohol, PCP, cocaine).
5. Management of agitated, overactive, acutely psychotic persons who leave open settings and are a serious danger to themselves because of confusion and disorganization.

These five indications for hospitalization represent those in an "ideal" system.

In addition to these few hospital beds, easy access to an emergency room is required as backup for community crisis intervention teams when, for example, they are uncertain of the proper disposition for an individual seen in the community or the clinic. The emergency room can provide experienced consultants, rapid medical diagnostic tests (e.g., for drugs), a longer period in which to evaluate the patient, and time to test whether or not a positive response will occur to removal from the site of the original crisis. To allow this we recommend that there be one or two crisis beds, available for up to 48 hours, in the emergency room. Basically, the emergency room should serve as a second triage point (after initial triage by the community team) for a selected subset of difficult cases.

CHAPTER 5

Is Psychotropic Drug Dependence Really Necessary?

CURRENT COMMUNITY MENTAL HEALTH PRACTICE with regard to psychotropic drugs is an accurate reflection of the wider culture: Quick, even magical, relief is sought from a pill. Nonprescription legal drugs like alcohol are widely used and abused; prescription drugs like Valium are widely used and abused; illegal drugs like marijuana are widely used and abused. Why then do we propose to violate our normalization principle and attempt to curb psychotropic drug use in community programs? Simply put, why, if everyone else is doing drugs, don't we? Five reasons come to mind:

1. Because many psychotropics separate persons from their experience of themselves. This intra-individual decontextualization (fragmentation) may actually make what might have been a temporary disorganization into a permanent split — one that may be immune to the psychosocial change methods we espouse.
2. Because a number of these drugs, especially the neuroleptics, have very serious short- and long-term side effects and toxicities. One of them, tardive dyskinesia, causes cosmetic disfigurement that makes community work more difficult because of the instant stigmatization it engenders.
3. Because the drugs are given in situations in which clients have little real choice about taking them or not. Doctor power is enormous and not usually a topic for discussion. Taking drugs puts the power

38

to help in someone else's hands. Options and the power to make one's own decisions are vital ingredients to good community programs.

4. Because they are major contributors to today's individual-defect, biologic zeitgeist. This zeitgeist is accompanied by hierarchical relationships and linear causality; both stand in contradistinction to the psychosocially oriented open systems view we believe is important for ongoing community-based work.

5. Because they seem to foster oversimplistic, reductionist thinking, such as the currently fashionable dopamine theory of schizophrenia: Neuroleptics are useful in schizophrenia; neuroleptics affect dopamine metabolism; therefore, schizophrenia is a neuroleptic deficiency disorder. Try this one: Digitalis is useful for heart failure; digitalis affects heart muscle contraction; therefore, heart failure is a digitalis deficiency disorder.

Since only M.D.'s can prescribe drugs, one might think that this should leave non M.D.'s in community programs free to be open-minded and innovative—both important staff characteristics (see Chapter 10). Unfortunately, in our experience this is not usually the case. M.D.'s tend to view themselves as being superior to the non M.D.'s, in part because they control an efficacious treatment. Over time, the non M.D.'s comply with this expectation and implicitly see their work as possible only because of the simultaneous use of psychotropics. Teamness (because the M.D.'s are set apart), innovation, and staff empowerment suffer as a consequence.

What never ceases to amaze us is the degree of collusion that goes on around the use of psychotropics between psychiatrists, non-M.D. staff, most clients, and the wider community. All seem tacitly to have agreed that pills are "the answer" to the problem of disturbed and disturbing behavior. There appears to be a shared need to have this belief be true despite the scientific evidence with regard to the limitations of drug treatment.

For example, if neuroleptics are the answer to the type of disturbed and disturbing behavior labeled "schizophrenia," why do about half of such persons relapse within two years despite being maintained on neuroleptics (Davis, 1980)? Why has the long-term prognosis for this group been unaffected by neuroleptics (Bleuler, 1968; Ciompi, 1980; Harding et al., 1987a,b; Huber et al., 1980; Niskanen & Achte, 1972)?

One might imagine that part of psychiatry's current preoccupation with being scientific would be serious attention to the implications of this (and other similar) evidence. Our perception is that data that don't fit current dogma are either completely disregarded or invalidated by ad hominem arguments regarding exclusivity (e.g., only in lower Slobovia is that so) or methodology (e.g., they weren't *really* schizophrenic). Investigators who persist in producing such deviant data are at high risk for marginalization, usually by highlighting a personal piccadillo (e.g., "you know he's a womanizer, don't you?").

THE PSYCHOLOGY OF PRESCRIBING

Over the years we've made several interesting sociopsychological observations about drug-prescribing practices among psychiatrists. We don't pretend that they're universally true; however, they are of some relevance here.

The drug treatment of schizophrenia seems to be subject to the greatest intensity of dogmatism. That is, for a variety of difficult (for us) to understand reasons, withholding neuroleptics from persons with this label is extraordinarily difficult. Attempts to do so are greeted with raised eyebrows, quizzical looks, "do you think they might?" or "what if?" questions from non-M.D. staff, and allusions to malpractice from other M.D.'s.

We must wonder if the dogmatism so prevalent with regard to maintaining schizophrenics on neuroleptic drugs really stems from psychiatrists' desire to keep a safe distance from these oftentimes difficult persons. Very short "medication visits" do not lend themselves to the development of the type of trusting, collaborative therapeutic relationships required if neuroleptics are to be used only when symptomatic exacerbations occur.

The party line that schizophrenia is a chronic biologic illness treatable only with medication has the field firmly in its grasp. What is labeled bipolar disorder is also subject to serious dogmatism around the issue of treatment with lithium. However, in our experience this disorder is viewed less negatively than schizophrenia, probably because of the notion that some persons with it may be quite creative. Hence, it is somewhat easier to hold open-minded discussions regarding medication of manic-depressives than of "schizophrenics."

Drug treatment of less disturbed and disturbing persons (i.e., neurotics and some personality disorders) tends to be less doctrinaire. The minor tranquilizers (e.g., benzodiazepines) and the antidepressants are used with them on a trial-and-error basis. There is no serious "party line" about their use, in part because the evidence for their efficacy is less clear. In addition, these lesser psychopathologic states have not achieved "disease" status in the minds of many psychiatrists. Psychiatry has less trouble acknowledging that this group of potential clients can be treated by others than is true for the four most serious categories—schizophrenia, bipolar, manic, and major depressive "disease"—which are seen as the real "property" of psychiatry.

Despite this rhetoric and territorial imperative, most American psychiatrists don't like to deal with persons labeled schizophrenic—a point made previously by us and by Torrey (1983). They're difficult, time-consuming, unresponsive, and unlikely to pay their bills. In fact, in the U.S., they are often without any means of paying for care. As a consequence, they are the largest single diagnostic group in the public mental health system. Manics, bipolars, and depressives are more attractive. They get better relatively rapidly, usually speak no language of social protest, have families who care about them, pay their bills, and can be pillars of society. To talk schizophreneze is to be incomprehensible; to talk maniaeze is to be funky, funny; to talk depresseze is to be boring, tiring. Most people find it much easier to stay with the last two.

PRESCRIBING PRINCIPLES

Although we are concerned about the overuse and misuse of psychopharmacologic agents, they are, unfortunately, a fact of current community mental health practice. The degree of shared fantasy around their efficacy makes it unlikely that the situation will soon change. Drugs are just too easy to use and too consistent with prevailing cultural norms to be given up easily. Nonetheless, we want to present principles that intelligent mental health workers and clients can use to make informed judgments about the psychopharmacologic practices of the group within which they are embedded. That non M.D.'s cannot write prescriptions is no excuse for their not being well informed, thoughtful, and critical of what is being done to their clients.

Furthermore, it is our hope that better informed clinicians will be drawn to conclusions similar to ours — that madness is all too understandable, and that it can be effectively treated by psychosocial methods, especially when the situation has not already been muddied by a course of psychotropic drug treatment. It must be pointed out in this context that the successful psychosocial treatment of very disturbed and disturbing behavior requires either a very supportive natural social network augmented by mental health staff or a properly organized, intensely supportive, residential therapeutic community designed specifically for this purpose.

Our principles are described below.

1. "A Well-Educated Consumer Is Our Best Customer."

Clients/users/customers/patients must have *knowledge about the chemicals they're being asked to ingest* (as well as about other treatments). One *cannot* rely on M.D.'s to provide this information in a way that will be heard and taken in by the disturbed person. Community mental health workers should know about the therapeutic and side effects of various *classes* of drugs.

A discussion of psychotropic agents does not have to be, and will usually not be, initiated by a doctor. Hence, workers at all levels should be familiar with what the five classes of psychotropic drugs do, and be able to outline phenomenologically what the experiences their clients are likely to have as a result of taking them. Appendix A (Medications for Mental Illness) should be studied and well learned by community mental health workers and users. The portions of it relevant to a particular patient's drug treatment regime should be given to him and discussed until clearly understood. These discussions should focus on what is to be expected, how the effects can be understood, and what other options there might be.

2. Power to the People.

A crucial ingredient of responsible community care, one that distinguishes it sharply from more dependency-inducing care that occurs in hospitals, is that it maintains individuals' power to be in control of their lives. Preservation of personal power, or reempowering if it has been eroded by a treatment system, is a sine qua non of successful community treatment. Psychotropic drugs must be dealt with in this context. How do you maintain a patient's power while giving him an agent that exerts powerful effects on his physiology, his self-perceptions, and his sense of who and what he is? We have found that the following paradigm, if well presented, and carried out honestly, will preserve most patients' power over their own bodies and make them partners in the treatment process. The example is drawn from giving a person labeled schizophrenic a major neuroleptic (e.g., haloperidol, chlorpromazine):

> I would like you to take a medicine that many persons with your type of problem(s) have found helpful in dealing with them. There is, of course, no guarantee that it will work. That's why it's so important that you regard your taking it as an *experiment* on yourself. By that I mean I'd like you to look at how you feel in terms of your emotional state, your sense of self, your perceptions of your body, your level of energy and overall comfort *before* you start the medicine. Then, beginning with the first pill, I'd like you to record, in writing, on at least a daily basis, changes in how you feel along all those parameters. I'll see you in one week and I want you to bring your diary into me. Based on that, and our discussion of how you feel at that time, we'll adjust the amount of drug you're taking. Between now and then, I'd like you to take the drug in the amount I've prescribed. If you begin to feel faint, weak and sweaty, stop the drug and call me. If you feel as if you must always keep moving, stop the drug and call me. If you feel spasms in your muscles, especially around the neck and shoulders, call me.
>
> *We* will sit down again in two weeks to assess what, if anything, the drug has done for you by that point in time. I will discuss your diary with you from my professional point of view and will ask you to tell me about your experi-

ence of the drug. I will also seek the opinions of those with whom you live about its effects on you. If the overall experience is positive, I will adjust the dosage and encourage you to continue the drug for a period of time. If the composite overall picture is negative, we'll stop and *may* try another. I cannot predict now. Remember, however, that it is your body that this drug is affecting. Pay close attention. I cannot force you to take the drug. But it should be given a fair trial. Only you can do that. We must work as a team. In the end the decision will be yours. I would like it to be a responsible one based on your experience with this drug.

Although the description of possible effects will vary with the drug, the basic "experiment on yourself" paradigm is the same for all drugs. In these discussions it is useful to find a drug the patient has previously taken — alcohol being the most common — and use it as a teaching example. This drug-taking process, because it involves very powerful and potentially toxic substances, must be addressed seriously; most critical is that the clinician take seriously the client's experience and questions. *Compliance is usually a relationship issue.* Properly handled, drug-taking should not be a serious problem between clinician and patient. If it becomes so, the clinician should look at what he is doing that has undermined the focus of a common goal: helping the client get his life back on track.

3. Have Available Psychosocial Intervention Alternatives.

Without other options drug treatment is almost inevitable. In particular, because long-term maintenance on the major neuroleptics is not usually warranted by the risk/benefit ratio, a variety of strategies and services need to be developed to serve in the place of neuroleptics. This is true of the other psychotropics as well, even though their long-term toxicities do not appear to be as severe as those of the major neuroleptics.

USE OF THE MAJOR NEUROLEPTICS

Our views on this subject are at variance with the predominant ethos in community mental health today, in which psychopharmacologic agents, especially neuroleptics for schizophrenia, are seen as *necessary* to the practice of community mental health. Their known and mythical effects are listed in Tables 5.1 and 5.2. Because tardive dyskinesia is an extraordinarily difficult and destructive iatrogenic disorder, *if* a proper social environment can be provided, every *newly* identified psychotic deserves several opportunities to recover without the use of neuroleptics. The evidence is reasonably clear that the vast majority of *newly* diagnosed psychotics *can recover without neuroleptics* (Bleuler, 1968; Huber et al., 1980; Mosher & Menn, 1978).

TABLE 5.1
Neuroleptic Drugs: Known Effects

1. Reduce "positive" symptoms
2. Shorten hospital stays
3. Reduce readmission rates
4. Produce tardive dyskinesia
5. Revitalized interest in schizophrenia
6. Produced large corporate profits

The challenge is to organize and present an appropriate intentional social environment. This type of environment, as well as its planning, organization, and implementation, is described in Chapter 9, p. 116). If, because an adequate therapeutic community is not available, clinicians are forced to use neuroleptics with newly identified clients, they should be used in as low a dose as possible for as short a time as possible. This may also be done with clients who have not responded to a fair trial of psychosocial treatment. This is actually a paradigm for the use of psychotropics in general: first a trial of psychosocial treatment, *then* a drug trial.

We do not believe in routine maintenance neuroleptic drug treatment for persons labeled schizophrenic. Basically, our argument against maintenance neuroleptic drugs runs as follows: Two-year relapse rates in random assignment double-blind studies of orally administered major neuroleptics run about 70–80% for placebo-treated patients and 40–50% for neuroleptic-maintained patients (Davis, 1980). In addition, the *annual* incidence of tardive dyskinesia in neuroleptic-maintained patients is about 5%. That is, by five years, about 25% of a neuroleptic-maintained cohort of newly treated patients will exhibit tardive dyskinesia (Kane et al., 1984). Based on these data, the risk/benefit ratio would seem *not* to favor long-term maintenance.

These 40–50% two-year relapse rates among drug-maintained patients have been attributed by many to noncompliance with medication. Certainly

TABLE 5.2
Neuroleptic Drugs: Mythical Effects

1. Cleared out psychiatric hospitals
2. Changed the long-term social recovery rates of schizophrenia
3. Enhance learning of coping skills
4. Address schizophrenia's specific etiology
5. Can reduce readmissions to nearly zero if drug compliance is assured

this is a reasonable position. The test of the noncompliance theory of relapse is the comparison of patients randomly assigned injectable neuroleptic or oral medication. If medication compliance is the critical variable, injectably treated patients should have substantially lower relapse rates than the orally treated ones. Four large-scale collaborative studies of this question have been carried out, the two most elegantly designed being Hogarty, Schooler, Ulrich, Mussare, Ferro, and Herron (1979) and Rifkin, Quitkin, Rabiner, and Klein (1977). The results of all four are extraordinarily similar. Relapse rates among orally maintained patients are no different from those of patients maintained on injectable neuroleptics, where compliance was assured. In addition, injectable neuroleptics had more unpleasant side effects than oral medication. What are the clinical implications of these studies?

1. For the 40–50% of patients already in the system who relapse *despite* maintenance neuroleptics, it is irresponsible to progressively increase their risk for tardive dyskinesia by progressively increasing the medication or by persisting in a search for another and another medication. They obviously need attention to their social environments so that stress can be reduced or avoided, thereby reducing the risk of relapse. For example, it has now been amply documented that offspring living in families with high levels of hostility, criticism, and overinvolvement relapse far more frequently than those living in families low on these characteristics (Leff & Vaughn, 1980, 1987; Vaughn, Synder, Jones, Freeman, & Falloon, 1984). A client living in such an environment could be encouraged and helped to move out, or a known effective family intervention (Falloon, Boyd, McGill, Razani, Moss, & Gilderman, 1982; Hogarty, Anderson, Reiss, Kornblith, Greenwald, Javna, & Madonia, 1986; Leff, Kuipers, Berkowitz, Vries, & Sturgeon, 1982) could be initiated to help reduce these stress-inducing characteristics, or he/she could be provided with an activity that reduces face-to-face contact with the family to a minimum. Thoughtful attention to the social environments of all clients, however labeled, should provide mental health workers with clues for the development of individualized psychosocial intervention strategies that will allow drug treatment to be avoided altogether, or at least kept to a minimum.

2. Patients who are not on maintenance medication but are at risk for relapse should be involved in therapeutic relationships in which their particular patterns of evolution of madness can be described and discussed. If the relationship is in order, clients will be able to tell their therapists if, and why, they're about to go crazy. At that point options can be discussed, only one of which should be institution of neuroleptic drug treatment.

When drug treatment is the only viable option, a "targeted" drug strategy (i.e., treatment of symptom exacerbations only) should be chosen. This results in no more relapses than long-term maintenance with neuroleptics (Carpenter & Heinrichs, 1983; Carpenter, Heinrichs & Hanlon, 1987; Carpenter, Heinrichs, Hanlon, Kirkpatrick & Summerfeld, in press). Even more importantly, it appears that persons who have not been maintained on neuroleptics respond more quickly (than do maintained patients) when drugs are introduced; i.e., they spend less time in the hospital if they have to be rehospitalized (Carpenter et al., in press). Carpenter has also recently shown that this "targeted" drug treatment strategy substantially reduces the risk of developing tardive dyskinesia, even though his "targeted" patients were on drugs roughly 50% of the time. The targeted drug strategy is also supported by the clinical and research observation that madness waxes and wanes. Common sense tells us that treating people with very powerful drugs during intervals of "wellness" is unwise.

3. If psychosocial programs are not available and clients are frequently rehospitalized despite the targeted drug approach, maintenance on as low a dose of neuroleptic as possible can be tried. Several investigators (Kane, 1983, 1984, 1987; and Marder, Van Putten, Mintz, Lebell, McKenzie, & May, 1987) have shown that this strategy is nearly as effective in preventing relapse as usual doses, has far fewer side effects, and is much better tolerated by patients.

We have found it very difficult to wean even relatively stable community-based patients completely off neuroleptics if they have been on them continuously for several years. We're not sure whether it's because their dopamine receptors are starving or because of a real addiction-like withdrawal syndrome, but ten days to two weeks after stopping most patients have what *looks like* the beginning of an exacerbation of psychosis (Chouinard, Bradwejn, Jones & Ross-Chouinard, 1984; Gardos, Cole & Torey, 1978; Luchons, Freed & Wyatt, 1980). To avoid the consequences of a serious crisis to the person from his community-based social field, we've pretty much given up trying to get clients *completely* off neuroleptics. Instead, we try to get them down to the vicinity of 25 mg. Thorazine equivalent a day. That usually keeps dopamine receptors happy enough (i.e., the levels of insomnia, anxiety, and restlessness experienced are tolerable) if it's the end point of a prolonged weaning process and levels of social stress are kept modest.

USE OF LITHIUM AND THE ANTIDEPRESSANTS

Recent data (Prien, Kupfer, Mansky, Small, Tuason, Voss, & Johnson, 1984) indicate that, despite combined lithium and imipramine maintenance, 62% of bipolar patients relapsed and were regarded as treatment failures during a 16-week minimum maintenance period. Furthermore, only 25% were considered "treatment successes." Unipolar patients, receiving the same drug regimen, had a 51% failure and a 36% maintenance success rate. This, taken in conjunction with lithium's known renal toxicity and the lethality of the tricyclics when used for self-destructive purposes, may indicate a need to reevaluate the practice of routine lithium maintenance in bipolar patients and the less common practice of routine tricyclic antidepressant maintenance in unipolar depressed patients. However, because of their lesser toxicity (as compared with neuroleptics), we will not take a strong position against such use of lithium and antidepressants. Their use can still cause the problems we noted at the beginning of this chapter.

CONCLUSIONS

Drugs and psychosocial interventions, when properly construed, need not be either/or interventions. Drugs will be more effective when given in a positive context rather than an antagonistic one. However, in many situations psychosocial interventions can be as effective as, or more effective than, drug interventions, *if properly organized*. See, for example, the recent studies of the cognitive-behavioral and interpersonal treatment of depression (Beck, Rush, Shaw & Emery, 1979; Klerman, Weissman, Rounsaville & Chevron, 1984; Murphy, Simons, Wetzel, & Lustman, 1984). The problem is that pills are easy to give, while psychosocial interventions dealing with particular types of problems are much more complicated, expensive to arrange, and difficult to sustain. However, if the patient were one of us, a relative, or close friend, a psychosocial intervention would be preferable, given the known toxicities of the chemicals.

Community mental health is psychosocial. The position we espouse is a psychosocial one. Psychotropic drugs are probably here to stay, so they must be contextualized in the overall approach. They should not be oversold and overrelied upon as they are so often today. Nonphysicians tend to accept their use far too uncritically because of the authority of M.D.ieties. To place them in proper context, non-M.D. community mental health workers must know both their value and limitations. They must know how to ask questions that call the prescribing practices of M.D.'s into question.

Community mental health workers must be very concerned about how much more difficult their work is when their clients have tardive dyskinesia or are experiencing the akinesic (demotivating) effects of neuroleptics. Community work must pay very careful attention to everything that makes the work easier or more difficult—drugs, families, stigma, etc. Leaving the drugs to the exclusive purview of M.D.'s is a common failing; on the other hand, physicians tend to overfocus on the drugs, leaving the psychosocial components to everyone else. The clients are the ones who suffer from this fragmentation in points of view.

Psychosocial Intervention

CHAPTER 6

Interviewing: Making All the Right Moves

IT IS NOT POSSIBLE TO DO EFFECTIVE community mental health without being able to establish and maintain a positive relationship between mental health worker and user. This chapter provides guidelines as to how this is best done and hence serves as the foundation for what follows. It should be read, reread and put into practice until it becomes instinctive.

INTERVIEWING

Every major mental health textbook contains a pro forma chapter on interviewing. There are entire books on the subject. With rare exception they emphasize history-taking, assessment of psychopathology, and the mental status exam, with the goal of enabling the student to make an accurate *DSM-III* diagnosis. In turn, this will purportedly allow an accurate treatment prescription (usually medication).

By way of contrast, the approach described here has as its principal emphasis the relationship between worker and user. We view making initial contact, building rapport, and establishing a collaborative working relationship as central to the work. In addition, we believe that our problem-focused, relationally oriented, contextualizing approach to the story the user brings, preserves, and enhances client self-control and power. Thus, the critical *therapeutic* process of remoralization is begun immediately.

We abhor today's trend to compartmentalize, and hence decontextualize, certain parts of assessment interviews. For example, one of us recently interviewed a 46-year-old chronically depressed, suicidal, unkempt, overweight man who had been confined to a wheelchair for several years since an auto accident. The interview focused on what kinds of things made him more or less suicidal, what, if anything, he had to live for, and events related to his most recent serious suicide attempt. It was only after the exploration of a number of areas in his life that we were able to agree upon something that presented a ray of hope for this otherwise hopeless, demoralized man. We agreed that he was lonesome for female company. He had let his personal appearance deteriorate because he didn't think he could ever again find a woman who would care for him (his last suicide attempt came after his then woman friend had left him). The discussion then focused on courting behavior, using his courtship of his ex-wife as an example. The interview concluded by our defining a number of specific things (e.g., lose weight, shave) he needed to accomplish before embarking on a new courtship. He looked revitalized. In the post-interview discussion, his worker remarked that she was afraid the interview would include a "real" suicide assessment! She obviously had been taught a format for such a decontextualized assessment. The interview, focused on suicide *in the context of events* in this man's life, didn't fit her format, hence didn't qualify as a "real" suicide assessment. For us there can be *no* valid assessment independent of context.

It is our position that mental health workers from several disciplines can be effective psychosocial change agents with very disturbed and disturbing clients. In our experience, the ability to implement a psychosocial intervention depends on a shared understanding of the client's current situation, of the life experiences involved in its development, and of the resources available for dealing with the problem, as defined by the client. The evaluative process should lead client and therapist to a shared, organized understanding of the client's world, which in turn will allow both players to act on a known and meaningful scenario. This sense of feeling understood is remarkably relationship-enhancing. Although the type, duration, and site of the intervention will vary, the evaluation process can be the similar across clients. Ideally, the evaluation will allow the development of a relatively specific plan in close collaboration with the client. No actions should be taken until both parties understand *what is going on* in the particular situation.

We are much more certain about the common nonspecific aspects of psychosocial treatments than we are about the applicability of specific types of treatments to particular patients. Although the type of interview we espouse is designed to result in maximizing the usefulness of these nonspecific factors, the techniques we describe to facilitate this process are quite specific in aim, content, and desired effect.

MAKING INITIAL CONTACT

One of the defining characteristics of persons coming for psychiatric help is difficulty establishing and maintaining interpersonal relationships. The extent of the difficulty and the reasons for this vary widely. However, very few persons labeled "chronically psychotic" will have an easy time beginning or sustaining a meaningful relationship—with a therapist or anyone else. Remember though—everyone deserves a fresh look and another chance. Thus, in approaching the assessment of a new client, the first and most critical task is to establish at least a thread of rapport. This can be achieved in a variety of ways. However, care must be exercised by interviewers so that their expectations are not unrealistic; otherwise they are likely to be disappointed. Approaching clients with a "what can I get out of them" attitude is likely to generate an unwinnable tug of war. Do not come on as a rescuer. Very often clients would rather "drown" than allow themselves to be rescued, with all the obligations (real or fantasied) engendered by the rescue process. Remember, the likelihood of your being the first person to try and save these clients is remote. They know, all too well, that disappointed rescuers usually give up when they find the rescuee is "uncooperative."

What are the elements in the interview that should be attended to? First, in order to be most effective you need to be as comfortable as possible. This means, for example, that you should do your evaluations in a setting in which you feel comfortable. Comfortable chairs, proper temperature, and uninterrupted quiet are essential. These ecological variables not only contribute to comfort but they also facilitate the rapport-establishing process by minimizing distractors and enabling the interviewer and the client to focus solely on the task at hand. Public settings tend not to take such ecological variables seriously. We do. You should be assertive with supervisors and colleagues about the need to be properly equipped.

What we describe here is what goes on when an evaluation takes place in your office; this is the setting where beginning interviewers feel most comfortable. With training and experience the contexts within which you feel comfortable should expand so that you feel comfortable working in other people's territories. Remember, the context in which an interview takes place affects both the content and evaluative process (Mosher, 1978). Metaphorically, your office is the zoo and the client's living place is the jungle; behavior may vary considerably across these contexts. We recommend in-home interviews when the client's living group plays a role in the problem and when the clinician wants to experience the situation first hand. There are, of course, realistic constraints on the frequency with which in home interviewing can be done. However, "it's too time-consuming" is an insufficient excuse if the real issue is lack of interviewer comfort with out-of-office contexts (see Burti & Mosher, 1986, for an example of the helpfulness of non-office-based interventions).

Setting the Context

It is important that you attempt to put yourself in your clients' shoes from the very beginning of your contact, i.e., the introduction (see Table 6.1). So, remember that they are bound to be nervous, unsure of what to expect, and hesitant—especially when seen in your office. Their interpersonal anxiety is often based on fear of rejection on the one hand and fear of being overwhelmed on the other. The interviewer must steer a course between these extremes; paying absolute attention to what clients say and do without being intrusive is a good guideline to follow. One way you can put yourself into the client's frame of mind is by thinking about times in your life when you've gone to a party in someone's home where you've never met the host or hostess and must introduce yourself. For us, this social context is analogous to the experience of the new client in an evaluator's office. So, like a good host or hostess, you should go out of your way to make the new guest comfortable. In psychologic terms this process can be called "active empathy." A warm hello, a firm, inviting-in handshake and a few words of small talk go a long way toward putting a new client at ease.

It is good practice to introduce yourself with your full name and ask the client for his. Call the client Mr., Mrs., or Ms. Jones and then ask him *how he would like to be addressed* in the interview—formally (Mr. Jones), by his first name, e.g., Richard, or by a contraction or nickname, e.g., "Dick" or "Rich." Too often a busy mental health worker will skip this process, introduce himself as "Dr. So and So" and addressing the client by his first name or nickname without first clearly showing respect by addressing him formally. Asking clients how they would like to be called, in addition to conveying respect, gives them some power and control in a still relatively undefined setting. There are sufficient power and status differences built into the situation without your contributing to them with the condescension implied when you don't feel obliged to follow usual social conventions. Clients are often very sensitive to this demeaning behavior on the part of mental health workers; in fact, a "veteran" (long-term system user) may be quite taken aback by being treated as a person entitled to the usual social amenities. It is also useful to answer clients' initial questions about the interviewer in a direct, honest, straightforward manner. It is important to remember that insofar as possible you want to treat clients as potential partners and attempt to recruit them into a collaborative relationship. Attention to these interpersonal nuances will facilitate this process.

For office-based evaluations we recommend directing the client to a particular chair as a means of providing anxiety-relieving structure. When on
their territory clients should be allowed to determine the seating arrangement. If possible, use two similar comfortable swivel armchairs placed at a
90° angle. This allows both client and evaluator to change distance and
degree of openness by turning the chairs from side to side and sitting forward or back (Figure 6.1). Similarity of the chairs is another way to avoid
reinforcing power and status differences. All too often the evaluator has a
large, soft, comfortable chair while the evaluatee is seated in a straightback
or metal fold-up chair. This makes it very clear who is in charge in that
context.

Assessing the Initial Relationship

Early in an initial interview distance will be defined mainly by the *physical* distance the client maintains. Psychological distance will be defined after
initial rapport has been established.

Early distance assessment begins with clients' response to the initial handshake. Try not to vary your handshake. It should be firm and used to lead
clients into the room. If their response is soft and their hand withdrawn
quickly, you have an immediate clue that, at least in the beginning, they
want to keep their distance. You may expect them to be rather passive. Initial
eye contact is another good guide. Look new clients directly in the eye while
you shake hands. If they respond by maintaining eye contact or looking you
over, you'll know they are willing to engage you, at least initially. If the eyes

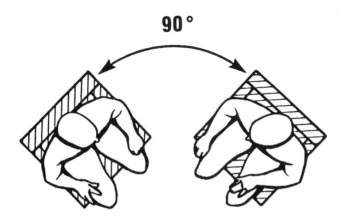

FIGURE 6.1
Interviewing: Optimal Seating Arrangement

do one thing and the hand another, you can presume that they're not really sure of how they're going to deal with you.

The few steps necessary between the handshake and the chair provide a good opportunity to get some sense of clients' physical presentation to the world. Do they carry themselves with head up and shoulders back and walk goal-directedly to the chair indicated, or do they move hesitantly, looking at the floor? Is the movement of their arms and legs free or do their joints seem to be filled with molasses? These physical movements are excellent indicators of such things as degree of situational intimidation, overall self-confidence, motor coordination, medication status, and passivity. Medication-influenced motor behavior is particularly relevant to an assessment of clients' ability to blend in with the rest of the people in the community. A grimacing, stoop-shouldered person with a shuffling gait typically evokes in others, including the interviewer, a response of "unusual," "odd," "peculiar," or "bizarre." Persons thus labeled are often avoided, if not actively rejected. Interviewers should be able to recognize and empathize with the client's position and not react as the client may have come to expect.

How persons seat themselves can also offer valuable clues to the amount of initial distance they require to be comfortable. Clients may sit as far away as possible in the chair or actually move it away. Others sit rigidly erect, equidistant from all sides. Others lean forward on the chair arms.

In addition to the physical (and by implication interpersonal) distance clients seek, it is very important to evaluate their initial degree of openness from their body language. Clients who sit far away, turned away, with their legs and arms tightly crossed, are giving a clear closed distant message. There are all kinds of variations on the open-closed, close-distant continua that should be assessed early on in the interview. These body movement variables provide an excellent nonverbal assessment of rapport parameters. Someone with whom you've been successful in establishing a relationship can go, in the course of an interview, from looking like a wilted plant to being firm, upright, and open. If they leave as wilted as when they came in, you've probably not been successful in establishing positive rapport. There are, of course, a number of clients with whom many contacts may occur before a relationship can be established.

In the beginning, it is important to respect clients' need for distance so as to avoid their feeling intruded upon and overwhelmed. For example, we recommend that with standoffish clients you push your chair back, lean back, and stare at the ceiling while beginning the interview with neutral, innocuous small talk about the weather or some similar topic. As the interview proceeds you can move in progressively with your chair, lean forward, and attempt to increase the amount of eye-to-eye contact as a test of the limits of their ability to tolerate closeness. When you get too close they will begin to withdraw. After a relationship has been established, their need to distance themselves can be commented on and the reasons for it questioned.

The "Joiner"

Joining is a technique whereby interviewers attempt to meet clients where they are, to share something about their world that is common to both. As part of interviewers' efforts to put themselves into clients' shoes, it is a good way to show active empathy.

Generally speaking, an informal, casual but respectful, open, interested, nonjudgmental, and *totally* attentive attitude is best. Informality will help undercut clients' attributions of extraordinary status and power to the interviewer. Attentiveness will both facilitate rapport-building and, in many instances, surprise clients. They may have gotten used to the all-too-common perfunctory "helper knows best" approach. Openness will allow you to meet clients empathetically, with a "fresh" eye.

Despite your very best efforts to begin a relationship, the client may still be wary of involvement. This can be a product of previous disappointment with "helpers," a lifelong need to maintain distance, or both. When you sense wariness (via the body movement patterns described above and a paucity of verbal response), it may be useful to begin the interview (while leaning back, staring at the ceiling) with a question focused on the client's geographical origins or recreational interests. These kinds of questions are usually nonthreatening and provide the interviewer access to an experience of the client's that he may, in at least an indirect way, share. In our experience even the most wary, almost mute clients will respond to a properly chosen joiner (although not always the first one).

> For example, one of us (LRM) opened an interview with a withdrawn, depressed 24-year-old woman with an obvious Texas accent by asking where she'd grown up (Houston) and then about the changes she'd seen there. She spoke of the high activity, boom-town, disorganized quality of the city and the interviewer replied that he'd experienced the same thing (with attendant discomfort) when he visited there some months earlier.

> In another interview a muscular, acutely psychotic 21-year-old man was asked if he like sports. He said he'd played football in high school and still followed the game. The interviewer acknowledged that he liked and followed football and then went on to discuss the ups and downs of the local professional team.

These seemingly mundane exchanges often prove to be remarkably facilitative to the rapport-establishing process. They involve limited self-disclosure by focusing on an experience the interviewer can acknowledge as having shared with the client. "Joiners" also serve to minimize status and power differences inherent to the context. Finally, "joiners" tend to counteract initial distortions and projections on the client's part by shifting the focus of attention to a shared, here-and-now, less threatening reality. Although these exchanges can be extraordinarily helpful, they should only be used when necessary and should not be used to provide the interviewer with a self-disclosure lecture format!

Another type of "joiner" found to be helpful in developing and maintaining rapport in an early interview is the use of the interviewees *exact* phraseology when clarification or additional information is sought.

> During a discussion of a 24-year-old male client's views on death and afterlife he said, "There's no way to know when your card will be pulled . . . it could be today or 50 years from now." The interviewer, following his lead, inquired, "When you let your imagination run free, when do you *think* your card will be pulled?"

Persistent attention to using the client's own language provides ongoing "joiners," keeps you on the client's level of expression and provides the client with an immediate, real experience of having been listened to carefully, and perhaps cared about. Clients surveyed at the end of successful psychotherapeutic relationships frequently report that what was most important to them was someone who *really* listened (i.e., understood their experience).

Minimizing Distortions and False Attributions

No matter how able you are to approach users with an open mind and a "fresh eye" (the phenomenological attitude), it is not likely that you will be accorded similar treatment by clients. They will come to your interview with varying amounts of baggage (i.e., unrealistic expectations, projections, false attributions, transference, misconceptions, preconceptions, etc.). One important aspect of the evaluation process is understanding the baggage but not letting it get in the way. To do this you must realize that clients will, to varying degrees, distort how you believe you are presenting yourself.

The type and amount of distortion will be a product of what both interviewer and client bring to the situaion. Sullivan was especially eloquent when he described therapists' need to understand what they bring to the interview.

> The psychiatrist must be alert to learn, insofar as possible, the immediate impression of him which is created in a stranger. It is useful for the therapist to review these details with great care at the start of his career, gradually catching on to what phenomena have made what impression on him; correspondingly,

by observing the larger context of what the other person has done after the formal beginning of the interview, he can begin to develop dependable impressions of how he himself must have affected that person. . . . Throughout the inception of the interview, the psychiatrist certainly, and any interviewer in some measure, should "know how he acts"—that is, he should have learned from experience the *usual* impression obtained of him in the particular circumstances of encountering the sort of stranger that the interviewee at first glance *seems* to be. In other words, the psychiatrist should have some idea of how he affects the stranger and how he facilitates or retards certain things that the stranger may have thought of doing. (Sullivan, 1970, p. 67)

It is sometimes helpful in attempting to understand one's self-presentation for a relatively inexperienced interviewer to review, for herself, how she "comes across" to strangers of various types in social situations. In general, we recommend review of self-presentation to younger and older males and females, to persons perceived to be authorities (by virtue of age, intellect, or power), to persons of very different cultural backgrounds, and to persons with some obvious handicap (e.g., blind, amputee). For inexperienced interviewers a review of their self-presentation can be accomplished with other trainees and supervisors, perhaps utilizing role-playing to enhance the reality of the situation. This process is a very important element in the evolving context of the interview. How it is dealt with will affect the nature of the relationship that is (or is not) established.

How can you deal with in-interview distortions effectively? First, we recommend that interviewers solicit clients' understanding of the reasons for and expectations of the interview. After affording clients enough time to explicate and clarify their understanding of it, interviewers should honestly and straightforwardly explain their own understanding of the reason(s) for the interview, about how long it will take and what the patient might reasonably expect from it. "I've been asked to see you with regard to the problems that resulted in your seeking (or being brought for) help. We'll spend 45 or so minutes discussing them, with the hope that we can evolve a plan together that may begin to address and solve some of them."

Although it is important not to fuel unrealistic expectations on the client's part, the interviewer should also not approach the interview with unduly low expectations, as these will only contribute to the demoralized state of the client. Under these circumstances, a dose of optimism tempered with reality can be extremely useful. For example, it may be helpful to say something like the following: "I don't know enough about you yet to say for sure that I can help you, but I will try and I believe that together we may be able to improve your situation. I wouldn't be here if I didn't believe that, even if you don't." For the demoralized veteran of the system, this sort of faith and optimism can be sustaining and mobilizing. It also establishes a precedent of honesty and openness that is likely to be experienced as reassuring and refreshing.

Above all, it is important to acknowledge the client's experiential basis for misattributions to the interviewer. This is another example of a crucial aspect of dealing with psychotic clients—*validating their experience*. A common problem with inexperienced interviewers dealing with psychotic clients is that they try to *convince* clients they are trustworthy. Clients' mistrust is based on experience. Hence, to try to convince them otherwise is to invalidate their experience. It's better to acknowledge their experience and advise them not to trust you until they know you well enough to warrant it. At this point it is often useful to inquire about clients' previous experiences with therapists.

A 25-year-old college graduate living at home with his parents after a year's hospitalization for schizophrenia was moved from the midwest to the east coast (at his parents', especially his father's, behest) to the city where his brother lived. During the initial interview, a major focus was what the client was going to do to get money. Each time the therapist mentioned going to work, the client would produce a litany of reasons why he couldn't. The therapist presumed, especially after having talked on the phone with the workaholic businessman father, that this was an attribution to him of the father's tremendous pressure on the client to "stop being so goddam lazy and go out and get a job." The therapist acknowledged the client's experience of his father's pressure about work and how that could certainly make him angry enough to resist. In fact, he hypothesized, the harder the father pushed, the stronger the resistance. The therapist also acknowledged that, since he'd been hired by the father, the client had *good reason* to believe the therapist would do the father's bidding, i.e., demand the client-son go to work immediately, if not sooner. At this point, the therapist returned to a previously agreed-upon goal—the client wanted to have his own source of support. The interviewer stated that how, when, and what the client did to get money was his responsibility, but that work was certainly the most common way in this culture. With that, the client began to focus on the types of jobs for which he might be qualified that might be available.

A second useful technique for dealing with in-interview projections is to shift the focus of discourse.

For example, a young woman who had made a suicide attempt by slitting her wrists came to the interview preoccupied with whether or not the therapist could ever see her as anything but a woman with an ugly scar on her wrist. Acknowledging her experience of her family's and friends' rejection-laden responses to her scar didn't defuse her preoccupation. She wanted to know the therapist's position. Did she "have any redeeming social value with a scarred wrist?" The therapist chose to use the client's metaphor—redeeming social value—and focus on it in its more usual context, that is, in the judgment of obscenity and pornography. This shifted the focus from an individual accept/reject response by the therapist to one of community acceptance of something it fears, but also "gets off on" by looking at. In discussing the application of this metaphor to her situation, the therapist placed himself in the position of an ordinary community member of his age and status and responded that, in fact, he was sorry but he probably wouldn't even notice the scar. Her plea for acceptance/approval, reassurance, and need to be special to the therapist was first shifted to the metaphor, then diffused and normalized within the reality context of community.

It is our intention to focus the interviewer's attention on the inevitable distortions that will occur in the interpersonal field with clients. As with so many other aspects of clienthood, the longer they've been in the system, the more hospitalizations they've experienced, and the larger the number of would-be rescuers they've seen, the more extensive and firmly held will be the projections. This is part of what causes so-called "chronic" patients to be viewed as very difficult and hence to be avoided if at all possible.

Avoiding Stereotypes

A preliminary, important aspect of a first interview is identifying the real "customer" of the intervention. In fact, in contrast to private office practice, where most patients go on their own, in public psychiatry, the patient often is brought to the attention of an agency by others or has been pushed by others: The patient is not the customer of the intervention.

This split in roles may be clear, as in the case of involuntary commitments. Often it is blurred or hidden and has to be actively looked for. It sometimes happens that a patient pretends to be cooperative but keeps being vague, generic, evasive, subtly "resistant." Usually this is because he only reluctantly agreed to see a mental health professional as a result of pressure from a spouse, a parent, or family doctor. In these cases the context is *not* therapeutic because there is no engagement. Pretending to do therapy is nonsense. It is advisable, instead, to conduct the interview in a way that brings to the surface how the patient has come to the attention of a provider, to show sincere understanding of his resistances and deal overtly with them, and to explain that therapy by force does not exist. However, we are available to treat him if he is willing. Sometimes, if motivation, however minimal, exists, it is possible to engage him. Also, paradoxically refusing to treat him may be the only therapeutic intervention possible.

In the case of involuntary commitments, it is hoped that every effort was already made to obtain the patient's consent. However, when a person has been committed involuntarily, it is still useful and necessary to explain to the patient the course of events that brought the therapist or some colleague, unwilling and compelled by the circumstances, to commit him. One explains that part of one's role as a responsible mental health professional is to do commitments and points out which behaviors of his were the most disturbing. A honest and realistic attitude may uncover in the patient an unpredicted awareness of the social disturbance he provoked and open the possibility for his cooperation in the treatment.

There may also be multiple layers of "customers," in which case one has to be concerned about who the ultimate purchaser of the intervention is; he will be considered to be "the" customer. A good way to recognize the real customer is to ask oneself: Who is most interested in the intervention? The inquiry about the customer may be complicated further if an institution is involved, for example, when a worker of another agency refers a case.

In the South-Verona (Italy) Psychiatric Register there is space to record who is the "customer" of each intervention. Alternatives provided are the following:

1. Patient
2. Relatives
3. Neighbor
4. Ourselves
5. Police
6. Family doctor
7. Psychiatrist
8. Other specialist
9. Agencies, other

There is also a very general "must" at the outset of any interview (or contact in general): Never take anything for granted. Information has to be probed in order to discriminate facts from assumptions and stereotypes, which tend to perpetuate problems and replicate the same answers and, therefore, make any change impossible.

For example, a common request in a case of someone who has had multiple previous hospitalizations is the following: "Come pick up Mr. X Y because he has gone crazy, just like the other time!" There are two important presuppositions (based on previous *institutional* practice) in a request worded like this: that X Y (1) actually has a mental illness, and therefore (2) actually needs hospitalization. No alternative is left to the mental health worker. He is regarded not as a professional, but as a mere executor. A request like this: "Come and see X Y because he does this and that — strange things!" does not require a higher level of sophistication; however, it is posed in a correct format.

An accurate inquiry has to be made right from the beginning, even over the phone. Proper questions include:

• What happened exactly?
• Who said it?

- From whom did you learn that?
- When did it happen?
- How long did it last?
- Who was there, etc.?

In general, facts in a context have to be collected. The classical 5 W's (who, what, where, when and why) are of help in guiding the inquiry. However, it should be kept in mind that *why* elicits an opinion and therefore is less reliable than *after what* is.

Collecting Information in the Initial Interview

In our view interviewing skills are better learned from clinical practice than from a book. However, some dos and don'ts to serve as broad, nonrestrictive guidelines can be helpful.

To reiterate, the initial segment of the interview should be aimed at maximizing comfort by use of active empathy, providing structure by setting the context, determining and respecting the amount of distance the client requires, facilitating rapport via small talk and "joiners," and defusing projections. Having done that you are ready to proceed.

Process Techniques: An interview is usefully separated into process and content elements. The latter will be described shortly. In terms of process, there are several ways by which an interviewer can both enhance the quantity and quality of it and have a positive therapeutic impact. These techniques also allow for the testing of client responsiveness to an interpersonal intervention.

Basically, we have found that it is useful for the interviewer to supply what is missing or underrespond to what is in oversupply in the interview. Three different variables—distance (relationship), verbal output (cognition), and body activity (affect)—should be observed and appropriate responses made based on these observations. Thus, when dealing with quiet, withdrawn, low energy (usually depressed) clients, interviewers should gradually change positions to sidle in closer, speak animatedly using lots of hand gestures (if it's comfortable to do so), while leaving plenty of time and space open to client response by asking open-ended questions and patiently waiting and gently prompting for responses. It is as if the interviewer is supplying the fuel for a stalled automobile with the expectation it will start as a result.

With an overactive, fast-talking, intrusive, but rather disorganized client the interviewer should exert control by moving in to meet the client face-to-face, by structuring the interview with short, focused, slowly and simply stated questions, by not allowing the client to respond tangentially, and by taking the stance of a firm, strong, and non-verbose person. The interviewer, once he has gotten in a face-to-face position, should move as little as possible and maintain as much eye-to-eye contact as possible while speaking slowly, quietly, and firmly. This is basically a containment technique using a highly structured interpersonal relationship.

With a withdrawn, quiet, frightened client, whose initial verbal responses are disorganized and contextually inappropriate, the interviewer's verbal behavior should be very structuring (simple, measured, quiet, focused), as with the overactive, intrusive client. However, the distance the client has established should be gradually decreased *only after* she has become less disorganized in response to the verbal structuring of the interview. Moving in too quickly will likely be experienced as overwhelming and lead to further disorganization and distancing.

What would be considered a positive response from each of these clients? From the first, depressed client we would look for more, and more animated, verbal output, increased motor activity, and an overall energized appearance. For the hypomanic person, a positive response to the interview would include decreased motor activity and intrusiveness and increased ability to stay on a subject without tangentiality or the intrusion of irrelevancies. The client should finish the interview in a much more mellow frame of mind. In the case of the disorganized acute psychotic, a positive response would include responding more promptly to the interviewer's questions and coherent speech that is clearly responsive to the questions asked (hence contextually appropriate). Finally, increased closeness will be tolerated without disorganization.

These interview process techniques are best learned through live supervision. However, an easy way to summarize what changing your in-interview behavior will do is to remember that greater structuring of the interview will result in greater organization and control but can also have the effect of dampening overall responsiveness and frightening clients who fear being controlled.

CONTENT—WHAT TO ASSESS

To begin with, it is important to acknowledge that your assessment must be somewhat limited and that it will change over time as your relationship with the client evolves. Since you can't do everything at once, priorities must be set. In general we recommend an overarching approach to assessment that focuses of what's *right* that can be expanded upon, rather than on what's wrong. Growth, development, learning, and competence are of greater interest to us than disease, disfunction and disability.

We recommend that answers to four questions be sought:

1. Why are you here? or, What is the problem? ("chief complaint")
2. What happened in your life that might relate to the development of the problem? ("precipitating events") (See Brown, 1981; Brown & Birley, 1968; Brown & Harris, 1978; Canton & Santonastoso, 1984; Caplan, 1974; Caplan & Killilea, 1976; Cobb, 1976; Day et al., 1987; Dohrenwend, 1975; Paykel, 1978; Pilisuk & Froland, 1978; Rabkin & Struening, 1976; Schwartz & Myers, 1977; Steinberg & Durrell, 1968 for research support of the importance of stressful life events in the precipitation of illness.)
3. What do you want? (What needs to happen to change things for the better?)
4. How can I help you get it?

Interviewers should be careful that they don't get so caught up obtaining a detailed history that they lose sight of the last two questions. The focus on client-defined needs is crucial to the preservation and enhancement of clients' control and power. In addition, it provides direct acknowledgment that they have a critical role to play in the resolution of the problem.

Question 4 explicitly states the interviewer's position that the interviewer and the client will be working collaboratively, following, insofar as possible, the client's lead. Questions 3 and 4 are *not* meant to invite the interviewer to suspend his judgment and common sense. Totally unrealistic needs or problem solutions should be labeled as such and the questions readdressed. We also find it useful to attempt to look for a client's sense of humor. This does at least two things: provides another way to build the relationship, and assesses the depth of the client's demoralization. It's always a hopeful sign, as well as a helpful intervention, if interviewer and interviewee can share a good laugh.

The answers to some or all of these four questions may not be clear immediately; however, they should continue to be focused on as the relationship evolves over time.

The first two questions are usually easier to address with clients who have not had long careers as patients. The further clients get from the initial episode that required mental health care, especially if it was serious psychosis requiring inpatient care, the harder it is to unravel the events that precipitated this original dramatic occurrence. However, even for long-term system veterans there is usually some event, however trivial it may seem to us, that precipitated a new need for "care." Focusing on the emotions associated with this event will both help establish empathic rapport and provide an opportunity to assess the degree to which the client is able to acknowledge and accept, rather than keep out of awareness, his feelings. Remember, the degree of difficulty encountered in attempting to establish a relationship and the degree to which content must be dissociated from the associated feelings will provide valuable clues as to how difficult it is going to be to involve the client in an ongoing therapeutic relationship. *Psychosocial interventions require relatedness.*

System veterans (the so-called "chronically mentally ill") are often distinguished by the degree of interpersonal scarring they manifest via active interpersonal distancing or passive disinterest in the interview. These interpersonal maneuvers are felt, by them, to be crucial to the prevention of further injury. Hence, they must be respected and approached with great care. The client's message is usually clear if we take the time to hear it: "I've been wounded and scarred too many times before by encounters like this one. Understand and respect my position." Inexperienced interviewers frequently make the mistake of trying to go too fast, of being pushy and unduly intrusive. Try to remember that it took a long time for clients to get where they are; you need not be in a hurry to unravel the story (heaven forbid that you even *think* of helping!). Instead say something like, "You don't have to talk now about things that make you uncomfortable or that you don't want to talk about. I hope that eventually you will." This usually enhances the patient's sense of control and autonomy and communicates respect. Clients have likely encountered many previous would-be rescuers; resist the urge to grab your lance and mount your white charger for the attack. The damsel has probably been at the dragon's mercy for a long time; nothing very serious is likely to result from waiting. We find it helpful to remember that when you begin to feel that you must *do* something, especially controlling action, something in the interaction is causing *you* to be nervous.

Another fantasy that commonly causes therapists problems (in addition to the rescue fantasy) is that something they do will cause irreparable damage to the weak, helpless client. This bit of omnipotence can be easily reality-tested by remembering something a great teacher, Dr. Elvin Semrad, said: "If you think schizophrenics are weak, try and change one."

However, there are times with very withdrawn "veterans" where no response at all can be elicited, despite various attempts. Waiting brings nothing. Providers, while not yielding to therapeutic furor, nevertheless have to become active, take the initiative, find their way through resistances, and seduce the patient into activity. Playing a two-person game or running errands together are examples of techniques that can be used. It often takes a long period of hard work before the patient becomes involved.

In other cases, especially with a person going through a psychotic experience, the patient may act out during the interview or overtly exhibit either disturbing behaviors or delusional ideas. To avoid being caught off balance, the interviewer should be aware of this possibility and remain tolerant while trying to understand the message hidden behind the behavior. It is a common observation that psychiatric patients produce more symptoms in the presence of the psychiatrist: How could it be different? How can a patient be helped by a mental health professional if he doesn't present what he is expected to, i.e., psychiatric symptoms? When he needs help, he simply plays his role as mental patient.

This concept may be better explained with an example:

> One day Piero and Maria show up for an appointment at the South Verona Community Center. They live in the territory; however, in spite of the fact that he is clearly a chronic schizophrenic, he is unknown to the register. So I ask why they come now; they explain that he needs a doctor from the public system to file a certificate for the renewal of his disability pension. Then he ventures into a stormy show of all psychotic behaviors he is able to perform, quite enough to result in an emergency admission if I (LB) had not the spirit to shout that I would sign the certificate right away. As if by magic, the show stopped; he did not need to play schizophrenic anymore.

An interpretation commonly made by professionals is that the patient, feeling uneasy and disturbed, unconsciously asks with his grossly disturbed and disturbing behavior to be stopped, controlled, sedated. We believe that this twisted interpretation serves only to relieve the conscience of the worker who resorts to such a drastic measure to deal with the crisis. More simply, we believe it is logical that a seriously disorganized person in great distress will communicate an urgent, dramatic need for help in a disorganized, "psychotic" way. The risk is to give the standard, institutional answer the patient expects or, as we think, reasonably fears: massive medication, seclusion, and the like. These answers reinforce withdrawal and dependency and miss the point of finding the reason for the crisis, an issue of tremendous importance for the patient. Taking measures to control him reinforces the idea that the crisis has come out of the blue, is beyond his control, and requires external means to be solved. In a relatively short period of time the person becomes unable to recognize any connection at all between events, feelings, and acts. Decontextualization has occurred.

> Lilly, a woman of 50, is a long-term patient in the South Verona community services. She has spent 15 years in various institutions. She is intelligent and capable of crystal clear speech but she usually utters a word salad; in her accounts facts and persons of her life history are mixed up and used interchangeably. From time to time she has tantrums; sometimes she hits people. Asked why she does this, she denies ever hitting anybody. When confronted with the victim she protests that the "pope" or the "government"* must have

*These are the two villains of her life: Catholic, she married a Protestant, an American soldier. She was pregnant and had to resort to a civilian wedding, a scandal in her times, because of delays in getting special permission from religious authorities. She believes it was a handicap that hampered the marriage (later disrupted) from the beginning. By definition the "government" represents the total institution.

hit that person, not her. An interested and careful questioning *always* reveals that a real frustration occurred before the "crisis" ensued and that she had *good reasons* for being upset. However, she is unable to recognize the correlation between being upset and acting-out.

In the course of piecing together the client's story, you should try to learn about certain historical and current aspects of his competence, both interpersonal and instrumental. These two related areas are critical for evaluations for psychosocial treatment because all such therapies involve at least two human beings interacting and usually have as an overarching goal the promotion of competence; that is, (1) the ability to be involved in a relationship (interpersonal competence); and (2) real world accomplishments (instrumental competence).

The initial aspects of interpersonal competence assessment have already been described in the section on Connecting in Initial Interview. These concern the in-interview experiential (in contrast to the historical) aspect of the evaluative process. The experiential assessment is perhaps more critical than the historical one in terms of one's potential to be helpful to a particular client. That is, clients may describe a litany of prior unsuccessful therapeutic endeavors; yet, if it is possible to establish rapport, a collaborative process, and a positive in-interview response from the client in an initial interview, the history of previous failures can be acknowledged but then set aside, for the time being at least.

Interpersonal Competence

It has now been amply documented (Cauce, 1986; Cohen & Syme, 1985; Cohen, Teresi & Holmes, 1985; Dean & Lin, 1977; Dohrenwend & Egri, 1981; Gottlieb, 1985; Gottlieb & Green, 1984; Gove, 1978; Greenblatt, Becerra & Serafetinides, 1982; Gove, 1978; Hammer, 1981, 1983; Hays & Oxley, 1986; Hirsch & Rapkin, 1986; Kaplan, Cassel & Gore, 1977; Lin, Simcone, Ensel, Kuo, 1979; Mitchell, 1982; Potasnik & Nelson, 1984) that the availability of a supportive social network is the single most important environmental factor in preventing the occurrence of physical and psychological disorders, in reducing related morbidity, and in promoting rehabilitation. As explicated elsewhere (Chapter 9), the social network can be "treated" or used as an adjunct to other psychosocial interventions; therefore, assessment of the social network is critical.

First and foremost, the size and quality of the person's *current* social network need to be assessed. A historical account will tell you whether past and present are similar and something about the vicissitudes of the client's social involvements. However, this is of secondary importance to the present status evaluation. We look for information about the size of the network

("How many people do you know with whom you have at least occasional contact?"), about its composition ("Of these people, how many are parental family generation, how many are your generation, and how many are unrelated peers?"), and about the intensity ("Whom do you see most frequently? How do you usually feel after seeing Joe, Jane, etc.?"). Seeing the entire family together, if possible, can expedite this social network assessment process.

The social network analysis will supplement and usually validate the information derived from the in-interview experience with regard to the person's ability to form relationships. For example, it is likely that someone with whom it is difficult to establish rapport will have a small, principally biologically-based network. If clients report a good-sized, positively evaluated social network and you are not able to establish rapport with them, you should examine your conduct of the interview for unrecognized problems. If that does not resolve the discrepancy between the historical and experiential information, you may wish to question the validity of the customer's reports.

Next we consider clients' level of independence. Assessment of this aspect of *current* psychosocial competence is relatively straightforward: Where is the person currently residing and how does that compare with the norms for his or her age, social class, and ethnic group? Because a number of clients may be living at home with their parents or in some other non-independent setting (e.g., halfway house), it is worthwhile to establish their best-ever level of independent functioning: Did they ever live alone or with nonfamily peers? If so, when and for how long?

Great care must be exercised to properly factor in cultural, religious, ethnic, and gender differences relevant to the assessment of independence. The interviewer's standards must take a back seat to factors relevant to the particular individual being seen. For example, in cultures where leaving home is not expected, the assessment can focus on the degree to which there is reciprocal versus exploitative dependency. In the former the participants each make a voluntary contribution to the common good; in the latter there is a usually covert agreement that each participant make a required, usually disliked, contribution. Another example of potential problems with this assessment can occur when a male is evaluating a female; he must remember that affiliation is more important than autonomy to many women and not judge living with parents as necessarily indicative of psychopathology.

This evaluation will allow you to set a current anchor point and a past best-ever one. The effectiveness of your efforts to facilitate independence (if this becomes an agreed upon goal) can be judged vis-à-vis these two anchor points.

Ideally, interpersonal and instrumental competencies are combined in sexual accomplishments. That is, having a loving sexual relationship demands the ability both to make a friend and to perform sexually. Wide variation is, of course, expected — from minimally sexual but very loving relationships to almost purely sexual and minimally loving ones. The important questions are:

1. Does the client have now, or did he/she have in the past, relationships where sex and affection were combined? If so, how many and for how long? When was the last one? What happened?
2. What was the nature of the relationships where sex and affection were not combined? Follow with other questions as above.

Needless to say, if the client is married it is important to know about that relationship. If possible, especially when the spouse is described as part of the problem, we recommend that the client and spouse be seen together. This can be very helpful for getting a different perspective on the problem (from the spouse) and for finding a way to address it at the level at which it developed. In fact, insofar as feasible, all problems brought in by customers should be addressed at the level at which they developed (e.g., the peer network, the family, the living group).

Generally speaking, the issue of suicide or violence to others will be assessed in the context of the client's various relationships. Except when drug intoxication is involved, it is usually a change in or threatened or real loss of relationships that causes persons to consider violence to themselves or others. If clients present as currently suicidal, this should be discussed in detail: How long have they felt this way? Have they made plans? What has to change in order to feel differently about killing themselves? How have they resolved their suicidal intentions previously? What has kept them from killing themselves so far? If they have made previous attempts what means were used? (Violent attempts — cutting, stabbing, hanging, shooting — should be taken *very* seriously.) To prevent the therapist from becoming subject to manipulation, it may be helpful to acknowledge that clients have ultimate control over their lives. If they really want to kill themselves badly enough, no one can stop them — even though the interviewer thinks it's a pretty dumb idea. Discussion of suicide should be matter-of-fact and detailed; otherwise the therapist's anxiety about it will probably be transmitted to the client. This will, in turn, make it more difficult to define and implement a helpful intervention.

Instrumental Competence

Basically, determining instrumental competence involves a rather straightforward assessment of clients' educational, vocational and recreational accomplishments. How far did they go in school? What kind of grades did they get? Why did they stop? What jobs have they held, for how long, and paid how much? Why did they leave? If currently unemployed, for how long? What do they do with their spare time?

This domain will allow you to derive, in concert with clients, reasonable expectations for their future educational and/or vocational goals. Remember, proven ability to hold a job is the best predictor of successful employment. This also applies to friendships and sex. Although these are useful generalizations, they should not be so overvalued as to prevent the setting of future goals that surpass past accomplishments. Here, phenomenologic openness tempered by knowledge and experience can be very helpful.

So-Called "Special Cases"

Some persons introduce themselves as "special cases" from the outset, for a variety of reasons (e.g., an important person has referred them; they are friends; they have special characteristics). This beginning is generally a handicap because important steps of a routine procedure may be skipped.

> For instance, during a team meeting one of the professional nurses speaks of a case he just referred to one of us (LB), the "doctor," after an unusually quick first interview. The patient, a teacher, had introduced himself as being "too dependent upon my mother" and extensively quoted Freud. The nurse, a born helper and an experienced counselor, had been caught off balance. He considered the case a "special" one, beyond his culture and therefore beyond his skills. He had even forgotten to fill out the register intake form. The author (LB) commented that considering a case as "special" exposes one to the risk of skipping important steps, as had actually happened. He also added that Freudian patients must receive the same treatment as all others — no more, no less — and suggested that the nurse see the teacher again and fill out the intake form.
>
> The author saw the patient two weeks later; he said he had come *only* to keep the appointment because he had already recognized and solved his presenting problem talking with the nurse. He added that he had been elected principal in his school and had gone through a period of disorganization in dealing with the new tasks. This had come out during the intake questioning; the nurse had seen him two more times and given very good, effective suggestions. As often happens, a reality orientation, together with the sincere interest of an experienced counseler, was effective in mobilizing the resources of the patient, without having to use a fancy psychotherapeutic technique.

STOCKTAKING AND CLOSING THE INTERVIEW

Although this discussion of the stocktaking process occurs near the end of this chapter, this is an activity that should be conducted throughout the interview. We presume that interviewers have by now learned to monitor clients' responses more or less continuously. It is just as important, but not always as easy, for interviewers to be aware of their responses to clients. It is virtually impossible not to respond affectively to clients. These responses are normal expressions of interviewers' humanity. Clients will excite, depress, turn on, turn off, anger, dismay, bore, frighten, perplex, amaze, stimulate, and confuse interviewers. Experiencing such feelings is not usually a problem — except when they are not recognized and acknowledged or are acted on without awareness. Acting on such feelings generally occurs, in fact, *because* interviewers have failed to recognize and acknowledge them to themselves. Generally speaking, acting on emotions generated in interviews will lead to either over- or underinvolvement with clients. In fact, this inappropriate level of involvement is a useful cue to supervisors for exploration of interviewer feelings toward clients. Keeping a watchful eye on one's own feelings, while simultaneously being totally attentive to the client, is something that can only be learned through experience and supervised client contact.

As is the case with clients, interviewers will have feelings generated both from the situation at hand (responses to the clients behavior) and from baggage they bring to the session from their own life experiences (countertransference, if you will). Earlier in this chapter we discussed the importance of knowing how you present yourself to various kinds of persons. It is also important that clinicians learn, over time, which kinds of clients consistently generate particular types of feelings in them.

For example, one of us (LRM) feels very sleepy, tired and bored when he interviews young men whose difficulties seem to stem from the lack of a well developed, functioning conscience. The response usually occurs within the first five minutes of an interview and is so predictable by now as to be a highly reliable indicator of a state of superegolessness. Clearly, these clients are not likely to be very positively regarded by this interviewer; acknowledging this helps avert problems by allowing anticipatory planning.

Basically, we advise inexperienced interviewers to ask themselves early in the interview whether or not they like the interviewee and/or find him/her interesting. If the answer is *negative*, the interviewer should try to assess quickly whether the response is generated by the client's interview behavior or whether something about the client is distasteful because of previous experiences with similar clients or because of the interviewer's particular mood that day or because something about the client triggers feelings that come from his/her own life experiences. This is, of course, easier said than done while continuing to conduct an interview. However, sorting out client, interviewer, and situational contributions to responses is important for deriving the best possible understanding of the client and his/her potential amenability to psychosocial interventions.

Clinicians should not expect to be saints. No one likes everyone. They are not expected to be able to hit it off with every client. Problems don't come from not liking some clients — they come from not recognizing that you don't like them. As long as strongly negative or positive feelings are recognized and acknowledged they will not usually cause trouble.

In addition to unrecognized affective responses, the rescue fantasy and overintrusiveness, discussed earlier, are potential sources of in-interview difficulties. A final, not uncommon source of problems between clinicians and clients is clinicians' unfulfillable expectations *of* clients. People who choose to work in mental health often do so because they enjoy helping people. Wanting to be helpful is an excellent motivation so long as it doesn't contain a "you must respond as I think you should to my ministrations" clause. Clinicians should keep in mind that the life of the client they're trying to help belongs to the client, not to the clinician. Clients have to be allowed to do what they decide to do, even if clinicians believe it is a mistaken course of action (barring imminent danger, of course). Clinicians who have a strong investment in clients' living up to their expectations are bound to be frustrated, disappointed, and disillusioned over time. If their expectations are not easily lowered to more realistic levels, they'll likely withdraw, be inattentive, or leave the field. Luckily, most unrealistic expectations stem from inexperience. Tincture of time and supervision are very useful medicines for the treatment of such disorders of expectation.

At the end of an interview there should be a sense of closure for both interviewer and client. After enough basic information has been gathered, a collaborative problem resolution strategy developed, and the client's response limits tested (in terms of relationship, affect, and cognition), the interviewer should initiate closure. Closure should *not* be determined primarily by how much time has elapsed. In our experience, 40 to 60 minutes are necessary to do what we have laid out above. However, if at all possible about 75 minutes should be *allowed* for an initial interview. Allowing a time "cushion" will help dispel interviewer anxiety that occurs when time is running short and much remains to be done. Many times an interview can be satisfactorily conducted in 30 to 35 minutes. However, time pressure may lead to shortcuts, insufficient attention to critical content areas and important nonverbal cues, and misuse of clinician power in a way that will detract from the establishment of the essential collaborative relationship.

It is the clinician's responsibility to set the context. To do so when ending an interview it is helpful to say something such as, "We've talked about lots of things in this interview and I'm wondering if there's anything more you think I ought to know about you and your situation so I will have as complete a picture as possible?" This is *not* a pro forma exercise. The interviewer should wait quietly for a response. If there is none, the question should be rephrased, "Again, before we stop, are you sure we've discussed everything that's relevant to your problem and its potential for resolution?" The interviewer must patiently await a response, if any.

Next, the interviewer should review and summarize with clients the mutu-

ally agreed-upon goals, as well as the ways they have collaboratively identified to attain them. This summary should be a 1-2-3 simple one, with
questions eliciting from clients their understanding of each: "Tell me as
clearly as possible your understanding of. . . ."

Finally, the interviewer should attempt to elicit clients' explicit affective
response to the interview and ask if they have any final questions to ask of
the interviewer. Questions raised should be responded to honestly and
straightforwardly. The client should be escorted to the door, the door
opened by the worker, and the client's hand shaken while goodbyes are
exchanged.

Departing from an effective initial interview, the client will likely look glob-
ally "better"—head held high, straight posture, firm stride and a smiling face.

This has been a long and complex, but important, chapter. Its content
should be mastered through reading and dialogues with clients, coworkers
and supervisors. Skillful interviewing is the bread and butter of effective
psychosocial change agents. To aid the learning and review process we have
provided, in summary outline form, the key elements that should be attended to in the course of an initial interview (Tables 6.1, 6.2, and 6.3).

TABLE 6.1
Making Initial Contact

1. Establishing rapport
   "the party"
   active empathy and respect
   understanding power and status differences
   condescension as a no-no
   partnership

2. Setting the context
   soliciting client expectations
   diffusion of projections
   providing structure
   defining the task

3. Assessing the initial relationship
   open–closed
   close–distant

4. The "Joiner"
   casualness
   commonality of experience
   exact replication of language

5. Dealing with distortions and false attributions

6. Avoiding stereotypes

TABLE 6.2
What to Assess

1. Critical Questions
   a. Why are you here?
   b. What happened that brought you here?
   c. What do you want?
   d. How can I help you get it?

2. Competence
   a. interpersonal
   b. instrumental

TABLE 6.3
Stocktaking and Closing

1. Impact of your interview
   a. client response; physical and verbal
   b. your response

2. Sources of problems
   a. the rescue fantasy
   b. excessive intrusiveness
   c. unfulfilled expectations
   d. failure to recognize your response

3. And in conclusion . . .
   a. reset context
   b. summarize
   c. check affective response

CHAPTER 7

Ongoing Involvement

GOOD COMMUNITY MENTAL HEALTH PROGRAMS are characterized by their ability to offer clients long-term staff involvement *as needed* in the clients' natural environments. This long process (and we mean *years*, if necessary) can be wearing on staff. In later chapters we describe how mental health programs are best organized to facilitate the development of these kinds of relationships (Chapter 8) and ways of detecting and dealing with staff burnout (Chapter 10).

Here we describe particular ways of being involved in ongoing staff-client relationships that will facilitate change without wearing staff out unduly.

It is in the arena of continuing facilitative relationships that nonspecific factors identified as important in all types of psychosocial interventions (independent of theory or technique) assume special importance. Keeping them firmly in mind and attempting to maximize them will help clinicians maintain positive helping relationships over time. In this chapter we first define and elaborate upon common nonspecific factors in psychosocial interventions and then describe a corollary series of relational styles whose use will enhance the overall psychosocial intervention process.

NONSPECIFIC FACTORS IN PSYCHOSOCIAL TREATMENT

Originally elaborated by Frank (1971), nonspecific factors include:

1. *Healing context.* That is, the client perceives the helper, facility, or program as helping or as providing the context in which the client can help him/herself.

2. *Confiding relationship with a helper.* This critical variable was addressed in Chapter 6. It further encompasses the more recently described working alliance variables of client and therapist involvement, liking the process and defining it as helpful (Frieswyk, Colson, & Allen, 1984; Gomes-Schwartz, 1978; Hartley & Strupp, 1983; Horowitz & Marmar, 1985; Marziali, 1984; Marziali, Marmar, & Krupnick, 1981; Morgan, Luborsky, Crits-Christoph, Curtis, & Solomon, 1982; Strupp, 1973).

3. *Plausible causal explanation.* Clinician and client should be able to evolve a shared definition of how and why the problem developed. Answers to the first two questions (What's the problem? What happened?) of the interview format described in Chapter 6, p. 65 should provide at least a preliminary working explanation. This in turn should lead to the development of agreed-upon goals and methods for achieving them. Recent work on the therapeutic alliance in psychotherapy has found a strong relationship between the goal and strategy consensus of therapist and client and good outcome (Bordin, 1979; Horvath & Greenberg, 1986). A goal and strategy consensus should evolve as the answers to questions three and four become clear (What do you want? How can I help you get it?). Having a shared, meaningful explanation for a phenomenon is useful for both client and worker and will help them sustain their work together over time.

4. *Therapist personal qualities generate positive expectations.* The relationally-focused, problem-solving approach, dosed with optimism, as described in Chapter 6, should enable clinicians to generate positive expectations over time. Clients almost always improve; this process can be facilitated by clear, consistent, realistic, positive expectations. Expectations are powerful determiners of behavior. Negative ones promote destructive behaviors and create negatively connoted definitions of contexts that can result in spiraling, destructive, self-fulfilling prophecies for clients and helpers. The personal qualities of hope and optimism displayed by staff via positive expectations can be critical for beginning the remoralization process needed by nearly all clients who seek psychological help. Indeed, realistic optimism is morale sustaining and enhancing for staff as well as clients.

5. *Provision of success experiences.* Low self-esteem and a lack of self-

confidence, competence, and a sense of efficacy define the demoralized person. It is a rare mental health system client who is not demoralized. The helping process can be viewed as one of remoralization, in which clients are given opportunities to develop options, solve problems, overcome obstacles, and accomplish goals. To do this, clients and clinicians need to agree upon goals and strategies (Bordin, 1979) and then proceed to put them into practice. Even the smallest accomplishment — like sprucing up one's appearance — is important to the process. Sitting with clients while they arrange job interviews is a simple example of how to use the working alliance to provide a success experience. Ongoing attention to redefining goals and strategies (What do you want? How can I help you get it?) will allow clinicians to facilitate success experiences that will feed back positively into the process, so that the user will continue to like the process and find it helpful (Frieswyk et al., 1984; Gomes-Schwartz, 1978; Hartley & Strupp, 1983; Horowitz & Marmar, 1985; Marziali, 1984; Marziali et al., 1981; Morgan et al., 1982; Strupp, 1973). A corollary of this is that staff should never do anything for clients that they can do for themselves. To do so promotes unnecessary dependency and prevents clients from assuming responsibility and developing competence via accomplishment.

RELATIONAL PRINCIPLES

The usefulness of these nonspecific therapeutic factors can be maximized if clinicians can also keep in mind certain relational styles in their day-to-day work with clients (see Table 7.1). Each relational principle will be paired with one or more of the nonspecific factors.

TABLE 7.1
Community Mental Health
Relational Principles

1. Atheoretical need to understand
2. Continuity across contexts
3. Response flexibility
4. "Being with," "standing by attentively"
5. Concrete problem focus
6. Consultation, facilitation
7. Peer-like reciprocity
8. Expectation of self-help

1. Atheoretical Need to Understand (Plausible Causal Explanation)

This is meant to encourage relationships that are open, nonjudgmental, tolerant, and respectful. The clinician tries to understand what's going on with clients while avoiding categorizations. Explanatory hypotheses may be collaboratively evolved to enhance shared understanding and meaningfulness, but these should be seen as always open to revision based on new information or new situations.

2. Continuity of Relationships (Confiding Relationship)

This is, in part, an administrative principle; unless a service is organized to allow and promote continuity, its implementation is difficult. Basically we propose that a *team* of three or more persons should be each client's primary therapeutic case manager/consultant. Thus, when a crisis arises that overwhelms the client's best self-help efforts, there will be someone with whom the person has an ongoing relationship available to help manage the situation. If a client is in some form of intensive residential care (e.g., alternative or hospital), the team's functions will be supplemented by facility staff. However, the team, in collaboration with the client and facility staff, will stay involved in an ongoing way. This can be accomplished in a number of ways, e.g., by team members' spending portions of their work day — in rotation — with the client in the facility. The team, or its representative, must be involved in all client-related meetings that might involve decisions.

3. Response Flexibility (Confiding Relationship, Success Experiences)

Basically this is intended to keep workers constantly alert and responsive to changes in the overall situation, in clients' clinical statuses and in their needs. It will be difficult to implement in hierarchical organizations, which tend to impair clinicians' abilities to respond to shifting situational demands, or in programs operating from a single theoretical perspective. It asks that facility rules and regulations be looked at in terms of their relevance to particular clients and requires that treatment plans be looked upon as guidelines rather than prescriptions. Absent bureaucratic or theoretical impediments, a plan will flow logically and easily from constant attention to and, as necessary, redefinition of the collaborative relationship established with the client. For example, it should allow the worker to recognize and implement a gradual shift from a predominantly "being with" interpersonal mode to a more down-to-earth, practical, problem-solving one as clients become more organized.

4. "Being With," "Standing by Attentively," "Letting Be" (Confiding Relationship)

This relational style will allow open nonjudgmental acceptance, empathic understanding, support, reassurance, validation, and containment *without* being overintrusive, overtalkative, or demanding, and without projecting unrealistic expectations. Its hallmark is a positive, attentive presence without an expectation of doing something *to* the client. It should be the major modus operandi with very fragmented, disorganized clients. As clients begin to reorganize, its use may be curtailed while practical problems are addressed. However, it should always be readily available to reorganizing clients, who will be facing increased levels of stress as they get their lives back on track. Remember, tincture of time is very powerful medicine.

5. Concrete Problem Focus (Success Experiences, Plausible Causal Explanation)

For many clients it will be difficult to begin addressing psychological and interpersonal issues until pressing financial, work, and housing issues are dealt with. It is not easy to approach a relational problem with someone who doesn't know how he's going to feed himself. Hence, the first priority in a problem-solving and relationship-building strategy should be practical, day-to-day issues. This approach will also provide opportunities for success that are remoralizing and self-esteem and confidence building. It will build a relationship because real needs are being acknowledged, addressed seriously and, we hope, filled. There's nothing like gratitude to help build a relationship!

In the course of accomplishing concrete tasks, a great deal will be learned about what has gone wrong. Staff will come to value "car therapy" highly. Much can be learned from a captive client audience while running errands. With this knowledge, devising a psychologically and interpersonally therapeutic program is much easier and will be more accurate (see below, The Spoken Word).

6. Consultation (Healing Context, Positive Expectations)

This relational mode of *"doing with"* denotes a somewhat more activist position than "being with," while avoiding the unfortunate "doing to" connotation of some forms of "therapy." As pointed out by Wynne, McDaniel, and Weber (1986), consultation involves stock-taking, agenda-setting, collaboration between consultant and consultee, an emphasis on constructive coping, education and option development, and the expectation of involvement of at least three people.

Like family therapy, the kind of consultative relational mode we are proposing will be more open and public than is common to most doctor-patient, therapist-client relationships. These traditional two-party relationships usually have the expectation of exclusivity and confidentiality. In contrast, our approach, involving a variety of players, cannot realistically guarantee complete confidentiality *within* the setting or program. The advantages of consultative relationships over these two-party relationships are: (1) They tend to be focused on a return to functioning rather than a "cure"; (2) they tend to be collaborative, self-help, peer-oriented types of relationships rather than those in which the therapist sets the agenda and is "one up" on the client; (3) the principal focus is on the development of competence rather than on psychopathology and dysfunction.

> For example, John, a 30-year-old single man, has lived with his widowed mother for many years. He comes to the treatment team because his mother can no longer stand his disturbing behavior. This pattern has resulted in several previous hospital admissions. John acknowledges that his relationship with his mother is difficult but he believes he must return to her home because he can't see any other option.
>
> It is recommended that the staff acknowledge the problematic nature of the relationship and then offer to meet with John and his mother to obtain her view as well. In the meeting other options can be explored with both of them. If it appears that going home is what they both want, even ambivalently, the conditions for it can be agreed upon and additional meetings — to include significant others like sibs, other relatives and friends — scheduled. Although staff may view this arrangement as less than optimal (but not clearly destructive), they should not attempt to interfere if it is what John and his mother evolve as their solution.
>
> One way of addressing the situation is to involve the social network (if there is one). The notion here is that the network may defuse some of the intensity of the mother-son relationship. Also, staff might look for ways to help mother and son spend more time with peers. If this can be done there won't be as many opportunities for the development of conflicts that result in the son's being ejected from the home.
>
> In this example it would probably be wise for staff, acting as consultants to both mother and son, to schedule ongoing but relatively infrequent network meetings and to put them in touch with peer support groups (e.g., an AMI group for the mother and an ex-client group for the son).

7. Peer-Like Reciprocity (Success Experiences)

It is good practice for staff to approach clients in a humble frame of mind. Each encounter should be viewed as one from which they may learn something new or understand something better about the client or themselves. It is easier to convey these attitudes if staff approach clients as they would friends, rather than as disturbed persons. Because of substantial age differences, "peer-like" may not be the best designation; however, if it's understood that what is meant is "as if" there should be no semantic difficulty.

This relational style will enable staff to avoid power struggles and attempts at manipulation. A peer orientation does not necessarily mean equality or complete reciprocity of relationship. Because of clients' inability to solve certain problems and staff's relevant life experience and training, it is likely clients will usually get more than they give. Hence, the relationships will have in-built status and power differences. They cannot be avoided. To minimize their potentially deleterious effects, they should be recognized, acknowledged, and discussed. The aim is to develop relationships that can evolve into more or less reciprocal (friend-like) ones over time.

Proper use of this peer orientation preserves client power, acknowledges the temporary nature of the need for help, and minimizes the staff's role as "experts." Staff can be usefully authoritative (e.g., by sharing what they've learned from their relevant life experiences) without being authoritarian. Temporary parent-like relationships are also fine, so long as they don't outlive their usefulness and become reified into *nonreciprocal* dependent ones.

8. Expectation of Self-Help (Healing Context)

To promote personal problem-solving skills, responsibility, and client power and control, clients should be encouraged to evolve potential problem-solving strategies themselves and be helped, as necessary, to try them. Staff should not set themselves up as the "experts." They should intervene only when a strategy that is *clearly* destructive is about to be tried.

Self-help is really mutual help. A minimalist orientation will keep staff focused on how they can help expand clients' use of their own networks. By thinking *group, group, group*, staff can help clients access or form one — preferably one that is not made up exclusively of mental health users. The ultimate goal is to get clients out of the mental health system — even though it must be recognized that many will not stay out.

By displaying these relational modes in a clear and consistent manner, staff are more likely to become persons whom clients will seek to imitate and identify with over time. This generic learning process can result in substantial client change if there is sufficient exposure to staff qualities relevant to the person's needs and those of his family and network. "Sufficient" will vary considerably from client to client, depending on need, intensity, and duration of exposure. Hence, for a relatively competent, interpersonally unscarred person, a few outpatient interventions will suffice. By way of contrast, an 18-year-old, ninth grade dropout who has stayed with his madness in his bedroom since retreating there two years ago may require many months of intensive residential care for this process to be effective.

For this reason we believe that arbitrary length of treatment rules are unwise. Treatment should, of course, be only as long as absolutely necessary. However, how long that will be is difficult to predict in advance. Basically, when an initial set of goals is achieved, treatment should probably stop. If there are questions or disagreements about stopping, a supervisory process should be used to avoid idiosyncratic definitions of "optimal" being applied without opportunity for scrutiny by knowledgeable peers, clients, and significant others.

THE SPOKEN WORD (PSYCHOTHERAPY)

There are volumes written on psychotherapy—this is not one of them. We believe that a good community mental health program should offer and use network, family, group, and individual verbal and expressive therapies. They need to be integrated into the overall community system. They are critical to addressing many clients' psychological needs. However, they are no more or less important than clients' social and medical needs. There should not be a best or worst treatment hierarchy. This means, for example, that the most disturbed and disturbing persons (usually labeled schizophrenic) should be able to obtain intensive individual psychotherapy as readily as less disturbed (let's say neurotic) ones. A focus on needs of all types will result in a treatment plan that will attempt to fill as many of them as possible—including a need for psychotherapy.

The principles so far explicated are ones that describe relational orientations for staff vis-à-vis users. We have begun with and emphasized them because of our perception that verbal interchange tends to be overvalued compared to relational issues in many mental health settings. We do not wish to reinforce community staff's becoming 50-minute hour, in-office psychotherapists—hence, the relegation of the use of talk to the end of this chapter. It should be obvious, of course, that the day-to-day practice of the various relational modes already outlined requires verbal exchange. What we want to stress is that the interactional style (form or process) is every bit as important as what is said (content).

What we describe now are *guidelines* and a *paradigm* (only) for having verbal discussions with clients in the context of a supportive relationship that may help them calm down, reorganize, behave in more socially acceptable ways, and identify new problem-solving options and strategies.

Based on our clinical experience, and supported by substantial research data (Mayer-Gross, 1920; McGlashan, Levy & Carpenter, 1975; Soskis &

Bowers, 1969), we believe that clients who are able to fit a life disrupting episode of disturbed and disturbing behavior into the *continuity of their lifes* will, over the long run, have better outcomes. Recovery and outcome are obviously not so simplistic as we're making them out to be here. For some persons, sealing over the disturbing events will be preferable. We believe that psychotherapy can be especially useful for the process of fitting an otherwise disjunctive experience into the continuity of a life. The process requires a relationship that can be sustained in difficult times. The quality of relationship needed may not be attainable with anyone in the client's immediate social field; hence, talking events through with that group of actors may not be helpful.

Some clients, for a variety of reasons, are never able to make a good enough relationship to sustain a formal psychotherapeutic process. Psychotherapy is not everyone's cup of tea. However, staff should always keep in mind that insofar as possible every encounter and intervention should be therapeutic—and they usually will be if staff are focused on responding to needs.

Tables 7.2 and 7.3 contain an incomplete laundry list of generic psychosocial intervention techniques arranged by approximate degree of activism required to carry them out. Readers should by now know that we prefer the *least activist* techniques. Most are usable in almost any context, including formal psychotherapy. Insight is notable for its absence from the list; for us, it is overused, usually not well defined, and difficult to assess as to its presence or absence. Psychosocial interventions of whatever type, if properly conducted, should result in clients' acquiring new information and applying it to their lives. This defines a therapeutic process. It is eminently researchable. Hence, we do not use the less precise term "insight."

Our basic atheoretical operational paradigm—one that is relatively easy

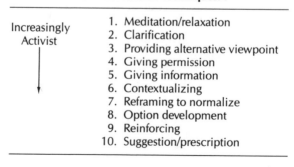

TABLE 7.2
Community Mental Health
Staff Intervention Techniques: I

Increasingly Activist	1. Meditation/relaxation
	2. Clarification
	3. Providing alternative viewpoint
	4. Giving permission
	5. Giving information
	6. Contextualizing
	7. Reframing to normalize
	8. Option development
	9. Reinforcing
	10. Suggestion/prescription

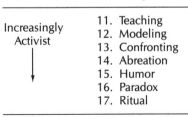

TABLE 7.3
Community Mental Health
Staff Intervention Techniques: II

Increasingly Activist	11. Teaching
	12. Modeling
	13. Confronting
	14. Abreation
	15. Humor
	16. Paradox
	17. Ritual

to teach (Table 7.4) – has the goal of helping clients fit an episode into the continuity of their lives. It begins by facilitating the connection of the emotions generated by a stressful life event to that event. The first step is to help clients *acknowledge or recognize*, with the worker, its occurrence and the emotional responses to it. Once this is accomplished the verbal process should be focused on helping clients come to terms with the consequences of the event and their reactions to it. The event and the associated emotions may need to be repeatedly discussed, until clients can *bear or experience* them without undue distress.

The last step in the process is to help clients get some distance from – to *put into perspective* or to contextualize – these occurrences while at the same time finding a way to encompass them, as well as their consequences, into their now changed life courses (Semrad, 1966; Semrad & Zaslow, 1964). This part of the process is basically one of helping the client expand his observing ego so as to encompass this painful event. The outcome of this process should be observable along the same parameters as in the initial interview, i.e., changes in relationship, affect and cognition (see Chapter 6). Note that

TABLE 7.4
Use of the Spoken Word:
A Paradigm

Fitting "the problem" into the continuity of one's life through a process of:
1. *acknowledging* the existence of the problem.
2. discussing it until it can be *borne*.
3. putting it into *perspective*.

the nature of the life events, types of emotions generated, clients' reactions, and the way they will fit into their lives are unspecified. This is deliberate so as to recognize the vast number of combinations and permutations that can be manifest clinically. A paradigm for the *process* is spelled out but the content is unspecified. The specification of the content must occur from the ongoing application of an investigatory, atheoretical need to understand.

An example of the application of this paradigm with a 22-year-old psychotic woman in Soteria House follows:

It was almost 6 a.m.; the sun was just coming up. Susan, a resident, had just set her bed on fire, hoping to cremate herself. After the fire was extinguished, she and a staff member began talking. Here is the staff member's report:

"I asked her what was happening with her. She sat quietly and without any show of emotion told me she was the devil, that the radio and TV had been giving her messages to 'burn, baby burn,' to feel the fire of hell. She subsequently said she'd gone to a Puritan gas station and decided that since the Puritans burned witches, she was a witch, and that because Halloween was coming, she would burn.

"I told her that it seemed to me she was saying she was bad in some sense, that she'd done something wrong and her way of handling these very painful feelings was to see herself as the devil.

"I then inquired of her as to recent life events which might have resulted in her feeling like a 'bad person.' She then related at first in a very disorganized way something about having had a fight with her sister in L.A. I asked again about other recent events of note; she gave me, in a much more organized way and with some real sadness, the story of how she'd not gone to her maternal grandfather's funeral last May although her sister had called and asked her to. She said she'd not gone because she was afraid of funerals, didn't want to see her grandmother hurt and crying, and feared trying to deal with her mother and sister. Both descriptions were punctuated with occasional silly giggles, questions of me as to whether I thought she was the devil, and assertions that she *was*, in fact. I said it seemed to me she talked about being the devil whenever she began to experience the pain of her sadness and badness.

"In time we agreed between us that her delusional beliefs and ideas of reference did seem to come to the forefront when she was confronting the pain of her life; later we agreed that in fact this might be her way of avoiding the experience of that pain. I went into some detail with her about her relationship with her grandfather, how she'd lived with him when things were bad for her at home. We also went into some detail about the funeral she hadn't attended; she knew her grandfather had wanted to be cremated and wondered what in fact had happened to him.

"She said then that the fire had been no accident; she had quite intended to cremate herself and had placed the lit cigarette in the mattress, watched it catch fire, and allowed it to burn her hair before deciding that burning the place up would be unfair to everyone else there. Then she went to get Greg.

"Our chat then returned to her sister. The story unfolded with pictures and a very heart-rending letter about how a year ago her sister had required gynecological surgery and had lost all her pelvic organs. Sister's letter described how empty, depressed, unfeminine and hopeless she felt. Several remarks Susan made about her sister made me feel she was in a self-destructive, competitive relationship with her in which she, Susan, was always the "bad one," the "irresponsible one," the loser in the eyes of her mother and sister. This made me feel that burning herself also had something to do with destroying her femininity. At this point she unravelled a tale of sexual promiscuity that began with her sister's surgery.

"Around 9 a.m. we switched to the living room couch and as we focused on these events she began to cry quietly. When I got inattentive and sleepy, she would bring up radio and TV messages. They told her how bad she was — I suggested maybe they were Susan talking to Susan and brought up some of the events we'd discussed about which she felt so guilty. She really delighted in that and we shared it many times over the next several days. During our time together I would often tell her I thought she was really all right but recognized how bad a person *she* felt she was; when she asked me what was good about her I told her I thought she was bright, competent, and pretty, each of which she was. I held her hand, stroked her burnt hair, and made small talk. Often I found myself reaching out to her because she was so sad and I wanted to comfort her and let her know that I could stand to share it with her."

As to Susan's outcome, by 11:00 a.m. she was very much in touch with her feelings, both pleasant and unpleasant. Her face was now mobile, and appropriately expressive. Her psychotic disorganization, delusions and ideas of reference had receded almost completely. While she clearly could not be called happy, she was very much in touch with us and herself. She no longer had the deadened "catatonic" appearance which characterized her between 6:00 a.m. and 9:00 a.m.

We chose to illustrate our psychotherapy with this example of a very disturbed person so readers could see its applicability to persons manifesting psychotic symptoms. It also illustrates how psychosis can recede in a matter of hours because of the application of a purely psychosocial intervention process. Finally, it illustrates how important an immediately responsive social environment is for dealing meaningfully with a crisis. Psychotherapy need not take place in an office for a specified amount of time.

Within the paradigm, any of the intervention techniques in Tables 7.2 and 7.3 might be applicable. It is expected that staff will be provided ongoing training and supervision around the proper use of these techniques. As this is best done in the context of ongoing clinical work, their use will not be discussed further here.

A Model for Effective Community Mental Health

CHAPTER 8

How to Organize a User Friendly System

THIS CHAPTER PRESENTS A DISTILLATE of the principles and practices we've found in one or more successful community mental health programs in the U.S. and Italy. In addition, we describe several administrative principles (horizontal authority and outcome-based bonuses) and three clinical ones which have not, to our knowledge, previously been explicitly applied to community mental health systems. For us, these clinical principles capture, in summary form, the essence of good community mental health practice. Because they will be set out without a specific geographic and administrative context, they may not all be applicable to a particular locale. They are meant to be modified and adapted to suit the needs and resources of a particular area. The distinction we've drawn between administrative and clinical principles is rather arbitrary; in practice they are complementary (see Table 8.1).

ADMINISTRATIVE PRINCIPLES

1. Absolute Responsibility for a Catchment Area

The mental health center should be administratively responsible for a catchment area of modest size (roughly 100,000 people). All entry points into the system (e.g., clinics, emergency rooms, etc.) must be under its control (see Figure 8.1). Catchment area boundaries should be drawn, insofar as possible, in a way that conforms to preexisting natural community

TABLE 8.1
Community Mental Health Administrative Principles

1. Catchmented responsibility.
2. Responsible teams.
3. Decentralized horizontal authority and responsibility.
4. Capitation payment.
5. Use of existing community resources.
6. Multi-purpose mental health center.
7. Non-institutionalization.
8. Outcome based bonus system.
9. Citizen/consumer participation.

divisions — e.g., ethnic, religious, geographic. A 100,000-person catchment area will probably need to be divided into three or four subareas with a team assigned responsibility for each of these. As with the catchment area itself, these subareas should be drawn insofar as possible with boundaries that are natural to the existing sense of community. As the teams will be competing for a year-end bonus from the capitation payment that supports the services (see principle 8) the subareas should be fair in terms of mix of socioeconomic groups and quality of the social fabric. That is, it's not fair for one team to have an area that either consists primarily of all newly arrived residents who have not yet developed a sense of community and have the predictable problems of new immigrants or contains mainly lower socioeconomic status residents with their known higher rates of all types of problems, including mental disorder. If natural boundary versus fairness of mix decisions must be made, we recommend that the former take precedence. The bonus calculation formula can be adjusted to compensate for socioeconomic differences.

2. Responsible Teams

Multidisciplinary teams of 3–5 workers should follow users from their point of initial system contact. The team should serve multiple functions for each client for whom it is responsible; crisis intervention and resolution, therapeutic case management, and formal psychotherapy (see also Chapter 9, Ongoing Outpatient Intervention). A multi-person group is required to allow continuity of *persons* across contexts (see Chapter 7, Relational Principles) despite departures, vacations and conflicting work demands. In addition, team members can provide each other support, consultation, and supervision with difficult cases. As noted below, they will function most effectively in a relatively non-hierarchical administrative structure that maximizes their autonomy.

3. Decentralized Horizontal Authority and Responsibility

Insofar as possible, authority and responsibility should reside at the lowest possible level within the hierarchy. As depicted in Figure 8.2, the system's organizational structure should be as flat as possible. Hence, only major

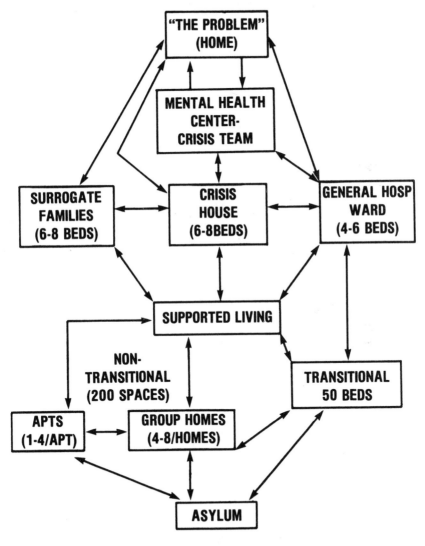

FIGURE 8.1
The Community Care System
Residential Care/100,000 Population

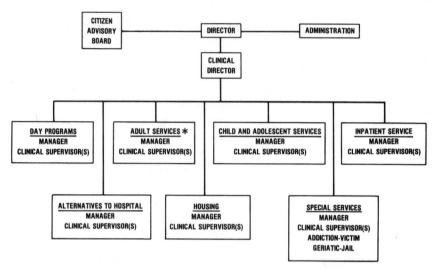

(The second service layer will more often be located away from the Mental Health Center
facility and may be operated on contract from the Mental Health Center rather than directly by it.)

*Includes: Emergency, community support, psychotherapies, medication

FIGURE 8.2
Organizational Chart
Model Community Mental Health Program

overall policy decisions will need to involve the top administrative-clinical
level. Each family-sized team or unit will make its own day-to-day clinical
decisions. This is the heart of the principle. In this context small is indeed
beautiful and normalizing (Table 8.2) (Schumacher, 1973). Interestingly, the
three American programs presented in this volume operate this way. The

TABLE 8.2
Community Mental Health
On Smallness

1. Small is beautiful.
2. Small is effective.
3. Small is tolerable.
4. Small is manageable.
5. Small is knowable.
6. Small is usual.
The bottom line: Small is normalizing.

Morrisania program (see Chapter 19) does it because of the theory its staff follows, while the others (see Chapters 17, 18) seemed to have arrived at it pragmatically. When teams can't reach consensus, a consultant from the center's specialists (see Chapter 10) should be called in to help, either through the provision of a needed technical skill or information or through group facilitation to resolve interpersonal issues that stand in the way of consensus. Should this process fail, the team supervisor, in consultation with the clinical director, will make a decision.

The aim here is to be sure line clinicians are empowered (Rose, 1985) in a meaningful way. The empowering process is enhanced by the fact that decision-making authority and responsibility are kept at the team's level while attempts are made to reach consensus. "Kicking something upstairs" for a decision should be an unusual occurrence.

4. Capitation Payment

According to our plan, the mental health center will receive at the beginning of each year a specified amount of money per resident in the catchment area to cover all mental health related needs, ranging from educationally oriented prevention to residential treatment and rehabilitation. In order to be effective the system must have direct control of its resources. We estimate this amount to be between 8% and 12% of the total health care budget. Each mental health center should have a minimum number of constraints, other than accounting ones, on how it decides to spend its money. A careful needs assessment should be conducted at regular intervals to define how the center will allocate its resources.

5. Use of Existing Community Resources

The mental health center should not duplicate anything that can be accessed in the adjacent community, including vocational, school, athletic or recreational programs. In addition to being more cost-effective, this will help keep the mental health center remain firmly embedded in, and in constant communication with, the community, which is vitally important from our perspective. This requires an activist stance vis-à-vis the community is accessing its resources, while at the same time inviting the community to use the center's facilities as well.

6. Multi-Purpose Mental Health Center

The center should be a *multi-purpose* facility accessible from and to the community and open a major portion of the day, such as from 8 a.m. until 10 p.m. Although it can be located anywhere, having it on the grounds of an affiliated general hospital does offer some advantages to the staff, since in this plan the same staff will be responsible for patients wherever they are in the system. Consequently, when patients are in the hospital, the teams will be expected to provide staffing for the hospital in proportion to the numbers of patients they have there.

By "multi-purpose" we mean that the center can house both mental health services, e.g., outpatient, emergency, day treatment, *and* nonmental health community activities, such as evening classes, art exhibits, and recitals. If, for example, there is not an adequate library in the community, the center's library should be used for this purpose. The basic point is that the center should be in active communication with its catchment area. It must not allow itself to be segregated from it.

7. Non-Institutionalization

As the hospital beds in the system will be the most expensive single service, and since the capitation payment is fixed, this is the area where the greatest administrative attention must be paid to controlling costs. We have described in Chapter 4 the legitimate and appropriate use of hospital beds. When one of these criteria is felt to be met by the emergency services director or his/her designate, a patient can be admitted, absent an emergency. Thus, all non-emergency hospital admissions would require prior clearance. We define an emergency as a situation in which the responsible clinician has explored all the other available options and has found neither one that meets the client's needs or one that is acceptable to the user. In practice, a candidate emergency for hospitalization is likely to be an agitated, overactive, acutely psychotic, new-to-the-system client.

From the Italian experience we have learned that once staff are firmly embedded in community work they quickly become disaffected with hospital-based work. Hence, requiring them to provide in-hospital staffing is, in and of itself, a great disincentive to hospitalization (see Chapters 15 and 16). Another disincentive is to make involuntary admission difficult and time-consuming, so that clinicians won't resort to it in the face of difficulty establishing rapport or persuading a patient that it is in his interest to go into some kind of residential care. Many observers believe this is the single most important factor in the dramatic decrease in involuntary commitment that took place in Italy after the reform of 1978 (see Chapters 13 and 16). Finally, the bonus system (see below) will provide a further disincentive by penalizing use of the hospital. We cannot emphasize enough that if a community system is to be cost-effective and comprehensive it must keep its use of hospital beds to a minimum. In this context, it should be remembered that at the present time about 70% of U.S. public mental health dollars are spent on inpatient care.

8. Outcome Based Bonus System

We propose that mental health centers devise year-end bonus systems based on the clinical outcomes of patients treated by each team. Ultimately each locale will have to put together its own formula for determining what elements will be weighted in what way, but for the system to work use of hospital will need to be penalized. Elements that will need to be considered for inclusion are: number of hospital days; number of readmissions; use of psychotropic drugs; percentage of patients returned to work (including homemaking) or school functioning; percentage of patients living in places appropriate for their age and social status; percentage of patients conducting a normal social life; client satisfaction with the services; client satisfaction with their lives and number of patients successfully emancipated from the mental health system. We suggest that the variables to be included be decided on in discussions between the independent research team and line staff and users.

Program directors can modify the weighting of individual variables to encourage certain kinds of practices. For example, we recommend that medication use be penalized to encourage the use of drug-free trials or low doses (Kane, 1983, 1984; Kane, Rifkin, Woerner, Reardon, Sarantakos, Schiebel, & Ramos-Lorenzi, 1983; Marder et al., 1987) or targeted neuroleptic drug strategies (Carpenter & Heinrichs, 1983; Carpenter, et al., 1987; Carpenter et al., in press) for the treatment of psychosis. At the same time psychosocial approaches to depression, anxiety, and phobic conditions might also be encouraged by the weighting of variables in the bonus formula.

Teams within each catchment area would be in competition with each other for parts of this year-end bonus. The bonus should be divided equally among team members regardless of educational background and experience. Giving all team members equal bonuses is a concrete means of reinforcing the notion of a nonhierarchical team with individuals on it having specialized functions based on education and experience (hence different base salary levels). The financial competition we envision may be offensive to some; in that instance we suggest that the most effective team and its clients share a properly ritualized ceremonial honor.

The bonus system we envision resembles those currently present in many HMO's in the U.S.A. However, it differs in two important ways. First, it is based more on actual client outcomes than on units of service. Second, it places greater value on more effective care rather than on less service of unknown quality. In HMO's, the incentive is to *not* serve. In our scheme the team that delivers the *most* units of service is likely to win the lion's share of the bonus.

Because our model is a "socialized" system, problems found in such systems are likely to occur: Employees may begin to see fewer patients for longer periods of time; they will try to select out the "easy" clients; and they can become so complacent as to appear institutionalized and hence non-innovative. Arranging the bonus system weighting of variables properly will help address these problems. This is a bonus system based on productivity, with productivity defined by client outcomes.

Finally, this bonus system will require an annual systematic program evaluation. As this research endeavor is directly relevant to clinicians' concerns, they will be highly motivated participants. Program evaluation, beyond units of service delivered, has historically been difficult to conduct in community mental health programs. The reasons for this are too many to detail here, but one of them is that it is difficult to convince clinicians of the relevance of research to their day-to-day clinical work. The type of careful research assessment needed to compute a bonus should both recruit them into the process and produce evidence that will validate (or not) their clinical practices. Thus, the bonus system provides an administrative mechanism that can be used to reinforce effective clinical practice.

9. Citizen/Consumer Participation

Most systems will have three, somewhat overlapping, types of public involvement: a citizens advisory board, consumer (user and ex-user) groups, and groups of involved others like parents and siblings.

The size, composition, and method of appointment to this Citizens Advisory Board will likely differ across locales. In general it should include representatives of local government, interested citizens, center staff, and consumers.

The board's function is to provide overall program policy and goals that will be translated into program activities by the center's directorship working with unit supervisors. Generally the board should not oversee the center's day-to-day operation. Rather, it should review it from congruence with expressed programatic policies and goals and quantity of resources available to put them into practice.

Several models for citizens boards have been developed and studied. Readers wishing more detailed information will find it in Bertelsen and Harris (1973), Bolman (1972), and Davis and Specht (1978).

USER AND EX-USER ORGANIZATIONS

"Ex-psychiatric inmate group" is the label the groups discussed here prefer. However, in order to make this section more inclusive and to simplify the language we will use the terms consumer, client, user, or patient, usually without the "ex."

The consumer movement in mental health began with the publication, in

1905, of Clifford Beers (1939) autobiographical account of his experiences in mental hospitals of the era. *The Mind That Found Itself*, because of its popular appeal, led over time to the development of the mental health associations and child guidance clinics. These were important background events to the subsequent development of community mental health movement, but did not stimulate widespread grass-roots, consumer-run self-help organizations. Basically, this early movement became professionalized, hence out of the direct control of consumers.

Recent mental health consumerism took hold and grew in the context of the civil rights movement, the legitimized antiauthority Viet Nam protest era, the widespread consumerism of the mid-'70s, and the women's movement. It is driven by shared feelings of outrage, hurt, degradation, and betrayal at the hands of the helping professions, especially psychiatry. The practices of forced hospitalization and medication to which these patients were subjected resulted in a great deal of anger that is being expressed in the movement. Being labeled "mental patient" (as conferred by institutional treatment in particular) led these patients to feel isolated and pariah-like. Promises of help that turned out to be social control led them to feel betrayed and disillusioned with the purveyors of "treatment." Being afflicted with tardive dyskinesia without having given their real informed consent led them to be suspicious of new, technologically advanced treatments. In sum, they have organized to fight for the restoration of their right to be first-class citizens.

The first groups formed in the early 1970s. Their early networking brought them together in 1973 at the first conference on Human Rights and Against Psychiatric Oppression. The ensuing series of conferences (lasting until 1985) brought together ex-patients from around the country. No organization emerged from these annual conferences because the major participants feared recreating the oppressive system they were protesting. In the late 1970s various individual ex-patients were invited (as were family members) to a series of NIMH-sponsored Community Support Program "learning conferences." These parallel series of conferences (Human Rights and CSP) enabled consumers to maintain contact, develop networks, and begin to organize on a local level.

Finally, in 1985, the NIMH awarded a Baltimore consumer group a grant to head a national "consumer conference." A split in the ex-patient movement began at this conference. The basic issue was whether or not the new organization would take a stand against forced treatment. In several subsequent meetings the differences could not be ironed out. By the spring of 1986 two ex-patient groups had been formed: the National Alliance of Mental Patients (NAMP) (Rae Unzicker, Coordinator) and National Mental Health Consumer Association (NMHCA) (headed by Joe Rogers).

Basically, NAMP is focused on developing programs totally outside the mental health system, while NMHCA is focused on working for change within the system, including aligning itself with NAMI (National Alliance for the Mentally Ill) goals. Despite this split, as we discussed the development of client-run mutual help groups with a number of persons participating in them, there seemed to emerge a modest consensus around the principles that should govern them. These are not specifically NAMP or NMHCA principles; rather, they are generic to a number of client-run programs:

1. Clients control major governance positions, including all hiring, firing and money management.
2. Participation is totally voluntary. No one will ever be forcibly sent to a hospital; they will not guide an individual's return to the mental health system.
3. Hierarchy is minimal.
4. Staff is responsible to membership and members control the staff.
5. The approach is nonmedical and nonclinical, involving support and caring, and includes consciousness-raising about issues of self-determination, personal responsibility, and autonomy.
6. Education, advocacy and one-to-one help with negotiating the system are high priority activities; that is, accessing entitlements, housing, and providing legal counsel when needed, especially when a person has been committed.
7. Information is provided about such things as psychiatric drugs, civil rights, and options within the psychiatric and other relevant systems.
8. Political action by the organization will be done in various ways, including joining with a variety of coalitions—the poor, the homeless, Grey Panthers, patient's rights advocates, etc. Other, more traditional forms of pressure (e.g., picketing) will also be used.

These principles are put into practice in drop-in centers staffed by a combination of paid and volunteer persons. The focus is on maximizing self-reliance while utilizing environmental (interpersonal) support as needed. A format that has been evolved is the "mutual speakout." By admitting their common situation, i.e., ex-patients, and criticizing the system in the context of mutual support, consumers find the occasion liberating, organizing, and passion-reviving. The goal is to get more and more distance from the identity as ex-patient so more normalizing activities can be undertaken. One example of this process would be moving from being a staff member or advocate in a self-help center to becoming a community organizer.

The focus of these groups is not so much on bashing psychiatry as it is developing a viable alternative to psychiatry's authority and control. Psychiatric (or other professional) help can be used so long as it is by choice. However, because of their experiences at the hands of psychiatry and the mental health system, ex-patients are very concerned about preservation of their integrity. They worry that cooperation *with* the mental health system will turn into co-optation *by* it.

Some consumer groups see mental health professionals as having a role in helping them form their group and establish their legitimacy. Once this is done they would like the mental health system to:

1. Provide technical information (i.e., regarding drugs, commitment, etc.);
2. Provide material support, such as office space, telephone, and photocopying;
3. Give access to persons who can help them attain goals they have decided upon as a group; and
4. Advocate with, or support their applications to, funding organizations.

There are other "consumer" organizations (e.g., the Manic-Depressive Association, Recovery, GROW, etc.); however, we've chosen not to describe them here, hoping this description will be prototypical enough to educate the average reader. Readers interested in more information about the ex-patient movement will find it in Frank (1986) and Miller (1983). Information about client-run programs can be found in Chamberlin (1978), Zinman (1986), Zinman, Harp, and Budd (1987), and from the journals *Phoenix Rising* and *Madness Network News*.

We believe that the development of a strong consumer mutual help group should be a high priority of every community mental health program. It is the most direct and clear statement of a program's commitment to the principle of preservation and enhancement of power. The nature of the relationship of the client-run program to the local community mental health system must be allowed to change over time and will vary between locales. What is most critical is that the mental health system *not* attempt to control it or take it over. The system's role should be to provide as much material support and *consultative* expertise as needed to get the program (as defined by users) up and running. After that, the community mental health system should make itself available as needed, with "needed" being defined by the users' group. The client-run program can be completely outside the mental health system and serve, for example, a watchdog function for it. Or, it can be at the boundary of the community mental health program by providing a way for clients to make the transition out of the mental health system via the peer support and advocacy offered in a drop-in center.

Boulder Colorado's application for a grant for its consumer group is one interesting prototype (Appendix B).

PARENTS OF USERS ORGANIZATIONS

The National Alliance for the Mentally Ill (NAMI) was founded in Madison, Wisconsin in 1979. The national organization brought a number of local organizations of the Alliance for the Mentally Ill under a single umbrella. There are now 856 affiliates with over 70,000 families involved nationwide. This national organization was presaged by the Schizophrenia Foundation and its local associations, an organization focused on the promulgation of megavitamins as *the* treatment for schizophrenia. A number of local Schizophrenia Association chapters (Schizophrenia Fellowship in Great Britain) changed their names to Alliance and joined NAMI. A number of local Alliance leaders were formerly Schizophrenia Association members.

The history of these local organizations and their various transformations is complex and convoluted and will not be further elaborated here. The essential point is that beginning in the early 1970s groups of parents with disturbed and disturbing children began to coalesce and attempt to make their wishes known. The parents involved were generally white, middle- and upper-middle-class professionals whose mostly male children had received extensive, but usually unsuccessful, psychiatric care. Many of them had spent, in addition to insurance, large sums of their own money for treatment of their disturbed offspring. They shared the common experience of feeling both ripped off and blamed by psychiatry. Many had been, at least implicitly, promised high-priced "cures" that were never delivered. In their interactions with treatment institutions they were frequently attributed responsibility for their offspring's condition. They were angry and highly sensitized to "family bashing," but continued to seek the magic bullet that would cure their offspring once and for all.

In the early '70s parent groups literally leapt on the Hofer-Osmond megavitamin bandwagon as it went by. What happened as a result of this movement was that parents with similar painful and frustrating experiences found each other. They formed support groups, circulated newsletters, had monthly meetings featuring invited professional speakers (megavitamin proponets only in those days), and began legislative lobbying efforts.

As the NIMH was gearing up its Community Support Program (1974–77), consumerism was the order of the day. For example, the 1975 CMHC act amendments were the first to mandate consumer representation (half) on

CMHC boards. The meetings convened as part of the Community Support Program's development included these *parents* as consumers. Subsequently the real users (the clients) were also included. These national meetings put local parent groups in touch with each other. We believe this was crucial to the eventual formation of NAMI (see Mosher, 1986). NAMI replaced the previous megavitamin ideology with a new one. It must be emphasized that the positions taken by the national organization on a number of issues are not uniformly supported by local alliance chapters. For example, many local chapters do not favor making involuntary commitment easier (see number 3 below of NAMI's political action platform). Also, local chapters are usually supportive of community mental health programs in their areas.

The basic tenets of the belief system being promulgated by the *National Alliance* are about as follows:

1. Major mental disorders (i.e., schizophrenia, major depression and bipolar illness) are brain diseases.
2. These disorders are genetic in origin.
3. Their genetic underpinning is played out via identifiable biological processes.
4. The family has no role in the production or maintenance of the disorders.
5. The only treatments of relevance are biological in nature.

From this ideology a political action platform has been drawn up by the national organization about as follows:

1. More research into the biologic bases of mental illness is needed. Because psychosocial (i.e., family) factors play no role, no psychosocial research should be supported.
2. As neuroleptic drugs are the only known effective treatment, new and better drugs should be developed and subjected to clinical trials. They will provide subjects for these trials (their offspring).
3. As a biologic illness psychosis should be treated in hospitals. Unfortunately, because of new admission policies, stricter commitment laws, and closing of hospital beds, it is not easy to have someone (their offspring) admitted to a hospital. Hence, it is advocated that mental hospital beds be reopened and commitment made easier.
4. Since mental illness is somatic/biologic like other illnesses, the National Institute of Mental Health should be renamed the National Institute of Mental Illness and moved back into the NIH fold. (In 1988 the Department of Health and Human Services refused to do so.)

5. Family therapy should be eradicated because it blames families, is really only intended to make families into better caretakers, prevents independence of the offspring, and leaves children no alternatives when parents die. No family therapy research should be supported.
6. Scientists who continue to conduct irrelevent (as defined by NAMI) psychosocially focused research should be educated as to the biologic nature of these disorders and their research carefully scrutinized for flaws, especially any hint of "family bashing." Scientific data that disagree with the ideology will be labeled invalid and disregarded.
7. Training in the relevant mental health disciplines must be carefully scrutinized to be sure students are being taught properly about the biologic basis of mental illness. The organization's curriculum committee will review training program content in psychiatry, psychology, nursing, and social work.
8. Practicing clinicians who continue to advocate psychosocial treatment (especially family therapy) or who question drug treatment for mental illness will be brought to the attention of the relevant licensing bodies as guilty of possible malpractice.

This ambitious program of thought reform has found a number of allies, especially within psychiatry's powerful biologic contingent. Their strong conviction as to the rightness of their cause and to the belief that a true "cure" is just around the corner fuels NAMI parents' fires. For interested readers this summary can be expanded by reading the NAMI newsletter or publications the organization recommends (Hatfield, 1984, 1985; Kanter, 1984; Torrey, 1983; Torrey & Wolfe, 1986; Walsh, 1985).

It is not likely that the family and systems psychosocial approach to community mental health we espouse—even though it never addresses the issue of causation—will be popular with the current NAMI leadership. However, as noted previously, there is a great deal of heterogeneity of point of view within the organization and a number of local affiliates are not in agreement with the national organization's aims. In our experience the local AMI organizations can, and have been, very helpful in advocating in the mental health system and legislatures for good community programs. A number of local chapters have developed quality housing and vocational programs. They, like all parents, want what is best for their individual offspring independent of the organization's firebrand rhetoric. Their functioning as reciprocal help groups (a more accurate term than self-help) is extremely useful.

What we advocate is quite consistent with these parents' stated wishes: They don't want to be the only care option available to their offspring. The community smorgasbord we describe gives users many options. The programs described should preserve and enhance their offspring's power so they won't need to be excessively dependent on their family. Our position is to try and give clients and their involved families what they want and need and to negotiate around problems that arise in the process. We recommend that support be offered to families of a disturbed offspring independent of whether he/she is living at home. We recommend that their participation be invited in planning processes as one set of players in a complex system.

Problems may be encountered around the issue of control. It is our position that no single participant in the system should be in control. However, users' wishes should be addressed first. Community programs should align themselves with parent groups but they should not let them, by themselves, dictate program policies. A proper mix of citizen participation will assure that all relevant points of view are attended to; a balanced position is required for ongoing program functioning.

Remembering again that the administrative/clinical distinctions we're drawing are somewhat arbitrary and that they operate in a complementary way in actual practice, we turn now to our clinical principles.

CLINICAL PRINCIPLES

There are three "umbrella" processes that must always be kept in mind by community mental health programs: (1) contextualization; (2) preservation and enhancement of personal power and control; and (3) normalization.

1. *Contextualization.* By this we mean keeping clients in as close contact with their usual surroundings, both geographic and interpersonal, as possible. In practice, the problem-focused approach explicated in Chapter 6 will serve to maintain persons in their context. To reiterate, we recommend that staff approach users so that they define the nature of the problem; then, staff can elucidate the environmental events temporally related to it, focus on clients' notions about problem solutions, and ask them what resources the team can help mobilize to deal with the problems. Validation of clients' subjective experience by the use of active empathy (see Chapter 6) will also help keep them in their context. The staff's job in this regard is to negotiate, over time, a compromise between the objective historical societal reality and the reality of clients' subjective experience. These two versions of reality need to be reconnected, since their disconnection has been part of the problem development. Contextualization is further facilitated by focusing on various aspects of clients' networks—their family and friends and the relevant professional network.

Even when clients are temporarily displaced from their usual surroundings—for example, by going into a transitional residential facility—staff must always keep their circumstances (context) in mind. Without this contextual thinking clients become difficult to understand and distant from staff. Implementation of the relational principles outlined in Chapter 7, pp. 78–83, depends on staff's being able to think contextually (also see Chapter 10).

  2. *Preservation and enhancement of personal power and control.* Although we have used the term "empowerment" (Rose, 1985) in reference to staff, we prefer the clumsier term "preservation and enhancement of power," when discussing power in relation to users. Empowerment implies that one person holds something he can give to the other, that is, power. We think it is important to recognize that the mental health worker is not handing out power packages.

  A major complaint we have with much of what goes on in today's mental health treatment is that the system immediately assumes the posture of knowing what is best for the users, especially if they are very disturbed and disturbing. This deprives clients of their power and undermines their sense of being in control of their lives – even though this is often a major feature of their problem. The system's job is to help them regain control over their lives or assert it for the first time – not to further erode their tenuous grasp on it. It's often easier to *do for* clients than to *help them with doing.* In our experience, unless this seductive process is kept under constant scrutiny, staff will soon create unnecessary dependency and deprive clients of opportunities to develop their own senses of autonomy and independence.

  There are a number of ways that staff can enhance personal power: by providing information, helping to identify options, role playing and practicing scenarios, exercising advocacy, and most particularly, spending a great deal of time and energy keeping the client engaged in the entire helping process. The primary modus operandi in community mental health programs should be to serve as facilitators for clients' identification, definition, development, and expansion of their personal cognitive and emotional resources. The ultimate goal is that of maximal self-help. Hence, relationships evolved within a program will need to be collaborative, interdependent, reciprocal, and facilitative. They will usually be characterized by a "being with," rather than a more activist "doing to," interaction process. Adherence to this kind of process will maintain and enhance client power and diminish splitting and blaming. The staff should see their roles more as consultants (a less powerful and less *activist* position) than therapists (a term that implies "doing"). Activism per se is not the problem; in fact, we firmly believe in the importance of adovcacy – a very activist function. However, the activism of "therapy" can be distorted in a way that aligns it with therapist, rather than client, goals or with adaptation to the status quo.

  When necessary, staff need to actively demystify medical issues that arise.

For example, how medications work, their effects and side effects, should be presented in ordinary language. Staff need to actively deinstitutionalize and destigmatize system veterans who have learned how to manipulate the mental health system to perpetuate unnecessary dependency. For example, they may need to call into question whether or not the particular function they are being asked to serve is necessary, and thus raise the possibility that clients could now do for themselves what, because of their previous training as patients, they have not previously seen themselves as being able to do.

Helpers must always keep a minimalist philosophy in mind. The less they do, the better. They should always be looking for ways to involve and support use of available nonmental-health network resources, e.g., friends, churches, Parents Without Partners. For clients with little previous experience in the mental health system, this orientation will help with critical aspects of normalization and maintenance of individuals in their natural contexts. This orientation will likely present problems for long-term patients who have evolved careers in the system and have come to expect that they will be taken care of by mental health workers. For them it is even more important that problem solutions be *evolved* from the client, not *prescribed* by a person in a high status role. Prescribing solutions results in a lack of personal responsibility on the part of the client for whom the solution is prescribed. Assumption of personal responsibility, and with it power and control, is a very important aspect of the deinstitutionalization process.

3. *Normalization (usualization)* (Wolfensberger, 1970, 1972, 1979, 1983). This principle overlaps to some extent with contextualization. However, they are distinguishable by time and reference frames: the process of contextualization includes an individualized longitudinal, historical point of view while normalization is principally a group cross-sectional, societal, or cultural norm perspective. That is, we mean there will always be times when clients are not able, by themselves, to generate the options they may need to solve a particular problem. It falls to the staff to help them develop options. In doing so, staff should think first of options that are most nearly normal. For example, if a client wants to work and has never really had the experience of finding a job, staff have at least two options: referring him to vocational rehabilitation or using the want ads. The preferred option is for staff to sit down with the client, discuss what kinds of things he might be interested in, and then go through the want ads with him. This option is preferable because this is the most normal or usual way of starting a job hunt. A referral to vocational rehabilitation is always possible if it becomes clear the user doesn't really know what he wants to do, or needs additional training, or isn't able to find and keep a job without extensive support.

Another good example of the application of the normalization principle concerns housing. For those users who cannot find, afford, or stay in housing without outside emotional support, community mental health systems have developed affiliated housing programs. Unfortunately, these are usually defined as transitional and "supervised." From our perspective it is preferable that they be *nontransitional* hence ascribing to clients the normal role of "tenant," and supported (something everyone needs) rather than supervised (a term connoting a non-normal dependent state on the part of the supervisee). The process of normalization will require a great deal of reframing, will exploit positive expectations, and will help enhance self-esteem and a sense of personal efficacy through real accomplishments, no matter how small, in a normal world.

PROGRAM VALUES

Three overarching principles described above should be translated into practice in programs that embody a consistent set of values and practices as follows:

1. Do no harm.
2. Do unto others as you would have done unto you (e.g., the same principles apply to clients and staff; everyone should treat each other with dignity and respect).
3. Be flexible and responsive.
4. In general, the user knows best.
5. Choice, the right to refuse, informed consent, and voluntarism are essential to program functioning.
6. Anger, dependency, sexuality, and development of potential are acceptable and expected.
7. Whenever possible, legitimate needs should be filled.
8. Take risks; if you don't take chances nothing ever happens.
9. Make power relationships explicit.

In the following chapters we turn to a description of the smorgasbord of facilities and approaches needed to operate a good community mental health program. It will be seen, quite easily, that these facilities and our view of the way they should be organized flows from the administrative and clinical principles discussed above.

CHAPTER 9

A Community Services Smorgasbord

OUTPATIENT SERVICES

The Heart of the Matter: Mobile Crisis Intervention

WE BELIEVE THE 24-HOUR MOBILE CRISIS intervention team should be the center of every community mental health program. In most situations it will function as the gatekeeper to the system (see Dane County, Chapter 18). Systematic research on the use of 24-hour mobile crisis teams has been shown that they reduce hospitalization by at least 50% (Gutstein, Rudd, Graham, & Rayha, in press; Hoult, 1986; Hoult & Reynolds, 1984; Hoult, Rosen, & Reynolds, 1984; Langsley & Kaplan, 1968; Reynolds & Hoult, 1984; Ruevini, 1977; Schoenfeld, Halvey, Hemley-van der Velden, & Ruhf, 1986; Stein & Test, 1978a,b; Test & Stein, 1978a). The experience in South Verona is that fully half of all patients labeled schizophrenic do not need residential care in any given year, principally because in-home crisis intervention is provided.

We expect that a substantial proportion of the work of the emergency services team will be done in the homes of the clients. This requires very good collaborative relationships with gatekeepers of different types: the

---

*Portions of the text in this chapter, titled Community Residential Programs/Alternatives to Hospitalization, appeared in Mosher (in press).

living group, the general practitioner, the police, and the mental health system staff. A community mental health program that is well embedded in its community will not have great difficulty educating these groups.

Whenever possible the work of the crisis team should take place in the living unit, for the following reasons:

1. Using a battle fatigue or shell shock paradigm, in-home intervention will often prevent evacuation to an unfamiliar setting like hospital or alternative to hospitalization. Hence, the client will be able to remain in relationship to the natural, known support group.
2. It provides externally generated social support in the individual's own territory. Meeting new people on foreign territory is always more difficult than meeting people on one's own ground. As a result, observations made in the home are likely to reflect family reality more accurately than those made in the clinic.
3. Meeting with the in-residence living group (usually, but not always, the family) provides an opportunity for the clinical team to frame the intervention as a healing ritual experience to help alleviate the problem behavior. The usefulness of rituals in facilitating change in social networks has been highlighted by Imber-Black, Roberts, and Whiting (1988) and others (Palazzoli, Boscolo, Cecchin & Prata, 1977).
4. The in-home context allows the crisis team to actively unlabel by use of positive reframing of "symptoms" or problem behaviors as normal, or at least understandable, responses to the stresses attendant to the particular situation.
5. By expecting the identified patient to be an ally/helper, maintenance of normal role functioning is promoted from the outset. This process helps preserve personal power and responsibility, goes on in the person's usual social context, and is framed in a normalizing way (see Chapter 8).

Basically, we believe that the in-home intervention paradigm mutes the potentially deleterious side affects of mental health system interventions by minimizing institutionalization and its inevitable decontextualization (even in community-based alternatives) of the individual. The process of repeated decontextualization and associated institutionalization — medicalization of an individual — is critical to the development of a view of that person, by the network and the system, as someone with a "chronic" illness. The disease-in-the-person view also provides the nidus around which the process of stigmatization forms; this process is a major culprit in the development and maintenance of "chronicity."

There are, of course, times when someone must be removed from a situation. Serious continued risk of violence or suicide, despite the family crisis intervention, requires that the situation be defused by removal of the person so disposed. This should be required in only a minority of instances.

We wish to draw readers' attention to the fact that, although for simplicity we label what the mobile team does as *"crisis intervention,"* whenever possible its work should be seen as involving *crisis resolution.* Crisis intervention is too frequently limited to assessment, triage and disposition. Our view is that the crisis team should continue to be involved until resolution occurs or an alternative course of action is clearly indicated.

There will also be situations in which the identified patient has already been taken out of the home and brought to an emergency room or some other intake point without the living group. In these instances it is often difficult to get the person back into the home and regroup the family or other persons in a way that will allow successful negotiation or settlement of the difficulties. However, approaching the problem from a systems perspective, even if it is not possible to send the patient home, will aid in the development of a plan that will facilitate returning there — or at least understanding of why it's not possible to do so. The availability of residential alternatives to hospitalization will allow a minimally decontextualizing response to the crisis; without alternatives, unwarranted institutionalization will take place.

Residential care must be considered when the person has no social network, when the person's social network is worn out physically and psychologically and in need of respite, when there is imminent danger to others, and when there is imminent danger to the self which clinicians judge cannot be successfully handled by a natural social network provided with mental health team support. A final indication for the use of residential care is when the in-home family crisis intervention has not led to a successful return of normal role functioning. Ergo, a situation in which the problem has not resolved or that continues to escalate despite the best ongoing efforts of the crisis intervention team necessitates the use of residential care. This response should be used infrequently.

The configuration of the crisis team will vary considerably across settings because of differences in geography, population density, manpower availability, and local regulations governing personnel use. One configuration used frequently in Italy is a four- or five-person team with two M.D.'s (staff and trainee), a nurse, and a social worker. Trainees from any other disciplines related to mental health may also be added to the team. A team configuration where psychiatric time is hard to find or very expensive and there are no M.D. trainees could be four non-M.D. mental health workers with psychiatric backup and consultation. However, each team should have at least *three* regular staff so as to provide continuity of persons, over time, for the clients.

Incoming calls are routed to the team responsible for the geographic area from which the call is coming. The call is then screened as to whether or not an immediate home visit is indicated. When it is unclear as to what the best response would be, we advise a home intervention. If a home visit is clearly not indicated, the case can be discussed in the team and a response made in a short period of time. This response can be anything from a call with some information to inviting the putative patient in for an individual or family evaluation.

If a home intervention is thought to be necessary the team *advises the caller of the plan and asks for his or her reaction*. If the plan is acceptable, the caller is asked to assemble the parties relevant to the problem and told that the team will arrive in about 15–20 minutes. If it is a call from police on site, they are asked to stay also.

A minimum of two team members, preferable a *male* and a *female*, should respond to in-home crises. A two-person response provides a feeling of safety and allows on-the-spot team consultation. On arrival the team evaluates the nature of the problem utilizing the interview techniques described in Chapter 6. If several people are present, the circular questioning style popularized by the Milan group (Palazzoli, Boscolo, Cecchin, & Prata, 1980) can be utilized to evolve an interactional picture of the problem and possible options for its solution.

Home visits can vary greatly in length; the team should allow at least one and one-half hours in the home but have the flexibility to stay longer if needed. The actual intervention will utilize a variety of techniques previously described, e.g., positive expectations, reframing, support, reassurance, and ritual. The initial evaluation may be followed by daily visits, if necessary, to stabilize the situation. The principle to be kept in mind is that the intervention should be tailored to the client's and family's needs — not to the needs of the mental health system.

Ongoing Outpatient Intervention

In our view all line mental health center staff should be members of a crisis team. However, when not involved in crisis work they will carry out a variety of other functions:

Individuals, families and social networks will need to be seen on an ongoing basis, either in their own environments or in the clinic. This caseload is derived from the team's crisis work. We advise that the ongoing interventions with individual clients or families be the responsibility of *at least two members of a team*. Both need not be involved in every session.

However, both should be up-to-date on developments. This arrangement will make continuity possible despite illness, vacations, departures, etc.

Specific therapies, such as cognitive-behavioral treatment of depression and behavioral approaches to phobias, can be provided by team members qualified to do so or by center "specialists" (see Chapter 10, p. 180). If a patient is referred to a specialist, the team should retain case responsibility. Specific interventions should be as focused and brief as possible. Group treatment should be highly valued and used to as great an extent as possible. It is in this part of the work that the relational principles and intervention techniques described in Chapters 6 and 7 will be used over and over again.

Case Managers Need to Be Therapeutic

The functions usually ascribed to case managers—case finding, assessment, service planning, linkage, coordination, monitoring, and advocacy—should, we believe, be the responsibility of the mental health center team with which a client makes initial contact. The reasoning behind our position is as follows:

1. Splitting out case management as a special role for one person outside the team complicates the situation unnecessarily and fragments responsibility for the client.
2. The role can be construed in such an activist doing-to way that the client becomes a bystander in the process. The development of competence and greater autonomy by the client via success experiences is very difficult when someone else takes care of everything. Institutional dependence can become case manager dependence.
3. As presently practiced, case managers are almost always individuals, not teams. What happens weekends, nights, and vacations? Clients will have a hard time finding someone they know and who knows them. In such situations, usually brought about by a crisis, a poor decision can be made. In addition to the problem with continuity of persons this engenders, a solo case manager has no peer support group with whom to discuss difficult clinical issues. Use of the generic mental health center team allows all of its members to know something about all the team's clients. Teams should have *no more than* about 20 active cases per member. Hence, a four-person team would have around 80 active cases, a manageable cognitive task for all team members.
4. The words planner, advocate, broker, monitor, and coordinator are not rife with connotations of support, empathy, and understanding. That is, as currently defined, case management does not explicitly

acknowledge the importance of a therapeutic relationship to its work. We believe this is a serious omission because case managers will come to see themselves principally as brokers and conduits, lacking a meaningful therapeutic role with clients. However, if their role is defined as therapeutic they can then share the morale boost a client gets from an accomplishment in which they have been involved. This will, in turn, help prevent burnout (see Chapter 10). Our point is that no plan should be developed and acted on until a respectful mutual understanding of the problem needing to be addressed, in the context of a positive relationship, has been evolved.

We also believe that case management can be more relationally focused if the mental health center has a designated concrete resources person(s). Thus, rather than many case managers having to know the ins and outs of all the relevant bureaucracies and the types of programs available, one person should be *very* knowledgeable on these matters and act as a consultant to the case managers and their clients. When relieved of the "doing for" task of identifying these resources, case managers can spend more of their time "doing with" clients, i.e., engaging in consultative activities that involve use of their collaborative relationships.

When mental health center teams are carrying out case management functions, we recommend they see themselves mainly as *consultants* to clients. Their consultative role should begin with a contextually valid empathic understanding of the problem(s) presented. Developing this kind of understanding will probably require team members to be with clients in several of their day-to-day activities. This down-to-earth orientation will also help dehierarchize consultant-client relationships so that they more nearly approximate our recommended peer orientation. Insofar as these conditions are met, the client will not be made *unduly* dependent, the consultation will be therapeutic, and case management functions will be performed successfully.

COMMUNITY RESIDENTIAL PROGRAMS

Community residential mental health system programs can be understood and compared by looking at three variables: (1) transitional versus nontransitional; (2) size; and (3) number of staff. For example, the Soteria/Crossing Place alternative to hospitalization we'll describe is transitional, small (six to eight beds), and intensively staffed (1.3 staff per resident). By way of contrast, the halfway house model we espouse shares only transitionalness with the Soteria model, as it is rather large (20–25 beds) and lightly staffed (.3 or .4 staff per resident).

Alternatives to Hospitalization

In a properly designed and functioning community mental health *system* community residential treatment facilities should serve the vast majority of disturbed and disturbing individuals in need of intensive interpersonal care who cannot be adequately treated by in-home crisis intervention. Use of these small home-like facilities in conjunction with 24-hour mobile crisis intervention will dramatically reduce the need for psychiatric beds in hospitals (Hoult, 1986; Langsley, Pittman, & Swank, 1969; Mosher, 1982; Stein & Test, 1985). That is, a 100,000 population catchment area will need about ten adult beds on a ward in a general hospital. More than ten beds per 100,000 may be needed in urban areas into which many former long-term state hospital inmates have migrated. This estimate presumes the existence of separate facilities for children and adolescents, geriatric, and addictions cases. We also presume there will be *no* backup state hospital beds. This estimate also presumes that the system will have affordable transitional (halfway, quarterway houses) and nontransitional (group homes, Fairweather lodges, foster care, apartments, etc.) supported (supervised) and unsupported housing readily available for its clientele's use after the intensive care phase. Without adequate numbers of these facilities, users will get "stuck" at home, in the hospital, or in shelters. This is both clinically unwise and unnecessarily expensive.

In contrast to hospital-based interventions, where various treatments are administered to patients on wards, residential alternative facilities are *themselves* the treatment. That is, the total social environment (place and persons) is the healing intervention. In more traditional language these social environments are conceived of as "therapeutic communities" or "treatment milieus" (Gunderson, Will, & Mosher, 1983).

Research (Braun, Kochansky, Shapiro, Greenberg, Gudeman, Johnson, & Shore, 1981; Kiesler, 1982a,b; Straw, 1982; Stroul, 1987) and clinical experience have shown that approximately 90% of functional psychotics presently treated in hospital, can be equally well or better treated, at less cost, in intensive residential community care. Only patients who are seriously assaultive, uncontrollably overactive, acutely intoxicated, have complicating medical problems, insist on walking or running away, or need special monitoring or diagnostic procedures should be treated in placed called hospitals (see Chapter 4).

Seriously disturbed and disturbing persons can be arbitrarily separated into two groups: those who have been recently identified and have not received much residential care (less than three months or so); and those who have been in the mental health system for a long time, usually more than two years, and have had more than three months of residential care (usually a year or more). For this latter group we prefer the term "veteran" to the more commonly used "chronic," as it has no illness association and is nonpejorative.

Community-based residential care is especially important for the first group. First, because these alternative facilities are minimally institutionalizing and maximally normalizing, they provide a means of preventing "instituationalism," a well-known iatrogenic disease (Barton, 1959; Wing & Brown, 1970) that contributes so much to what becomes labeled "chronicity." Second, because of their being relatively inexpensive (averaging about $100 a day), they provide a setting in which an adequate trial of a psychosocial treatment, with minimal or no use of neuroleptics, can be conducted. Low cost is important to a trial of treatment without antipsychotic drugs because the initial episode in residence will likely be longer than is generally allowed presently in hospitals for the treatment of acute psychoses. That is, given the current pressure to shorten hospital lengths of stay for economic (not clinical) reasons, use of neuroleptics becomes almost obligatory. In alternative care settings a three-month average initial length of stay (usually adequate to allow remission to occur) is not economically prohibitive. Thus, these environments allow an attempt to avoid two of today's most recalcitrant mental health problems: "chronicity" and tardive dyskinesia.

The design, implementation, and results of the use of residential alternative care without antipsychotic medication with newly diagnosed psychotic patients has been well researched in random assignment studies (Matthews, Roper, Mosher, & Menn, 1979; Mosher, Menn, & Matthews, 1975; Mosher & Menn, 1978; Mosher, Vallone, & Menn, 1988).

Of relevance to our recommendation of a drug-free psychosocial treatment trial are Soteria study data (Mosher, et al., 1988) from two separate cohorts of clients treated without neuroleptics that indicate that this psychosocial intervention was able to produce reductions in levels of psychopathology at 6 weeks post admission comparable to those found in the neuroleptic treated control group. The power of this milieu intervention to produce short term symptom change in newly diagnosed schizophrenics provides clear scientific support for a seemingly heretical recommendation. Interestingly, there is no random assignment study presently available to definitively support the usefulness of these types of facilities for "veteran" clients. However, there are a number of clinical studies (Kresky-Wolff, Matthews, Kalibat, & Mosher, 1984; Lamb & Lamb, 1984; Weisman, 1985a,b) that consistently demonstrate that these types of social environments can be successfully adapted for use with longer-term clients.

DEFINING THE SOCIAL ENVIRONMENTS: MILIEU CHARACTERISTICS

Expanding on Gunderson's (1978) seven essential milieu functions we have identified ten: control of stimulation; respite or asylum; protection or containment; support; validation; structure; involvement; socialization; collaboration or negotiation; and planning. They are listed in approximate order of increasing complexity and need for active participation of the client in the process. That is, early in an acutely psychotic patient's stay in a therapeutic milieu the staff will be making sure the environment is quiet, stable, safe, and predictable. They will provide interpersonal support, validation, and structure with only minimal expectations regarding the client's involvement in the process. As the acute phase of the psychosis subsides the latter four functions (involvement through planning) will predominate. Each requires progressively more client collaboration in the process. For example, planning requires extensive client participation and collaboration while involvement can occur with only minimal effort on the part of the patient.

These functions are served to varying degrees in all of our living and working environments. However, an *intentional* social environment whose focus is recovery from psychosis provides them consciously, explicitly, and with ongoing attention to their maintenance and adequacy.

The variables are basically self-explanatory, with the possible exception of validation. By validation we mean that staff are instructed to let clients know that what they are experiencing is quite *real*, even though it cannot sometimes be *consensually* validated. For example, hallucinations can be discussed for what they are, what they mean, and how they make the person feel, but they should not be labeled as not real and "part of their illness." Relating to hallucinations as not real only serves to reify the fragmentation the client is already likely to be experiencing.

The literature also provides differing descriptions of how milieus should be organized to deal with newly identified acutely disordered persons (Table 9.1) and with long-term "veterans" (Table 9.2) of the system. Basically, these descriptions provide more specific approaches that are to be carried out within the overall generic milieu functions listed above. The two types of effective milieus have a number of overlapping characteristics; however, they differ to some extent with regard to what should be done when. That is, time

TABLE 9.1
Effective Milieus for Acute Psychosis

1. Small (6-10 patients)
2. High staff/patient ratio
3. High interaction
4. Real involvement of line staff and patients in decisions
5. Emphasis on autonomy
6. Focus on practical problems (e.g., living arrangements, money)
7. Positive expectations
8. Minimal hierarchy

From Mosher & Gunderson, 1979.

TABLE 9.2
Effective Milieus for Hospitalization Veterans ("Chronic")

1. Clearly defined, specific behaviors requiring change
2. Action (not explanation) oriented, structured program
3. Reasonable, positive, *progressive*, practical expectations with increasing client responsibility
4. Continuation of residential treatment program into in-vivo community settings
5. Continuity of persons
6. Extensive use of groups to facilitate socialization and network-building

From Paul, 1969; Paul & Lentz, 1977.

needs to be allowed for the gross disorganization associated with acute psychosis to begin to recede before focusing on practical problems or decision-making processes. With system veterans this initial reorganization period may be either unnecessary or short and practical problems may be focused on almost immediately. For long-term clients we have found that often the presenting "acute" symptoms are really only a way of accessing help. Once help is assured by being admitted to residential care, these "symptoms" often recede quickly to the background.

If both acute and veteran clients are admitted to the same facility, staff will have to develop the skill necessary to distinguish between their differing needs. Of course, a number of clients will fall in a gray area between the two. Unfortunately, there are no research data and only limited clinical experience to address the issue of whether or not these two populations do better when mixed together or maintained in separate, more homogenous, groups. We believe, but can't prove, that a separate facility for newly identified psychotic persons would be the preferred arrangement. The issue will likely be decided on economic grounds; that is, are there enough newly identified clients deemed in need of hospitalization to keep 10 alternative beds (six in a surrogate peer facility and four in homes of surrogate parents) full in a catchment area of 100,000?

A calculation for the U.S. is almost impossible because of our two track (public/private) mental health system and the lack of mobile crisis intervention. However, in Italy, with its universal national health insurance coverage and in-home crisis intervention, roughly 10 to 15 hospital beds/100,000 population are used (Mosher, 1982). Assuming that 10 of these beds could be replaced by community residential alternatives and that they would have somewhat longer lengths of stay, it would seem that one six-to-eight-bed alternative facility per catchment area serving a mixture of clients would be the most practical arrangement. Whatever configuration is decided upon, newly identified clients should be given first priority for use of these facilities so that they are maintained in as normalizing an environment as possible. Even with adequate numbers of spaces (i.e., 10 per 100,000) in residential alternatives to hospitalization, ten hospital beds will probably still be needed.

IMPLEMENTATION ISSUES

Given the substantial body of research that consistently favors alternative care over hospitalization, it can be legitimately asked why such care is not widely available. We have detailed some of the reasons for this:

> First and foremost, because all alternative care is by definition not given in a hospital it is classified by third-party payers as outpatient treatment. There are limitations on, and disincentives to, outpatient psychiatric care in nearly all health-insurance plans (including Medicare and Medicaid). For example, the federal employees' Blue Cross/Blue Shield high-option plan currently covers nearly all the costs of 60 days of psychiatric hospitalization but limits outpatient visits to 50 per year, with a 30 percent copayment. However, the 50-visit limit includes all physician-outpatient contacts. Thus, even in a "generous" plan, the actual number of psychiatric visits per year that are paid for by the insurance will be fewer than the maximum allowable. For its part, Medicare treats care in psychiatric wards of general hospitals like other types of inpatient care but has a $250 maximal annual reimbursement for psychiatric outpatient care. Payment is based on a formula requiring that $500 worth of care be delivered for the patient to receive the maximal reimbursement. The disincentives to outpatient care in these two large reimbursement schemes are representative examples of third-party-payment plans. Alternative care is usually intensive and may involve a residential (but nonhospital) component; outpatient coverage is rarely sufficient to cover professional fees and never covers residential care, because outpatient means nonresidential by definition. Hence, psychiatric treatment that is offered instead of hospitalization is a true Catch-22 with respect to health-insurance plans.
>
> Secondly, since early in our history American physicians, patients, and the public at large have come to expect that serious mental disorders will be dealt with in hospitals. After a century and a half or more, culturally sanctioned expectations are a powerful force and are not easily modified. An attitude of "out of mind, out of sight" is pervasive. Hence, alternatives to psychiatric hospitalization tend to be unacceptable because they run contrary to conventional wisdom.
>
> Thirdly, today's psychiatry prides itself on being scientific. The *Diagnostic and Statistical Manual* is the obsessional person's dream and the medical student's nightmare. Psychiatry's research on brain pathophysiology uses the latest biomedical technology. Its clinical research, especially into drug efficacy, uses highly sophisticated methods. Over the past several decades psychiatry has experienced a rapprochement with the rest of medicine, partly because of its scientific achievements. The growth of psychiatric wards in general hospitals has been part of this process. To ask psychiatry to move many of its therapeutic endeavors out of hospitals would be regarded as a disruption of its new relation with the rest of medicine. Hence, data about the effectiveness of

alternatives are not greeted with great enthusiasm by the profession. (Mosher, 1983c, p. 1479)

In addition to the three reasons described above, alternatives to hospitalization have failed to be developed because of a combined training and critical mass problem. That is, those alternatives that exist are mainly in the public/community mental health system. The present-day image of community mental health is not a very positive one. It is fashionable to criticize it for having been irresponsible with the deinstitutionalization process and for not having given priority to serving the most disturbed and disturbing persons. This system traditionally pays less well and has more bureaucratic barriers to good care than the private system. It serves the disenfranchised, minorities, the poor, the homeless, and the truly mad. It is, in sum, not very attractive.

Training in social work, psychology, and psychiatry tends to be focused on preparing students to be private practitioners. Community mental health, along with alternatives to hospitalization, is doubly afflicted; its clientele tends to be unattractive and few potential staff have training relevant to working with them.

This training issue is compounded in the case of residential alternatives to hospital; there are so few of them that it's impossible to provide training sites for more than a handful of students (the critical mass problem). With rare exception, line staff in residential alternative programs have had no previous experience in a similar setting. Hence, they are all basically trained on the job. On-the-job training can be excellent if experienced supervision is available. Here again, because there are so few of these facilities, there are not substantial numbers of experienced professionals available to organize, administer, and supervise these programs — another aspect of the critical mass problem.

This problem could be addressed if professional schools recognized the existence of the phenomenon of alternatives and began to include them in curricula. Over time a cadre of trained persons would be developed to provide the leadership and expertise necessary to implement these programs. We have described elsewhere a model for such community-based training (Burti & Mosher, 1986). Until this image and training issue is addressed it will be difficult to plan, develop, and implement the types of intensive residential community-based care described here.

CLINICAL MODELS

Two models of intensive community residential treatment have been extensively written about: the surrogate parent model developed in Southwest Denver (Polak & Kirby, 1976; Polak, Kirby, & Dietchman, 1979) and the

Soteria/Crossing Place surrogate peer model developed by Mosher and co-workers (Mosher & Menn, 1977; Mosher & Menn, 1978; Mosher & Menn, 1979; Mosher & Menn, 1983; Wendt, Mosher, Matthews, & Menn, 1983). The Polak and Kirby model has not been formally researched in a random assignment study. The Soteria portion of the Soteria/Crossing Place model has been intensively and extensively studied in a random assignment two-year follow-up design. Crossing Place has published a clinical (i.e., nonran-dom, no controls) short-term outcome study of its first 150 clients (Kresky-Wolff et al., 1984).

THE SURROGATE PARENT MODEL

The Southwest Denver model was developed in conjunction with the program's use of mobile in-home interventions as their major form of emergency service. They found, logically enough, that a certain percentage of in-home crisis interventions were not successful enough so that they felt safe in leaving all the parties at home. The program's leadership (principally Paul Polak) was moderately hospital phobic, so they devised their surrogate parent program to be used in those instances where someone needed to be temporarily taken out of the home.

The program's design capitalizes on the empty nest syndrome. By means of ads in local papers and word-of-mouth, the CMHC recruited families whose children had grown up and left home. In this mostly suburban part of Denver many couples had substantial homes with two or more empty bedrooms. Couples who responded to the ad were interviewed by CMHC staff and, if accepted, provided with a modest amount of information about, and training for dealing with, disturbed and disturbing persons. There were no hard and fast selection criteria, but they preferred to use couples with a previous record of some type of community service whose offspring were leading reasonably successful lives (i.e., not in jails or the mental health system). Each couple was asked to set aside one or two bedrooms for use by CMHC clients. The rooms were paid for whether or not they were occupied.

The program's success (as it is judged by the CMHC and the families) was due to a variety of factors: First, the CMHC's mobile community team promised a 15-minute response time to any crisis that evolved in the surrogate parents' homes. Early in the program's life this availability was tested several times. As the parent couples became more comfortable with their roles, the need to call the backup team became quite rare.

Second, all acutely psychotic patients admitted to one of the homes were treated vigorously with neuroleptics, often via intramuscular "rapid neuro-lepticization." Hence, they attempted to minimize the occurrence of disruptive behavior through chemical restraint. Whether this type of high-dose neuroleptic treatment was still necessary when the parents became more experienced was never really tested.

Third, the parent couples who stayed with the program were natural healers. They approached their temporary children with a great deal of support, reassurance, and gentle firmness. As they got to know them, the parents began to involve themselves in helping clients with problem-solving. They gradually integrated clients into the family's ongoing life. Although there were no length-of-stay rules, most clients stayed two-to-three weeks and left gradually. Even after they were no longer sleeping in the surrogate parents' home, ex-clients would be invited to visit, to have dinner, or to share in a family event.

Fourth, the parent couples were highly respected by the CMHC staff. They were seen as an integral part of their program. They were identified and highlighted as the persons responsible for the CMHC's ability to use only one bed (on average) in the nearby state hospital—a statistic many people found astounding given a 75,000 person catchment area. Parent couples were sent to professional meetings to speak. They were visited by professionals, officials, and dignitaries of various types. All in all they felt themselves to be important contributors to a groundbreaking, innovative program. The parents became advocates for better community-based care.

Fifth, it provided the couples with a new career to be pursued during their retirement years. In addition, the predictable income from the program allowed many of them to keep and maintain family homes that otherwise might have had to have been sold.

In a sense the program provided preventive mental health care to the parent couples by refilling the empty nest. To us, the Polak and Kirby model is ideal for use in areas with low population density—i.e., semi-rural to rural areas. It is very economical even if the beds are not filled. Current replications provide stipends to the couples of $800–$900 per month per bed. With this model excellent care can be provided in the client's own, or a very nearby, community even in rural areas, thus minimizing disruption of ties with the natural support system. There are many rural areas where the nearest psychiatric inpatient care is 100 or more miles away; in this context hospitalization is extremely disruptive for patient, family and network.

Although the surrogate parent model is particularly well suited to rural settings, we believe that urban and suburban community programs should have two or more (i.e., four beds) of these settings available per 100,000 population. Clinically, they would seem to best suited to the treatment of unemancipated psychotic persons, i.e., those in the 16–22-year-old age range with whom in-home family intervention has not been successful. Living in an alternate family environment affords many opportunities for these young people to experience, relate to, and learn from less highly emotionally charged parent figures. When properly planned, these settings can also provide the *client's parents* with an opportunity to share their difficulties with another set of parents, get support and understanding, and perhaps learn new ways of coping with their offspring from the surrogate parents' examples.

Utilizing empty nest parents allows the community program to actually address a problem of many seniors—feeling put out to pasture too soon and unnecessarily. These parents constitute a much underutilized natural resource—the experience, knowledge, and wisdom that accrues to people as they get older. Successful child-rearing capabilities should be a highly prized commodity. Yet, these qualities are rarely explicitly acknowledged and used for the benefit of others. This is an excellent illustration of a principle of good community psychiatry—using already available community resources. These include school and recreational programs, libraries, gyms, *and* personal skills.

SURROGATE PEER MODEL

The model developed by Mosher and coworkers has its roots in the era of moral treatment in psychiatry (Bockoven, 1963), in the psychoanalytic tradition of intensive interpersonal treatment (especially Sullivan, 1931; Fromm-Reichmann, 1948), therapists who have described growth from psychosis (Perry, 1962), research on community-based treatment for schizophrenia (Fairweather, Sanders, Cressler, & Maynard, 1969; Pasamanick, Scarpitti, & Dinitz, 1967) and to some extent in the so-called "antipsychiatry" movement (Laing, 1967). The Soteria project opened its first house in San Jose, California, in the fall of 1971. A replication house, Emanon, opened in another Northern California town in 1974. The original house closed because of lack of funding in October of 1983; the replication closed January 1980 for the same reason.

The basic notion behind the project was that the first treated psychotic episode was a critical intervention point. That is, the project's developers believed that the way the first episode of psychosis is dealt with will likely have great impact on long-term outcome. The project selected young, unmarried, newly diagnosed *DSM-II* schizophrenics because, statistically, the literature clearly indicated that they are the most likely to become disabled (Klorman, Strauss, & Kokes, 1977; Phillips, 1966; Rosen, Klein, & Gittelman-Klein, 1971). Hence, the project took clients with whom a successful intervention might save society a great deal of money over the long run in terms of hospital days, medications, and welfare costs.

An additional reason for taking only newly identified patients was our wish to avoid having to deal with the learned mental patient role that veteran patients have frequently acquired. Neuroleptics were not given for an initial six-week period so that a fair trial of a pure psychosocial intervention could take place. An additional reason for withholding antipsychotic drugs is that no, or minimal, neuroleptic treatment is the only certain way to prevent tardive dyskinesia.

Although the program's individual elements were not new, bringing them under a single roof in a 1915 vintage, six-bedroom house on a busy street in a suburban northern California town was. The program was designed to offer an alternative not only to hospitalization but also to neuroleptic drugs and professional staffing of intensive residential care. The program's psychiatrist, for example, was a consultant who did initial client interviews and staff training but had no ongoing contact with the clients. As the program matured, the psychiatrists came to be seen, and to see themselves, as mostly peripheral to it.

Given the three areas to which the Soteria project was designed to provide an alternative (i.e., hospitals, neuroleptics, and professionals), it is not surprising that over its 13-year life the project was regarded by the field with ambivalence at best and suspicion and hostility at worst. Its research grant applications set NIMH records for numbers of site visits, reviews, and opinions sought. It was, and to some extent still is, viewed as a threat to psychiatry's current biomedical zeitgeist. Nevertheless, as a demonstration, Soteria and its successor Crossing Place have provided the field with successful alternative clinical models. At the present time the only Soteria replication (i.e., with newly identified psychotics) under way is in Berne, Switzerland, under the direction of Professor Luc Ciompi. There are a number of facilities similar to Crossing Place (i.e., ones that deal with the whole spectrum of clientele). An accurate count is difficult because of definitional and identification problems, but there are certainly 20 or more, almost all in the public sector.

The 11 most important elements of the surrogate peer model we have identified are listed in Table 9.3. They are, for the most part, self-explanatory. However, a comment on the size issue appears warranted. We believe, based on our extensive experience, the Soteria data, the literature on extended families, communes, experimental psychology task groups, group therapy, and the Tavistock model, that for a community to be able to maximize its healing potential no more than eight to ten persons should sleep under the same roof. Larger groups require more space than most ordinary houses provide; moreover, the interaction patterns and organizational governance needed are very different. Hence, economy of scale, i.e., facilities of 15 or more beds, is clinically unwise. Ideally, six clients, two staff, and one or two others (e.g., students, volunteers) should sleep in the facility at any one time. Eight clients can be accommodated, but this begins to tax the limits of

TABLE 9.3
Soteria and Crossing Place: Essential Characteristics

1. Small (6 clients), homelike
2. Ideologically uncommitted staff
3. Peer/fraternal relationship orientation
4. Preservation of personal power valued
5. Open social system (easy access and departure)
6. Participants responsible for house maintenance
7. Minimal role differentiation
8. Minimal hierarchy
9. Use of community resources encouraged
10. Postdischarge contacts allowed/encouraged
11. No formal in-house "therapy"

the size of the social group and stretch staff availability if half or more of the clients are in acute distress. Actually, we believe that a 50–50 mix of disturbed and disturbing persons with nondisturbed persons is about ideal for the functioning of the house as a therapeutic community. This equation of six clients, two or three of whom have been in residence long enough to have reorganized sufficiently to appear relatively undisturbed, and two or three quasi-normal staff (including students) makes for an optimal mix.

There are a number of residential alternatives in existence that have 15 or so client beds (Lamb & Lamb, 1984; Weisman, 1985b). We believe that the home-like atmosphere is so absolutely crucial to the therapeutic functioning of community-based alternatives that we would *not* include such programs as examples of the Soteria/Crossing Place model. It is likely that when the NIMH or state departments of mental health get involved in the development of these facilities they will like the cost-savings of these larger units. However, it seems clear from recent research (Rappaport, Goldman, Thornton, Moltzen, Stegner, Hall, Gurevitz, & Attkisson, 1987) that they sacrifice clinical effectiveness when they grow to the size of small hospital units, especially if they are located on hospital grounds. Their non-institutional character is compromised, and with it that compromise the treatment milieu is changed. To reiterate: to be family-like, their critical and unique characteristic, these facilities should have no more than six, or at most eight, client beds and must be real *community* homes – not institutional appendages.

Minimal role differentiation is a term that is sometimes misunderstood and responded to by comments like "what these clients need are examples of clear roles and boundaries." What we mean is that, for the most part, each line staff member will be able to do anything needed by a particular client. For example, the same staff member may accompany a client to apply for an apartment, go with him to the welfare office to see about SSI benefits, and meet with his family that evening. Only the program director and psychiatric consultants have different, and differentiated, roles. Having staff as generalists makes it easier to use the natural pairings that occur to accomplish particular client goals without having to assign a "special" staff member to the task.

A comment is also in order about the absence of formal in-house therapy. As noted previously, we view the entire facility "package" as providing the therapeutic social environment. Hence, everything that goes on in and out of it can be viewed as therapeutic. However, there are no time-limited in-office therapy sessions—individual, group or family—*in the facility.* We believe that because of this policy client fragmentation and community suspicion about what's going on behind closed doors are prevented and a treatment value hierarchy does not become established. That is, for the environment to be the treatment, the "real" treatment cannot be a one-to-one hour in the office with a therapist. Individual clients may be referred out, as indicated, to receive these types of therapy away from the setting itself. Having said there is no formal in-house therapy, we must go on to say that a great deal of therapeutic interaction takes place in dyads, in groups, and with families in the setting. Much of it is spontaneous, but not infrequently staff will take clients aside to discuss particular issues or behaviors.

Specific therapies can be made available in the house to persons living there as long as these therapies are invited in based on the approval of a majority of the participants and are made available to everyone who wishes to become involved. Hence, art therapy, bibliotherapy, yoga, massage, acupuncture, special diets, etc., have come and gone in the settings depending on the group's wishes and the therapies' availability.

Group meetings are also held. Some, like the house meeting, occur on a regularly scheduled basis. Others, like family meetings, usually occur soon after the client is admitted and on an as-needed basis thereafter. Morning "what are you doing today?" and evening "how was your day?" meetings occur regularly but are not formalized. The Crossing Place brochure describes the social environment that should characterize this type of intensive residential community care:

> The basic therapeutic modality is one-to-one, intensive interpersonal support. Specially selected and trained staff members are with the client for as long as intensive care and supervision are required. The staff members all have experience in crisis-care.
>
> The program's home-like environment is also an important therapeutic element: it minimizes the stress of going into residential care and re-entry into the community because it resembles the client's ordinary environment. Individuals focus on coping with their life-crisis in a real-life setting. In addition,

the environment minimizes the potential for severe acting-out by being small, intimate, and rapidly responsive. This setting tends to elicit the best from clients by regarding them as responsible members of a temporary family.

The staff members work closely with the director and psychiatrists to help individual clients formulate goals and plans. The entire staff meets regularly to discuss problems encountered in the helping process. The program director and psychiatrists are available to give individual attention to clients with particularly difficult situations.

The length of stay varies from a few days to several months, depending on individual needs. Discharge is effected when the crisis has subsided and adequate plans have been worked out for important aspects of post-discharge living and treatment.

When we compare Soteria with its successor Crossing Place, we find a number of differences: Soteria House was a carefully designed research project that limited its intake to young, newly diagnosed schizophrenic patients. Crossing Place takes adult clients of all ages, diagnoses, and lengths of illness. Soteria House existed mostly outside the public treatment system in its city. Its clients came from only one entry point and were carefully screened to be sure they met the research criteria before being randomly assigned to Soteria House or to the hospital-treated control group. Because of its restrictive admission criteria (about three or four of 100 functional psychotic patients admitted per month met them), Soteria House was not seen as a real treatment resource within that system.

Crossing Place, on the other hand, is firmly embedded in the Washington, DC public mental health system. It was founded by Woodley House, a long-established private nonprofit agency whose programs include a 22-bed halfway house, a 50-bed supervised apartment program, and a thrift shop with a work support program. Because of contractual arrangements with the District of Columbia mental health system, Crossing Place accepts referrals from a variety of entry points. Its clients are primarily system veterans whose care is paid for by one of these contracts. Although it officially excludes only persons who have medical problems or whose primary problem is substance abuse, it has little control over the actual referral criteria used by a variety of clinicians.

Thus, in contrast to Soteria House, Crossing Place clientele are a less well-defined, more heterogeneous group. They *may* be less ill, violent, or suicidal (unfortunately it's not possible to know for sure) than those sent to St. Elizabeth's Hospital, the main residential treatment setting for public patients in Washington. Compared with Soteria subjects, Crossing Place clients are older (32 versus 21), are more frequently members of minority groups, and have extensive hospitalization experience (4.5 versus no admissions). Basic subject data comparing the two settings is shown in Table 9.4. Thus, although the characteristics of the Crossing Place client population

TABLE 9.4
Patient Demographic Data

	SOTERIA (N = 30)	CROSSING PLACE (N = 155)
Age	21	32
Marital status:		
unmarried	100%	96%
Education	13 years	12 years
Employment:		
any prior to admission	73%	47%
Diagnosis	All schizophrenic	62% schizophrenic
		26% affective psychosis
		17% nonpsychotic
Previous hospitalizations:		
percent of sample	3%	92%
average number	1	4.5
weeks hospitalized		
previous year	0	8
Initial length of stay	166 days	32 days
Neuroleptic drug Rx		
during initial admission	8%	96%

are not as precisely known as those of the Soteria patients, the former group can be characterized as "veterans" ("chronic") and the latter as newly identified ("acute").

In their presentations to the world, Crossing Place is conventional and Soteria was unconventional. Despite this major difference, the actual in-house interpersonal interactions are similar in their informality, earthiness, honesty, and lack of professional jargon. These similarities arise partially from the fact that neither program ascribes the usual patient role to the clientele. Both programs use male-female staff pairs who work 24- or 48-hour shifts.

Soteria's research funding viewed length of stay as a dependent research variable. This allowed it to vary according to the clinical needs of the newly diagnosed patients. The initial lengths of stay averaged just over five months. Crossing Place's contract contains length-of-stay standards (one to two months). Hence, the initial focus of the Crossing Place staff must be: What do the clients need to accomplish so they can resume living in the community as quickly as possible? This focus on personal responsibility is a technique that Woodley House has used successfully for many years. At Soteria, such questions were not ordinarily raised until the acutely psychotic state had subsided — usually four to six weeks after entry. This span exceeds the average length of stay at Crossing Place (32 days).

In part, the shorter average length of stay at Crossing Place is made possible by the almost routine use of neuroleptics to control the most flagrant symptoms of its clientele. At Soteria, neuroleptics were never used during the first six weeks of a patient's stay and were rarely given thereafter. Time constraints also dictate that Crossing Place will have a more formalized social structure than Soteria. That is, when goals are identified rapidly, there must be a well organized social structure to allow them to be pursued expeditiously.

The two Crossing Place consulting psychiatrists evaluate each client on admission and each spends an hour a week with the staff reviewing each client's progress, addressing particularly difficult issues, and helping develop a consensus on initial and revised treatment plans. Soteria had a variety of meetings but averaged one client-staff meeting per week. The role of consulting psychiatrists was more peripheral at Soteria than at Crossing Place. They were not ordinarily involved in treatment planning and no regular treatment meeting was held.

In summary, compared to Soteria, Crossing Place is more organized, structured, and oriented toward practical goals. Expectations of Crossing Place staff members tend to be positive but more limited than those of Soteria staff members. At Crossing Place, psychosis is frequently talked *around* by staff members, while at Soteria the client's experience of acute psychosis was an important subject of interpersonal communication. At Crossing Place, the use of neuroleptics limits psychotic episodes. The immediate social problems of Crossing Place clients (secondary to being system veterans and having come from lower-class minority families) must be addressed quickly: no money, no place to live, no one with whom to talk. Basic survival is often the issue. Among the Soteria clients, because they came from less economically disadvantaged families, these problems were sometimes present but much less pressing. Basic survival was usually not an issue.

Crossing Place staff members spend a lot of time keeping other parts of the mental health community involved in the process of addressing client needs. Since the clients are known to many other players in the system, just contacting everyone with a role in the life of any given client can be an all-day process. In contrast, Soteria clients, being new to the system, had no such cadre of involved mental health workers. While in residence, Crossing Place clients continue their involvement with other programs. At Soteria, only the project director and house director dealt with the rest of the mental health system. At Crossing Place, all staff members negotiate with the system. The house director supervises this process and administers the house itself. Because of the shorter lengths of stay, the focus on immediate practical problem-solving, and the absence of most clients from the house during the daytime, Crossing Place tends to be less consistently intimate in feeling than Soteria. Individual relationships between staff members and clients can be very intimate at Crossing Place, especially with returning clients, but it is easier to get in and out of Crossing Place without having a significant relationship than was the case at Soteria.

One aspect of the Crossing Place program that deserves special mention is the ex-residents' evening. It is based in part on the Soteria experience, but also grew out of the emphasis at Crossing Place and Woodley House on alumni involvement. An art therapist supervises the session, to which former and current residents are invited. Attendance varies considerably, but the formal time, place, and the nature of the activity make returning much easier for persons who might otherwise not be sure they are "really" welcome. The evening provides social contact, a place to find friends, and a chance to meet new people. Art seems to be an ideal medium around which to focus a meeting of long-term clients. Almost anyone can draw, and the critical comments of others can be easily deflected by saying, "Well, I've never drawn before." Although a large informal social network of clients existed around Soteria, the house never had a formal arrangement with ex-residents. Again, this program difference would appear to be best explained by differences in clientele.

Both Soteria and Crossing Place use non-degreed paraprofessionals as staff. Although some of the staff may, in fact, have college or graduate degrees, they are not required in the application process. These facilities seek staff who are interested, invested, and enthusiastic about the type of work they anticipate doing, independent of credentials. The down side of this practice is that there is often no career ladder available to them. Additional problems with using non-degreed paraprofessional staff are the generally low salaries paid them and a lack of recognition of their value in the professional mental health community. Hence, staff turnover is usually a consequence of returning to school to get graduate degrees, most frequently MSW's.

Our experience is that the more accurately the reality of the job is described, the less likely it is that a misfit between job and person will occur. Thus, we like to make very explicit exactly what will be expected of staff in ads and job descriptions provided to them. Our view is that the *self-selection process is the primary determinant of the quality of staff.* The requisite values and attitudes predate their employment; the setting only serves to reinforce and expand them.

The job description should contain sufficient substance to allow candidates to easily identify the major activities that will be part of their job. These include:

1. *Client assessment.* Staff are required to evaluate each client's strengths and weaknesses, with an emphasis on expandable areas of

strength. The task is to respect and *understand*, in context, what's going on with the client. Psychopathology will be factored in, but in a manner that preserves the focus on health, positive assets, and normalization of functioning. This assessment will also include a future planning element, since in these transitional programs the *process of leaving begins at entry.*

2. *Relationships, "being with."* Staff will be expected to form some modest relationship with most clients. It is expected that they will form close relationships with a minority of clients. The relationships are expected to be peer-oriented, fraternal, nonexploitative, attentive but not intrusive, warm, nurturant, supportive, and responsive. Staff are not expected to like everyone, nor are they expected to have a close relationship with the majority of clients. They are not expected to see themselves as psychotherapists, even with those clients with whom they form close relationships. Quiet, attentive, nondemanding support is highly valued.

3. *Advocacy/empowerment.* Staff will work with clients on *their* goals. If this requires involvement with specialists or others outside the facility, they will be involved as required. Client goals are always primary, even if they require staff to go out of their way. Staff take clients and stay with them, if necessary, to the welfare, vocational, housing, socializing, and recreating systems. Their goal vis-à-vis the clients' goals is to facilitate the process of normalization and integration back into the mainstream of society. They are to view themselves as being clients' employees and should treat them as "the boss" insofar as their requests are at all reasonable. Even seemingly unreasonable requests (if not dangerous to anyone) should be pursued. Staff are not to see themselves as necessarily knowing what is "best" for the client. A truly unreasonable request will likely be treated as such by the entire social environment. Hence, staff need not make it their responsibility to define this "reality." Also, they need not necessarily try to protect clients from the impact of pursuing their requests (absent real risk of serious harm). Doing so would deprive the client of an in-vivo learning experience.

Basically, staff should be able to put themselves, flexibly and non-judgmentally, into the client's shoes. This ability will allow them to accept a variety of wishes, needs and goals from the client without a predetermined staff-derived hierarchical scale of importance or "rightness." This is why we try *not* to hire staff with a strong commitment to a particular mental health ideology—psychoanalytic, behaviorist or what-have-you. In our experience adherence to a particular theory inhibits the staff person's ability to be immediately and flexibly responsive.

What follows are three illustrative excerpts of staff-client interactions taken from the Soteria treatment manual (*Soteria: A Manual*, 1972, available from LRM). This document attempts to provide management guidelines and case examples of how Soteria staff dealt with various difficult behaviors and states of mind without using seclusion, restraints or medications. Major headings include: aggression, withdrawal, regression, sexuality, relationships, contagion, and leaving.

The first example illustrates the course of a series of interactions around a young woman's firmly held, but not consensually validatable, belief system. It is not uncommon for an individual staff member to spend entire shifts for weeks on end with one resident, often sleeping in the same room with him.

> For a long time it was Monday through Wednesday, which is my shift. I'd spend the whole time with Hope when she wasn't asleep. She went through a long period where she just didn't sleep at all at night, like, you know, we'd watch the sun come up every morning talking. Hope was an all-nighter—one of the most famous all-nighters.
>
> She was consumed by the devil in the beginning, but she wouldn't talk about it as much after a while because she knew that people would try to talk her out of it. Then when she really started to believe that there was something inside her besides the devil, and the closer she would come to figuring out things for herself, she would talk back to you a lot of times, really getting a lot of garbage out. She needed a sounding board. She'd suddenly become more and more rational. She would talk about how she really knew she wasn't the devil, yet inside, she felt so awful. Sometimes I argued with her about it. She would talk about how she was the devil, then together we would find these coincidences that could prove that anybody was the devil or that she wasn't the devil. After a while, when she really became aware that nobody in the house believed that she was the devil, she was sort of pissed off. She really would try hard to prove it. Sometimes I'd get angry at her if she was really carrying on trying to prove she was the devil. I'd tell her about the parts of her that weren't the devil.

The next example is taken from the manual's section on regression:

> I had had three hours of sleep, and even that had been broken sleep. Sleeping with and guarding Sara is not especially conducive to good resting. I was sleeping on the floor by the door so that I would waken if she tried to leave. She awakened at 6 o'clock demanding food. I got up and started to fix her breakfast. She was sitting at the table waiting more impatiently; she then urinated on the bench she was sitting on. I took her to the bathroom, changed her pants and we went back to the kitchen. I fed her at the table. She finished and sat quietly for about two minutes. Then she looked at me with a fearful expression on her face and asked me what day it was. I told her it was Sunday, and she said, "No, I mean what day is it *really. You* know what I mean!" I told her that it was Sunday, September 5th. I knew that it was Sara's birthday but for some reason I didn't want to deal with it then. I was tired, I was sad—it was

Sara's 16th birthday, "Sweet 16." It was Sara's special day to celebrate, and there sat Sara in Soteria, soiling herself, terrified of dying, of being alone, of being with people, of spiders, of noises, of being loved, of being unloved. Happy Birthday, Sara—it was so goddamned sad.

Anyway, when I told her the date she was stunned. She sat completely still and stared at me. Then came the change—fear, anxiety, joy, little-girl pleasure, sorrow, and pain all flashed over her face in seconds. Then she started to cry, a slow, sad, and painful cry. And then she said, "It's my birthday, say 'Happy Birthday' to me." And I did. Then she got up and came over to me and sat down. She took my hand in both of hers and said, "Hold me!" I held her while she cried for a few minutes. Then she sat up and said, "Give me a present. Give me something. Give me anything. Give me something you don't want anymore. Give me something you hate. Just give me anything of yours and I'll love it forever." I told her that she would be getting birthday presents later in the day—that we hadn't forgotten her.

I was wearing a T-shirt that morning, one that Sara liked. She asked me then if I would wear her shirt and could she wear mine, just for her birthday. No one else in the house was awake—it was early and it was Sara's birthday—so we exchanged shirts.

When I took my shirt off Sara stared at my breasts and seemed to freeze for a few seconds. I can't describe even to myself the expression that was on her face, so I won't try here. She collapsed into my chest with her eyes closed, she was completely limp. I almost fell under her weight. Her face was toward my chest and she moved it a little and started sucking my breast. For a very brief moment I panicked and feared being bitten and wanted to pull away. But that feeling passed very quickly, because I didn't pull away at all. I guess it could have been instinctive, it just all felt so *right* to me then. Without thinking of appropriate therapeutic moves or words, I held her, cuddled her, nursed her, cooed to her—all very freely and naturally—and it ended.

Sara moved away from me and said, "I'm not your baby, you're mine." She then ignored it and went on to deal with the rest of the day. It was a brief happening, a quiet one, but an important one. It was the kind of incident that makes our house a special and more-than-good place for me and for my people that live there.

Regression, while not induced, is allowed and tolerated when it occurs naturally. Staff feel that it is often an important step toward reintegration.

The last excerpt is a marvelous example of the concept of "being with," both physically and psychologically:

While we were talking he kept talking about how his father was Howard Hughes. And at this point he was just laying on the bed and I think I was sitting on the floor next to him. And he was saying he had to find out where his Lear Jet was parked. I asked him why he wanted it and he said he had to get back to Nevada to see his mother. He was saying his back was very sore, so I gave him a back massage. He talked more about his mother. He wanted to see his mother and bring her back here. He'd start crying a little bit. This went on for pretty close to an hour. Afterwards he said his back felt better. He said he could wait to go see his mother but he still wanted to find his Lear Jet. He thought it was parked on the driveway. So we went out to the driveway and it wasn't there. He said it must be at the airport. We came back in the house and we went to his room again. He was talking about things that happened in the war between him and Harly Bird. And then I wanted some coffee so we went over to Spivey's (a nearby restaurant). And I bought him a hamburger. He was telling me all about when he was a kid—the childhood he had and the paper routes and about school. About every two or three minutes he'd stop and laugh and say, "Well, this is silly for me to tell you; you're my father; you already know all this." As we were coming back, he stopped and said, "That was really nice. I knew you were going to take me out to dinner some night, Dad. And now we've done it." When we got back to the house he began telling me the Venutians were going to come down and visit him that night. He says "I can see them coming down now. They're going to be waiting for us." So then we went across the street under the stoplights, because he had to see the sun at the same time he saw Venus, and the sun was just coming up the other side. And he had to be between them for the Venutians to find him. So we were waiting there for maybe a half hour or 45 minutes, and he figured, well, they weren't going to come today, after all. It was getting light and Venus was disappearing from the sky, and they hadn't shown up yet, so he figured they weren't going to come. We came back to his room and it was maybe 5:30 or 6 in the morning by this time. He was talking about this belt that Harly Bird had given him that allowed him to go through space and time and it was a seat belt for the Lear Jet. Somewhere thereabouts he fell asleep, and I fell asleep too.

We hope these examples convey the flavor of the very unusual ways of dealing with madness that evolved at Soteria House. These descriptions should be compared with Dr. Holly Wilson's account of the treatment process on the ward where comparison group clients were sent (Chapter 4, pp. 33–35).

Systematic research comparison of the Soteria and Crossing Place treatment milieus has taken place. Moos' Community Oriented Program Environment Scale (COPES) (Moos, 1974, 1975), a 100-item true-false measure of participants' perceptions of their social environment, was administered at regular intervals to staff and clients in both programs. This measure has both "real" (i.e., "How do you see it?") and ideal (i.e., "How would you like it to be?") forms.

Although staff and client real and ideal data were collected, only staff real data are reported here (see Figure 9.1). According to these data, Crossing Place staff members, as compared with Soteria staff members, see their environment as three standard deviations higher in practical orientation and two standard deviations higher on order and organization and staff control. Both programs are one or more standard deviations lower than norms derived from other community-based programs on autonomy, practicality, and order and organization. They are one or more standard deviations higher on the three psychotherapy variables—involvement, support, and spontanei-

COPES REAL PROFILES

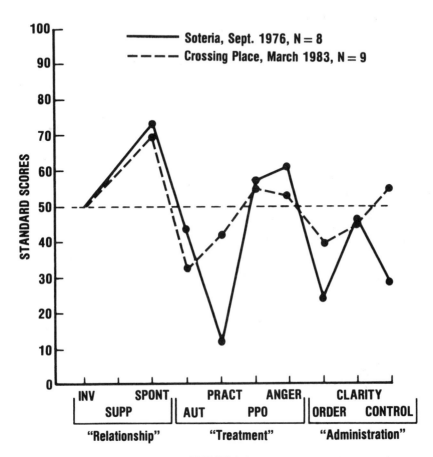

FIGURE 9.1
Program Comparisons: Staff
Soteria and Crossing Place

ty — and on the treatment variables of perceived personal problem orientation and staff tolerance of anger. The overall shapes of the two profiles have
almost point-by-point correspondence on six variables and similar profile
shapes on the other four. The congruence between clinical descriptive and
standardized assessment findings is both noteworthy and gratifying (Mosher
et al., 1986).

The two programs also conform well, by both clinical description and systematic assessment, to the literature-derived descriptions of effective therapeutic milieus for acute and "veteran" clients outlined earlier.

Basic two-year outcome data from the Soteria project are shown in Tables 9.5 and 9.6. One surprising finding not contained in the tables, was that Soteria treated subjects experienced reductions in psychopathology over the initial six-week period of treatment that were comparable to those found among the neuroleptic treated controls. This was true for both the 1972–76 and 1976–80 patient cohorts (Mosher et al., 1988). The clients in the Soteria control group were all treated with neuroleptics for an average of 28 days on a 30-bed ward in a community hospital that was used as a training site by a nearby university medical school. Forty-three percent of control subjects were maintained on them for the two-year follow-up period.

Despite minimal neuroleptic use (57% never received neuroleptics and only 4% were maintained on them during the two-year study period), experi-

TABLE 9.5
Soteria Outcome Data
Postdischarge Resource Use, Cumulative to Two-year Follow-up

VARIABLE	EXPERIMENTAL GROUP	CONTROL GROUP	EXACT PROBABILITY
*Readmissions**			
N	30	33	
Total readmissions	28	37	n.s.
N readmitted	16	22	
% readmitted	53%	67%	
Neuroleptic drug treatment			
N	23	23	
Continuous	4%	43%	.00001
Intermittent**	30%	52%	
Occasional	9%	4%	
None	57%	0	
Other mental health contacts			
N	22	22	
Any contact	59%	100%	.0007
Outpatient therapy	45%	100%	.0001
Day or night hospital	19%	41%	.04
Total days of day or night hospitalization	110	1215	

*Includes readmissions to other psychiatric hospitals as well as original treatment facilities.
**At least two weeks of continuous medication.
From Mosher & Menn, 1978.

Mental Illness: My Personal Story

My Life is but a Weaving

My Life is but a weaving between my God and me,
I do not choose the colors, He worketh steadily.
Ofttimes He weaveth sorrow, and I in foolish pride,
Forget He sees the upper, and I the underside.

Not till the loom is silent, and shuttles cease to fly,
Will God unroll the canvas and explain the reason why.
The dark threads are as needful in the skillful Weaver's hand,
As the threads of gold and silver in the pattern He has planned.

Author: Unknown[1]

TABLE 9.6
Soteria Outcome Data
Psychosocial Adjustment before Admission and at Two-year Follow-up

VARIABLE	EXPERIMENTAL GROUP	CONTROL GROUP	EXACT PROBABILITY
Work status			
Before admission			
N	36	28	
Full-time work*	64%	64%	n.s.
Part-time work	19%	21%	
Not working	17%	14%	
Two-year follow-up			
N	25	29	
Full-time work	32%	28%	n.s.
Part-time work	44%	52%	
Not working	24%	21%	
Occupational level**	2.71 + .56	2.33 + .49	.05
Living arrangements			
Before admission			
N	37	39	
With parents or relatives	68%	62%	n.s.
Independently	30%	36%	
Board and care or similar	3%	3%	
Two-year follow-up			
N	33	30	
With parents or relatives	33%	37%	.02
Independently	58%	33%	
Board and care or similar	0%	23%	
Soteria or hospital (readmission)	9%	7%	
Friendships***	1.95 + .59	1.56 + .92	n.s.

*Includes patients attending school full time.
**A rating of 2 indicates fallen, 3 the same, and 4 risen.
***A rating of 0 indicates none and 3 many.
From Mosher & Menn, 1978.

mental group patients were less often readmitted, were more often able to leave home to live on their own or with peers, and had higher level jobs as compared to control group patients. These data, especially the six week psychopathology findings cited above, support our contention that all newly identified psychotics deserve a trial of pure psychosocial intervention if a proper therapeutic environment can be provided.

Based on 12 years of experience and several hundred clients in the Soteria project and 10 years and more than 500 clients in Crossing Place, we have identified what we consider to be the nine essential therapeutic ingredients of these special social environments. They are:

1. Positive expectations of recovery and learning from psychosis.
2. Flexibility of roles, relationships and responses.
3. Acceptance of psychotic persons' experience of themselves as real — even if not consensually validatable.
4. Staff's primary task is to *be with* the disorganized client; it must be specifically acknowledged that staff need not *do* anything.
5. Normalization and usualization of the experience of psychosis by contextualizing it, framing it in positive terms, and referring to it in everyday language.
6. Tolerance of extremes of human behavior without need to control it except when there is imminent danger.
7. Sufficient time in residence (one to three months) for development of surrogate family relationships that allow imitation and identification with positive characteristics of staff and other clients.
8. Sufficient exposure to positively valued role models to identify, experiment with, and internalize strategies for problem-solving that provide a new sense of efficacy, mastery and competence.
9. Readily available post-discharge peer-oriented social network with which contact is begun while in residence.

The reader will note that most of these have been previously described in Chapter 7.

Transitional Residential Programs

Transitional housing is a clear departure from usual living arrangements and therefore not optimally *normalizing*. Transitional facilities and program should be arranged in a way that delivers the "this is a temporary arrangement" message clearly and consistently. In contrast to what we espouse for both alternatives to hospitalization and supported nontransitional housing, we believe that halfway houses should be somewhat institutional and have a social organization that expects, promotes, and reinforces independence in the context of support. Their social structure will produce the desired independence-promoting effect only if they are closely associated with supported nontransitional housing programs. Repeated separations from friends and family and housing instability are known to be associated with increased rates of psychiatric disorder. For these reasons, the thrust of transitional programs should be toward helping clients establish permanent housing and stable social networks.

What kind of "institutional" characteristics should such facilities have?

1. They should house more persons than an extended family. Hence, 15 to 25 clients is a good number of clients for such places.
2. Program rules should specify the independence-oriented behaviors desired:
   a. Length of stay should be limited.
   b. There should be few private rooms and clients should have only minimal say in roommate selection.
   c. Outside the house day-time activity should be required. Consistent school attendance or paid work should result in paying less rent.
   d. All therapy should take place outside the facility.
   e. Residents should be involved in the day-to-day running of the house as training and practice for their own living environment.
   f. Attendance at client-run in-house meetings focused on dividing up chores and planning educational, social, and recreational events should be required.
3. The program should be relatively lightly staffed so that staff are forced to focus on helping the client group develop into a reciprocal-help, peer-based support network. Foremost in each staff member's mind should be the question: "How can I foster groupness?" Ideally, instead of turning to staff for help, clients will use each other. Subsets of the networks that develop can be helped to move out together into the associated housing program.
4. The setting should be regarded by staff (and thence transmitted to clients) *as if* it were a college dormitory. The resident managers (not counselors or therapists) should be there after 4 p.m. and overnight and leave in the morning as clients are expected to do.

The rules should function to prevent settling in and the dependency it tends to foster. This is intended to help minimize problems with leaving. It is an intentional social environment focused on restricting in-house freedom for the sake of promoting out-of-house autonomy. It is meant to make the nontransitional housing program look very attractive by comparison. The program should provide individualized training to those who need it in cooking, cleaning, doing laundry, and personal care. This training can be continued as clients make the transition to new residences.

Halfway houses in the 15–25-bed range can also provide on site (if space is available) a variety of general health-oriented activities—aerobics, yoga, meditation, safe sex education, etc. The literature contains a number of specific models for these types of programs (Budson, 1978; Budson, Meehan & Barclay, 1974; Coulton, Fitch & Holland, 1985; Glasscote, Cumming, Rutman, Sussex & Glassman, 1971; Golomb & Kocsis, 1988; Jansen, 1970; Landy & Greenblatt, 1965; Lowenstein, 1981; Parks & Pilisuk, 1984; Pratt, Luszcz & Brown, 1980; Purnell, Sachson & Wallace, 1982; Rausch & Rausch, 1968; Rothwell & Doniger, 1966; Spivak, 1974; Task Force on Community Mental Health Program Components, 1975). Above we've attempted to provide flexible principles that can be adapted to fit local conditions.

A 100,000-person catchment area will need about 50 halfway house spaces. Their daily cost should be about $30 per client.

Supported Non-Transitional Housing

There are a number of contextual factors in the U.S. that make the inclusion of decent, affordable housing a critical element in an effective community mental health system. They are:

1. At the present time, because of its progressive nuclearization and frequent disorganization as a consequence of divorce, remarriage, and absent fathers, the American family is not a reliable source of housing for its adult children or the grandparental generation. In the U.S. fewer than half of community-based mental health clients live with their families. By way of contrast, about 80% of such clients in Italy live with their families.
2. Politicization of the homelessness problem has added fuel to the "irresponsible deinstitutionalization" fire surrounding mental health policies and programs. This attribution has further eroded public confidence in community mental health programs and resulted in a call for a return to institutional care. Mental health programs must become able to absorb into their programs those homeless individuals who are truly disturbed and disturbing and seek permanent housing. This is not only humane but good public relations for community mental health. It is worthwhile in this context to point out that Italy's closing of its large psychiatric institutions nearly 10 years ago has not resulted in a substantial increase in the homeless population in that country. This cross-cultural difference is probably due both to the strength of the Italian extended family and the system's focus on *preventing* institutionalization rather than on deinstitutionalization.
3. Users of the public system are almost by definition poor. SSI recipients receiving about $350 a month (the present Washington, DC

rate) cannot, by themselves, afford housing in most urban areas. By seeking housing in an ongoing way, a mental health program can find bargains, negotiate leases, guarantee payment and upkeep to landlords, and serve as housemate brokers for the clientele. Program staff can also develop the expertise necessary to access the local housing subsidy program on behalf of its users. There are, of course, other ways of assuring the availability of housing to mental health system users. In fact, setting aside a percentage of units in public housing programs is in many ways a more normalizing option and should be used if feasible. There are many ways to skin the housing cat; all should be tried.

We estimate that the average U.S. public psychiatry program will need about 200 supported independent living *spaces* (beds) for a 100,000-person catchment area. Clients should not have to pay more than about a third of their incomes for housing. Programs may add a modest consultation fee to the amount paid for rent (e.g., $20 per month) to help the program pay for itself. Doing so (assuming clients cover the rent one way or another) will result in a very economical housing program; the equivalent of six or seven full-time staff for 100 spaces will cost approximately $1500 per space per year after startup costs.

In keeping with the principle of normalization, we believe that community residences (group homes, apartments, Fairweather lodges) developed by mental health programs should be labeled *nontransitional.* This is designed to promote security, stability, predictability, and "ownership" in the lives of users. Persons seeking housing who are not mental health system clients are not ordinarily (assuming the terms of the lease are met) subject to arbitrary length-of-stay rules or required to leave places they've leased to make room for others who also need a place to live. So we believe it is best, *insofar as feasible,* for programs to make clear to clients that the program will turn over its lease to the clients in residence if they wish to remain there. It should also make clear that they are always free to leave to find a place of their own choosing. This policy most nearly approximates what ordinary citizens experience in the role of "tenant." This means that mental health programs will need to seek replacement housing units in an ongoing way. However, we also recognize that the transfer of a lease to a client group will probably not be the modal experience. It is just too difficult when groupings are formed at least in part based on program needs for a three-, four-, or five-person group to be compatible enough to remain together.

So *in practice* many units in housing programs will be transitional and thereby remain in the program. The important point is that if clients know there is no *programmatic* barrier to their making the unit into "home" it will tend to encourage them to take care of it as if it were theirs. Thus, an important normalizing expectation is facilitated by program policies. Creative program staff will attempt to be housing matchmakers; for example, when program users find friends in the group, staff should facilitate their efforts to move in together and eventually take over a lease.

Most community mental health experts agree that ghettoization of the mentally ill in community-based residences is just another form of segregation from so-called normal society. Hence, it is typically recommended that housing for clients be scattered in the community and only a minority of units in multi-unit apartment buildings be leased to them. We agree completely. However, is restricting the types of persons eligible for the housing to the mentally ill not also a form of segregation? We therefore recommend that community mental health housing programs attempt to make their units available to nonmental-health-program-related persons in need of housing. Although administratively cumbersome, having a mix of mental health clients and "normal" people in the housing has several things to recommend it:

1. It continues the process of desegregating the so-called mentally ill.
2. For a "normal" person it provides direct day-to-day experience with a person carrying a "mentally ill" label and vice versa. This is the most effective way to destigmatize mental health clients.
3. The "normals" provide role models clients can imitate and identify with and from whom they can learn various coping skills. The users provide the "normals" with access to life experiences they've likely never had.
4. It provides housing that some of the "normals" might not have been able to afford.

Where are such persons to be found? Students and persons on public housing waiting lists come immediately to mind. Actually, persons with limited incomes might be recruited via newspaper ads.

This mixing of populations may prove difficult to implement because of bureaucratic and administrative issues, but it does highlight a continuing problem with segregation of the mentally ill even in good community programs. It will need to be addressed before clients can be truly embedded in the community.

We like to apply our oft-used analogy of the smorgasbord to the types of living arrangements possible in housing programs. The nontransitional housing smorgasbord should vary widely along two continua: type of living arrangement (e.g., group home, apartment, Fairweather lodge) and amount of interpersonal *support* provided by the mental health system. We prefer the term "supported" independent housing to the more commonly used "supervised," as it has less of a child-like, dependency connotation. This is in keeping with the normalization principle; everyone needs support, whereas only specially designated groups, like children, need supervision. No living group should be larger than an extended family, i.e., six to eight persons. If possible, the group should decide whether or not it will be mixed or of one gender only.

Ideally, program support should be flexibly available to all living arrangements in the system, so that it is *brought to clients* when they need it—including those living at home with their families. This arrangement makes it possible for individual units to become independent of mental system support—a salutory development when it occurs. Having to move into a new living situation when more support is needed only adds the stress of moving to those already being experienced; hence, bringing support to the client to prevent this stress makes good clinical sense. Of course, if sufficient in-residence support can't be arranged or if the family or house or apartment mates are feeling no longer able to tolerate the crisis, then a move to a hospital alternative or some other intensively staffed transitional facility is warranted. One interesting way to structure a program is to have the staff consultants based in an apartment that can also be used as needed for temporary intensive respite care.

We recognize that a comprehensive housing program will need to include nontransitional settings that provide 24-hour on-site supervision and care-taking. Foster care, board and care, boarding houses, single room occupancy hotels, and nursing homes will be required to care for a subset of the population. Staff support should be available to clients and caregivers as needed. We have not highlighted these settings because we believe it's better to aim a bit high rather than too low with regard to the degree of independence clients are able to sustain in the community. However, clients should be free to trade some of their freedom and autonomy for reliable on-site caretaking if they so choose.

An array of support and intervention should be available in housing programs—family meetings, house meetings, single and multi-apartment group meetings. In-residence training sessions focused on cooking, cleaning, doing laundry, and personal appearance should be provided as needed, usually to clients new to the program. It must be remembered that what clients learned in other settings will not necessarily transfer to new ones. Staff should generally view themselves as consultants to *households* (i.e., the living group), not to individuals. This attitude will help foster collectivity in the group and self-help and independence on the part of the individuals. Staff should focus their efforts on helping clients learn to solve their own in-residence issues by modeling an approach that attempts to deal with problems at the level at which they occur. For example, a problem between two roommates should be dealt with by meeting with them (assuming they've already tried to solve it themselves), *excluding* others in the same apartment if they're not *directly* involved in the problem.

If housing program developers keep in mind the principles of normalization and preservation of power we've described, program policies should flow logically from them. Doing so will enable the program to avoid the oft-made mistake of creating mini total institutions in the community. For example, we are frequently asked what kind of rules should be made with regard to sex and alcohol in residences. Our response is that *insofar as feasible* the clients in each unit should make whatever rules are needed. We advise that program staff look at the issue from the perspective of their *own* group living experiences. Externally introduced (i.e., program) rules should be kept to the absolute minimum consistent with the program's functioning. Society's views on the particular issue should be used as guidelines in developing program rules. That is, society allows alcohol consumption, so a housing program should not have a *blanket* rule against it. However, individual units should be free to decide to not allow alcohol. Also, if a unit seems to be having a problem with alcohol that is unresolved after a series of staff consultations, a temporary, externally imposed (from staff) rule against it can be made. By way of contrast, we believe that housing programs affiliated with the mental health system should have an explicit rule against illegal drugs in their facilities.

Staff should remember that rules are easier to make than to do away with. Also, given the realities concerning the amount of staff time available to supported housing, staff's ability to enforce externally applied rules is limited. For example, in a discussion of a program's rule against having sex in its housing, a staff member wryly remarked, "Yes, they don't have sex in the house between 4 and 8 p.m. — when we're there!"

Many clients in these residences will have had long institutional experiences. A large part of their difficulties adjusting to the community will stem from their expectation that, if they agree to abide by a series of institutional rules governing their behavior, they will be totally taken care of. A good community program should not replicate this institutional experience in its housing. This is not to say that clients with long institutional experiences can be expected immediately to be individually self-governing and to participate appropriately in within-unit discussions. However, these should be overarching long-term goals to be pursued in collaborative relationships between staff and users. Deinstitutionalization should be an active process — not a state designated by the fact the clients are no longer in the hospital. Because the degree of institutionalism evident in clients will vary widely, it will take experience and good clinical acumen to be able to walk the ever shifting line between expecting too much and asking too little of individual clients.

Supported independent housing programs are fortunate that their rental units do not usually require a special permit or license that would bring their presence to the attention of the community. Halfway houses, because of the number of residents involved (e.g., 10–15), are not usually so fortunate. Community opposition to such facilities is a reality. What is needed is patience, strong backing from official agencies, good legal counsel, and good diplomacy with and responsible reassurance of the community by the program.

Discriminatory zoning regulations have been consistently struck down in the courts. Hence, the most frequent legal grounds used in support of community protest is not usually viable when court tested. In addition, evidence from the study of the implementation of the Willowbrook decision indicates that community fears were unfounded and quieted rapidly as group homes in the community were established and filled (Rothman, 1980). Hence, if programs can quietly and consistently maintain pressure they will eventually overcome opposition. Once in place they can actually begin to expect a rather neutral or even positive view of them by the community. This process is easier if the agency has a good reputation, if it does something that actually enhances property value (e.g., repair and renovation), and if staff are sensitive to the needs of the neighbors. Tincture of time seems once again to be a useful medicine, this time for dealing with community opposition to mental health clients living in its midst.

There are a number of mental health housing program models (Arce & Vergare, 1985b; Carling, 1984; Carpenter, 1978; Chien & Cole, 1973; Cournos, 1987; Fairweather et al., 1969; Goldmeir, Shore, & Mannino, 1977; Hodgman & Stein, 1966; Kresky, Maeda, & Rothwell, 1976; Mannino, Ott, & Shore, 1977; Meddars & Colman, 1985; Murphy, Engelsmann, & Tcheng-Laroche, 1976; Orndoff, 1975; Randolph, Lanx, & Carling, 1988; Segal, Baumohl, & Moyles, 1980; Sinnett & Sachson, 1970; Solomon & Davis, 1984; Weinman, Kleiner, Yu, & Tillson, 1974). Unfortunately (at least from our perspective), they are too often designated as "transitional" and "supervised." We believe that calling them *nontransitional* while expecting that most will in fact be used as transitional housing is preferable in terms of the expectations engendered. Readers interested in day-to-day implementation, administrative and program management issues can find that information in these publications.

In many locales bureaucratic regulations will make adherence to the principles outlined above difficult. However, they do set out relatively ideal program guidelines against which current program realities can be compared.

The Problem of Homelessness

It is a sign of the times that a book on community mental health has a section devoted to something that really is *not* a mental health problem. Mental health workers like ourselves are quite sensitive to the context within which we operate. Attributions of mental health as being responsible for the homelessness problem abound. The mental health field seems to be responding with a combination of guilt and compliance. Psychiatrists are being recruited to volunteer their time in shelters. Psychiatric residents are being trained in them. These dreadful, inhumane institutions have sprung up like topsy. Professionals of every stripe are in attendance in them. All of the activity and rhetoric about the problem seems, to us at least, mostly designed to avoid asking, much less answering, this question: *How can a seemingly civilized, highly affluent society like ours allow somewhere between two and four million of its members to be homeless? What are its root causes and how can we, as a society, address them?* Europeans find this situation inexplicable and unbelievable. Volumes (for example, Lamb, 1984) have been written about it, research on it is proceeding apace, but as a fundamental political and social issue it remains largely unaddressed. The scarcity of decent affordable housing has not yet been thrust into the political limelight as a major domestic issue.

Despite what we're being told, mental illness does not cause homelessness. That many homeless persons are "mentally ill" is not at all surprising. There is probably no more demoralizing experience than the double stress of being without work and having no place to live. A number of those who *do* work (at minimum wage) cannot afford housing in expensive urban areas like New York City, Boston, Washington, Los Angeles, etc. Actually, about 20% (estimates vary greatly) of shelter inhabitants have regular jobs. Most welfare recipients can't afford decent housing in those areas either. Mentally ill or not, these groups are all exposed to the same degrading and dehumanizing conditions in the new urban almshouses — the shelters.

There exists today a belief that most homeless persons are deinstitutionalized mental patients. Let us examine the evidence. Roughly 400,000 patients were deinstitutionalized between 1960 and 1980 (Goldman et al., 1983). About half went home to live with their families. So there is a maximum of 200,000 available to the homeless person pool. Actually, the maximum available is probably less than 100,000 because most persons deinstitutionalized in the 1960–70 decade were geriatric patients placed in nursing homes. Recent studies have found that between 10 and 20% of shelter inhabitants are deinstitutionalized persons (Struening, 1986; Susser & Struening, 1987). Estimates of the numbers of mentally ill in shelter populations vary widely, but 30–40% seems like a fair ballpark figure (Lamb, 1984). The estimates of the number of homeless in 1984 varied between two and four million (Lamb, 1984). Where did they all come from? Clearly, there is no simple answer.

Our analysis of the problem runs like this: Homelessness is basically an economic problem — not enough money to pay for housing. Which groups in our society have the least money? Welfare recipients, the working poor, and the unemployed (obviously overlapping to some extent). Which of these groups increased dramatically in size concomitant with the discovery of the homeless problem in the winter of 1981–82? Between 1980 and 83 unemployment rose from about 7.5% to 10.5%. This represents about three million persons.

In addition to these three million new poor being added to the potentially homeless pool, other factors were at work:

1. The rise in the cost of housing in the 1970–80 decade far outstripped wage and welfare payment increases for the working poor and welfare recipients.
2. The Reagan administration reduced support for development of low income housing and housing subsidy programs.
3. Because of both rapidly rising rents and urban gentrification (there was a 60% decline in the number of single room occupancy hotel rooms in New York City between 1973 and 1980), the cost of available housing moved out of reach for an increasingly large percentage of these groups. The economics of the social context forced them into homelessness.

Thus, when the cohort of new poor, i.e., three million new persons collecting unemployment (who became really poor when their unemployment ran out six months or a year later), was added to the preexisting pool, homelessness increased dramatically. It is not surprising that a substantial subset might have *become* mentally ill as a consequence of the confluence of two stressors—unemployment and homelessness.

Based on this analysis, the solution to the problem should be straight forward: Provide either enough money to these people to buy housing on the open market or develop a rent subsidy program in conjunction with buying and rehabilitating housing for which subsidies can be used. With each barrack space in shelters in New York City costing $20,000 and hotel space for families over $300,000 a year, such a program makes good economic—and humanitarian—sense.

Although federal legislation (the "McKinney" Act) has been passed to attempt to deal with the problem, there is no real sense of national urgency about building, rehabilitating, and subsidizing enough housing to assure all Americans access to decent, affordable, permanent housing. This bill has an unfortunate feature; it separates programs for mentally ill persons without housing from those for persons without mental illness. It identifies and segregates one subset of persons without housing. This not only serves to divert attention from the larger problem (so that it won't be seriously addressed), but also does a grave disservice to these persons.

Housing programs will not, of course, deal with the unfortunate sequelae of homelessness:

1. Demoralization for so long as to render persons so hopeless that they lose all motivation to work — especially at entry level jobs that won't enable them to leave the shelter system.
2. A new form of institutionalism — homeless shelter institutionalism (an interesting oxymoron), stemming from a situation not unlike the one in traditional total institutions, where one group with no other options (the homeless) is required to subjugate itself to another (the shelter providers) in order to obtain the basic necessities of life. Many of the "new" homeless have by now been on the streets for five or more years. Many have become dependent on the shelter system and reluctant to leave it (see Chapter 19).
3. Many of the homeless have serious medical and psychological complications as a result of poor nutrition, exposure, involvement in endemic shelter violence, rape, drug abuse, etc.

Unfortunately, because of a short-sighted social policy that is attempting to repair a deep rent in the fabric of society with a stitch here and there (i.e., shelters), we have likely created a new group of more or less permanently demoralized and disenfranchised Americans. The shelter system is developing into a permanent set of new institutions that will need to continue to recruit clients to maintain itself. An institution-clientele marriage has been cemented by the political system's failure to address the problem with a real long-range solution.

Good community mental health programs should have enough affordable housing and intervention available to take in a share of the homeless — those with the most serious psychological difficulties who are *willing* to come in from the cold. Getting the maximum number of homeless into housing and treatment programs will be a test of community program's ability to be flexible and innovative, especially around the use of incentives. That is, the problem now emerging with the homeless is that many of them — some seriously disturbed but many who are not — have embarked on *careers* as homeless persons. They are likely to be unwilling to participate in a process that will reintegrate them into society because they perceive the homeless subculture as more caretaking than the wider society. Innovative approaches to reacculturating these persons and families will need to be developed if this career path is to be interrupted. Developing incentives that will really get their attention is going to be a tall order.*

*Readers wishing additional information on programs for homeless mentally ill persons should contact CHAMP, c/o Macro Systems, Silver Spring, Maryland; also, Goldman & Morrissey, 1985; Levine, 1984; Levine, Lezak & Goldman, 1986.

DAY AND EVENING PROGRAMS

The literature indicates that only 20–25% of *all* persons discharged from psychiatric hospitals are competitively employed (Anthony & Dion, 1986). Hence, the majority of mental health clients lack the organizing, structuring, expectant daytime environment associated with working. They also lack the rewards for accomplishment that flow from successful work.

Community-based day and evening programs should be focused on providing intentional social environments that address the interpersonal and instrumental competence deficiencies of the clientele. They should provide concrete vocational and social success experiences in the context of a supportive group. Optimally, these success experiences will come from learning the skills they lack, or are deficient in, and from flexible programmatic attention to their individual needs. The expectation should be one of making the transition, with proper training and support, to a more normal way of life (including a job) in the community.

While functioning as nonresidential alternatives to hospitalization, day programs should also be able to provide for clients who are either unwilling or unable to be involved in an organized, structured group exercise. That is, acutely disorganized clients using the program as an alternative often find the environment of a large, well-organized psychosocial rehabilitation center or day hospital just too stimulating, confusing, and overwhelming. This is also true of a number of clients recently discharged from intensive residential care (e.g., alternative or hospital). They will drop out or appear only irregularly. For these clients a low intensity, low demand, simple, casual, "drop in" social environment should be provided. This requires a sound-dampened room with soft, comfortable furniture and the availability of optional low-key activities like art, cards, checkers, VCR movies, community outings, and the like. The social interaction should be mostly dyadic or triadic. Staff should be patient, non-intrusive and nondemanding. Small groups discussing sports, the soaps, the VCR movie, etc., can be organized. We highlight this need early in this chapter because in our experience day programs do not often attend to the special needs of this subset of clients. This results in unnecessary utilization of the system's most expensive component — intensive residential care.

Two different types of day programs have proliferated over the past three decades and dominate the field: day hospitals and psychosocial rehabilitation centers based on the Fountain House Model. Both have been shown to be effective in shortening inpatient stays and reducing relapse rates (to 10% a year as compared with an expected rate of 40% per year) among formerly hospitalized patients (Anthony, Buell, Sharratt, & Althoff, 1972; Beard, Malamud & Rossman, 1978; Bond, Witheridge, Setze, & Dincin, 1985; Dincin & Witheridge, 1982; Malamud, 1985). Day hospitals have, in addition, been shown to be an effective alternative to 24-hour inpatient care for selected clients (usually those with involved families) (Glasscote, Kraft, Glassman, & Jepson, 1969; Herz, Endicott, Spitzer, & Mesnikoff, 1971; Washburn, Vannicelli, Longabaugh, & Scheff, 1976; Wilder, Levin, & Zwerling, 1966; Zwerling & Wilder, 1964). Both seem to be ideal environments in which to implement the kinds of individual social skills and family intervention programs recently found to be effective in reducing relapse and enhancing community adjustment (Bellack, Turner, Hersen, & Luber, 1984; Falloon et al., 1982; Hogarty et al., 1986; Leff et al., 1982).

Although day hospitals and psychosocial rehabilitation centers grew out of different cultures (medical versus rehabilitation), the social environments they provide serve the generic milieu functions we describe in the chapter on residential alternatives for their clientele. Most day hospitals are what the name denotes: an eight-hour-a-day hospital staffed mostly by medical personnel. Their focus is on providing specific treatments (medications; individual, group, and family psychotherapy) in the context of a highly organized, structured program format. The usual medical hierarchy may be muted but M.D.'s are usually in charge. Psychosocial rehabilitation centers tend to have a practical down-to-earth focus, while day hospitals tend to focus on resolution of personal problems. Day hospitals tend to be smaller— 20–40 persons versus 75–150 in rehabilitation programs. Psychosocial rehabilitation centers frequently have their own housing programs; day hospitals usually do not. Day hospitals generally take patients with involved families; psychosocial programs take persons from any type of living arrangement.

Propelled by a key NIMH training grant, active involvement in the development of the NIMH Community Support Program (see Mosher, 1986, for a more complete explication), and the development of two centers focused on the rehabilitation of the mentally ill (at Boston University and Albert Einstein College of Medicine in the Bronx), psychosocial rehabilitation programs have proliferated rapidly. At the present time there are about 300 "clubhouses" attended by about 25,000 clients throughout the U.S. It is for this reason we are reprinting the classic article on the Fountain House model of psychosocial rehabilitation—a model that dominates the field at the moment. It, or a variant, should be included in the smorgasbord of community-based facilities.

Because of day hospitals' medical/psychiatric/individual psychopathology focus, we are ambivalent about recommending their inclusion in a community array. If reframed as day centers and focused on family, network and systems interventions, they can provide a useful additional element in a community array. This is especially true if they are not in, or on, the grounds of a hospital. Day hospitals have often been established because they are sufficiently medical in their orientation, programming, and staffing to qualify for third-party reimbursement. To the authors this seems to be an example of penny wise and pound foolish. They usually cost $100–150 per day as compared with $20–30 per client per day for psychosocial rehabilitation centers. Unfortunately, there are no random assignment studies comparing outcomes of clients seen in psychosocial rehabilitation centers with those in day hospitals. Until the issue can be resolved empirically we advise program planners to chose the less costly option. Having said this, we suspect that day hospitals *may* be best suited to the treatment of a subset of clients: middle- and upper-class depressed persons with well established occupations as housewives or white collar workers and only temporary loss of social competence. For this group, something called "hospital" may be more legitimate and acceptable than a rehabilitation center, a term they tend to associate with serious physical disabilities.

We estimate that a catchment area of 100,000 persons will need about 100 or so day program spaces. This is a crude estimate that will need to be modified in areas that have large numbers of veteran clients.

THE FOUNTAIN HOUSE MODEL*

The Fountain House model is a social invention in community rehabilitation of the severely disabled psychiatric patient. Fountain House itself is an intentional community designed to create a restorative environment within which individuals who have been socially and vocationally disabled by mental illness can be helped to achieve or regain the confidence and skills necessary to lead vocationally productive and socially satisfying lives.

Fountain House conveys four profoundly important messages to every individual who chooses to become involved in its program:

1. Fountain House is a club and, as in all clubs, it belongs to those who participate in it and who make it come alive. As with all clubs, participants in the programs at Fountain House are called, and are, members. The membership concept is considered a fundamental element of the Fountain House model. Membership, as opposed to patient status or client status, is regarded as a far more enabling designation, one that creates a sense of the participant's belonging, and especially of belonging to a vital and significant society to which one can make an important contribution and in which one can work together with fellow members in all of the activities that make up the clubhouse program.

*From Beard, J. H., Propst, R., & Malamud, T. J. (1982). The Fountain House Model of Psychiatric Rehabilitation. *Psychosocial Rehabilitation Journal, 5,* 1, 47–53. Reprinted with permission.

2. All members are made to feel, on a daily basis, that their presence is expected, that someone actually anticipates their coming to the program each morning and that their coming makes a difference to someone, indeed to everyone, in the program. At the door each morning every member is greeted by staff and members of the house, and in all ways each member is made to feel welcome in coming to the clubhouse.

3. All program elements are constructed in such a way as to ensure that each member feels wanted as a contributor to the program. Each program is intentionally set up so that it will not work without the cooperation of the members; indeed, the entire program would collapse if members did not contribute. Every function of the program is shared by members working side by side with staff; staff never ask members to carry out functions which they do not also perform themselves.

   To create a climate in which each participant feels wanted by the program is the third intentional element in the Fountain House model. It is to be seen in stark and radical contrast to the atmosphere created in more traditional day programs, especially the attitude, almost universal in such programs, that persons coming to participate are doing so not because they are wanted by the program but because they are in need of the services provided to them by the program.

4. Following from the conscious design of the program to make each member feel *wanted* as a contributor is the intention to make every member feel *needed* in the program. All clerical functions, all food purchases and food service, all tours, all maintenance, and every other ongoing function of the clubhouse program are carried out jointly by the staff and members working together. Fountain House thus meets the profoundly human desire to be needed, to be felt as an important member of a meaningful group, and at the same time conveys to each member the sense that each is concerned with all. Mutual support, mutually caring for the well-being, the success, and the celebration of every member is at the heart of the Fountain House concept and underlies everything that is done to ensure that every member feels needed in the program.

These four messages, then, of membership, of being expected, being wanted, and being needed constitute the heart and center of the Fountain House model.

Additionally the model is informed with four fundamental and closely related beliefs:

1. A belief in the potential productivity of the most severely disabled psychiatric client.
2. A belief that work, especially the opportunity to aspire to and achieve gainful employment, is a deeply generative and reintegrative force in the life of every human being; that work, therefore, must be a central ingredient of the Fountain House model; that work must underlie, pervade, and inform all of the activities that make up the lifeblood of the clubhouse.

   Thus, not only are all activities of the house carried out by members working alongside staff, but no opportunity is lost to convert every activity generated by the clubhouse into a potential productive contribution by members. Such involvement in the work of the clubhouse is a splendid preparation for and source of increased confidence in each member's ability to take gainful employment in the outside world.

   Further in support of this profoundly held belief, Fountain House guarantees to every member the opportunity to go to work in commerce and industry at regular wages in nonsubsidized jobs (see Transitional Employment Program, below). Indeed, Fountain House considers this guarantee part of the social contract that it makes with every member.
3. As a parallel concept to that of the importance of work and the opportunity to work is the belief that men and women require opportunities to be together socially. The clubhouse provides a place for social interchange, relaxation, and social support on evenings, weekends, and especially holidays, seven days a week, 365 days a year.
4. Finally, Fountain House believes that a program is incomplete if it offers a full set of vocational opportunities and a rich offering of social and recreational opportunities and yet neglects the circumstances in which its members live. It follows that the Fountain House model includes the development of an apartment program, which ensures that every member can live in adequate housing that is pleasant and affordable and that provides supportive companionship.

Program Components

The following program components of the Fountain House model will be seen to flow naturally and logically from the underlying concepts discussed above.

- the prevocational day program
- the transitional employment program (TEP)
- the evening and weekend program (seven days a week)
- the apartment program
- reach-out programs
- the thrift shop program
- clubhouse newspapers
- clubhouse name
- medication, psychiatric consultation, and health
- evaluation and clubhouse accountability

PREVOCATIONAL DAY PROGRAM

Fountain House believes that regardless of a member's apparent level of disability, each member has a significant contribution to make that is needed by the clubhouse setting and that will be valued and appreciated by others. Each has skills and talents that, when discovered and utilized, can make the experience of each day worthwhile. Fountain House believes that this process provides a new and nourishing foundation for the future.

The psychiatric patient returning to the community faces extraordinary difficulties in achieving vocational objectives. Employment interviewers in industry do not look favorably on previous psychiatric hospitalization. The psychiatric patient often lacks self-confidence in his or her ability to perform a job and typically does not have the job references essential in securing employment. The Fountain House prevocational day program provides many opportunities for members to regain vocational skills and capacities.

All of the day program activities are performed by members and staff working together. What everyone does is clearly necessary to the operation of the clubhouse. In working side by side with members the staff become aware of each member's vocational and social potential and the Fountain House member begins to discover personal abilities and talents that can lead to greater social effectiveness and more meaningful work.

In designing a program in which staff and members work together, Fountain House has brought about a major change in staff role from the role assigned in other, more traditional day programs. Role change necessitates attitude change on the part of the staff, specifically, that staff come to appreciate the members, to respect their contributions. In more traditional day programs the patients frequently respect and appreciate staff, but staff rarely have the experience necessary to appreciate and respect their patients.

Members find it helpful to work with staff and other members in the snack bar and kitchen/dining room areas, serving food to other members, helping to keep the area clean, maintaining equipment, and planning menus. Others find a meaningful experience in the clerical area, operating the busy switchboard, helping publish a daily newspaper or a monthly magazine, using typing skills as well as helping with essential clerical routines. There are also members who have talent in art and photography, and their skills can be further developed in the day program of Fountain House. Those who have special academic skills can utilize them in tutoring fellow members. Still others will find the thrift shop an environment where they can assist in sorting, pricing merchandise, and other warehouse activities, as well as acting as sales clerks and having opportunities to learn to use the cash register.

Where the educational background or interest of the members is appropriate, they can assist in research activities as well as educational programs, especially in the introduction of new members and visitors to Fountain House, in welcoming fellow members at the front door, in providing orientation for new members, and in conducting tours for the many visitors.

Members become involved in a profoundly important role, visiting other members who are at home or in the hospital, reaching out to those who have stopped coming to the clubhouse for whatever reason. Members also assist each other in working out their problems with welfare or social security regulations.

At Fountain House, as in other clubhouse settings, members view their daily participation in the prevocational day program as a "natural process" that is essential to the growth and well-being of all individuals. They are members of a club and voluntarily provide their help and assistance. They do not regard themselves as undergoing a formal rehabilitation process, in which something is being done to them. The goal is to establish a foundation of better work habits, enriched social skills, and a more helpful view of the future. Many discover that although they are viewed as disabled, there are many ways they can still be constructive, helpful, and needed.

In time, this newly discovered self-awareness can be translated into a more rewarding, nondisabling way of life, free of financial dependency and perpetual patienthood.

In brief, the prevocational day program provides a diversified range of clubhouse activities that clearly need to be performed and that, if reasonably well done over a period of time, will not only be personally rewarding to individual members but in a most fundamental sense will give them the self-confidence and awareness that they can successfully handle a job of their own or an entry-level job in the business community. These opportunities are guaranteed to all Fountain House members through the transitional employment program.

TRANSITIONAL EMPLOYMENT PROGRAM (TEP)

Successful participation in the prevocational day program encourages many members to look forward to independent employment in the community. However, because they have often experienced considerable vocational failure, they lack confidence and necessary job references and are typically unable to secure employment on their own. The Fountain House transitional employment program makes it possible for members to work at jobs that other members have held before them and that industry has made available specifically to Fountain House to facilitate the work adjustment of the vocationally disabled.

The major ingredients of the transitional employment program are as follows:

1. All job placements for the severely disabled mentally ill are located in normal places of business, ranging from large national corporations to small local firms employing only a few individuals.
2. All job placements are essentially entry-level employment, requiring minimal training or job skills.
3. The prevailing wage rate is paid by all employers for each job position, ranging from the minimum wage to considerably above minimum wage.
4. Almost all jobs are worked on a half-time basis so that one full-time job can serve two members. A few TEP placements, however, are available on a full-time basis.
5. Most job positions are performed individually by a member in the presence of other workers or employees. Some job responsibilities, however, are shared by a group of six, eight, or even ten individuals from a community-based rehabilitation facility. In that case members relate primarily to one another on the job.
6. All placements, both individual and group, are temporary or "transitional" in design, providing employment for as little as three months to as long as nine months or a year.
7. TEP provides a guaranteed opportunity for disabled members to maintain temporary, entry-level employment through a series of TEP placements or to use such employment as a link or step to eventual full-time, independent employment.
8. Job placements are maintained only if the individual member meets the work requirements of the employer. No adjustment or lowering of work standards is made by employers.
9. Job failures on a TEP placement are viewed as a legitimate and essential experience for most vocationally disabled members in their effort to eventually achieve a successful work adjustment.

Fountain House believes that the opportunity to fail on a job is a part of the total learning experience of working and that, although the sting cannot be totally eliminated from a member's experience of failure, it need not be the catastrophe it would be if it were perceived by the staff as a major defeat. In guaranteeing the member the right to fail, the transitional employment program at the same time guarantees the employer a worker. In setting up a TEP with employers Fountain House agrees that if a member does not come to work, another member or a staff person will be selected to do the job. No matter what an individual member's vicissitudes may be, employers can count on the job assigned to Fountain House being done every day.

10. In the work experiences of normal or nondisabled individuals, failure or withdrawal from entry-level employment often occurs, and TEP employers emphasize that job turnover rates are not typically greater for the vocationally disabled mentally ill on TEP placements than for the normal or nondisabled employee.

11. New TEP placements in the business community are always first performed by a staff worker for a few hours, longer if necessary, so that an accurate assessment can be made of the requirements that must be met if the job is to be handled successfully by individual members. Staff initiating new TEP placements are also able to evaluate the work environment and its compatibility with the needs of the vocationally disabled individual.

12. Through direct familiarity with the work environment, staff have immediate access to a work site whenever vocational difficulties occur that require prompt evaluation and assessment of a member's performance.

13. All TEP placements are allocated to Fountain House by the employer and the selection process to fill TEP placements rests with Fountain House and the individual members its serves.

14. No subsidy is provided to the employer with respect to wages paid by the employer to a member on a TEP placement.

15. The unique collaboration or rehabilitation partnership between the business community and Fountain House is not a charitable act on the part of the employer. It is an agreed-upon arrangement that is of mutual benefit to the employer and the member who is seeking a higher, more rewarding level of work adjustment through the vocational services of the TEP.

16. The TEP provides a unique opportunity to enrich and expand the evaluation process concerning vocational potential and work adjustment. Assessment is made through guaranteed positions in a

normal work environment, one that only the business community can provide, rather than through evaluations based solely on an individual's past work adjustment, performance in sheltered environments, or personal interviews and psychological assessment.

17. In the TEP it is not assumed that a member's prior history of vocational disability or handicap is necessarily indicative of his or her inability to successfully meet the minimal requirements of entry-level employment provided as a primary service within the supportive, comprehensive delivery system of a community-based clubhouse.

18. TEP placements remove or circumvent barriers that typically preclude or diminish the possibility that psychiatric patients will seek and secure entry-level employment:

    a. A history of psychiatric hospitalization does not prevent the member from having the opportunity to secure entry-level employment.

    b. No attention is given to the duration of a member's hospitalization, which may frequently be as long as 20 or 30 years or more.

    c. The number of psychiatric hospitalizations is irrelevant to a member's opportunity to assume a TEP placement.

    d. The absence of a work history, the presence of an extremely poor work adjustment, or lack of, or very poor, job references does not prevent or serve as a barrier to TEP work opportunities.

    e. An individual's inability to pass a job interview is not viewed as a relevant to working on a TEP placement.

    f. A TEP job placement is an opportunity guaranteed to all clubhouse members. It is not a requirement, therefore, for the disabled member to have sufficient motivation to seek employment independently. In the TEP it is believed that the ability of a member to perform a TEP placement productively is not necessarily correlated to the individual's motivation to seek employment independently.

The presence of guaranteed part-time, entry-level work opportunities within the rehabilitative environment emphasizes to the members that mental illness is not viewed as the sole or even primary explanation for vocational disability. It is, rather, a personal experience, one that typically prevented members from having normal opportunities to experience the real world of work and to develop capabilities to perform work productively and meet job requirements.

Transitional employment programs have been developed as a rehabilitative function of the normal work community. Although designed to meet the needs of the more severely disabled mentally ill, TEP placements have been integrated from the beginning with the work community rather than intentionally simulating the real world of work, yet clearly separate and apart, as in the case of the sheltered workshop.

THE EVENING AND WEEKEND PROGRAM

A primary difficulty for the more severely disabled psychiatric patient has been the inability to get along socially with others in the community. Discharged psychiatric patients typically find few opportunities for successful social interaction, remaining lonely and isolated in the community. This isolation is one of the crucial variables underlying the inability of many discharged patients to maintain their adjustment in the community and it often results in their return to the hospital.

The evening, weekend, and holiday social-recreational programs offered by Fountain House are designed to meet the members' needs for companionship and socialization. Fountain House members can experience being with each other, taking part in art programs, photography, chess and other table games, dramatics, chorus singing—indeed, in a rich and varied program. In addition members have the opportunity to be participants in outside volunteer-led activities such as bowling, movies, tours, theater, and sporting events.

It is important to note that the social-recreational programs of Fountain House are all conducted in the evening, on weekends, and on holidays, not during regular work hours as is often the case in other psychiatric day programs. They are specifically carried out during evening, weekend, and holiday periods because these are times when all other people are able to engage in social and recreational activities. Fountain House considers it counterproductive to the psychiatric patient's reintegration and success in the community to be engaged in recreational activities during what would otherwise be normal working hours.

The evening and weekend program enables members to maintain long-term contact with the clubhouse after they have become fully employed, which is of primary importance to their adjustment in the community. Such contact enables the member to continue to benefit from the supportive relationships developed at Fountain House, as well as from specific services such as the educational and employment programs. Members must know that there is assistance and encouragement available to them in their efforts to obtain a better job or to pursue their educational aspirations.

The evening program is also helpful to members when difficulties arise, such as when a job is lost or there is a recurrence of illness. Through the evening program, staff and members become aware of such problems and are able to assist the member who is in difficulty. This might involve helping someone to get to a clinic for a change in medication, or to become hospitalized, or to return to full-time participation in the Fountain House day program.

It has been found that the informality and openness of the evening and weekend program also eases reentry into the rehabilitation environment for a member who has, for one reason or another, stopped coming to the program for a time or who has been rehospitalized.

THE APARTMENT PROGRAM

Many psychiatric patients are without financial resources of their own when they are discharged to the community. Their sole support is often minimal income from public sources, which makes it extremely difficult to secure adequate housing. In the past the only alternative has been residence in a single room occupancy hotel, a woefully undesirable alternative. More recently, discharged patients have been placed in other kinds of facilities such as family care homes, community residences, and halfway houses.

In an effort to provide less institutional, more normalized housing alternatives, Fountain House some years ago began to lease modestly priced apartments and to make them available to two or three members living together. It was felt that not only could Fountain House provide much more attractive apartments, furnishing them with contributions to the thrift shop, but that members living together could provide support, comfort, and understanding for each other. All apartments have kitchen facilities so that members may cook their own meals. Members pay their fair share of the rent and utilities.

Although the leases are initially held by Fountain house itself, it is entirely possible for a member or members to take on the lease once they have become stable and employed in the community. Apartments are located in various neighborhoods of New York City and many of them are located just across the street or in the immediate neighborhood of the clubhouse.

The apartments serve other important purposes. Resident members often host a new member who is still hospitalized and who is interested in exploring the kinds of living arrangements Fountain House provides as well as the activities of the clubhouse itself. With assistance from staff and other members, apartment residents have the opportunity to learn or relearn needed living skills, including housekeeping, cooking, budgeting, and getting along with a roommate.

Unlike almost all other community residential programs for mentally ill patients, residence in a Fountain House apartment is not time-limited; indeed, Fountain House does not perceive that any of its programs should be conceived of or presented to members as time-limited. On the contrary,

Fountain House believes that members have the same right to seek independence at their own pace as do all persons growing up in a family and that if their growing is successful they have the same likelihood of achieving independence and separateness from the clubhouse family as does the growing person from his or her family. Just as in the family, where certainly no time limit is placed on membership, no time limit is placed on membership in any of the programs of Fountain House, including the apartment program.

Residence in a Fountain House apartment carries with it continuing active involvement in the clubhouse program as long as such participation facilitates the adjustment of the member. Fountain House does not provide apartments to individuals who are in need of housing but who are not at the same time seeking membership in the full Fountain House program.

REACH-OUT PROGRAMS

Often a member stops coming to Fountain House and it is not clear why he or she has done so. At other times a member requires rehospitalization. In both instances Fountain House feels that a reach-out effort from the clubhouse to the member is important, both to carry the message that the member is missed by fellow members and staff and to ascertain whether there is some way in which the clubhouse can help the member.

Both staff and members are involved in this critical reach-out effort. Increasingly it is felt at Fountain House that the reach-out function is peculiarly suited to members. It is often the members who first realize that a person has stopped coming; it is often other members who recognize that a person is becoming upset again and may need some counseling, some change of medication, or even a brief period of rehospitalization. It has also been learned that members take pride in and are effective in providing reach-out to fellow members.

The reach-out function is intended to convey important messages to members — not that they must come back to the clubhouse, but that they are cared about, that they are missed when they don't come, and that Fountain House will try to supply whatever assistance they may require.

THE THRIFT SHOP PROGRAM

Many years ago Fountain House began to receive a number of telephone calls and written inquiries from people interested in its programs, some of whom expressed their willingness to make donations of goods they thought might be of value to Fountain House. A number of these inquiries came from individuals who knew of the Fountain House apartment program and who had furniture that they no longer needed but that was still serviceable and that they hoped might help furnish an apartment for Fountain House members.

In response to these generous offers Fountain House established a thrift shop with several goals in mind. First, the shop makes possible the sale of donated goods at reasonable prices both to community residents and to members of Fountain House. The income from these sales converts donated goods into cash donations to the Fountain House program. Second, operation of the thrift shop provides opportunities for a variety of prevocational experiences for the members: warehousing, classifying, sorting and pricing merchandise, arranging merchandise attractively in the store, and meeting the public both as salespersons and as operators of the cash register. Volunteering in the thrift shop has been particularly appealing to, and effective for, older members.

Over the years, the thrift shop has grown both in the volume and in the variety of the items donated and subsequently offered for sale. Furniture, clothing, jewelry, and merchandise suitable for gifts are all available. The cash income derived from sales now makes a significant contribution to the total budget of Fountain House. The effort to attract donations from department stores and other retail outlets, factories, and individuals has led to a greater public awareness of the program and in some instances has led directly to active, invaluable involvement of individuals in Fountain House. For all of these reasons, the thrift shop has become a significant component of the Fountain House model.

CLUBHOUSE NEWSPAPERS

Some years ago it was felt that there should be a vehicle for alerting members of Fountain House to the activities available within it and to current news about fellow members and staff. A clubhouse newspaper was established that from the beginning was a cooperative effort of staff and members. The newspaper contributes to bringing the membership together, it provides a variety of work activities in the prevocational day program, and it also serves as a very powerful communicating tool that informs staff and members of other clubhouses about Fountain House activities.

Members have the freedom to say what they wish about the programs of Fountain House, about experiences in the house, about successes and failures, in articles that they are free to publish. This helps both the members who write articles and the members who read them to experience a deepening sense of participant contribution to and shared responsibility for the club that they and the staff bring to life and help to flourish.

CLUBHOUSE NAME

Fountain House believes that one of the very significant acts a clubhouse program can undertake is to establish its own name. In many instances — and there are many — when a clubhouse is a component of a larger mental health consortium, such as a community mental health center, it is critical that the clubhouse establish its own identity and a separate location in its own building. The name of the clubhouse thus comes to signify not only its identity but also its independence as a program. The name also can reflect the feeling the program is meant to convey. For example, The Green Door suggests a welcoming place; more traditional names of facilities are often not as suggestive.

MEDICATION, PSYCHIATRIC CONSULTATION, AND HEALTH

Fountain House plays an important role in helping members maintain themselves on prescribed medication and in ensuring that they get required psychiatric care. Most of the members view medication as both necessary and helpful in their adjustment and they are of significant assistance in reinforcing this attitude among other members. Staff and members become aware when other members seem to be suffering a relapse and often help the member in getting to the clinic or hospital for assistance. Part-time psychiatric consultation is also available at Fountain House in emergencies.

Members and staff also help other members utilize community health facilities. This is extremely important to members who do not have the financial and personal resources to secure such help independently. In this important sense, Fountain House plays a crucial family role in encouraging members to get the care they are entitled to and require.

EVALUATION AND CLUBHOUSE ACCOUNTABILITY

Fountain House believes it is imperative that a continuing effort be made to evaluate the effectiveness of its programs, a belief shared by responsible community-based day programs for chronically mentally ill patients living in the community. Characteristically, however, the justification for the necessity of evaluations has been the staff's need to know the effectiveness of programs. Fountain House believes that this central reason for evaluation must include the members' right and need to know what kinds of successes and failures each of the programs of Fountain House is contributing to in the lives of fellow members.

In taking this position Fountain House considers itself to be in harmony with the concept emerging in the medical community that the patient has the right to know his or her temperature, pulse, diagnosis, and, further, that the fact of knowing will in itself positively contribute to the patient's recovery of health. Fountain House, in this analogy as in the family, is persuaded that the members' involvement in all aspects of the life of the clubhouse will have the same salutary effect, that is, that it will contribute to assisting members in achieving a high degree of self-confidence and productivity.

Fountain House considers it both natural and desirable that members themselves become significantly involved in the procedures that are utilized to evaluate program effectiveness. The major evaluation effort currently undertaken by Fountain House and other clubhouse programs, the Categories of Community Adjustment Study, is therefore to a very large extent being carried on by members of Fountain House with the assistance and guidance of staff.

In our view Fountain House type rehabilitation programs are especially well suited to persons with substantial institutional experience who are in the process of leaving, or have recently left, hospitals. Their comprehensiveness and steady, gentle tug toward community reintegration is responsible deinstitutionalization at its best. The potential problems with such programs have to do with their size, which invites hierarchization, and their sometimes doctrinaire commitment to *the* Fountain House Model. Also, in day-to-day operation they seem to have bought into the genetic-biologic-chronic-disease model of disturbed and disturbing behavior that's so fashionable among today's biologic psychiatrists and Alliance for the Mentally Ill members. This ideology runs counter to the program's push for true community integration of clients and makes us somewhat uncomfortable.

VOCATIONAL REHABILITATION

Transitional employment has been a feature of Fountain House Model programs for many years. This form of in-vivo paid work training and adjustment is clearly more normalizing than more traditional approaches centered on sheltered workshops and training for placement. In the U.S. there are presently 148 TEP programs, with 850 employers, providing over 2000 jobs, yielding earnings of over nine million dollars. The Fountain House research team recently surveyed the results of TEP programs. They found:

1. Following the start of a TE placement, the percentage of those who are independently employed steadily increases from 11% at the end of one year to 40% working on independent jobs at the end of three and a half years. Studies elsewhere report only 10–20% employment rates for similar populations.
2. Those who spent the longest period of time in Fountain House *prior* to entering the study also had the highest rate of independent employment—66%.
3. Length of time spent by individuals on TE was significantly related to the securing of subsequent independent employment.
4. The entire study sample represents the "target population"—severely vocationally disabled chronic psychiatric patients—and, in addi-

tion, no significant differences in background descriptive characteristics were found for those independently employed versus those who were not.

5. Psychiatric rehospitalizations following TE placement were both few (from 2 to 4% at any time) and of short duration (an average stay of only 26 days). Both of these figures represent a substantial change in pattern in the prior histories of the study sample. (Fountain House, 1985)

More recently, the rehabilitation field has begun to focus on "supported employment." This movement began in the early 1980s among the advocates and providers for the mentally retarded. By the mid-80s, after strong multi-organization lobbying efforts, the U.S. Congress passed a series of amendments to the Rehabilitation Act of 1973 that mandated supported work programs for persons with serious mental health problems. Supported work is of interest because, while overlapping with transitional employment, it is different from it in several more normalizing respects (Anthony & Blanch, 1987):

1. The trainees are involved in identifying work slots for themselves that are commensurate with their interests, abilities, career aspirations, and likes and dislikes. Hence, *non-entry-level jobs are possible.*
2. The jobs are sought via the usual application process (TEP's are usually given to programs). The difference between job complexity and job *stress* is factored into the process.
3. The reality of stigma is acknowledged and attempts to get around it are made. That is, for example, program support to the employee may not be given on the job site, and the employer may not know his employee has a history of mental health involvement. Support and a low stress environment during non-work hours are seen as critical.
4. The jobs are permanent and have, hopefully, career ladders.

For readers wishing more information, the entire October 1987 issue of *Psychosocial Rehabilitation* is devoted to supported work.

A brief note about several other work-oriented community-based rehabilitation programs is warranted:

The Fairweather Lodge program (Fairweather et al., 1969) provides a model that combines housing and work. It is a program that has been replicated many times across the U.S. As always, there are local variations, but the basic notion is to form a living group of mental health clients that will also sell their services in the open marketplace (e.g., maintenance, gardening, etc.).

In Italy, the cooperative (see Chapter 13) is a common form of client-operated business. Prototypical cooperative activities are cleaning, gardening, and working in restaurants that feed both mental health clients and the public at large. Housing is not generally part of the arrangement.

The Boston Center for Psychiatric Rehabilitation, directed by William Anthony, Ph.D., has recently developed a new vocationally focused continuing education program that is both innovative and promising. Their brochure describes it as follows:

What is a Career Development Program?

A career development program is an innovative rehabilitation program that teaches young adults with psychiatric disabilities how to develop and implement a career plan. Students attend classes on a university campus to learn new skills that enable them to make decisions about choosing an occupation or additional education or training that leads to an occupation. With support from staff and other resources, students are helped to take the steps necessary to change their role from patient to student and worker.

Students learn how to develop a profile of themselves as workers and then to match these profiles to occupations. They develop short-term and long-term goals to begin the process of acquiring the occupations of their choice.

We have mentioned sheltered workshops only in passing for several reasons:

1. These traditional work programs are well-known and extensively used already (Bennett & Wing, 1963; Black, 1970; Wadsworth, Wells, & Scott, 1962; Wansbrough & Miles, 1968).
2. They are mostly nontransitional (in practice, if not theory), hence more dependency-producing and perpetuating than we like.
3. They violate our normalization principle. We would like their use to be kept to a minimum.

The Incentive Issue

Despite extensive experience with vocationally focused programs, there remains a major problem in the field around incentives. That is, at the present time most clients who successfully obtain work in entry-level jobs do not earn enough to make it worth their while to go off welfare. Mental-health-affiliated transitional employment programs basically train clients (when successful) to become members of the working poor. Whether this will also be true of supported work programs remains to be seen. The notion is only now really beginning to catch on. In many respects the working poor are the most disadvantaged group in American society; they usually can't afford decent housing, have no health insurance, and have jobs with no career ladders. The principal reward successful clients get is the satisfaction that comes from accomplishing the work task — but at the price of considerable security if they give up their welfare benefits.

Supported work and transitional employment programs are clearly preferable to sheltered workshops, "make work" in day programs, or long-term "employment" in clubhouse maintenance or volunteer work without prospects of eventually becoming paid. However, they have not yet solved the incentive conundrum described above. What appears to be needed now is a variety of experimental programs that focus on the issue of how to enable clients to get themselves out of the welfare-poverty-dependency cycle via truly rewarding work. Unfortunately, such programs have to operate within the United States' current welfare context. It is this context that makes it so difficult for clients to step out of the ranks of the poor and dependent. We wish we had a solution to offer to this very important problem but we do not. We hope that identifying and acknowledging it will begin a problem-solving process.

CHAPTER 10

Power to the People: Staffing

THE QUALITY OF PROGRAM STAFF, assuming a reasonable administration, is probably the single most important factor in creating a quality program. Staff qualities we will describe are, in our view, *generic* for clinicians working in community mental health programs. Hence, we believe a similar selection process can be used to hire staff for the mental health center team, adolescent and child and specialized addiction programs, and mental health affiliated housing.

We believe today's trend to train highly specialized "counselors" with limited range and flexibility of function is unwise. For example, persons trained in highly specialized alcoholism treatment programs who have only limited experience with other types of clients are likely to be very uncomfortable and unsure when attempting to deal with functionally psychotic persons. Staff who have learned to deal pretty much exclusively with mental health system "veterans" will likewise tend to feel at sea when the veteran has a simultaneous substance abuse problem; yet, at least among urban public sector long-term clients in the U.S., substance abuse is endemic—at least for the first few days of each month after an SSI check has been received.

In part because of a lack of breadth in training and experience among many front-line clinicians, the so-called "dually diagnosed" (mental illness and substance abuse) client may get short shrift in both systems. We believe there should be only *one system*, staffed mainly with broadly trained and experienced clinical generalists, to minimize the numbers of clients who are hard to serve because they don't "fit." This would represent a substantial improvement over the situation as it exists in most programs today. In our problem- and needs-oriented view, the same clinicians should be able to deal with substance abuse, depression or psychosis, especially since they not infrequently coexist or are serially present in the same client.

In our experience there is no necessary association between desirable attitudes and values and particular mental health relevant academic degrees. In fact, some of the characteristics of good staff (e.g., openmindedness, flexibility, and tolerance), are sometimes inversely related to the amount of formal training persons have received. This is particularly true of persons trained in institutions with a single dominant theoretical orientation. We recommend a staff selection process based more on competence than on degrees.

It is an unfortunate reality that pay is generally determined by training (i.e., type of degree) and experience using that degree. Time spent taking care of an ill relative or friend, being a volunteer community organizer, expanding one's personal strength and resources through reflective self-discipline (e.g., martial arts, psychotherapy) aren't usually rewarded with a higher salary. To develop an applicant pool that will contain properly degreed persons who also have such experiences, we advise that a wide advertising net be cast in terms of acceptable educational and experiential background. Selection can then take place from among a group of equally *formally* qualified candidates on the basis of the *informal* experiential and personality characteristics of known effective staff. A large net will also be more likely to produce an appropriate (i.e., to the particular locale) mix of socioeconomic strata of origin, race, ethnicity, and religion in the candidate pool.

We recommend that candidates be interviewed by as many persons as possible from the team they will join. In addition, the team manager (administrator), clinical supervisor, and the program's clinical director should see all viable candidates. Finally, if feasible, a representative of the consumer group associated with the center should be involved in the process. Final selection should be by consensus development among line team members and their immediate clinical supervisor. If the program director or consumer representative has a strong opinion that runs counter to the consensus selection, he must meet with this group to discuss his concerns; if his concerns are still unresolved after discussion, the team's selection should be hired. Note that this practice is in keeping with the principles of horizontal authority and responsibility, staff empowerment (Rose, 1985), and program unit independence we've already described.

We recommend that mental health center team staff also work on the associated 10-bed ward in a general hospital. This arrangement serves to ensure continuity of persons and proper service coordination for hospital-ized users. However, ward staff will need to be supplemented with additional staff, mostly nurses, to meet hospital staffing requirements, provide conti-nuity in the milieu, and allow mental health center staff to perform their ongoing outpatient duties. Residential alternatives to hospitalization and housing programs will need to have their own separate staffs with coordina-tion (a case management function) provided by the mental health center's staff teams. Members of mental health center in-house teams will need to be the most flexible and contextually thinking of all the staff. Their job de-scriptions include in-residence and walk-in emergency crisis assessment and intervention, case management, and in-office and in-home psychotherapies. They provide the critical element of continuity of persons for the clientele. In addition, some of the mental health center team staff should have exten-sive experience with individual, group, and family therapy so they can su-pervise these therapeutic activities with less experienced staff. These "renais-sance" staff will require a great deal of morale attention, through opportunities to interact with colleagues, live case supervision, seminars, problem-focused groups, formal educational opportunities, and the like.

Although most clinical supervisory personnel will have professional de-grees and extensive experience, we see no reason why experienced, equally competent, nondegreed persons should be excluded from these positions. Unfortunately, community mental health programs are usually embedded in city, county or state personnel systems that don't readily allow persons with competence and experience, but without an advanced mental health degree, to be eligible for supervisory positions (see, for example, the Morrisania experience, Chapter 19). The absence of a career advancement ladder can be very demoralizing for highly motivated, experienced, competent nonprofes-sionals. If career ladders can't be erected for them, we recommend the development of mental-health-center-supported work-study programs lead-ing to advanced degrees.

SELECTION

Based on the Soteria and Crossing Place experiences (Hirschfeld, Mat-thews, Mosher, & Menn, 1977; Mosher, Reifman, & Menn, 1973), the litera-ture on the characteristics of effective psychotherapists (Rogers, 1957; Van-denbos & Karon, 1971; Newton, 1973; Schaffer, 1982, 1983a, 1983b; Strupp, Hadley, & Gomes-Schwartz, 1977), and consulting experiences in a widely varied array of community programs, we have been able to distill a set of personality attributes and life experiences of potential staff that should allow employers to be discriminating in their hiring practices. These attributes and experiences outlined in Tables 10.1, 10.2, and 10.3, are, we

TABLE 10.1
Community Mental Health Staff Selection:
Desirable Personality Characteristics

1. Strong sense of self; comfort with uncertainty
2. Open minded, accepting, nonjudgmental
3. Patient and non-intrusive
4. Practical, problem-solving orientation
5. Flexible
6. Empathic
7. Optimistic and supportive
8. Gentle firmness
9. Humorous
10. Humble
11. Thinks contextually

TABLE 10.2
Staff Selection:
Relevant Experience

1. Dealt with real life problem
2. Lived with madpersons
3. Martial arts
4. Local community involvement
5. Training to look at and understand their reactions
   (e.g., psychotherapy, supervision)
6. Ex-user

TABLE 10.3
Staff Selection:
Deselection Characteristics

1. The rescue fantasy
2. Consistent distortion of information
3. Pessimistic outlook
4. Exploit clients for own needs
5. Overcontrolling and needing to *do* for others
6. Suspicious and blaming others

believe, relevant to the hiring process of all community mental health staff (including volunteers). They are guidelines, not recipes! They will need to be adapted to suit local hiring practices and work conditions.

We believe that self-selection, based on a complete and accurate job description, is probably the most important single factor in obtaining the right kind of staff for a particular program. We have found that most good staff bring the requisite values and attitudes with them. The program only provides a vehicle for their expression.

One reason we recommend that degree and relevant experience not be sole selection criteria for work in community mental health programs is the wish to avoid, as much as feasible, staff who have been taught tightly organized, overexplanatory theories of the etiology or treatment of disturbed and disturbing behavior. We believe it is easier to interact with individual mad persons from a phenomenologic stance (i.e., open, accepting, without preconceptions) if previous learning does not have to be unlearned. It is also easier to learn and practice a family, network, and open systems point of view without a previously learned individual defect theory.

Hence, when interviewing potential staff it is useful to ask about their ideas about the nature and treatment of madness. Most people have some theory of madness. However, in our experience, tentative, open-minded, non-exclusive theoretical preconceptions do not create difficulties. However, doctrinaire adherence to *a* theory—no matter what its content—may create subsequent interactional difficulties. Research on harmful psychotherapists supports this clinically derived notion of ours (Grunebaum, 1986).

The characteristics that tend to make for effective staff are listed in Table 10.1. These attributes are clearly easier to list than to accurately assess in a pre-employment interview. Careful attention to applicants' in-interview language and behavior will usually allow the interviewer to evaluate their degree of self-confidence (#1). Asking interviewees their opinion of a hypothetical case of a person with a strong belief in a nontraditional religion or living an unorthodox lifestyle will often elicit information as to how open-minded and accepting they are (#2). Patience (#3) can be looked at in terms of persons' life histories; did they stay with jobs or family obligations that required them to postpone satisfying their own needs in favor of those of others? In relating information in this area their capacity to be empathic (#6) will also be assessable, because fulfilling other persons' needs requires empathic identification.

Number four—practical, down-to-earth, problem-solving orientation—can be assessed by asking the questions: How do you see your role with the clients? What will your overall orientation towards them be? We like to hear some version of a practical, problem-solving approach. Responses such as, "Those folks have real problems—maybe I can help them deal with them," or, "Life seems to have dealt them a bad hand—maybe I can help them learn to play their cards better," are used as positive selection criteria. Responses indicating a psychotherapy view of their role with clients, e.g., "I'd like to help them understand how they got that way," help to deselect potential staff persons.

Presenting a decontextualized case history and asking the candidate to generate an approach or a solution to the problem will allow contextual thinking (#11) to be evaluated by means of the kinds of additional information sought (if any) before answering. Flexibility (#5) can be looked at in terms of how a candidate can change from one possible problem solution to another when the interviewer arbitrarily designates the chosen one as a nonsolution. Firmness (#8) can be evaluated from the response to a child-rearing problem or from historical material. Sense of humor (#9) can be assessed by means of jokes inserted into the interview after a relationship has been established.

Braggarts (#10) will go out of their way to impress potential employers with their wonderfulness. After a great deal of experience with charismatic therapists and the mischief they can create, we've come to believe that humor and humility are very important characteristics. Good staff don't generally take themselves too seriously.

The six relevant experience variables (Table 10.2) are much easier to assess than the ones that have to do with personality. All one needs to do is ask candidates about their lives with these areas in mind. In terms of having dealt with a significant life problem, it has been our experience that persons who've had a modal American middle-class, suburban, intact, no-problem family upbringing don't generally make good staff.

In our original group of Soteria staff we found a surprisingly large number who had been invulnerable children in "vulnerable," problem-laden families. That is, they were frequently the rather neutrally regarded (by the problem parent in particular) caretaker child in the family. For example, one staff member was his fatherless family's principal housekeeper (at age nine) while his mother was nonfunctional because of an 18-month-long episode of unlabeled and untreated psychosis. His older brother, who was much closer to, and involved with, the mother, grew up with serious psychological difficulties, while our staff member developed into a highly competent person without serious problems.

We now look for this type of overcoming of serious adversity in the backgrounds of potential staff members. While obviously it is not always present, when it is we are more confident in our selection. We believe that the test-measured personality trait of high ego strength (Hirschfeld et al., 1977) we found in Soteria staff is also related to the process of successfully coping with these difficult life experiences. These experiences also seem to contribute to the responsiveness, flexibility, and tolerance needed to work in these settings. Without such experiences we found that staff had substantial difficulties relating to newly diagnosed, unmedicated psychotic clients for prolonged periods. At Crossing Place, with its "veteran" clientele, on-the-job development of the ability to "hang in there" can take place more easily than was the case at Soteria, because the amount of externally manifest madness is diminished, primarily because of the use of neuroleptics.

The attributes and experiences we've set out here must be taken with a grain of salt in the hiring process. They're helpful, but in no way exact. It is especially important to remember the context of the assessment interview — this situation can bring out the worst in some persons. We tend to believe that people who show up with a good understanding of the job, who are motivated out of real interest in doing what it entails, who have had difficulties in their lives, and whom we like will probably make good staff. It's probably unrealistic to expect them to exhibit a number of the personality characteristics we'd like to see in a short interview. These are better looked at in vivo, that is, on the job, over time. In our lighter moments we like to say that sainthood, i.e., having all these wonderful characteristics, can only become apparent after seeing someone actually working miracles.

Deselection

In terms of characteristics to watch out for (Table 10.3): The rescue fantasy (#1) can be tapped by asking applicants why they want to do this kind of work. Knights ready to grab their lances and mount their chargers will usually make themselves known by detailing an experience(s) that makes it vitally important for them to provide a better life for the clientele. However, we continue to be impressed by how many job applicants are truly motivated by altruism — a real interest in helping others, but without rescue fantasies.

Distortion (#2) can be picked up by asking candidates to convey their understanding of the job description to the interviewer. The last three variables on the list can be assessed by asking potential employees to describe their most and least successful interpersonal experiences or interventions with users. The "yes but" person is readily identified as a pessimist (#3). Overconcern with "what if" and liability issues generally indicate a rigid, frightened, moralistic person who won't be a good staff member.

MORALE MAINTENANCE

Burnout is a dysfunctional psychological state that seems to be most common among persons working in job settings characterized by a great deal of close interpersonal interaction under conditions of chronic stress and tension (Maslach & Jackson, 1979). The literature contains descriptions of it among the following mental-health-related disciplines: rehabilitation workers (Emener, 1979), counselors (Watkins, 1983), mental health workers (Pines & Maslach, 1978), social workers (Borland, 1981), special therapeutic community workers (Freudenberger, 1980, 1986), and physicians (Battle, 1981). Clearly, the conditions under which it occurs are endemic to community mental health settings and systems.

In our experience, this state involves various depression-like symptoms: low energy, disinterest, touchiness, unhappiness, and physical illnesses. Staff views of clients are affected by it as well; they will discuss clients in terms of hopelessness, chronicity, noncompliance, etc. (see Table 10.4). In fact, the symptoms of burnout generally parallel, in a less severe way, those of the clientele; low energy, lack of motivation, poor self-esteem, and a level of hopelessness that results in demoralization are generally sine qua non's of being a patient in the public mental health system.

The conventional view is that burnout stems, for the most part, from working with this difficult population, from the sense of powerlessness, helplessness, and frustration experienced by staff in their day-to-day work. While this is clearly an important factor, our experience has taught us that a more complete explanatory view is that burnout is an interactional product of setting, staff person, and client. Conventional wisdom attributes it almost exclusively to the client. In contrast, we ascribe great causal significance for burnout to the way in which the setting structures the staff's day-to-day working relationship with it and the clients it serves. The major issue is whether or not staff perceive themselves as being empowered to make, and feel responsible for, on-the-spot clinical decisions (see Table 10.5). The degree to which this empowered state can be truly experientially validated (thus preventing burnout) is closely tied to the size of the setting, number of layers in the organization's hierarchy, and the organization of the work group. We believe that these variables operate to reduce or produce burnout at all

TABLE 10.4
Staff Burnout:
Description

1. No energy
2. No interest in clients
3. Clients frustrating, hopeless, chronic, unmotivated, untreatable, non compliant, acting out, etc.
4. High absenteeism
5. High turnover
The bottom line: Demoralization

TABLE 10.5
Staff Burnout:
Causes

---

1. Setting too hierarchical—staff not empowered
2. Too many externally introduced rules—no local authority and responsibility
3. Work group too large or noncohesive—no sense of "teamness"
4. Too many clients—not able to "understand," feels overwhelmed
5. Too little stimulation—routinization

The bottom line: Demoralization

---

salary levels. Adequate pay, while it may reduce the incidence of burnout to some extent, will not, in and of itself, eliminate it.

An example: For intensive residential treatment settings the two ends of the hierarchy/size continuum are the large state hospital and small community alternatives. Twenty-to-thirty-bed wards in general hospitals fall midway on the continuum. In the large hospital hierarchy the lowest level of personnel ("aides," "technicians") have the most direct contact with patients and the least power. Clinical decisions must be cleared by a series of more powerful persons—the nursing staff, the head nurse, the ward administrator, the multi-unit administrator, and (occasionally) the hospital superintendent. Hierarchies like these tend to engender paralysis in the lowest level staff; they fear making important on-the-spot decisions as they may misstep; they fear taking responsibility as they may subsequently be blamed for a mistake. They want a rule from on high telling them what to do. These externally introduced constraints on their decision-making abilities in clinical situations are analogous to those often experienced by their clients in the mental health system. A similar psychological state results: learned helplessness, dependency, demoralization, and lack of motivation to participate actively in the planning and treatment processes.

For mental health center generalists, embedded in a context with a large number of actors, how the work is organized becomes crucial to whether or not burnout will be a frequent or unusual event. Mental health centers that pay reasonably, operate with small collegial teams, have reasonable workloads, and provide non-monetary educational "perks" will have a lower incidence of burnout than ones that don't organize the work this way. No matter how cleverly organized, community mental health programs must keep a watchful eye out for the sometimes subtle, but always pernicious, presence of burnout. Understanding why it occurs will allow its ongoing prevention and active treatment.

Regarding treatment and prevention of burnout (see Table 10.6), what must always be remembered is that, if the needs of clients are to be met, the staff must feel they have an accessible reservoir of energy from which to draw. Hence, meeting staff needs is no less important than meeting those of the clients. In fact, to avoid staff's exploiting clients, acting out against them, or being unresponsive to their needs requires constant attention to staff's own reasonable demands in the setting. Supervisor-staff relational processes should parallel those of staff-client relationships.

The principles involved in the "treatment" of burnout flow logically from the major causative factors outlined in Table 10.5. They are straightforward but may be difficult to apply in larger organizational units dealing with very disturbed and disturbing clients. The required elements: small working group size; minimal hierarchy; staff empowerment; and staff feeling they are valued members of a team whose needs will be responded to by the bosses. These conditions are hard to attain in large hierarchical units. The importance of mutual support, consultative help, and a sense of trust and belonging that accrues from working in a small (six to ten person) collegial group should not be underestimated. Small is, once again, beautiful. The work

---

TABLE 10.6
Staff Burnout:
Prevention and Treatment

A. Principles
   1. Concrete accomplishments enhance morale.
   2. Staff must be empowered.
   3. Staff should feel membership in supportive team.
   4. Group experiences used to promote mutual trust and collectivity.
   5. Provide challenging new learning.

B. Specific techniques
   1. Group didactic teaching (e.g., incest, addiction, etc.).
   2. P.R.N. interpersonal problem resolution group.
   3. Regular problem case discussions with consultant.
   4. Staff teams learn and apply new techniques.
   5. Supervision (live, if possible).
   6. Parties.
   7. Coupling.

group is the staff's social network in that context; as such, it is as deserving of care and attention as the clients' network.

A touching example of what can happen when staff are empowered and able to make decisions based on current circumstances is worth recounting:

> A 30-year-old woman came to Crossing Place after having been picked up wandering in a daze around the bus station. She arrived still dazed, very tired, uncommunicative and quasi-catatonic. She was able to tell us she was from a midwestern city and give a name and address. Her family (mother and uncle), had no phone so staff contacted the nearest police station and asked them to have family call Crossing Place. The relatives were overjoyed when they called because they had thought our client was dead since her purse had been found in New York City some days before. The uncle came by bus the next day to fetch his niece; our client came out of her daze when she saw her uncle. Staff offered them a ride to the bus station. In a simple, extraordinarily human gesture, the staff member asked the uncle if he'd ever been to Washington before. He said no. The staff member then took uncle and client on a whirlwind tour of the monuments, White House, and Capital Hill before dropping them at the bus station.

This is an example of immediately therapeutic interactions that occur frequently in settings where staff are empowered. The staff member's kindness, humaness, and generosity were subsequently acknowledged and complimented by staff-peers, director, and consultants.

A psychological principle underlying many helpful interventions is that restoration or maintenance of self-esteem, self-confidence, and morale is dependent on visible and acknowledged accomplishments or successes. Without being empowered, neither staff nor clients will be very willing to try things that might result in noticeable accomplishments. Hence, staff burnout is prevented by their feeling empowered so that their actions can facilitate success experiences with a notably unsuccessful clientele. In turn, they must both acknowledge clients' accomplishments, however small, and be acknowledged by peers and supervisors for having facilitated clients' successes.

For example, a client tells a staff person that he doesn't feel able to negotiate the process of getting into an apartment program (often based on a previous failure in trying to do so). Based on their judgment of that person's clinical state and knowledge of the nature of the application process to the apartment program, staff decide that the client will probably be successful if accompanied. If the process *is* then successfully negotiated, everybody wins; both staff and client have accomplished something that is real and visible. The staff person delivers lots of positive strokes to the client (who is also stroked by client-peers and other staff), and the staff person's role in the success is acknowledged by the client, supervisor, and staff-peer group. Remoralization is the outcome for client and maintenance of morale is the outcome for staff and setting.

There are a number of specific techniques for burnout prevention that flow from the five principles elucidated above:

1. *Didactic training exercises* focused around specific topics or techniques, such as dealing with incest victims or violence, use of trance, etc. They can be led by outside "experts" brought in specifically for the occasion or by in-house specialists. This provides the staff as a group with an opportunity to gain new knowledge and perhaps practice a new technique via role-playing. They grow together.

2. *Regular staff-only meetings focused on problems that have arisen between staff members.* These meetings can be led by the clinical supervisor. However, if similar issues keep resurfacing over time, we've found it's generally helpful to invite an outside "neutral" facilitator in to lead them. These therapy-like meetings not only solve problems, but also enhance group cohesion.

   These meetings (training and staff group with an outside facilitator) should be scheduled in response to problems as they arise. It is part of the clinical supervisor's job to be sure these needs are responded to in a timely and appropriate fashion.

3. *User-oriented group consensus development meetings.* This activity is focused on perplexing and difficult clinical problems as related to individual and group relationship issues with clients and between staff. This meeting should be problem-focused, relationship-building, and supportive of both individual positions and differences among staff, while operating with the overall expectation that a consensus plan will eventually emerge. In our experience, this user-oriented meeting is best led by a consultant who knows the clients but doesn't run the program. It is focused on developing individualized approaches to each user's particular problems. These occasions would be called treatment planning meetings in most settings. Because of our emphasis on a collaborative planning and goal-setting process, we have tried, at times, to have clients attend these meetings. We've tried having one client at a time routinely present in these sessions, but this was experienced by many clients as an inquisition or at least as overwhelming (there are usually 12–15 persons in the room because of students, split positions, etc.). We've also tried having several clients in attendance; this was difficult logistically and proved rather inefficient. It was also impossible to discuss certain background facts about clients (incest, abuse, etc.) in front

of other clients because of issues of confidentiality. Our current practice is to ask individual clients to come to these meetings when there is a staff consensus and user agreement that it would be useful to hear their point of view firsthand.

4. and 5. *Team learning of new techniques* can occur didactically, by demonstration, by live supervision, or by case discussions. What is important is that staff continue to practice their new techniques within supportive peer groups. This will further mutual trust, collectivity, and validation of their acquisition of new techniques – a success, an accomplishment.

6. *Parties* are really just another way to ensure cohesion, trust, and mutual respect among staff. The basic paradigm is simple – parties away from the clinical setting. In the early phases of programs they are best organized by the power figures: the program director, supervisors, or specialist consultants. As a program becomes more settled and routinized, these events are best rotated among willing staff, whatever their programmatic role. We have found that two or three evening parties a year are important for maintenance of morale.

7. *Coupling.* Staff relationships outside the setting are another means by which staff treat or prevent burnout in themselves. These will generally evolve naturally out of the close working relationships established in family-like teams. They should be regarded by the program's leaders as interesting but basically none of their business. In our experience a number of such pairings have produced enduring relationships.

There are too many events over which individuals or groups have no control to ever guarantee minimal levels of burnout: Parents die, lovers leave, coworkers move on. However, careful attention to this burnout paradigm will at least allow the work setting to minimize its contribution to the demoralization that has come to be called "burnout."

CLINICAL SPECIALISTS

There are a number of persons with special technical knowledge and expertise who should be readily available as consultants to generic staff.

Concrete resources. At least one person should be specifically knowledgeable about what resources are available in the system, their criteria for eligibility, and how to facilitate client access to them. A non-inclusive list includes: jobs and job training; independent and supported housing; financial assistance (general relief, SSI, SSDI, housing subsidies, etc.); medical coverage and care.

Specialized therapeutic modalities. Consultation around these will require a psychiatrist and a Ph.D. clinical psychologist in most settings. A psychiatrist is unique in his psychopharmacologic and overall biopsychosocial integrative consultative expertise. Nurses can also provide this biopsychosocial integration, and hence are very valuable to programs, but they cannot prescribe and regulate medications.

A psychologist and in some instances a psychiatrist or other appropriately trained person can provide consultation/intervention around the use of trance and hypnosis, biofeedback, bioenergetics, acupuncture, meditation and relaxation, Gestalt practice, behavioral programming, social skills training, etc. Centers should attempt to have as many of these areas as possible covered by their own staff. It is also useful to have staff consultants in areas of family, individual, group, occupational, and art therapy. It is our view that these areas are best dealt with when these consultants are individuals drawn from the generic staff pool who have special training, expertise, and interest in teaching.

Variety of therapeutic approach is as important to us as the heterogeneity of programs we expose (our smorgasbord). Because of their focus on accomplishable tasks, occupational and art therapists are usually good staff for settings with acutely disorganized clients. As with other staff specialists, their roles should not be confined to the exercise of their unique skills.

In addition to providing consultation, teaching, and supervision around specific therapeutic techniques, Ph.D. psychologists give centers important research capabilities. This is particularly important because of our espousal of an outcome-based bonus system for clinicians. Its design requires considerable research expertise, sophistication, and experience. On-site psychologist(s) have the virtue of being part of the territory they will be researching — always an advantage for designing *relevant* research. They are more likely to be trusted to design evaluation research that taps variables clinicians define as appropriate to their approaches.

Good community mental health programs do not confine psychiatrists' or psychologists' roles to the areas of their *unique* competence. Doing so would artificially separate them from the team's overall functioning, provide them with decontextualized (hence limited) views of clients, and prevent their applying a variety of other skills they've acquired to a particular clinical situation. In sum, it would do the client and doctor a disservice. In the U.S. such selective use of highly degreed professionals is usually rationalized by the fact M.D.'s and Ph.D.'s are relatively expensive as compared with other disciplines. In Italy, with its doctor glut and flatter salary schedule, it is not a problem; in fact, M.D.'s usually outnumber social workers on the teams (see Chapter 16, Verona South).

For us, to be able to recruit and retain highly trained professionals, who have a great deal to contribute if their training has been community oriented, it is important to have them apply the entire spectrum of what they know to clinical situations. In fact, these highly paid persons should be constantly challenged to expand and refine the breadth and depth of their skills. Although specialists in some respects, they are very useful generalists in others. The context should define their roles in a way that they are team players rather than solo experts. As team players they will obtain the morale-enhancing benefits that flow from collegial participation in research, seminars, and didactic exercises.

The three American model programs included in this volume (Chapters 17, 18, 19) use their psychiatrists and Ph.D. psychologists in this way. Because their work is structured so that it provides them with the kinds of experiences described above, they are happy and stay despite pay that is lower than in private practice. Doctors, especially M.D.'s, have often been trained to believe that they are being poorly utilized if they are not "fully responsible for" or "in charge of" a patient's care. Experience in community mental health has shown that this is not only a false belief but one that gets in the way of being most effective in those contexts where authority and responsibility need to be widely shared. The consultative model we've described and recommended involves role reframing that should make the issue of professional territoriality moot for doctors. The staff teams in the Morrisania program are organized in this way; we detected little territorial concern and lots of job satisfaction.

In the system we propose there should be no financial reason not to hire as many doctoral-level persons as needed to maximize program effectiveness. Even without our proposed system of capitation-based national health insurance, the system's greatly reduced use of expensive hospital beds should free up adequate resources to hire "expensive" personnel. These savings are possible *now* within the public part of the American two-tier public/private mental health system. At the present time the average state spends 70% of its mental health budget on hospital care. As this percentage is reduced, a large number of dollars can be transferred to community programs. Proper planning on the state level will make *anticipated* savings from decreased bed utilization available to community programs on a 50 cents on the dollar basis a year or more *before* the savings actually occur. This will allow a transition period and provide money that community programs can use to start or expand the parts of their programs that will decrease hospital use (usually community residential alternatives). Reallocation of money from hospitals to community should be the highest priority. Experience has shown that it can be accomplished, despite institutional counter pressure, by a combination of strong leadership from the top and guaranteeing hospital workers continued employment, perhaps in a different setting.

ADMINISTRATORS

In our experience good clinicians find administration difficult and unrewarding. Hence, we believe that program administrators should be persons with relevant management training and experience. It is usually a mistake to use M.D.'s or Ph.D.'s in these roles. Their special expertise is more readily put to use if they do not have major administrative responsibilities. Their consultative roles are actually made more difficult if they are simultaneously "the boss."

There are, of course, clinicians who find administration challenging, interesting, and rewarding, and who have had sufficient experience with it to develop competence. These individuals (usually social workers in our experience) are extremely useful because they can manage programs in the context of their clinical knowledge.

Each program unit (e.g., adult services, alternatives to hospitalization, day programs; see Figure 8.2) should have one manager—an administrator—and one or more clinical supervisors. To ensure an ongoing mutual feedback and education process between clinicians and administrators, regular problem-focused meetings should be held involving all managers and program supervisors. In most cases one manager is sufficient for each service, whereas we estimate that one clinical supervisor will be needed for each extended family-size clinician group (six or eight or so). A relatively nonhierarchical organization of the mental health system preserves contact between individual program units and "the boss," while allowing each unit to operate relatively independently. Each unit has both responsibility for, and control over, its activities. Units that become larger than eight or ten clinical persons (as adult services would in this arrangement) should be subdivided. Again, small is not only beautiful, but functionally more effective as well.

The Italian Experience

CHAPTER 11

Mental Health Italian Style, Pre 1978

FROM THE 1800s TO 1961

IN THE 1960S, WHEN A MOVEMENT FOR deinstitutionalization first started in Italy, the mental health care system was characterized by a massive institutionalization of mental patients, generally involuntarily committed, in large state hospitals. Such a condition had its roots in the 1800s, when mental hospitals were established and increased in number and size. The first modern Italian mental hospital, the S. Bonifacio Hospital, was built in Florence in 1788. It was directed by Vincenzo Chiarugi (1759–1820), who supervised the preparation of hospital regulations (1789) according to his enlightened and philanthropic ideas, thus paralleling the freeing of mental patients from the chains by Philippe Pinel (1793) and William Tuke (1796), in France and England, respectively.

Between the end of the 18th and the beginning of the 19th centuries, other Italian states opened institutions for the insane. However, in comparison to other European, more industrialized countries, like England, France and Germany, in Italy the admission of deviants to institutions occurred on a much smaller scale, probably because of a more tolerant, somewhat archaic society, based on agriculture and handicraft. The process was also moderated by the influence of the philanthropic attitudes towards the poor and the marginal propagated by the Catholic Church. The "great hospitalization" occurred later, in the last decades of the 19th century and the beginning of the 20th. Between 1875 and 1914 the number of institutions increased from 43 to 152, and the number of inpatients increased from about 13,000 to about 54,000 (Direzione Generale della Statistica, 1888, quoted by Canosa, 1979). Since the Italian population increased from about 27 to about 35 million in the same period, there was a threefold net increase of the rate of hospitalization, from 0.5 per 1,000 population, to 1.5.

The phenomenon has been correlated to factors like an increase in social awareness and concern for the mentally ill, the need to assure a quality care and the like, but it seems more a consequence of the great social changes of society, especially the deteriorating conditions of lower classes. Galzigna and Terzian (1980) show that institutions and patients increased in number only in the northern, more industrialized regions, while they did not change much in the south during the century.

After its consolidation as a nation (1860), Italy confronted social problems correlated to industrialization that other, more advanced European nations like England, Germany, and France, had experienced decades before. The flow of large masses of people to the cities could not be absorbed by a still primitive industrial system and resulted in a growing number of underemployed and unemployed. As a consequence there was an increase of those who became homeless, tramps, thieves *by necessity*. These uprooted and vagrant people, often living on more or less illicit activities, posed serious problems of public order; many were eventually incarcerated in institutions suitable to contain and manage them in a disciplined way (Galzigna & Terzian, 1980). (See the section on homelessness in Chapter 9.)

The correlation with specific poverty markers like the composition of diet (Canosa, 1979) has also been investigated. There was an impressive over-representation of patients affected by pellagra in mental hospitals. In fact, the poor would live on a low cost diet, scarce in daily allowances of vitamins — essentially "polenta" (a pudding of maize) and wine — hence, pellagra and alcoholism, two conditions characterized by dementing symptoms that justified admission to the asylum, were common. Percentages of patients with pellagra as high as 8.8% nationwide were reported around the turn of the century (Canosa, 1979). Galzigna and Terzian show also an impressive coincidence of geographical distribution among alcoholism, pellagra, and clustering of mental hospitals in the North (Figures 11.1, 11.2, and 11.3).

THE STRIVING FOR A PSYCHIATRIC LEGISLATION

In the 19th century the history of Italian psychiatry was closely intertwined with that of the process by which Italy became a nation. It has been pointed out (Giacanelli, 1975) that it was only after the Italian nation was established that Italian psychiatry could strive for recognition. The process

FIGURE 11.1
Italy: Mental Hospitals (1886)

took about five decades and can be considered accomplished with the passage of the 1904 law "Provisions on Public and Private Mental Hospitals," which actually ratified Italian psychiatry as a defined scientific discipline and as a function of the state. This law (No. 36), proposed by the prime minister Giolitti, consisted of 11 articles (see appendix C); main provisions had to do with the mental hospital, of course.

Article 1 opened: "People affected by mental illness *have to* be guarded and treated in mental hospitals when they are dangerous to themselves or

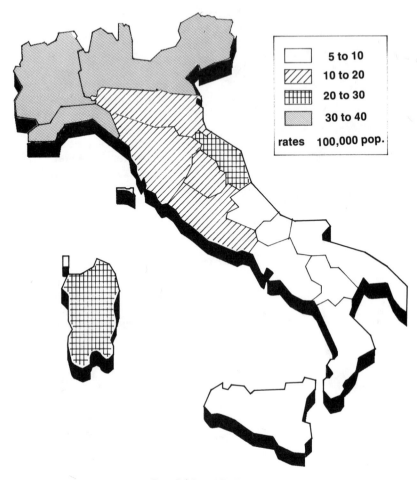

From Galzigna & Terzian, 1980.

FIGURE 11.2
Italy: Mortality for Alcoholism (1887–1898)

others or of public scandal and are not, and cannot, be guarded and treated elsewhere." Initial admission, for up to one month of evaluation, was issued by the police magistrate, or in the case of an emergency by the police, after a medical certificate. Admission was entered on the person's criminal record. At the end of the evaluation, the patient was either discharged, or admitted permanently by court order. This implied the loss of his civil rights. In case of recovery, discharge was ordered by the court after the proposal of the superintendent of the hospital.

The law addressed two somehow opposite needs: the good of the patient and that of society, hence, the recurrent swing between provisions dealing with patients' health and civil rights, and those dealing with the protection of society from the mentally ill. Thus, it was not just a public order law, as it dealt with treatment, care etc.; but it was not just a health law either, as it referred to dimensions of public concern, like dangerousness, as criteria for

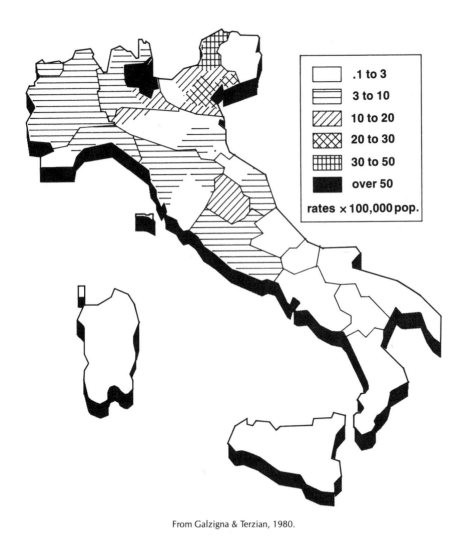

.1 to 3
3 to 10
10 to 20
20 to 30
30 to 50
over 50

rates × 100,000 pop.

From Galzigna & Terzian, 1980.

FIGURE 11.3
Italy: Epidemiology of Pellagra (1899)

admission to the mental hospital. Interestingly, the task of supervising the mental hospitals was given to the governmental department in charge of public order and the police. There was a serious shortcoming in the law, which was criticized right from the beginning: dangerousness was a *necessary* requisite for admission! Either quiet patients were not admitted or their degree of dangerousness was exaggerated in the doctors certificate (which was almost the rule, in practice). Leonardo Bianchi, a leading Italian alienist and a congressman, chairman of the commission for law 36, wrote a few years later:

> The 1904 law orders admission only when the patient is dangerous to himself and others. This criterion is detrimental and cruel. It is detrimental because mental patients are sick people and have to be treated *as any other patients* . . . A developed country must not exclude from admission to the hospital those mental patients who are not dangerous. (Bianchi, 1925, quoted by Canosa, 1979)

Forensic hospitals were established in 1889 as a provision of the new penal code, thus completing the organization of psychiatric residential facilities. The regulations governing these facilities are the same today as when they were established.

Following enactment of the 1904 law, the number of inmates in mental hospitals continued to increase. The need for revision of the law became apparent after World War II. During the 1946 and 1948 conventions of the Italian Psychiatric Association, the need for an essentially medical, non-judiciary law was expressed and it was asked that psychiatric hospitals be "put on the same level with all other hospitals with respect to health service organization" (Proceedings of the 24th Congress of the Italian Psychiatric Association, 1949, quoted by Maj, 1985).

In the following years several propositions were presented before the parliament, but it was only in 1968, under the pressure of an already strong movement for psychiatric renewal, that amendments were issued as Law No. 431. This introduced several important innovations. First of all, voluntary admissions were finally allowed. Also the provision that admission to mental hospital be recorded on criminal record was revoked. The size of hospitals, and of single wards and staff-to-patients ratios were also set. Extramural facilities were established for aftercare and prevention; each service was connected with the hospital ward referring to the same catchment area in order to assure continuity of care, prevention, and rehabilitation. The system was designed after the French model of the Psychiatrie de Secteur. All the sections on commitment in the 1904 law remained unchanged.

Unfortunately, the overall reform was never fully implemented, and law 431, although inspired by innovative ideas, did not bring forth a real change because of the limits imposed by the 1904 law, still in existence. However, the more liberal legislation of 1968 made it possible for dedicated workers to start working in the community. This gave momentum to some pilot initiatives in a number of cities: Arezzo, Ferrara, Gorizia, Parma, Perugia, Reggio Emilia, Trieste, etc.

THE ROLE OF THE MENTAL HOSPITAL

From the late 19th century until most recent years, it was clear that psychiatry practically *consisted of* the mental hospital, so that Basaglia (1968) could righteously affirm that the "affair" of psychiatry was the "affair" of the *manicomio*. And how could it be otherwise? The mental hospital perfectly met the societal needs. The progress of a positivistic science demanded order and rationality, while the industrialized society required that the marginal, those who were unable to find a social role in a fast changing environment, be contained in separate spaces.

By the means of incarceration in the asylum, psychiatry provided a well-refined, scientifically sound, and therefore acceptable, means of social control. Humanitarian concern for the prevention of exploitation and violence against deviants had been instrumental in first developing asylums. The fact that hospitalization might in fact allow more abuses than it prevents, in the form of institutional violence, has always been considered of secondary importance, and an exceptional, avoidable occurrence — a "scandal." As to the psychiatrists, they were well paid for their services: They were given a lot of power; it was practically absolute in the case of the superintendent of the mental hospital. The fact that doctors had so much power made it more difficult to begin deinstitutionalization, with its concomitant erosion of their power. For all these reasons, the late 19th and first half of the 20th century witnessed an enormous expansion of mental hospital populations in Italy.

DISSENT, 1961–78

In 1961 a group of radical psychiatrists led by the late Dr. Franco Basaglia took over the state hospital of Gorizia, a small city in northeastern Italy. They were deeply concerned about the terrible conditions of the inmates of the manicomio, 600 hundred people, mostly long-stay, chronic patients, in old, crowded buildings.

Basaglia had visited eminent English psychiatrist Maxwell-Jones and been impressed by his ideas and clinical achievements. He and his coworkers were imbued with the ideas of existential philosophy and shared a phenomenological approach. They were convinced that:

> . . . the effect of institutionalization has covered up the primitive illness, in
> such a way as to make it practically impossible to decide how much of the
> present condition [of patients] depends from the former or the latter . . . the
> mentally ill is "ill" mostly because he is a "marginal," deserted by everybody
> . . . we reject that the dehumanization is the natural outcome of the illness,
> and attribute it to the violence of the asylum . . . (Basaglia, 1968, p. 33)

At Gorizia they started to reorganize the hospital according to the principles of therapeutic community. Soon, however, as a consequence of interrupting the rigid patterns of the institutional organization and getting a new
perspective, a number of pseudoscientific stereotypes of institutional psychiatry became apparent. It became clear that it was neither a specific
technique nor a single apparatus that was antitherapeutic and destructive;
rather, the whole organization of the hospital, by aiming for system efficiency instead of caring for patients as individuals, was ultimately responsible
for inmates becoming victims of institutional deterioration. From then on
the therapeutic community was considered only as a temporary stage and
action was directed towards "dismantling the mental hospital from within."

Basaglia's approach was clearly sociological in orientation, nonmedical,
and to some extent antipsychiatric. However, it differed substantially from
English antipsychiatry and the American radical movement in that it was
less radical in principle and more pragmatic and action-oriented. Basaglia
and associates were especially critical of the American radical movement,
whose extreme libertarianism, in their eyes, could actually result in abandoning patients, especially in the case of the nonconsenting ones.

Basaglia did not question the existence of mental illness. He often used
the term "bracketing," i.e., the suspension of judgments, applied to mental
illness as disease (Scheper-Hughes & Lovell, 1987). The problem, he said, is
not about the illness per se (its nature, causes, prognosis) but about the
consequences of the illness. The consequences are very different according
to the *kind of relationship* that exists between patient and treater, which in
turn largely depends upon the social and economic status of the patient. He
contended that if the patient is empowered because of his socioeconomic
status, he has a "reciprocal" relationship with the treater, maintains his role
and has control over therapeutic actions. In the case of the institutional
relationship instead, he has no right:

> . . . the patient, for the very fact of being admitted to an asylum, becomes,
> necessarily, a citizen without rights, entrusted to the power of doctors and
> nurses, who may do anything they wish with him, without any possibility of
> appeal . . . "
>
> A rich schizophrenic, admitted to a private hospital, will have a different
> prognosis from that of a poor schizophrenic, committed to the asylum . . . A
> private admission does not always interrupt the existential continuum of the

patient, neither reduces nor abolishes, irreversibly, his social role . . . while those people who have no other alternative to the state hospital are exposed to the decontextualizing, destructive, institutional power of the asylum. . . . (Basaglia, 1968, pp. 122–123)

Thus the illness, as a clinical entity, plays just a secondary role; in fact, the same illness may result in very different outcomes depending on the degree to which the person's social role is preserved.

According to Basaglia, treatment is possible only if mental patients are free and have a relationship with clinicians characterized by reciprocity and empowerment. Within the institution, treatment is just another form of violence in that it aims at helping the patients adjust to the condition of being discriminated against.

What, then, can psychiatrists do? They can refuse to submit to, and carry out the institutional power mandate. Hence, they should "deny" or "negate" the institution. In this reframing of the role of the psychiatrist and of mental health workers in general, Basaglia and followers were influenced by the theories of Antonio Gramsci (1891–1937), a leading Italian politician and philosopher, who was incarcerated by the fascists for his ideas and political activities. Gramsci had stressed the importance of cultural components in the struggle between conservative and reforming forces and assigned a key role to the intellectuals in this respect.

> Intellectuals are the "clerks" of the dominant group for the fulfillment of the subordinate functions of social hegemony and of political government . . . [they have the task of assuring] the social consensus of large masses of population to the trend given by the basic dominant group to social life . . . [and run] the apparatus of state coercion "legally" assuring the discipline of non 'consenting' groups. . . . (Gramsci 1955, quoted in Basaglia & Ongaro Basaglia, 1975, p. 3)

Expanding these concepts, Basaglia suggested that psychiatrists, being aware of their being the "clerks and the government officials" of the dominating group in their own field of activity, should reject their role not by simply dropping it and preaching absolute libertarianism, but by creating " . . . the conditions enabling the recognition of patients' needs and their fulfillment . . . " (Basaglia and Ongaro Basaglia, 1975, p. 7).

These ideas are synthesized in the Basaglian concept of "denial": The denied institutional mandate is replaced by attending to the real needs of individual patients. But the denial has to go beyond one's own professional activity and involve the institutional apparatus as a whole: "A system is negated when it is turned upside down, and when its specific field of activity is called into question and thereby thrown into crisis" (Scheper-Hughes &

Lovell, 1987). When somebody commented that they were doing anti-psychiatry, Basaglia objected: "No, we are doing non-psychiatry" (Basaglia, 1968, p. 269).

The actual work within the hospital consisted in gradually removing all institutional barriers and restrictive practices. The wards were opened one after the other, allowing patients to move freely inside the hospital and even outside, in the city. Practices considered violent, like electroconvulsive treatment, isolation, and restraints were banned. In the case of an agitated person, members of the staff would remain with him as long as necessary; he would not be restrained.

Modalities to retrain the personnel to accommodate such dramatic changes in their activities were inspired by the same principles discussed above. Training was not separated from doing and took place in team assemblies where everybody was listened to and criticism from anyone was welcomed. Instead of being either disregarded or repressed, disagreement between classes of workers, and between workers and patients, was welcomed as an expression of the underlying institutional contradictions that had to be negotiated. Trade-union claims of mental health workers were dealt with in a similar way.

Partial forms of patient government started within the first two years. A relatively small group of patients, the most active and motivated, formed a club and organized leisure activities. In 1964 a therapeutic community involving all the patients of a ward started, followed by other wards in succession. A bar completely run by the patients was also opened in the same period.

Meetings and assemblies were held in a great number. It is reported that in 1967 there were about 50 of them per week in the whole hospital. Every day started with a brief staff meeting, followed by a general assembly of about an hour and an evaluation meeting (staff plus assembly leaders) to review the contents of the assembly. In the afternoon single-ward assemblies (daily, biweekly, or weekly, according to the ward) were held, as well as ad hoc committees and professional meetings. Everybody was invited to attend and express his own ideas. Especially "hot" institutional topics were welcomed and discussed animatedly. The classic therapeutic community was criticized because, while being more "human," it still left the structure of the institution unaffected. This would be clear in meetings, where patient government could take only minor decision, not those regarding institutional cornerstones like hierarchy, general policies etc. (Schittar, 1968). This was in accord with the theoretical assumption that patients had to become aware of the violence they had suffered, to discover a feeling of aggressive opposition, in order to find the strength and motivation to react.

Around 1970, the members of the original Gorizia group moved on to different cities (Arezzo, Ferrara, Parma and Reggio Emilia) where they showed that the model could be replicated in different geographic and sociocultural contexts. Basaglia moved to Trieste in 1971, where during the next six years he was able to phase out the state hospital and replace it with a comprehensive network of community services. Trieste became the prototype of the new Italian psychiatry, served as a model program for the reform, and was studied and publicized extensively (Bennett 1985; Jones & Poletti, 1985; Mosher, 1982).

In addition to deinstitutionalization other happenings in Trieste are notable, including:

"Marco Cavallo" (Mark the horse). In March 1973 the members of the hospital—patients and workers—went on a parade through the streets of the city towing a big, papier-mâché horse, painted bright blue. It was to symbolize patients returning to the city as the Greeks did in Troy. The event had a great emotional impact on the city population and on the people of the hospital and marked a milestone in the process of deinstitutionalization.

The guests. Given the great difficulty of finding alternative living arrangements for patients ready to be discharged, a new status was invented. They were formally discharged but remained on the hospital grounds, board and care was provided by the administration. They were housed in the buildings that the deinstitutionalization had emptied. They were considered recovered and could come and go to their will; staff supervision was minimal. However, community residential alternatives were also developed at the same time, as well as sheltered apartments.

Work cooperative. Since ex-mental patients had great difficulty in finding a regular job on the open market in a country with a high unemployment rate, a work cooperative was established. It was originally developed as a reaction to work therapy, considered mystifying and exploitative. The patients would be given rights similar to those of regular workers and the status of members of a corporation. Initially the cooperative was in charge of cleaning hospital buildings. Later on the administration offered contracts to clean other public buildings. Eventually several cooperatives developed, competitive as any private corporation. Work cooperatives of ex-mental patients are presently very successful in Italy and probably the most important single source of job positions for these people.

The pilot experiences described and others that developed throughout Italy both established a broad base of mental health workers committed to and experienced in deinstitutionalization and attracted the attention of the public. In fact, these activities were accompanied by the dedicated work of publicizing the conditions of patients in state hospitals and enlisting individuals and organizations willing to cooperate. In those years of student and worker upheaval, the cause of the mental patients became part of the demands for social change. Professional workers were supported by a vast number of volunteers, especially students, who spent time working in the institutions and had an important political part in movement for the renewal of psychiatry.

In 1973 Psichiatria Democratica (The Society for Democratic Psychiatry) was established, an organization constituted by the fathers and the followers of the movement. The founding manifesto clearly summarizes the principles of the movement and states what the mental health worker has to do:

1. Identify and fight one's own power role in relation to the user (term for patient).
2. Identify, in the individual, unmet social needs that confinement wipes out by concealing them under the diagnosis of illness.
3. Identify therapeutic interventions that are implicit in one's specific role performance, after having freed oneself from the instrumentalization that social system exerts by delegating control and power.
4. Identify and recognize individuals and social forces already involved, and those to be involved, in the fight.

CHAPTER 12

The Revolution Succeeds:
Law 180 of 1978

BACKGROUND

BESIDES SPREADING THEIR IDEAS among mental health workers, administrators and the public domain, Democratic Psychiatry was also concerned about getting political support. The members of the group, who shared a leftist political orientation, looked for the support of the labor unions and the left wing parties. In the early '70s, left wing parties officially included the liberation of the mental patient and the reform of the psychiatric legislation in their political agenda. In the mid '70s, with the increase in power of the Italian left (especially the Communist Party, the P.C.I.) and of the workers' movement, a number of social reforms regarding the family, workers' rights, more permissive regulations concerning drug addiction, etc., were brought forward. Those were also the times of the so-called "historic compromise," i.e., an agreement between the Christian Democrats and the Communists on a set of political objectives in social reforms. All these factors created favorable political conditions for psychiatric reform.

In the mid '70s lay people, independent of political affiliation, had become sensitive to the "psychiatric affair." Publicity gained from the movement and public pronouncements about the terrible conditions of the asylums contributed to this awareness. The national conventions of the Society for Democratic Psychiatry attracted many people, especially the young and the elite of radical intellectuals (Laing, Cooper, Sartre, etc.); they included a number of social events and had a vast resonance. Basaglia's books became best-sellers (*L'istituzione Negat* [*The Denial of the Institution*], Basaglia 1968; *La Maggioranza Deviante* [*The Deviant Majority*], Basaglia and Ongaro-Basaglia, 1971; *Che Cos'e' la Psichiatria?* [*What is Psychiatry?*], Basaglia 1973; *Crimini di Pace* [*Peace Crimes*], Basaglia and Ongaro-Basaglia, 1975) and movies were produced (*Matti da Slegare* [*Madmen to untie*]).

For sake of brevity and simplicity we have limited our historical description to the movement connected with Psichiatria Democratica, which was the most famous and probably the most important body in preparing the way for reform; however, this does not do justice of a great number of individual and group actions that took place in those years. Among these groups there was rather consistent agreement on the need for reform and on most basic topics, including the controversial ones like the critique of state hospitals and social components of mental illness. Also, the official bodies of Italian professionals, such as the Italian Psychiatric Association, shared the principal themes of the movement, including phasing down the state hospitals and replacing them with general hospital wards, developing community-based alternative services, and incorporating the psychiatric system within that of general public medicine (see, for example, the motion of the Italian Psychiatric Association in Appendix D).

However, in spite of the interest and the relatively universal agreement around the reform, nothing had been done legislatively by 1977. Then a small but very dynamic party, the Radical Party (holding about 5% of the seats in the parliament), which had successfully used the constitutional device of referendum to promote liberal reforms, launched a campaign to collect the 500,000 signatures prescribed to bring to referendum the 1904 psychiatric law (actually, 750,000 signatures were collected). They succeeded and the referendum was scheduled for the summer of 1978. If the referendum passed, the existing psychiatric legislation would be completely repealed and the nation would be without a mental health system (no legal basis for the operation of mental hospitals and admissions, no budget, etc.).

Facing this possibility, the government quickly appointed a commission to compile a new law. Although Basaglia was not on the commission, he was consulted extensively and certainly set out its basic characteristics (although there were areas of compromise), so much so that the resulting law is popularly known as "the Basaglia law." The Italian Psychiatric Association gave its assent to the reform and contributed to it. Prof. Balestrieri, the Director of the Institute of Psychiatry of Verona, who supported the reform was president of the Italian Psychiatric Association at that time, a fortunate coincidence. He actively promoted the new law and helped obtain the assent of the Association.

The law was ready and passed on May 13, 1978, just in time to avoid the referendum, as law N. 180: Voluntary and Compulsory Health Treatments. The title does not do justice to the scope of the law, which actually revolutionized the legislation on mental illness: Although it is true that many provisions refer to the legal modalities for commitment, it is their logical consequences and a few other provisions (see Appendix E) that make this law so innovative and unconventional in contemporary world.

The main features of the law are the following:

1. Gradual phasing out of state mental hospitals by blocking all admissions. As an immediate provision of the law, no new patients could be admitted to state mental hospitals. Until December 31, 1980 (deadline postponed to December 31, 1981, in some regions), ex-hospital patients could be readmitted voluntarily; after the deadline no patient could be admitted.

   It is prohibited to construct new mental hospitals and to use the already existing ones as psychiatric facilities of general hospitals.

   New services to be developed have to be staffed by existing personnel, i.e., drawn from mental hospitals. The status of all inpatients had to be reconsidered and for those deemed in need of continuing commitment, a complete procedure had to be done, as if they were new patients; the probable duration of the treatment had to be specified.

2. Treatment will ordinarily take place outside the hospital, with community-based facilities responsible for definite geographical areas, for which they have to provide the full range of psychiatric interventions. These facilities have to be organized in a departmental way so as to ensure connection with the inpatient units in the general hospital and the state hospitals and thereby to provide comprehensive interventions in the fields of prevention and rehabilitation, as well as in the care of mental illness.

3. Hospitalization (either voluntary or compulsory) is regarded as an exceptional intervention, to be used only if community treatment is not feasible or has already failed, and can take place only in small units located in general hospitals (no more than one 15-bed unit per hospital). Such units have to be associated with community facilities (see above) and are not considered as actual psychiatric wards (whose construction is prohibited, as is the transformation of existing neurological or neuropsychiatric wards into psychiatric wards) but as functional inpatient units. In some places (see Arezzo) even beds scattered in other medical departments are used for psychiatric

patients and activated only when needed. However, this alternative is not explicitly mentioned in the law.

4. Compulsory evaluation and treatment in the hospital may take place only if (a) urgent intervention is required, (b) the necessary treatment is refused, (c) community treatment cannot be opportunely implemented. Certificates by two doctors (one must be from the National Health Service) making independent evaluations are required to initiate the compulsory action, which then has to be approved and actually ordered by the mayor, or his designate, acting as local health authority. The duration of compulsory hospitalization is limited to seven days, but extensions may be requested by the attending psychiatrist, specifying and justifying the length of stay. Independent judicial review is required at two and seven days. The patient and any interested party may make a court appeal. Patient's civil rights must be safeguarded, including freedom of choice of physician and hospital, as far as possible; efforts to enlist the consent and cooperation of the patient have to be made.

COMMENT

The Italian approach to deinstitutionalization is radical and gradual at the same time and is actually a preventive one (Mosher, 1983a), the primary target being the system rather than the patients. The closing of the "front door" of mental hospitals by blocking all admissions drastically interrupts the path of institutionalization and will eventually make the mental hospital disappear "by extinction." At the same time, existing mental hospital patients are not "dumped" in the community since the law does not force their discharge, instead recommending a gradual process of rehabilitation. Hence, it is better seen as a *non-institutionalization* rather than a deinstitutionalization law.

In contrast to other countries with community psychiatry, where alternative services have simply been added to those already existing, including the mental hospital, Italy has developed a psychiatric system without the mental hospital, knowing that the adding of new services eventually recruits new patients but leaves the mental hospital unaffected. Interestingly enough, the law dictates that the new services are to be staffed with the existing mental health personnel, thus stressing again the principle of reallocating the resources in order to change the system.

As to the provisions for involuntary commitment, notice that the criterion of dangerousness is not listed. In fact, Law 180 is conceived as a public health law and therefore deals with treatment, not with custody. In this it differs fundamentally from the 1904 law. The legislated characteristics of the inpatient facilities demonstrate concern with the risk of reproducing the mental hospital on a smaller scale.

On December 23, 1978, the law was incorporated in the act that launched the Italian National Health Service, Law N. 833. This fact, which deeply influenced the implementation process, is important in that it framed the psychiatric reform in a profound and comprehensive reform of the whole health system.

The Italian National Health service made health care available to all citizens and created a local administration (Unitá Sanitaria Locale, i.e., Local Health Unit) that is responsible for planning and implementing the local health system and for distributing resources within each catchment area (50,000 to 200,000 inhabitants). The government of the Unitá Sanitaria Locale (U.S.L.) is comprised of the general assembly and the president. The general assembly is made up of city councilmen appointed to it. From among its members the general assembly selects the president and a management committee, whose principal function is planning. The office of the president is the technical body of the U.S.L. and cares for the implementation of plans.

Although revolutionary and demanding a strong commitment from professionals, administrators, patients, and families, the law was almost universally approved and greeted with satisfaction by Italian society; after all, it had been designed and approved by a broad political coalition. However, it was primarily regarded as a success of progressive forces and especially of the Society for Democratic Psychiatry and as an official recognition of the deinstitutionalization (or better, *non-institutionalization*) movement. Basaglia was appointed a special position, created for him in Rome, of superintendent of psychiatric services of the city and the surrounding region. Unfortunately, he died shortly afterwards, in August 1980; with his death the movement lost its charismatic leader and the law its promoter and principal supporter.

CHAPTER 13

So Who Said It Couldn't Be Done: Implementation of Law 180

IMPLEMENTATION

ACCORDING TO THE ITALIAN ADMINISTRATIVE SYSTEM, regional governments had to pass implementing legislation for Law 180. There are 20 regions in Italy, which differ broadly from one another in terms of geographical, historical, cultural, political, and socioeconomic characteristics (see Figure 13.1). Therefore, across regions the pace of developing the new services varied greatly. According to a survey by Misiti et al. (1981), in December 1979 the number of psychiatric beds in general hospitals varied between 13.55 and 2.28 (rates per 100,000 inhabitants). An even greater variance occurred in relation to community services. In those regions where previous experiences of deinstitutionalization and alternative work had occurred, some community services existed already and others were rapidly implemented in order to provide a comprehensive system; therefore, a small number of hospital beds was required.

Especially in southern regions, new services were implemented slowly, the more traditional and less problematic hospital-based ones being opened first. Thus, a low rate of hospital beds may indicate two opposite phenomena: either a lack of facilities in general, or the presence of an effective comprehensive community network of services. There is a third possibility, exemplified by Rome, where for a resident population of about 3.5 million, only 45 (that is right—45!) public beds exist out of about 300 required.

FIGURE 13.1
Italy: Regions and Major Cities

Although a network of community services was developed, the number of beds is clearly inadequate for the needs of a large and socially problematic metropolis. Some have argued that the number of public beds developed is so low because of the lobbying of private hospitals (16, with a total of 1400 beds, only half of which are occupied by Rome citizens [Bacigalupi, Crepet, & Levato, 1982]).

Regional differences apart, the reform was implemented slowly and is not yet complete. In 1984, six years after the reform, only 3,113 general hospital beds were available in the whole country (5.5 beds per 100,000 population), out of the total number of 5,126 planned (9.0 per 100,000 population; CENSIS, 1985). The development of community-based facilities was also slow because the law gave only general recommendations about them; it specified neither a budget to develop and run them nor sanctions for non-compliance.

The psychiatric reform has also been affected by problems encountered in the implementation of the National Health Service at large. Such a momentous enterprise was not easy in times of economic recession and political instability. The passage from the old to the new system implied enormous administrative problems. The N.H.S. inherited an already terrible debt. In order to collect money a new tax was imposed, a very unpopular one (it is currently called "the tax for the health"), judged most unfair to the poor. An appeal to the Constitutional Court recently resulted in a most curious verdict—that it "might" be unconstitutional, but, given the severity of public debt, we cannot get away without it! There is presently a general dissatisfaction with the N.H.S. and especially with its local administrative bodies, the U.S.L.s, which are accused of being too bureaucratic, ineffective, and little concerned about the consumer. Reform of the organization of the U.S.L.s has been proposed recently.

Another important problem had to do with personnel. Since the law prescribed that existing personnel be used to staff the new services, there have been difficulties and delays in moving people around. Some of the workers, especially senior ones, showed resistance to changing jobs, and the decrease of staff of state hospitals has been slower than that of patients (see below). Retraining staff of closed institutions has been and remains still a major endeavor.

The economic recession affecting Italy in late '70s and early '80s, with a rate of inflation that passed 15%, an unemployment rate that almost doubled in ten years (5.9% in 1975; 10.6% in 1985, according to the Central Institute of Statistics, ISTAT 1986; the rate is steadily increasing: 12.6 in 1987), and a public debt that increased tremendously in ten years and in 1985 reached 95,000 billion lire (77 billion dollars), cooled the enthusiasm for social reforms of the '70s, and had a negative influence on the implementation of Law 180 (see Figure 13.2).* Slashes in an already limited budget for social services afflicted the reform right from the beginning. For instance, between 1980 and 1985 no replacement of personnel was allowed, not even when somebody retired; therefore, services had to be run understaffed.

There is also another essential factor to be taken into account—reallocation of money. One could easily affirm that, in actuality, there was *no reallocation* at all. Even now 80% of the psychiatry budget goes to maintain the closed, but still existing, mental hospitals (Ongaro-Basaglia, 1987)! In spite of the fact that they presently house fewer than 30,000 patients, they

---

*Public debt is still increasing: in 1988 it is expected to exceed 123,000 billion lire.

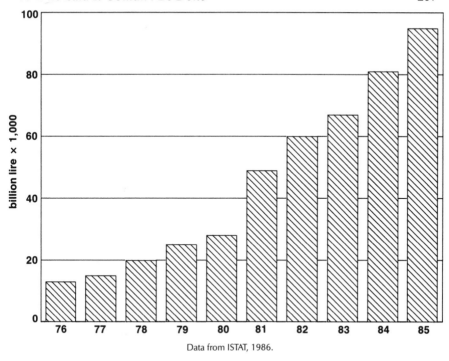

Data from ISTAT, 1986.

FIGURE 13.2
Italy: Public Debt (1976–1985)

still cost as much as when they housed twice as many. In addition, the overall budget for psychiatry is quite meager. In fact, it seems that less than 8% of the National Health Service budget (which amounted to about 42,000 billion lire in 1986 [ISTAT, 1987] goes to psychiatry, compared to 15% in Europe at large (Ongaro-Basaglia et al., 1987). For this reason Senator Franca Ongaro-Basaglia (the widow of Franco Basaglia) has presented a law requiring that at least 8% of the medical budget go to psychiatry.

The instability so characteristic of Italian politics has also had a negative effect on the development of new programs. Between 1978 and 1983 there were seven government crises. In 1979-80 the "historic compromise" between the Christian Democrats and the Communists broke down, because of attrition, change in political balance, and probably, the kidnapping and assassination of Aldo Moro, its principal and most prominent supporter. No event in recent history so profoundly affected so many Italians. It was followed by the kind of universal outpouring of grief and outrage that was seen in America after John Kennedy's assassination in 1963. Moro had begun to travel a course which might have brought the Communists into the

Italian government. He commanded respect from a wide range of the political spectrum. He was regarded as someone who might at last establish a government in Italy that would not exist in almost perpetual crisis.

The stories circulating about Moro's abduction and killing rival those surrounding the Kennedy assassination. Rumors of both CIA and KGB involvement were rife. Fears of an Allende-type overthrow were also fairly widely engendered. Repressive antiterrorist measures running counter to traditional Italian anti-authoritarianism were allowed. Political activity became more muted and careful; the national reaction can be best described as widespread demoralization. In this context the energy, dedication, and zeal necessary to implement already legislated reforms was difficult to sustain. Security consciousness, control, and caution became the order of the day. Incidentally, Moro's body was found May 9; Law 180 was passed May 13, 1978.

In 1983, after an electoral success of the Socialist party and the concurrent fall of the Christian Democrats (who scored the lowest number of votes in their history), the ebullient socialist leader, Bettino Craxi, was appointed prime minister and, somehow paradoxically for a socialist, launched a program of political and economic realism. This also resulted in cuts in social programs, which directly affected the implementation of the psychiatric reform.

Because the law was not being implemented at the same pace throughout the country, discontent grew and fed opposition to the law. A number of proposals were presented from different parties to modify Law 180, mitigating its revolutionary character. Although confirming the goal of phasing out existing mental hospitals, these proposals included a provision to allow the opening of departments for intermediate and long-term care of chronic patients. Family organizations were also instrumental in voicing discontent (but there is also a movement of families *in favor of* Law 180).

However, no proposal went very far. In addition, a proposal presented by the government in 1986, trying to integrate all previous ones, was abandoned *because there was no economic coverage.* Counterreformation is troubled, even before it starts, by the same problem as the reform!

In sum, Law 180 has certainly not been fully, and especially *evenly*, implemented yet. No question, then, that it elicits a fierce controversy. In the international literature, comments span from full and enthusiastic support (Lacey, 1984; Mosher 1982, 1983a, 1983b) to a very critical and pessimistic stance (Jones & Poletti, 1985). Official appraisals of the services of specific areas have been very positive (Bennett, 1975, Jablensky & Henderson, 1983). In addition, there is already a bulk of data, regarding specific services, showing that where the reform has been appropriately implemented, it works well (Burti et al., 1986; Martini et al., 1985; Tansella & De Salvia, 1986; Torre & Marinoni, 1985). However, criticism regarding the applicability of the reform on a national scale persists. Existing national data do not support such criticism. Data are extensively presented hereafter. The hurried reader may skip to the notes of recapitulation and conclusion, at the end of the section.

1984 CENSIS DATA

Nine years after the implementation of Law 180, a nationwide comprehensive analysis of the effects of the reform has not yet been published.

In 1984 the Ministry of Health appointed a distinguished organization, the CENSIS (*Centro Studi Investimenti Sociali*) to perform a comprehensive survey. The survey was performed "in all services and in all regions" and a report delivered to the Department of Health. However, at present (fall 1987), the report has not been released for publication by the department and circulates only as mimeographed copies of the original report, although partial data and summaries have been published (CENSIS, 1984; Fri sanco, 1987; Maranesi & Piazza, 1986). The long delay on the part of the Department of Health has elicited rumors that there may be political reasons for withholding the data. Besides this survey, the evaluation of the effects of the reform relies on data coming from sectorial and ad hoc studies at local or regional level and official national statistics.

The Istituto Centrale di Statistica (ISTAT), Roma (Central Institute of Statistics), collects and publishes data on hospitalization and other gross variables on hospitals; it relies on a routine health information system involving all Italian hospitals, public and private. No information is collected on community services and even data on hospitals are considered of limited reliability (De Salvia, 1983). The same can be said of the Information System of the Department of Health, which started to collect data in 1984. Also the results of the CENSIS survey were questioned by some, because data were collected from key persons within services, using questionnaires. Therefore reliability depends upon the objectivity and accountability of the respondents.

TYPES OF PSYCHIATRIC FACILITIES

The present organization of psychiatric services in Italy includes the following major types of facilities:

- State mental hospitals: 89 in number, as of 1984 (ISTAT source); they are the traditional, large (still housing more than an average of 300 patients each) psychiatric asylums.
- Private mental hospitals (*ospedali psichiatrici privati convenzionati*); there are 11 of them, with an average population of more

than 500 patients each (CENSIS, 1985). They are run by private organizations, but patient expenses are paid for by the National Health Service; they do not differ much from state hospitals. They cluster in the south. They will be described with the state hospitals, as to their characteristics, but data are merged with those of other private institutions.

- *Cliniche private* or *Case di Cura*: private, relatively small, inpatient facilities, that, as to size, structure, type of patients, and length of stay, occupy an intermediate position between general hospital units and the mental hospitals mentioned above. Most of their beds are *convenzionati*, i.e., hospital expenses are paid for by the National Health Service.
- Psychiatric units in general hospitals (usually called *Servizi Psichiatrici di Diagnosi e Cura: S.P.D.C.*); these are the units created by the reform. They are located within general hospitals and cannot exceed 15 beds; beds scattered in other medical and surgical departments may be used instead, but this is the exception rather than the rule.
- Community Mental Health Centers (*Servizi Psichiatrici Territoriali: S.P.T.* or *Servizi di Igiene Mentale: S.I.M.*); also created by the reform, they are catchmented community facilities that provide on-site interventions and are responsible for cooperation with inpatient facilities.
- University departments: There are 27 of them; about half are involved, at varying degrees, with the public system and operate as S.P.D.C.s (also accepting involuntary commitments) (CENSIS, 1985).
- Residential alternatives: They vary a lot as to size, characteristics of the members, degree of staff supervision, length of stay, goals, etc.
- Day hospitals, usually located in a community mental health center, but other locations are reported as well.
- Workers cooperatives: Formed by ex-psychiatric patients and often including other categories of people with handicaps, they provide job opportunities.

STATE MENTAL HOSPITALS

Table 13.1 and Figure 13.3 show annual data regarding Italian state mental hospitals at five-year intervals between 1962 and 1981,* plus the most recent available year (1984), as to the number of institutes, number of beds, physicians, paramedical staff, inpatients on one day, admissions in the year,

*Data for 1982 are not available.

TABLE 13.1
State Mental Hospitals in Italy (1962–1984)
Indices of Hospital Activity

Year	No of inst.	No of beds	No of M.D.s	Param. staff	Pts. on cens. day	Admiss. one yr.	Disch. one yr.	Deaths one yr.	Pts. in the yr.	H. days (x1000)	% bed occ.	L. of stay
1962	94	97,946	913	19,170	91,237	72,290	66,564	5,095	163,527	34,137	95.5	209
1967	89	91,594	1,025	21,401	86,063	82,128	78,291	4,742	168,191	31,974	95.6	190
1972	97	85,000	1,334	25,537	77,987	102,617	101,797	4,517	180,604	28,503	91.6	158
1977	97	70,070	1,670	25,825	58,445	92,212	93,546	3,225	150,657	21,384	83.6	142
1981	96	47,871	1,202	17,621	38,358	27,322	29,071	1,634	65,680	13,423	76.8	204
1984	89	38,928	989	13,967	30,672	15,995*	16,224	1,227	46,667	11,027	77.4	236

Census day = Dec. 31st of the previous year.

Pts. in the yr. = patients on census day + admissions in the year. It implies that the same patient is counted more than once if he has multiple admissions. This somehow incorrect way of presenting a dimension depends from the modalities of data collection used by ISTAT.

% bed occ.(upancy) = daily average number of hospital days per 100 beds.

L(ength) of stay = hospital days divided by the number of patients in the year.

*It may be surprising that in a country where admissions to state hospitals are prohibited by law almost 16,000 admissions are reported in calendar year 1984. The phenomenon is largely an administrative artifact: for instance, state hospital inpatients temporarily transferred to medical or surgical departments of a general hospital for the treatment of intervening physical illnesses result in the statistics as been discharged and, when back, readmitted to the state hospital. The same applies to all those patients who are allowed to spend some time (varying between a few days to some weeks) with their families, usually during holidays or summer vacations. This is a rather common practice for the patients who are relatively well, who have a family or significant others of any sort, who can benefit from these temporary permissions to spend some time in the community, or who may be in the process of getting ready for a final discharge. Another explanation is that some neuropsychiatric institutes, where admissions are allowed, are still computed with the state hospitals. Nevertheless, a number of admissions are true admissions, because of regional wavings of the law and other special situations; however, only those who were inpatients before the 1978 reform may be readmitted and a special procedure must be employed, to prevent any abuse. The number of these cases seems to be rather low; unfortunately, no objective figures are available to measure this phenomenon.
Data base: Istituto Centrale di Statistica (ISTAT), 1964–1986.

211

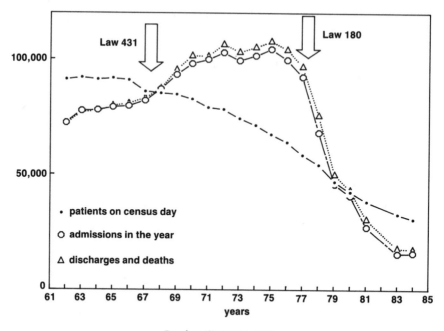

Data from ISTAT, 1964–1986.

FIGURE 13.3
Italy: State Mental Hospitals (1962–1984)
Indices of Hospital Activity

discharges in the year, deaths in the year, patients in the year, hospital days
(per 1,000), daily bed occupancy, length of stay. Up to the mid '60s there was
an increase in the number of beds, patients on census day, and hospital days.
Top figures were scored in 1963: 98,544 beds, 91,868 patients on census day,
and 34,199,000 hospital days. In the late '60s, and even more in the '70s,
there was a steady decrease on these three parameters.

In 1963 there were 1.73 public mental hospital beds per thousand population; the rate became .76 in 1983. The decline occurred at an increasing rate:
the average decrement of beds per year being 1,390 between 1963 and 1968;
3,305 in the prereform half-decade (1973–1978), and 4,140 in the years
1979–1983 (Tansella & Williams, 1987). The number of patients in the year
reached top figures in 1972 and has declined ever since. They were 180,604 in
1972 and 65,680 in 1981, the average decrement of patients per year being
5,989 in the prereform half-decade (1972–1977), and 21,244 in the years
1977–1981. The average length of stay increased steadily after the reform,

from 142 days in 1977 to 236 days in 1984. In fact, those people who could be discharged were released after the reform and only the most serious cases remained; for them the hospital is most likely a dead end.

Interestingly enough, until 1975, the decrease in patients was the consequence of the number of discharges plus deaths exceeding admissions. After 1975, there was also a decrease in admissions. This was a consequence of the movement for deinstitutionalization, the development of alternative services in the community, and the implementation of Law 180 of 1978. De Salvia (1984) pointed out that Law 180 just accelerated a process of deinstitutionalization already in progress. See, in Figure 13.3, that Law 180 did not affect much the slope of graph representing the number of resident inpatients, while it deeply increased the slope of the graphs representing admissions and discharges. As already mentioned, the reform was not designed to bring about a rapid deinstitutionalization, but rather to *prevent institutionalization*. Note that there are two intersections between the graph of patients on one day (census day) and that of admissions. This is characteristic of the Italian situation, and does not occur, for instance, in the U.S., where there is no decreasing trend in the number of admissions (De Salvia, 1985, Figure 13.4).

It is usually assumed that the principal reason for deinstitutionalization in the last quarter of this century comes from the discovery of psychotropic drugs. This mythical role of neuroleptics has been seriously questioned for many years (Kramer & Pollack, 1958) and other factors, such as changes in legislation and welfare policies, have been shown to correlate more consistently (Goldman, Adams, & Taube 1983) with the patterns of deinstitutionalization. The several years' delay between the introduction of neuroleptics and the initial decrease of hospital patients in Italy supports the doubts mentioned above. As to the importance of legislative and policy-related factors, Italy provides the rule of the thumb: the most effective means to decrease the population of (state) mental hospitals is to prohibit admissions, i.e., a change in the legislation.

Also noteworthy is the decrease in the number of hospital staff, as they are transferred to the new services. However, the overall decrement of staff, although substantial, and almost parallel to that of inpatients on census day, thus reflecting the impact of the reform, has been quite uneven, thus reflecting local difficulties and delays of this process. While the number of patients on census day decreased from 58,445 in 1977 to 30,672 in 1984 (-47.5%), the number of physicians decreased from 1,670 to 989 (-40.7%) and that of paramedical staff from 25,825 to 13,967 (-45.9%) in the same period (Figure 13.5). But the transfer of mental health workers to the new services was substantial in just over one-fifth of the hospitals, while in more than one-fourth of the hospitals there has been *no* transfer at all (CENSIS, 1985).

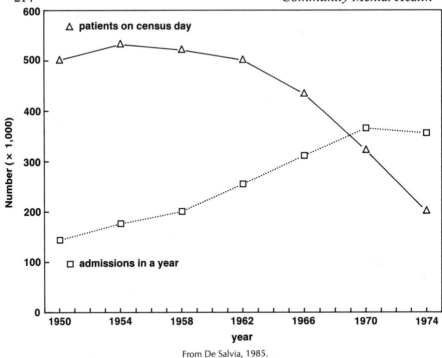

From De Salvia, 1985.

FIGURE 13.4
Number of State Hospital Patients on Census Day and Admissions in the Year
U.S.A. (1950–74)

COMPARISON WITH OTHER COUNTRIES

A decrease of the number of patients in state hospitals accompanied by a shift to alternative, community-based services is a trend common to most industrialized countries, at least in the Western world. Table 13.2 shows the variations of the number of beds in state hospitals per 100,000 adult (> 14 years) population in several European countries, the United States, and Canada, in a given period, as specified (ISIS News, 1985). It can be noted that the rate of hospital beds varies greatly between countries and probably reflects different phases in the development of mental health services; i.e., a low number of hospital beds may mean either that the system was never fully developed or that it has already shifted to community care. It may also be noted that the decrease in Italy, albeit noteworthy, is not that dramatic in comparison to other developed countries considering the fact that the datum of 38.8% of Table 13.2 refers to a six year period, while data for other countries refer to different years and to shorter periods of time because of different methods of data collection. In addition, it must be remembered that the decrease in Italy was the effect of an exceptional event such as a national psychiatric reform, while changes in other countries reflect just a routine evolution of services and practices. In fact, in Italy, there has not been a rapid discharge of patients as happened, for instance, in some areas of the U.S., such as California and New York State and very little "dumping" has been reported (Misiti et al., 1981): the decrease was rather the consequence of the blocking of admissions and readmissions, as already mentioned.

PRESENT SITUATION OF STATE MENTAL HOSPITALS*

Two opposite situations are described in the large hospitals (CENSIS, 1985). The first is one of extreme disinterest and abandonment, where gradual exhaustion because of the death of the inpatients is the only ongoing process. In these instances two major trends have coincided: the continued employment of most conservative and less motivated staff in the institution

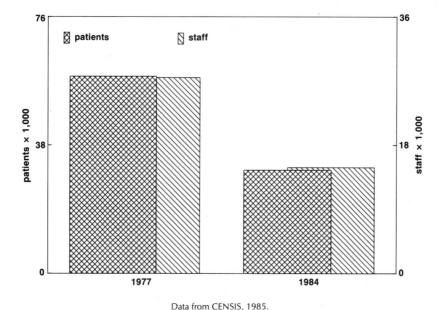

Data from CENSIS, 1985.

FIGURE 13.5
Italian State Mental Hospitals: 1977 vs 1984
Patients and Staff

*The picture presented here applies also to the 11 large *ospedali psichiatrici privati convenzionati* mentioned above.

TABLE 13.2
Trends in the Number of Beds in Public Mental
Hospitals in Europe, U.S.A., and Canada

Country	Period	+/– %	No of beds*
Austria	1978–81	– 2.4	219.4
Belgium	1977–81	– 3.0	307.8
Bulgaria	1977–81	+ 8.3	108.4
Canada	1977–78	+ 2.1	87.5
Czechoslovakia	1980–81	+ 0.9	146.1
Denmark	1975–79	– 17.6	233.7
Finland	1978–80	– 2.9	526.5
Greece	1978–81	– 2.0	170.8
Holland	1978–80	+ 6.2	238.2
Hungary	1978–81	+ 10.5	156.2
Ireland	1978–80	– 8.7	576.4
Italy	1977–83	– 38.8	94.0
Luxembourg	1978–81	– 6.9	440.7
Norway	1978–81	– 11.7	204.6
Poland	1978–79	– 1.1	143.9
Rumania	1978–81	+ 8.3	107.2
Scotland	1978–80	– 2.8	406.9
Spain	1976–79	– 5.1	151.5
Sweden	1977–80	– 12.6	277.9
U.S.A.	1978–80	– 8.7	112.0
West Germany	1978–80	– 3.0	206.1
Yugoslavia	1977–80	– 5.7	62.3

*Rate per 100,000 inhabitants aged 14 and over
Data base: WHO, 1983.
From Cecere, 1985.

and a gap with community services overburdened by new cases and organizational problems. The second occurs in a considerable number of institutes (this is more true in the case of private institutions) that have been able to bring about change. Interestingly enough, positive changes in mental hospitals do not seem related to their geographical location; good examples are reported in the less progressive southern regions. Another interesting finding is that changes start from within the hospital itself, not from outside community services. This would again confirm Basaglia's classic axiom that the asylum cannot be changed from outside, only from within.

These changes include: discharge of patients and reduction of the number of beds (73% of the hospitals); demolition of large wards (58%); renewal of buildings (53%); hiring new professional staff for rehabilitation (33%); transforming patients into "guests" and preparing residential, self-run communities on the hospital grounds (47%); providing job opportunities outside the hospital (51%), etc. Other innovations concern the use of psychotherapy and rehabilitation techniques, trips and summer vacations, contacts with the family on a regular basis, etc. (CENSIS, 1985).

PRIVATE INSTITUTIONS

Deinstitutionalization also involved private institutions, although to a lesser extent and with a different pattern. Table 13.3 shows their number, the number of beds, inpatients on one day, admissions in the year, discharges in the year, deaths in the year, patients in the year, hospital days (per 1,000), daily bed occupancy, and length of stay, at five year intervals between 1962 and 1981,* plus the most recent available (1984). Differently from in public institutions, in private hospitals the number of beds, patients on one day, and hospital days diminished slightly. In addition, the number of patients in the year increased until 1977 and has leveled off only recently.

Note also the length of stay: 127 days in 1972; 87 days in 1984. This has been interpreted to mean that private institutions are serving — and becoming more and more specialized with — a different population: short- and, especially, medium-stay patients, who did not use the state hospital before the reform and do not use the short-stay general hospital units now (CENSIS, 1984). These interpretations apart, data reveal that, since 1978, *there has been no appreciable shift from the public to the private hospitalization*, as predicted by some.

FORENSIC PSYCHIATRIC HOSPITALS

Forensic hospitals have not been affected by the reform, although a debate on urgent changes has gone on for a long while, because they fall under the jurisdiction of the Department of Justice. There was an expectation that there would be an increase of admissions to these hospitals. It occurred only to a moderate degree. The overall number of beds is relatively small (Table 13.4).

PSYCHIATRIC UNITS IN GENERAL HOSPITALS

Implementation

As of June 1984 regional governments had planned and approved 389 units for a total number of 5,126 beds. However, on December 31, 1984, only 236 units (3,113 beds — 60% of those planned) were active (CENSIS,

---

*Data for 1982 are not available.

TABLE 13.3
Private Psychiatric Institutions (1962–1984)
Indices of Hospital Activity

Year	No of inst.	No of beds	Pts. on cens. day	Admiss. one yr.	Disch. one yr.	Deaths one yr.	Pts. in the yr.	H. days (x1000)	% bed occ.	L. of stay
1962	83	16,371	13,316	23,989	22,938	743	37,305	5,009	83.8	134
1967	95	23,037	20,116	31,283	30,084	988	51,399	7,356	87.5	143
1972	105	26,278	22,042	42,859	41,667	1,127	64,901	8,227	85.5	127
1977	97	24,177	19,663	49,582	48,983	1,116	69,245	7,351	83.3	106
1981	90	21,905	16,872	47,864	47,386	958	64,736	6,279	78.5	97
1984	87	18,345	15,025	49,719	49,330	754	64,744	5,639	84.0	87

Census day = Dec. 31st of the previous year.
Pts. in the yr. = patients on census day + admissions in the year. (See also the corresponding note of table 1.)
% bed occ.(upancy) = daily average number of hospital days per 100 beds.
Data base: Istituto Centrale di Statistica (ISTAT), 1964–1986.

TABLE 13.4
Hospital Days in Italian Forensic Hospitals (1976–1981)

Year	Hospital days	Trend (in%)
1976	623,450	100
1977	602,333	96.6
1978	560,170	89.8
1979	585,516	93.9
1980	612,117	98.2
1981	645,507	103.5

There are 6 forensic hospitals in Italy, with 1907 beds total.
Data base: Calvaruso et al., 1982.
From De Salvia, 1984.

1985). Great variations among regions are also reported, providing evidence for the uneven state of implementation of the reform. In Table 13.5 and Figure 13.6 the situation of psychiatric units in general hospitals on December 31, 1984 is described by region. Regions are divided by geographical area.

It must be noted that bed rates depend on two very different factors: regional policy towards the development of inpatient settings and delays in the implementation of services. A comparison between beds due and active gives a gross idea of which factor is more likely involved. For instance, in northern Italy, Veneto offers an example of a hospital-oriented policy with some delay in developing services; Emilia Romagna, instead, has a system that is practically already completed but with few hospital beds planned. Note that in the south all the regions but Molise still have to develop some of the beds planned; this is *one* of the aspects of the *global* delay in developing services that affects the south of Italy.

The average number of beds per service is 13, lower than the number allowed by law (15). However, in order to comply with a widely accepted standard of about 1 bed per 10,000 population, 173 new units, for an overall number of 2,595 beds, should be developed. Does the existing number of beds meet the needs? It does not seem so, at least for 60% of the services: that is in fact the percentage of services that had to refuse patients on some occasion in 1984 because of lack of beds available; 28% refused more than 20 requests for admission in the same period. In the south this percentage was 42.3%.

Characteristics

Inpatient facilities were the services developed first after the reform, to provide an alternative to the block of admissions to the state hospitals: 54% were developed in 1978, the first year; 23% in 1979–80, and the remaining

TABLE 13.5
Psychiatric Units in General Hospitals, By Region (Dec. 31st 1984)

| | PLANNED | | ACTIVE | | |
REGION	No. of units	No. of beds	No. of units	No. of beds	Rate of beds*
Piemonte	21	255	20	240	5.4
Valle d'Aosta	1	15	1	15	13.2
Lombardia	51	758	38	601	6.7
Liguria	10	200	8	126	7.1
NORTHWEST	83	1,228	67	982	6.5
Trentino A. Adige	5	75	5	73	8.3
Veneto	43	645	34	460	10.5
Friuli V. Giulia	12	180	4	48	3.9
Emilia Romagna	11	170	9	160	4.0
NORTHEAST	71	1,070	52	741	7.1
Toscana	23	345	16	172	4.8
Umbria	2	30	2	16	2.0
Marche	18	194	14	162	11.4
Lazio	18	250	5	70	1.4
CENTRAL ITALY	61	819	37	420	3.8
Abruzzo	15	203	3	42	3.4
Molise	3	35	3	35	10.5
Campania	29	437	17	215	3.8
Puglia	32	480	12	150	3.8
Basilicata	11	86	5	53	8.6
Calabria	19	158	10	85	4.0
SOUTH	109	1,399	50	580	4.2
Sicilia	59	520	26	304	6.0
Sardegna	6	90	4	86	5.3
ISLANDS	65	610	30	390	5.8
ITALY	389	5,126	236	3,113	5.4

*Per 100,000 population
From CENSIS, 1984; 1985.

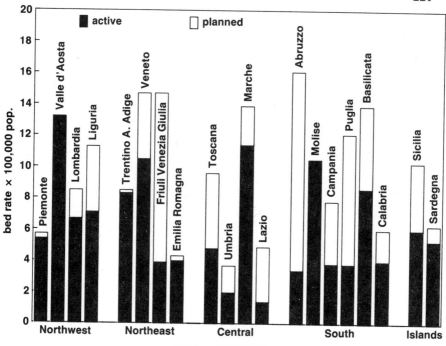

Data from CENSIS, 1985.

FIGURE 13.6
Psychiatric Units in General Hospitals by Region
Italy (Dec. 31, 1984)

23%, located mainly in the south, in the following four years (Figure 13.7). The prevailing location is within a general hospital, as a definite and separate unit (85%); 5.5% are classified as part of another department; 5.1% are defined as separate facilities outside a hospital, and 4.2 have another location, without further specification. The majority of the units (78%) have an on-call service at the hospital emergency room. As to the degree of freedom allowed to patients, 57% are reported to be open "always" or "most of the time," and only 17% "always closed" (CENSIS, 1985).

Data on Patients

Table 13.6 summarizes data regarding number of patients, number of admissions, hospital days, daily bed occupancy, and length of stay. Data were collected by the CENSIS and are based on respondent units, as specified. According to these data, there are an estimated 78,000 admissions per year to the general hospital units, one-fifth of which are involuntary com-

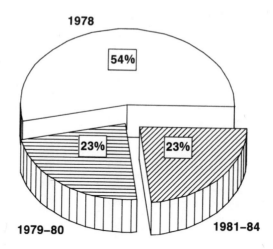

Data from CENSIS, 1985.

FIGURE 13.7
Italian Psychiatric Units in General Hospitals
Year(s) of Development

TABLE 13.6
Psychiatric Units in General Hospitals (1984)
Indices of Patient Movement (% in parenthesis)

	Pts. in the yr.		Admiss. one yr.		H. days (x1000)		% bed occ.	L. of stay
Number of respondent units	186		229		181		181	181
Voluntary admission	30,746	(77.0)	60,257	(79.7)	531	(78.6)	61.8	12.4
Involunt. admission	9,201	(23.0)	15,344	(20.3)	145	(21.4)	16.9	12.8
Total	39,947	(100.0)	75,601	(100.0)	676	(100.0)	78.7	12.5

%bed occ.(upancy) = daily average number of hospital days per 100 beds.*
L(ength) of stay = hospital days divided by the number of admissions in the year.*
*based on 181 services that provided both data.
From CENSIS, 1985.

mitments. The percentage of patients admitted involuntarily varies among regions and from unit to unit and may be interpreted as an index of the comprehensiveness and integration of community services; it is higher in the south (about one-third of all admissions are involuntary commitments) than in the north (one-sixth to one-seventh of admissions). The average national annual rate is about 36 per 100,000 adult (>14 years) population. Average length of stay is about 12 days, with minimal differences between voluntary and involuntary admissions. As to readmissions, they are about one-third (34.1%) of all admissions (CENSIS, 1985).

The Personnel

The overall staff working in the 236 units amounts to 6,775 individuals, i.e., 29 per unit. In general, the units are understaffed, since even in the north only 35% of units have complete staffing. The professional composition is represented in Figure 13.8 (CENSIS, 1985). All mental health professionals are represented in about one-third of the units, while almost 40% of the units have only medical personnel (physicians, aides, and nurses).

Where do these personnel come from? The great majority (58.6%) come from state hospitals, where they had worked before; 18% come from other services, and only 23% have been hired anew, after the reform. Data regard-

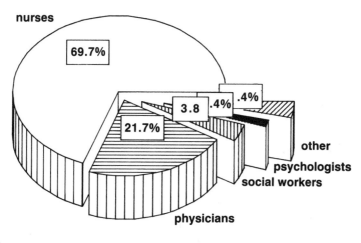

Data from CENSIS, 1985.

FIGURE 13.8
Italian Psychiatric Units in General Hospitals
Composition of Personnel

ing training and continuing education within the units give a rather unsatisfactory picture: More than two-thirds of the units have not offered *any* courses to their personnel since their existence. However, if the service is based on multiprofessional teamwork, training takes place while actually working in the team (Burti & Mosher, 1986). This seems to be the case on a good percentage of units: According to the CENSIS survey, 25 to 30% of units have daily staff meetings, while another 30% have "many," at least weekly. Information on training of various staff members is given in Appendix F.

As to the therapeutic style, while it is true that the medical model prevails, most units report including some form of individual psychotherapy (80%), while 30% offer group activities and 40% provide interventions in the community.

In sum, units in general hospitals are unevenly distributed in the nation, and their staffing is mainly medical, having come from the mental hospitals and generally lacking formal training for the new job. Although there are wide differences from region to region, in general these units do not seem to be overburdened by their caseloads — this is especially true where community services are effective and integrated. Data on commitments, readmissions, and length of stay are also quite positive.

COMMUNITY SERVICES

Implementation

The CENSIS survey reports 675 community services active as of December 31, 1984, out of 694 U.S.L.s existing in Italy. Their distribution by region is summarized in Table 13.7, and represented in Figure 13.9. Note that, as a rule, the ratio of services to resident population becomes less favorable going from north to south (one service to about 70,000 pop. in the north; one to 80,000 in central Italy; one to 100,000 in the south; one to 149,000 in Sicily). However, when single regions are considered, the pattern of distribution is more complicated and not completely consistent with a north to south gradient (Figure 13.9). Extremes are represented by the region Friuli-Venezia Giulia (northeast), with one to 47,000, on one side, and Molise (south), with one to 333,000, on the other (CENSIS, 1985).

Interestingly enough, 36.7% of the services had been developed *before* Law 180; i.e., the process towards community care was already in motion. The reform certainly gave momentum to the process, especially between 1978 and 1980; since then there has been a general slowdown (Figure 13.10), and 132 are still due. The number of U.S.L.s without a community service also increases from north to south, where about one-third of the population

TABLE 13.7
Number of Psychiatric Services by Region (Dec. 31st 1984)

REGION	USL	Community services	Hospital units	State* hospitals	Private hospitals	University dep. s.**	Residential facilities	Day hospitals	Total services
Piemonte	76	78	20	6	7	1	17	1	130
Valle d'Aosta	1	1	1	—	—	—	—	—	2
Lombardia	98	97	38	15	5	1	28	17	201
Liguria	20	20	8	2	1	1	4	1	37
NORTHWEST	195	196	67	23	13	3	49	19	370
Trentino A. Adige	14	15	5	2	—	—	6	3	31
Veneto	36	45	34	18	5	—	30	1	133
Friuli V. Giulia	12	26	4	6	—	1	20	9	66
Emilia Romagna	41	65	9	14	7	3	35	7	140
NORTHEAST	103	151	52	40	12	4	91	20	370
Toscana	41	35	16	7	—	2	25	5	90
Umbria	12	13	2	1	—	—	15	—	31
Marche	24	27	14	4	1	—	3	—	49
Lazio	59	58	5	5	21	2	9	4	104
CENTRAL ITALY	136	133	37	17	22	4	52	9	274

(continued)

225

TABLE 13.7 (Continued)
Number of Psychiatric Services by Region (Dec. 31st 1984)

REGION	USL	Community services	Hospital units	State* hospitals	Private hospitals	University dep. s.**	Residential facilities	Day hospitals	Total services
Abruzzo	15	9	3	2	3	—	—	—	17
Molise	7	1	3	—	1	—	—	—	5
Campania	61	46	17	6	7	—	7	—	83
Puglia	55	45	12	3	3	1	9	2	75
Basilicata	7	7	5	1	—	—	8	—	21
Calabria	31	34	10	2	6	0	9	—	61
SOUTH	176	142	50	14	20	1	33	2	262
Sicilia	62	34	26	6	4	1	2	—	73
Sardegna	22	19	4	3	—	1	21	—	48
ISLANDS	88	53	30	9	4	2	23	—	121
ITALY	694	675	236	103	71	14	248	50	1,397

*Private mental hospitals (11) are counted here. **University departments admitting involuntary patients are listed with hospital units.
From CENSIS, 1984, 1985.

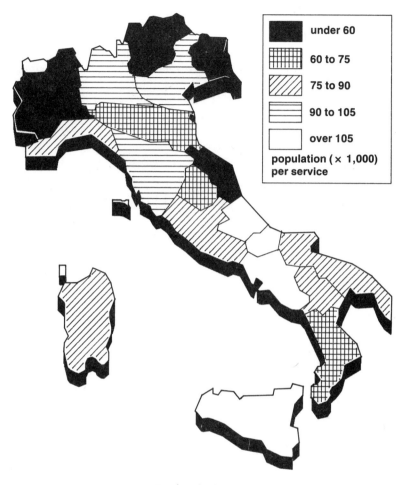

Data from CENSIS, 1985.

FIGURE 13.9
Italy: Community Services by Region

lives in U.S.L.s without a psychiatric community service (the national ratio is one of six).

Characteristics

In terms of physical space, they tend to be rather small (140 sq. m/1,500 sq. ft.) and two-thirds of the space are used as offices; only 66% of services have common spaces; 13% have beds, but in only 1.8% may beds be used

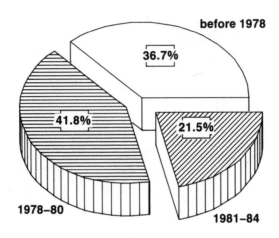

Data from CENSIS, 1985.

FIGURE 13.10
Italian Psychiatric Community Services
Years of Development

overnight. Forty percent of services have also other offices in the territory, for outpatient activities. Twenty-one percent provide a day hospital, but only 6.7% provide meals, and only 12% have a specific space for rehabilitation and resocialization activities.

The majority of services (60%) are open six days a week; 26% Monday through Friday; 5% seven days a week.

Personnel

As to staffing, there are broad variations among regions and services: 22 staff average in northeastern and central Italy regions; 17 and 13 in the northwestern and southern regions, respectively; 8 in the islands. In particular, the number of psychiatrists and nurses reflects these differences. Only one-third of the services have all professional types represented.

As to their origins, 33.2% of all staff were expressly hired after Law 180; 43.4% were transferred from state mental hospitals; 17.4% from preexisting extramural services (those implemented after Law 431); 6% from nonpsychiatric services. In half of the services there has been no formal training initiative.

Patient Load

In 1984, about 360,000 patients used the community services, of which one-third were new to the service. The majority of interventions (60%) were office consultations, 29% home visits, and 11% other community interventions. Average number of all annual interventions per service was 4,094: 480 per 10,000 population. Differences between areas were substantial: 656 per 10,000 population in northern regions; 230 and 119 in southern regions and the islands, respectively. Differences were even more dramatic if data are broken down according to the site of intervention: community interventions are 265, 82, and 28, per 10,000 pop., respectively.

As to the *type* of intervention, 50.3% were reported as mostly pharmacological, 32.4% as mostly psychotherapeutic, and 17.3% as mostly social. Again, the south and the islands were characterized by a higher predominance of pharmacological interventions, because of a more medical and office-based kind of approach.

Style of Work

As to staff meetings, 67% of services have some, at least weekly (78% in the north; 50% in the south). However, in the south, 19% of services never have meetings (3.1% national average).

The degree of integration with inpatient facilities does not look very good, even nationwide: only half of services have at least occasional contacts, while 8% have none, ever. The percentage of services where the same staff also runs the inpatient facility is 17% (see South Verona as an example). There seems to be relatively little coordination with other medical and social agencies (G.P.s, public administrations, jail, nursing homes) in terms of frequency, and especially, type of contacts: Most consist of exchange of information; program and patient-oriented meetings are far less frequent.

Other indicators are also not very encouraging: 72% of services never organized encounters (conferences, discussions, parties, festivals) with the population and 63% never organized vacations and trips for the patients. Finally, as to data collection, only one-third has instruments (register of interventions, therapeutic plans, etc.) other than individual clinical charts. However, there is a number of services with efficient psychiatric registers and active epidemiological research activity (Lomest, South Verona, Portogruaro, just to note those that have already published extensively).

Summary

Although services are still lacking and considerable differences among regions exist, the CENSIS survey actually provides a picture of a comprehensive network of community services extended to the whole nation—a tangible sign that the implementation of the reform has actually progressed.

In an effort to outline a typology of these services, a cluster analysis was performed. Five types of community services were identified (CENSIS, 1985): In brief, in terms of overall qualitative appraisal, only one type (representing 11.4% of the services) has to be considered inadequate; three types (representing 55.2% of services) could be defined as satisfactory, to different degrees. One (33.4%) may be considered less adequate, but still acceptable. Areas of special concern are the degree of integration with other services in the community, the style of intervention (excessively pharmacological), and the lack of training.

RESIDENTIAL FACILITIES

As to alternative facilities, CENSIS reports 248 residential facilities.* Over half (56.5%) of these alternative services are in the northern regions, but there are exceptions: Friuli Venezia Giulia has 30 (1 to 39,500 pop.); Umbria, 15 (1 to 54,000 pop.); Emilia Romagna, 35 (1 to 94,000 pop.); Trentino Alto Adige, 6 (1 to 97,000 pop.).

These facilities are almost equally distributed among high (24 hours a day), middle (9 to 18 hours), and low (less than 8 hours) levels of supervision. Most of them (90%) are public and have been implemented since the reform (80%). Over a third (39%) are located in a specific building; 24% are within the boundaries of a reformed state hospital; very few (less than 3%) are in a condominium. About one-third of them has a day program, while another third refers members to other services for day activities.

As to the personnel, two-thirds are nurses, one-tenth M.D.s, another tenth psychologists and social workers; the rest are other types of caretakers. The majority of the personnel comes from the state hospitals (54%).

The number of patients amounted to 2,901 on January 1, 1984; 897 entered during the year; 845 were either discharged or died in the year.

Predominant activities are those of generic rehabilitation (expressive and occupational activities) and resocialization in the community; administering and monitoring drugs is also reported, together with some psychotherapy (individual supportive therapy and group psychotherapy). Very few facilities report that they actively pursue finding a job for the members. Community meetings occur at least weekly in over 50% of these facilities, daily in 15%.

Most residential facilities (88.2%) report having good connections with community psychiatric services; the same is true for other human services in

---

*Only facilities with at least four hours per day of staff supervision were recorded. Group homes were not included.

the community. As to relationships with the surrounding community at large, they are described as generally good, but conflicts are reported in about one-fifth of the cases.

WORK COOPERATIVES

The CENSIS survey reports 50 work cooperatives (19 in the north; 23 in central Italy; 8 in the south and islands). Most of them (38) were established after the reform. The total number of members is 1420. The members are very heterogeneous: 127 are still inpatients of the state hospital; 402 are ex-state hospital patients; 431 were never admitted to a psychiatric institute; 208 are nonpsychiatric members; 252 are administrative personnel. Most members are young adults.

Income is still rather low: In 36% of cooperatives each member receives less than 200,000 lire monthly; in 26% between 200,000 and 500,000 lire; in 16% more than 500,000 lire (100,000 lire equal about $80).

Although still limited in number, cooperatives are developing at a steady pace and are part of a well organized nationwide movement. In recent years they have more and more attracted the attention of the public administration (and some regions are offering economic incentives) because of their potential for finding viable job alternatives for people that have practically no hope in the public market, given the high unemployment rate in Italy.

THE OVERALL SCENARIO

Table 13.7 summarizes the situation of psychiatric services in Italy as to December 31, 1984. Besides the units in general hospitals, community and alternative services, public mental hospitals, private hospitals funded with public money and university departments are reported by region.

Global Inpatient Care in Italy

Using available data, we can tentatively outline the pattern of inpatient care before and after the reform (Table 13.8). It should be noted that between 1974 and 1984 the rates for inpatient care, public and private, show a steady decrease in the 70s and seem to level off after the reform, thus indicating that the process of deinstitutionalization and the shift of inpatient care from state hospitals to general hospitals, as an effect of Law 180, neither increased the rate of admissions — in other words the phenomenon of the revolving door did not occur, as some feared — nor brought about a shift from the public sector to the private one.

These data are depicted in Figure 13.11. A visual inspection of the picture

TABLE 13.8
Global Inpatient Care in Italy (1974–1984)
(Rates per 100,000 General Population)

Year	Public inst.s	Units in gen. hosp.s	Total public	Private inst.s	Global
1974	311	—	311	119	430
1975	307	—	307	120	427
1976	291	—	291	122	413
1977	267	—	267	122	389
1978	215	41	256	120	376
1979	163	70	233	113	346
1980	145	105	250	117	367
1981	117	105	222	115	337
1982	94	116*	210	(**)	—
1983	86	127*	213	112	325
1984	82	137	219	113	332

*estimated. **not available.
Data base: ISTAT 1976–86; Calvaruso et al. 1982.
From De Salvia 1983, modified.

shows that after the reform the overall rate of inpatient care did not increase, but remained stable, with the general hospital units progressively taking over the patient load at the expense of state hospitals, while private institutions maintain their positions. The most dramatic change occurred with regard to compulsory hospitalizations, which dropped from 32,521 in 1977 to 13,375 in 1979, with corresponding rates of 57 and 23 per 100,000 population, respectively (Misiti et al., 1981). In 1984 compulsory hospitalizations were about 15,800. In the areas with effective and comprehensive community services rates were even lower than 10 per 100,000 (De Salvia, 1984; Tansella et al., 1987).

Indices of Quality of Care

The impact of the reform on the quality of life of psychiatric patients, on their families, and on general population, has not been assessed nor have outcome studies been completed. Some projects are in progress (Mignolli, 1987), but results are not available yet.

However, studies are available on suicide rates before and after the reform. In a study of the Consiglio Nazionale delle Ricerche (C.N.R.) the rate of suicide due to mental illness did not show a substantial increase two years after the reform (Debernardi, 1980). Williams et al. (1986) also studied the effect of the reform on the suicide rate, using data collected by the police. They found that the national suicide rate in Italy had increased since 1978, but such increase was largely confined to the more developed regions of northern and central Italy (Figure 13.12). However, they found no increase in the proportion of suicides attributed by the police to mental illness (Figure 13.13). Using an ecological approach, they compared the pre-post reform change in the trend in suicide with four measures of psychiatric service provision (mental hospital beds, general hospital beds, community mental health services, transitional housing). The only significant correlation found was a negative correlation with the number of *general* hospital beds, i.e., the increase in the suicide rate was lower in regions with higher bed rate.

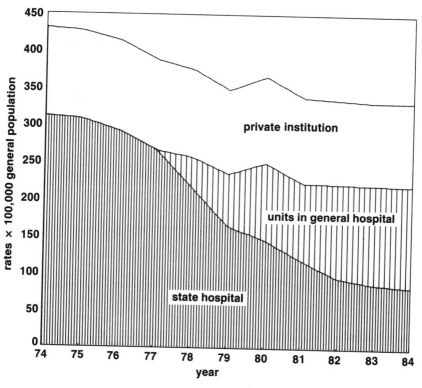

Data from De Salvia 1983, modified.

FIGURE 13.11
Global Inpatient Care in Italy (1974–84)

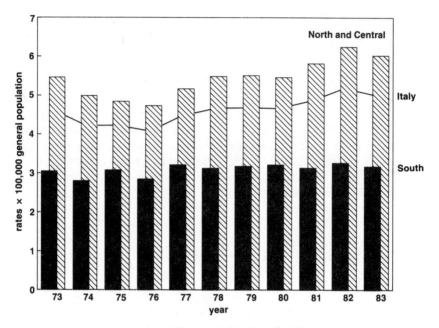

Data from Williams, De Salvia & Tansella, 1986.

FIGURE 13.12
Suicide in Italy (1973–1983)

CONCLUSIONS

The Italian reform has been described in terms varying from "the most advanced in the world" to the "aborted" reform. Let the reader make up his or her own mind and decide according to the "evidence" (Tansella et al., 1987), rather than from preconceptions and stereotypes; there is enough literature already on the topic.

This much is known:

1. While previous literature showed that " . . . there are many places in Italy . . . where the psychiatric reform has been in fact implemented and is actually functioning . . . " (Tansella et al., 1987), the CENSIS report clearly shows that these "many places" are more numerous than it seemed before. In fact, it appears that the 1978 law is being widely, but not uniformly, implemented.

2. The number of mental hospital inpatients has decreased from about 60,000 before the reform to less than 30,000. More importantly, closing of the front doors of the state mental hospitals *prevented* the

institutionalization of new patients or the reinstitutionalization of those discharged. This has occurred without either an increase in the number of admissions to private hospitals or an increase of short-term admissions to general hospital units. Actually, the *overall* inpatient care rate (including admissions) has remained stable since the reform, with general hospital units replacing the state hospital.

3. Both inpatient services (general hospital units) and outpatient services (community mental health centers) have been developed throughout the country and are available to more than 80% of the Italian population in their own catchment areas (U.S.L.s).

4. The flaws have mainly to do with limited resources. The reform has been made more difficult from the beginning by cuts in the health budget. In addition, the state hospital system still consumes about 80% of the national mental health budget, in spite of the fact that the number of patients has been reduced by 50% since the reform.

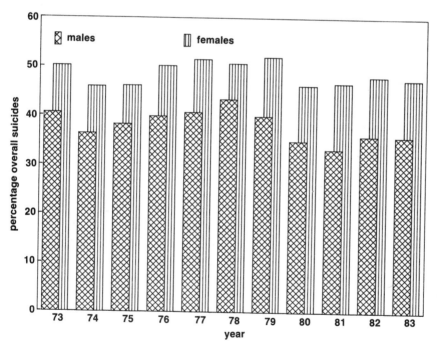

Data from Williams, De Salvia & Tansella, 1986.

FIGURE 13.13
Percentages of Suicides by Sex Attributed to Mental Illness in Italy (1973–1983)

There is also a delay in the transfer of the personnel from the mental hospitals to community services. All this results in delays in the development of community services. This is especially true of those regions in the south which were already lacking in social services. Other problems identified are poor integration of services, poorly trained personnel, and lack of routine participation by the medical schools.

However, the evidence is that where both hospital and community services have been developed, i.e., in a vast part of the country, the reform has been implemented successfully.

CHAPTER 14

Making It Work in a Big City: Genoa

GENOA PSYCHIATRIC SYSTEM

WE CHOSE TO ASSESS THE SITUATION IN GENOA for a number of reasons: First of all, it is a large city, which may serve as the prototype of a modern metropolis, with all the related social and organizational problems. In the literature on the Italian reform, the following stereotype frequently appears: The reform might work in a small city or in a stable rural community, but not in a metropolis. OK, there is Trieste, but it is a small, quiet, residential city, without harsh social contrasts; the same is true of Arezzo, Ferrara, Perugia, etc. All these folks of democratic psychiatry picked nice, small cities to do their gimmicks, but what about a big city, with the "real" problems, the homeless etc.?

We could have chosen Turin, Milan, Venice, or Bologna as well (as to Rome, or the south, that is another issue, as it is discussed in the section on the implementation of the reform. I (LB) chose Genoa because I had visited the services before and felt great rapport with the one responsible for the catchmented community services, Prof. Antonio Slavich who, because of his past positions, is an excellent source of information. He had been a member of the original Gorizia group and coauthor of the books by Basaglia. Afterwards he moved to Ferrara, where he accomplished a well-known deinstitutionalization experiment; in 1978 he had been appointed to the directorship of the Mental Hospital of Quarto, one of two in Genoa.

In 1979 I had met Slavich and visited the services with a group of colleagues and nurses from South Verona. At that time we were setting up our service and visiting several sites known for their good community work in order to get ideas and experience. In Genoa we found a comprehensive and efficient organization and a mature working team with a high standard of expertise at both professional and paraprofessional levels. We participated in the weekly coordination meeting held at the headquarters. Observing these people going through all the intricacies of social support and community resources with the ease of the experienced, we were all very much encouraged.

THE VISIT

The Mental Hospital

The visit took place in midsummer 1987. My appointment with Prof. Slavich was arranged at his office, on the mental hospital grounds in Quarto, a nice residential suburb of Genoa. As I walk along the fence towards the gate, I am summoned by a female patient who asks me to buy some tobacco and cigarette paper at the drugstore across the street; she hands me some money, which turns out to be the exact amount for the purchase. Returning to her with the tobacco, I ask why she did not come out herself to buy what she needed (I know already that patients are welcome to walk around; they are discreetly checked by the nurse at the gate, who makes sure they dress and behave appropriately). "I am lazy," she states with genuine impudence, and leaves.

I meet Slavich at his office; he is as friendly and hospitable as ever. He is with a young assistant, Dr. Marco Lussetti, who is doing clinical work at the hospital and also studying biomedical statistics in Pavia (where there is a psychiatric case register, as in South Verona, and a tradition of studies in psychiatric epidemiology). I learn that they are trying to keep up with a great demand for statistical data in Genoa (I will come back to this issue later).

Slavich is the coordinator of psychiatric services of U.S.L. No. 16, and therefore he is responsible for the mental hospital as well, which is located in the territory. However, he is no longer director of the hospital, since the two positions were considered incompatible. He interprets this as a political decision of the administration in order to limit his power.

He rapidly updates me on the situation: Since 1980 there have been no new important initiatives; rather there has been, in his eyes, some regression. Alternatives to hospitalization have not been created yet and the work of deinstitutionalization at the mental hospital has slowed down to a large extent — or even reversed. In the first years of his mandate he had started a process of devoting the buildings which were made available by the discharge of patients to other social purposes. A new pavilion built in the mid '70s to house another ward had been transformed into a high school; empty wards had been recycled as a "social center" with a theater, serving both the patients of the hospital and the population. An amateur dramatic company as well as a ballet and a jazz group, had been given hospitality on the hospital grounds.

But in 1980, after a political change, a more conservative administration took over, which has maintained a legalistic attitude ever since, thus opposing these unconventional initiatives. Things worsened after the Cabinet decree of August 8, 1985 (the so-called "Craxi decree," from the name of the prime minister) which, in practice, brought about the division of health and social budgets. Psychiatry has become more medical since that law and social initiatives more difficult. The ballet company is likely to be removed soon, as well as the jazz center. The drama company left already. Instead, and for the same reason, the headquarters of the local U.S.L. were established on the hospital grounds, so part of the administrative personnel of the hospital (and of the budget for psychiatry) has been redirected to the administration of the U.S.L.

However, there are also positive outcomes of the situation: Because of the availability of buildings and valuable ground very conveniently located within the city, and the U.S.L.'s chronic need for money, the administration might accept an offer from the C.N.R. (the National Research Council), which wants to open a large research center in basic and applied sciences. The administration could sell part of the area to C.N.R., earning enough money to restore the remaining buildings, most of which require major work. It has been estimated that simply upgrading the electrical system in accordance with C.E.E. norms would cost 900,000,000 lire.

Some work is already in process: A ward is being restored and will provide decent and comfortable accommodations for elderly patients. Another building is being remodeled to become the day center for the surrounding territory. The work is worthwhile, since the position (a hilltop not far from the sea), the general layout, and architectural style of the hospital are quite good.

We take a little walk in the hospital, see the work in progress, and then stop at the bar. It has been run by the patients since the late '70s; service is not fast, but it is friendly and the atmosphere is nice. Today's cashier becomes a little disorganized, so another takes over, kindly, paying attention not to hurt his feelings.

We also go to visit the ballet company. Over the years, this group has become fairly well-known in Italy and abroad. They certainly worked hard, having restored the building they use practically by themselves. Between performances and tours they teach students. In exchange for the hospitality they give shows for the patients and do body work with them. They also give performances to attract the public to the hospital. These cultural anchors were an important ingredient of the deinstitutionalization process in the '70s, reflecting the efforts to bring the patients back to the things of normal life, including culture. Nowadays these things seem less fashionable and certainly do not fit the matter-of-fact contemporary attitude of many administrations.

In general Slavich regrets that there has been a gradual decrease of enthusiasm and involvement over the years, especially regarding the mental hospital, which presently has a rather poor turnover and is clearly becoming a deadend for the inmates. He says it was the administration's fault, but there are other reasons: The original group, with several representatives of Democratic Psychiatry, eventually was fragmented because of the assignment of people to different services, and lost momentum. Community services also have their flaws, adds he (as it will be discussed later). In general they tend to act more as outpatient clinics than as alternatives to hospitalization with around-the-clock accessibility.

We go to see two of the remaining eight wards. They are quite similar as to layout, organization, and kind of patients (wards accommodate patients according to catchment areas). Doors are kept locked most of the time, says Slavich, but our first trial contradicts him: The side door leading directly to the women's dormitory is, in fact, open. Inside female patients are loudly reciting the rosary, under the supervision of an elderly nun. The men's section is on the other side of the wing; the communicating door is usually open. People inside look like the usual Italian *manicomio* population. Most are geriatric, chronic patients; a significant proportion seems affected by psycho-organic conditions. The atmosphere is relaxed and the patients do not look heavily medicated. I ask Slavich about restraints and electroconvulsive therapy. He looks at me surprised: Neither has been used during the past 15 years; they had already been abolished when he was appointed director. In addition, none of the patients is involuntarily committed. "There is no overt violence," he says, "it is just a squalid place, poor in *active* therapeutic and caring interventions." An old lady, clearly demented, follows us, asking repeatedly to go outside. We ask the nurses about her; they say they have taken her out several times, but each time, when out, she asks, same style, to go back inside. More than half of the patients go out, some alone, some with the nurses. Slavich comments that the door could be easily kept open all the time, with just a nurse to check the passage; he is absolutely right.

Back in the director's office, I ask for more data about Genoa and the Liguria region in general; he has plenty of valuable information, which I report below. Slavich also hands me the mimeographed copy of a draft version of the famous CENSIS study, to which he contributed (CENSIS, 1985). I refer to it widely in the following paragraphs.

Sociodemographic characteristics of the region (ISTAT, 1986): Genoa is the capital of Liguria, a region located in northwestern Italy, a strip of land enclosed between the Mediterranean sea and the steep slopes of the Apennines, which separate the region from the Po valley. The overall population (1981 census) is 1,807,893, subdivided into four provinces corresponding to the four major cities: Genoa (pop. 1,045,109); Savona (pop. 297,675); La Spezia (pop. 241,371); and Imperia (pop. 223,738).

A maritime country since the Middle Ages (Genoa is the home town of Christopher Columbus), it went through a process of industrialization in this century. Now it is affected by the general industrial recession in Italy. Resident population is decreasing in both the city and the region: a decrease of 3.9% and 2.5% respectively between 1971 and 1981 censuses (the Italian population was increasing by 4.5% in the same period). Both the city and the region are well above the national average as to the mean population age and single person households, while the marriage rate is one of the lowest in the nation.

As to the occupational situation, the percentage of professional and self-employed workers is higher than the national average and the unemployment rate is slightly lower (8.5% vs. 10.6%); however, in the recent years, because of the recession, there has been a more substantial loss of jobs than in the rest of Italy. Indices of quality of life, such as annual per capita income and expenses, availability of public health services, and per capita medical and welfare expenses, are substantially superior to national averages. The suicide rate is also higher; however, there has been a decreasing trend in the most recent years. In brief, Liguria consistently presents the social characteristics of a developed and relatively wealthy region in comparison to the rest of Italy.

History of Services in Genoa and Liguria

Until the 1978 reform, Liguria was characterized by an uneven distribution of services. The two mental hospitals (the only ones in the region), Quarto and Cogoleto, were both in Genoa. Savona referred the patients to Cogoleto, while both Imperia and La Spezia referred their patients to institutions *outside* the region. Paradoxically, this may have favored the implementation of a consistent and balanced network of community services after the reform.

Although scarcely important* in a psychiatric system dominated by the mental hospital, Genoa may proudly affirm that a community service,

*The C.I.M. has always accounted for less than 5% of psychiatric costs.

the so-called *Centro di Igiene Mentale* (C.I.M.) was opened as early as 1929, the first in Italy to my knowledge.

As in all other regions, most of psychiatric work took place in the two mental hospitals. Quarto, initially opened in 1894, was enlarged and remodeled over the years; its last department was built in 1974. Cogoleto was built little after, during the first decade of this century.

Data on patients in the two mental hospitals are summarized in Figure 14.1. It can be noted that deinstitutionalization started late — more than five years later than in Italy at large. The process of deinstitutionalization started in a fairly usual way — following a scandal regarding the conditions of the inmates denounced publicly by the left wing parties. A popularly supported "health workers council," constituted of nurses, some doctors, and a few other paraprofessionals, was founded; it started to put pressure on the director and the administration (1971–1974).

In this atmosphere, the president of the province had an agenda approved forbidding the construction of new hospitals (note the coincidence with what happened in Arezzo) and favoring a community orientation for pro-

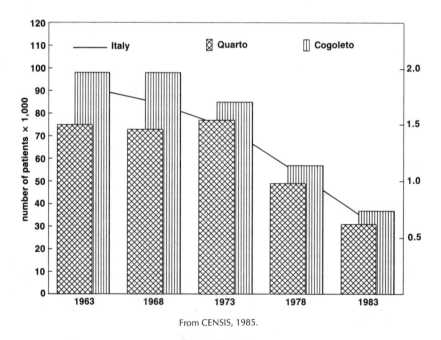

From CENSIS, 1985.

FIGURE 14.1
Number of State Hospital Patients on Census Day (1963–1983)
Italy (left scale) vs. Genoa (Quarto & Cogoleto, right scale)

spective services. A commission was nominated, with the participation of Dr. Franco Basaglia. As a provision of this commission, psychiatric services were reorganized. The territory was subdivided into 14 areas, each one referring to a specific ward and a therapeutic team within the hospital, in order to provide continuity of care.

In June 1975 elections of the communist and socialist parties were victorious. A leftist government was inaugurated and a communist psychiatrist was designated as councilor responsible for the health department. This gave momentum to the sectorial reorganization of the hospital and to the establishment of strongly democratic and egalitarian teams in the hospital. In the following period, the number of involuntary commitments decreased slightly and the number of patients in both hospitals steadily decreased; however, the number of admissions did not show any decrease because of the revolving-door phenomenon.

Teams followed the patients discharged in their own homes, facilitating the successful and permanent resettlement of a number of patients; moreover, there was no piling up of new chronics. However, as a consequence of the sectorial organization, the hospital remained the hub of any activity. The workers spent much more time in the hospital than in the territory, and no effort was made to start alternative services.

At the beginning of 1978, two new directors of the mental hospitals (one was Antonio Slavich), a number of doctors, professionals, and paraprofessionals were hired; many of them had experience in deinstitutionalization and community psychiatry. Then Law 180 was passed on May 13, 1978. Incidentally, one of key persons involved with the passage of the law, the Vice Minister of Health at the time, Bruno Orsini, was one of the head physicians of the mental hospital of Quarto.

The provinces of Liguria promptly issued regulations regarding implementation of Law 180. Eight hospital units, the *Servizi Psichiatrici di Diagnosi e Cura* (S.P.D.C.), as they are currently called, were planned, five of these in the province of Genoa (two in the two general hospitals of the metropolitan area). All the services had to be implemented by July 17, 1978; they had to be staffed with two doctors and 18 nurses each, using the personnel of the mental hospitals. By the deadline all the services were operational, a total of 105 beds. Readmissions to the mental hospitals was forbidden after December 31, 1979.

Community-based services (the so-called S.S.M.s: *Servizi di Salute Mentale*) were prescribed by the regional Law No. 45, 1978, issued soon thereafter. There should be 20 areas in the region (11 in the province of Genoa; 5 in the city), each served by its own community service, separated from the S.P.D.C., and therefore, with a different director and staff. However, community services would be preeminent as compared to the hospital services and related to them in a departmental way (this provision was never implemented); they would be also in charge of programs for the drug-addicts.

This regional law also implied a separation between the social and the mental health compartment, the municipalities being in charge of the first, the U.S.L.s of the second (Art. 17); services for the children, the elderly, the handicapped, etc., were assigned to the social compartment. This would produce serious shortcomings in the following years; in fact, while programs for the handicapped received attention and money and good alternative services for them were developed, such as home care and vocational rehabilitation programs, similar initiatives were not developed for the mentally ill. No housing program was ever developed; existing municipal contributions for lodging and subsistence to patients discharged from the mental hospital were gradually withdrawn; even subsidies were blocked at one time and restored only after difficult negotiations and individual, special certifications by the doctor in charge.

As to the staffing of the S.S.M.s, in general it was implemented as planned, with only few exceptions. Procedures for transferring the staff from the mental hospitals and other health agencies (drug addiction programs; preexisting community agencies) were implemented in a relatively brief time, and the new services were operational by October 1979. Open for 12 hours on working days, these services certainly reduced the initial burden on hospital units.

What about alternative facilities? In 1980 the regional government assigned 6.5 billion lire for their development (this money would *never* be spent).

In the meantime there was an important political shift. After the left was defeated in the 1980 elections, there was no longer a major political commitment for the implementation of social services. Besides, a period of political uncertainty followed, with four different persons responsible for the health department in five years.

Two important regional laws need to be mentioned: Both were passed in April 1983. One prescribed that the two mental hospitals would be transformed into nonmedical facilities; this allowed readmissions of previous hospital patients without going against the Law 180. This law was clearly a tricky compromise. However, the total number of patients admitted under this procedure is actually minimal, because of strict norms for its implementation. The other increased the number of beds in general hospital units to 135; the number of doctors was increased to four and the university psychiatric department was included among the S.P.D.C.s (however, to date, summer 1987, its involvement is only partial). As an effect of this increase in resources, the average length of stay in hospital units passed from five days to about 10–15 days.

The separation of the budget for health and social expenses was accomplished: this brought with it the danger of interrupting even the subsidies to patients discharged to the mental hospital and the users of the S.S.M., as mentioned before.

Any other need for planning was postponed to a future general regional plan for public health, a plan that was never issued. Therefore, the organization of psychiatric services was never fully accomplished. The most important problems were dealt with through ad hoc compromises. The continuation of efficient services, both hospital and community-based, was assured; however, there was no development of alternative services, and therefore the system remained only partially developed. Most important, in absence of a regional plan, the hiring of new personnel was impossible; it was only in 1985 that, given the obvious delay in planning, some hiring was permitted to U.S.L.s.

As to the attitude of the population: Given the general social orientation of the population of the region, the debate has never included reestablishing the mental hospital. In 1982, when a nationwide collection of signatures to request the full implementation of the Law 180 was launched, 14,000 were promptly collected in Liguria (only 10,000 were requested). In sum, even without brilliant innovations, the psychiatric system of the region in general, and of Genoa in particular, is unanimously considered as an efficient one: No serious problems are reported regarding the homeless, the accumulation of new long-stay patients, and cases of abandonment.

The Services

There are 20 U.S.L.s in Liguria; 11 in the province of Genoa, and 5 in the metropolitan area. Population served by each U.S.L. varies between 35,000 and 120,000 inhabitants.

There is one S.S.M. per U.S.L. Tasks involve coordination of all activities, including consultations, home visits, social work, training of workers, etc.; they are also in charge of the care and treatment of drug addicts. They may have peripheral sites, which generally work as part-time outpatient services. Usually open 12 hours a day on working days, they follow both new and old patients, with the basic goal of preventing admissions as far as possible. However, urgent interventions are made only for cases already known to the services. Crisis interventions for new cases go to the emergency room of the local S.P.D.C. The same applies when the S.S.M. is closed, at night and during weekends and holidays. There is no on-call service. The

S.S.M. provides consultations in the hospital(s), nursing homes of the catchment area, and the jail.

As to the drug addicts, generally a subgroup of workers deals specifically with them. The S.S.M. is expected to provide community care and psychological counseling to the drug addicts; it is also responsible for prescribing and monitoring methadone, which is provided in a hospital setting.

There are wide variations among services in the number of personnel. In general, in each S.S.M. in Genoa there are five to eight doctors, seven to twelve nurses, one to seven social workers, and one to three psychologists. In addition, there are counselors and teachers, varying in number between none and eight; there may also be administrative personnel (up to three) and a number of technicians and aides (two to six).

There are eight S.P.D.C.s, general hospital units (four in the province of Genoa; two in the metropolitan area). The one at the university psychiatric department is not officially operational yet; patients are already admitted, indeed, but only on a voluntary basis. The overall number of beds is 135. The staffing of each service includes four psychiatrists, and 18 nurses. The style is a medical one. They are generally locked facilities, with a prevailing diagnostic attitude and a psychopharmacological orientation. Average caseload per S.P.D.C. (data from two S.P.D.C.s in Genoa, 1983) consists of 466 voluntary admissions and 99 compulsory admissions; hospital days were 4,961, average length of stay 8.8 days, and average daily bed occupancy 13.6.

The state mental hospitals, officially transformed into *sociosanitary facilities* (May 1983) are part of U.S.L.s Nos. 8 and 16. Admissions of previous hospital patients are allowed after an accurate evaluation of the community service responsible. As of December 31, 1986, a total of 92 patients has been admitted this way; 36 of them are still in the hospital. In the course of 1986 the number of these admissions amounts to 31. Patients are accommodated in wards according to the area of origin. There is one ward that operates as a community for about 50 patients who have been discharged but are allowed to live on the hospital grounds as "guests." On December 31, 1986, there were 555 patients at Quarto, 730 at Cogoleto. As to the personnel, there are 16 psychiatrists, 261 nurses, and 101 aides at Quarto, and 15 psychiatrists, 343 nurses, and 84 aides at Cogoleto (Slavich, 1987).

As to alternative facilities, there are only a few—two day centers and a therapeutic community for addicts. Three more day centers are going to be opened soon. Private facilities are practically irrelevant, as to the number of beds. In addition, relatively few elderly mentally ill are admitted to nursing homes. Interestingly, two provinces, Imperia and La Spezia, still have chronic patients in institutions of other regions. There are also three private therapeutic communities, two of these in Genoa.

Site Visit to S.S.M.

Dr. Lussetti, who accompanies me in the visit, tells me on the way about the information system that is being implemented in the whole region. The *Istituto di Scienze Sanitarie Applicate* of the University of Pavia is in charge of the planning, implementation, and training of the personnel. Starting January 1, 1989, each U.S.L. in the region will be provided with a psychiatric register and one for the drug addicts. Although relatively late on the scene, Liguria can soon count on an excellent information system.

We visit the S.S.M. of U.S.L. 15. It is several miles from downtown, yet still within city limits. Genoa, constricted between the sea and the mountains, expands deeply along the valleys. Level ground is very limited in the city; this accounts for the chaotic development of modern Genoa and the chronic housing problem. The service is located in a large comfortable building which also houses a geriatric nursing home. We are half an hour late because of the traffic, but the primario, Dr. Luigi Ferrannini, and some of his colleagues have waited patiently.

The catchment area includes three town districts and 11 villages (200 to 3,000 pop.) scattered in the Trebbia valley, a mountainous district; there are, therefore, great differences in terms of needs and population characteristics within the area. This service is also in charge of drug addicts, as are the other S.S.M.s.

The personnel includes six M.D.s, two Ph.D.s, five social workers, and seven nurses, two aides, two counselors, and two administrative staff. Soon two more M.D.s, two Ph.D.s, two social workers, and seven nurses will be hired in order to staff the planned day center. A minority of professional staff comes from the mental hospital, but all nurses do. The primario and a significant number of workers have been there since the opening of the service in 1979; the team looks mature and well integrated. The service is open 12 hours a day, Monday through Friday, and six hours on Saturday.

In 1986 there were 10,900 contacts total: 9,255 with psychiatric patients and 1,645 with drug addicts. Of these, 284 with psychiatric patients and 20 with addicts were first contacts. The percentage of contacts with drug addicts was higher in the past; it was 30% in 1983, but has subsided ever since. About 550 psychiatric patients and 250 drug addicts are estimated to be in contact at any given time.

As to the site of interventions, about 60% of them are consultations at the S.S.M.; 10% are home visits; the rest are evenly distributed between the hospital, other residential facilities (nursing homes, the jail, a therapeutic community for drug addicts), and contacts with other agencies. Two beds are available at the S.S.M. for partial hospitalization during working hours. They are used for both psychiatric patients and drug addicts as needed, especially if i.v. treatment is considered. The planned day center will provide a therapeutic-community type of setting for six to ten young psychotics. Group psychotherapy and occupational therapy will be used in combination. Three sheltered apartments already exist and more are planned. Organizing a mobile crisis intervention team has been considered, but the idea of having several U.S.L.s share one is preferred (Ferrannini, 1987).

When an admission is necessary, the service refers patients to the psychiatric unit in the San Martino hospital, where there are 20 beds for U.S.L.s 13 through 16 (overall population: 380,000). Admissions are also possible at the university psychiatric department (40 beds) which, however, to date does not accept involuntary commitments. In 1986, 110 patients were admitted, of which 23 were involuntary commitments; 14 were initiated by the S.S.M. and 9 by the doctor on duty at the emergency room of the hospital. None was initiated in the territory independently from the S.S.M. Doctors always consult with the S.S.M. before making any decision about psychiatric cases. Drug addicts are referred to medical departments if they need to be admitted.

Medications seem to be used in moderate dosages: 3–6 mg. of haloperidol is considered a reasonable dose for a patient in an active psychotic episode. Only 15 patients are on depot neuroleptics. Lithium is rarely used. Patients are generally seen weekly. The style of therapeutic encounters seems to encourage a one-to-one, supportive relationship, with one eye on basic needs and the other on psychodynamic theory. Social interventions are used extensively; by the way, the primario and the others participating in the meeting demonstrated formidable expertise in welfare norms and regulations. Family therapy is also practiced, following a systemic model.

The personnel is divided into three teams, each being in charge of a subdivision of the territory. There is no separate team for the drug addicts, but some workers tend to see more of them than the others. The teams have a case-oriented meeting each week. A general, systems-oriented meeting is also held weekly. There are also a number of task groups on specific goals. Two private psychotherapists, a psychoanalyst, and a systemic family therapist, provide on-site clinical supervision once a week. They are paid for by the administration.

The impression is one of a well-staffed, well-organized service. The primario is active and enthusiastic; the same is true of anybody else I meet there. People share the feeling that they are doing a good job. Efforts are now directed to improving treatment of young psychotics and to offering more alternatives to hospitalization.

Costs

Data on costs were collected for the CENSIS study referring to three index years: 1972, 1977, and 1984. Sums were computed in terms of the 1983 value of the Italian lire. It must be mentioned that while data for 1972 and 1979 are fairly reliable, those for 1984 are not, because after the passage of the competences to the U.S.L.s expenses for psychiatric services were pooled with other medical expenses and so are not easily distinguished; another reason is the proverbial bureaucratic inefficiency of U.S.L.s, especially as to collecting and recording data. However, after some recalculations, 1984 data are considered realistic by the CENSIS researchers. Data available refer to the whole region.

Two things in Table 14.1 are especially noteworthy:

1. The two mental hospitals still consume 63% of the overall budget for psychiatry, in spite of the fact that their role is presently marginal, in that they house less than half (41%) of the patients they had in 1972, with practically no turnover. This happened for two reasons: First, the personnel is moving out of the hospital far more slowly than the decrease of patients (while the ratio staff to patients was 1 to 3 in 1974, it is 1 to 1.7 in 1984!), and second, the hospital maintains its costs because of general expenses, independently from the number of staff and patients.

2. The other important aspect is that, after the reform, there has been a *decrease* of expenses! This finding throws a completely new light on the implementation of the reform, which may account for the limits of the implementation itself. These two findings seem to be common all over the nation.

In sum, the reform was implemented in Liguria with monetary resources which were largely inferior to those of 1977 by as much as 10 billion lire (14% less)!

TABLE 14.1
Annual Expenses for Psychiatric Services
in Liguria

	1972	1977	1984
Total regional costs (*)	65.83	65.34	55.75
Mental Hospital costs (*)	48.06	49.75	35.20
% costs M.H.	73%	76%	63%

(*) in billions of lire (adjusted for inflation; 1983 = standard).
From CENSIS, 1985.

(Re)training of the Personnel

As in other regions, laws and resolutions, while stressing the importance of training and retraining, did not provide any practical direction; therefore, community services developed their own programs. There are two basic components of training: One is teamwork and clinical supervision within each team; the other is teaching and supervision provided by an expert from outside, contracted privately. The two principal areas of supervision are psychoanalysis and systemic family therapy. It must be noted, however, that those who attend are especially professionals, with nurses and paraprofessionals being involved to a lesser degree. However, starting in 1986, a regional series of continuing education seminars has been implemented successfully.

In addition, cooperation is developing with the university department of psychiatry, which in December 1983 was allocated funds by the region in order to provide training to the community services personnel. In turn, residents in psychiatry rotate through community services during their training period. These initiatives, however, are limited to community services, while the S.P.D.C.s and the two mental hospitals do not participate in them.

DISCUSSION

There are a number of problems in Genoa. One has to do with the lack of coordination between the S.S.M.s and he S.P.D.C.s and between the S.S.M.s and other social services, like those for the elderly and the handicapped and those for child psychiatry. In practice, however, social workers maintain communication and assure cooperation. Another problem regards the lack of an information system to date: even basic data required by law are often missing. As to single S.S.M.s, only one in Genoa and two in the whole region have a recording and information system on interventions and activities; therefore, an objective evaluation of the functioning of services is practically impossible. However, the situation is going to change in the near future, since an information system is being initiated in all U.S.L.s.

In conclusion, the situation of the region Liguria was rather peculiar at the time of the reform (May 1978): Out of four provinces, only one, Genoa, had a mental hospital and a public psychiatric system at all; with the reform, the three remaining provinces had to start practically from scratch. Within two years, thanks to enlightened administrations both at the regional and provincial levels and the professional competence and enthusiasm of a number of workers, a correct, comprehensive framework of community and hospital psychiatric services was laid out.

Because of a reforming attitude even before Law 180 in the city of Genoa, community services were rapidly developed, using personnel from those in the mental hospital. Within two years the transformation into community psychiatry was accomplished, each area having its own S.S.M., and S.P.D.C. of reference, and a section of the mental hospital.

However, since July 1979 there has been no further substantial growth. It is meaningful that no comprehensive set of norms has been issued by the region: because of a political change and the transfer of the administrative organization to single, mostly unprepared, and therefore inefficient U.S.L.s, there has been a lack of planning and a fragmentation of initiatives. This lack of growth is particularly evident in the fields of alternative residential facilities, training of personnel, and information systems.

Notwithstanding these shortcomings, the judgment on the services of Genoa is certainly positive. It shows that it is possible to implement the reform in a large city. It shows also that a standard network of relatively traditional psychiatric services (even without sophisticated alternative facilities) can provide a satisfactory level of community-based services.

CHAPTER 15

Utopia at Work: The Mental Health Service of Arezzo

AREZZO IS ONE OF THE WELL-KNOWN PLACES of Italian deinstitutionalization since the mid 1970s. It is presented here as an example of a model program where concern for developing alternatives for existing hospital patients matches that for the implementation of effective community services to prevent the institutionalization of new patients. The impressive results derive from at least three factors: the commitment of policymakers, the early opening of community services, and a constant commitment of mental health workers to both preventing and treating institutionalism. However, it must also be remembered that Arezzo is not an isolated example; there are several model programs like this in Italy, with a long tradition of deinstitutionalization and a good system of community services: Ferrara, Perugia, Reggio Emilia, Torino, Trieste, just to mention a few.

BACKGROUND

Arezzo is a city of 92,000 inhabitants in central Italy, about 100 km. from Florence. It has a beautiful medieval historical center, rich of monuments and rare paintings, like the frescoes by Piero della Francesca, in the church of the Franciscans.

For centuries it was basically an agricultural area, with relatively little industrial development; however, in the recent years, it has been characterized by a rapid development of the tertiary sector and presently the majority

(48.9%) of workers are employed in the service industries. Left wing parties have been in power for many years and have always had a strong commitment to developing good and efficient social services.

In 1969 the local government unanimously decided not to build a new state mental hospital and to devote "all the available resources to implement comprehensive mental health services in order to reduce admissions to the hospital and fight the psychiatric marginality" (Amm. Prov. Arezzo, 1974). Two years later, Dr. Agostino Pirella, a close coworker of Dr. Basaglia since the times of Gorizia, was appointed director of the psychiatric services of the province of Arezzo. He soon started a program of deinstitutionalization of the mental hospital and of developing alternative services in the community.

In 1972 the regional administration organized a conference on Mental Health: From the Marginalizing Institutions to a Community Organization of Social Security. The final resolution contained a number of enlightened recommendations.

1. No construction of new facilities which engender segregation, such as mental hospitals and special institutions for children, adolescents, and the elderly.
2. Immediate establishment of alternative community services for mental health, functionally integrated with the broader system of human services.
3. Gradual passage of institutional staff to the new community services.
4. There should be the possibility of using the general hospital for the acute phase of mental illness in close cooperation with community services. This implies "no psychiatric wards in general hospitals, but hospital-based services for the presenting needs."

The resemblance of these recommendations to the cornerstones of the 1978 reform is certainly impressive and shows the widespread influence of the deinstitutionalization movement.

TRANSFORMING THE MENTAL HOSPITAL

Changing the mental hospital implied removing physical barriers, modifying routines, and changing the roles, tasks, and competences of the staff. The unions were involved in this process and had an important part in promoting change.

Locked wards were opened one after the other, grates and nets were removed, and walls moved to allow freedom to patients. Seclusion rooms and restraints were abolished.

Nurses were encouraged to take the initiative and to participate fully in regular daily and weekly team meetings. Before this the education and status of psychiatric nurses were rather low — their task was to obey orders and follow rules and routines, without questions on creativity. The professional staff directed much effort to educating nurses, less by formal teaching than by setting examples and encouraging discussion and free communication of ideas and experience in meetings. General assemblies were started; staff and patients were encouraged to attend and freely express themselves in a spirit of democratic cooperation.

The workers started to get in touch with the families of chronic patients; relatives were invited to visit the patient any time they wished, while patients were taken to visit their families on a regular basis. The families as well as the community, were invited to attend social events given on the hospital grounds. In 1976 a cafeteria, run by the patients, was started on the hospital grounds. It was patronized not only by the patients but also by students and workers by the nearby community.

All these efforts to reestablish connections with the outside world resulted in active discharge of patients (Table 15.1). Two wards, cleared of patients, were remodeled and transformed into hostels.

At the end of 1974 two community mental health services (S.I.M., Servizio di Igiene Mentale) were started in the province: one in Arezzo, and one in Valdarno, another catchment area. The activities of these two services, covering about two-thirds of the population of the province, resulted in a dramatic decrease of admissions to the mental hospital: from 784 in 1975 to 649 in 1976 (see Table 15.1 and Figure 15.1). Later, three more community services were implemented, one per U.S.L.

As part of our study of model programs, I visited Arezzo in early 1987. The following is a recount of the visit.

THE VISIT

My colleague host, Dr. Franco Domenici, meets me at the train station. He is young, confident, and energetic and sounds, from the beginning, quite happy with his job and proud of it. However, he is free of any triumphal attitude, or even overtone, and describes the situation with a realistic and pragmatic attitude.

The "Manicomio"

We start our visit to the facilities "clockwise," from the old *manicomio*, which dates back to the early 1900s. The hospital lies in the flat — a nice,

TABLE 15.1
Mental Hospital Patients (1966–1976)

Year	Pts. on census day		Admitted in the yr.		1st admissions			Discharged in the yr.		Dead in the yr.	
	Tot.	Vol.*	Tot.	Vol.	Inv.**	Vol.	Tot.	Tot.	Vol.	Tot.	%
1966	720	—	446	—	190	—	190	413	—	35	4.8%
1967	701	—	406	—	124	—	124	407	—	43	6.1%
1968	695	1.4%	462	17.3%	131	70	201	418	16.0%	43	6.1%
1969	659	6.1%	570	44.7%	97	117	214	563	37.4%	45	6.8%
1970	646	10.5%	723	53.6%	92	162	254	691	53.8%	36	5.5%
1971	605	11.5%	657	60.5%	65	146	211	727	54.6%	36	5.9%
1972	497	14.0%	582	55.1%	35	45	80	633	47.3%	19	3.8%
1973	450	16.7%	527	56.3%	16	31	47	529	48.7%	8	1.7%
1974	423	31.7%	548	70.8%	16	49	65	577	60.3%	10	2.3%
1975	404	41.2%	784	76.9%	19	203	222	769	74.9%	12	2.9%
1976	377	48.9%	649	76.4	15	112	127	659	71.9%	9	2.3%

*Vol. = voluntary. **Inv. = involuntary.
From Amministrazione Provincialed: Arezzo, 1974.

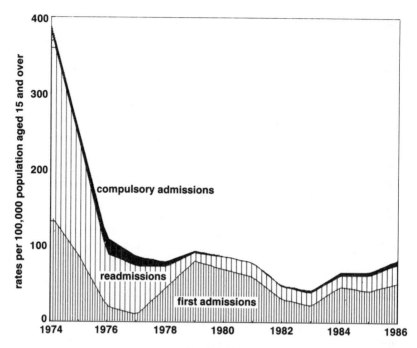

FIGURE 15.1
Admissions* to the Hospital for Mental Illness
Arezzo Catchment Area (1974–86)

*Unduplicated patients
Data from Corlito, Martini, Domenici, Cesari & Petrillo, 1987.

greenish area outside the mighty medieval walls that surround the city. The pavilions of the hospital lie in a park carefully designed in the "Italian garden" style; although clean and still cared for, it shows signs of some abandon—grass and bushes grow wild and flowerbeds are missing. The paintings of the buildings also reflect some decay. You can see patients around: Some are busy doing gardening or working with the cleaning squad; most are sitting around, doing nothing. However, they do not show any of the behaviors characteristic of chronic mental hospital patients, like begging for money or cigarettes or exhibiting mannerisms. They wear their own clothes and are conventionally groomed—in a word, they look like retired people relaxing in a park.

As of December 31, 1986, there were still 58 inpatients from the U.S.L. corresponding to the city of Arezzo. The overall number of patients still in the mental hospital, including those from other four U.S.L.s, was 120 at the same date. Dr. Domenici tells me that there are plans to complete the process of deinstitutionalization, moving the patients to their own families if possible, or to sheltered apartments, and recycling the buildings of the hospital for other social purposes. For 23 patients with serious disabilities, deemed in need of continuous care, accommodation in two hostels established in the community is being prepared.

A *Centro Sociale* (social center) is already housed on the hospital grounds, and an amateur theater company has been assigned a place; plans exist to accommodate a school and some apartments for the employees of the municipality. Using mental hospital buildings for other, nonpsychiatric purposes is common in the process of deinstitutionalization in Italy, following the tenets of *Psychiatria Democratica*: Stigma and marginality are lessened if physical barriers are removed and the hospital becomes *physically* part of the community at large.

We enter a ward housing patients from the city of Arezzo (patients are generally assigned to a ward according to their area of origin). The door is open, and there is no formal control. The patients in the ward are mostly elderly people who have physical problems and require continuing nursing assistance; this is the main reason why they are still in the hospital. Only a minority have functional psychosis and are waiting to be discharged to their families or to sheltered apartments. There is no sign of restriction to free movement or of excitement or anger.

We talk to the psychiatrist in charge, who gives us some information about the ward. There are 20 nurses on the staff; they cover the shifts in the ward and are also available for providing shifts in the general hospital when necessary. In fact, in Arezzo there is no psychiatric unit in the general hospital, and mental patients are admitted to beds scattered in other departments; shifts of psychiatric nurses are organized only if needed, as happens in the case of an involuntary commitment. In this way, all the nurses are available for community work unless needed for the shifts, and admissions are more thoughtfully planned.

We move on to see one of the two wards which operates as *casa albergo* (hostel). People housed here are not considered as patients, but as guests who have not yet found a place to live on their own. They have been officially discharged and therefore have the freedom to come and go as they wish. The level of supervision is relatively low.

We are escorted by Maria, a nurse who has been working here since the beginning of the deinstitutionalization in the early '70s. She voices regret that plans to discharge residual patients are going slowly because alternatives are not presently available. However, this problem concerns only the province, since downtown Arezzo has good alternative residential facilities. Patients here usually share a room or have one to themselves.

Maria asks a woman patient who passes by to show her room to "the two doctors who came to visit the hospital." The patient seems flattered and greets us with enthusiasm. She has a single; the room is clean and kept with care. Maria compliments the patient, who cares for the room by herself. The donated furniture is not typical hospital style, but rather, the traditional style of popular furniture of the early 1900s. The patient likes artificial flowers and has many in the room, as well as old snapshots and a variety of souvenirs and memorabilia. The overall result is a very personalized room. The patient plays shy when we compliment her.

Then Maria suggests that we visit the "room of the assembly," impressive for a huge fresco on the wall. General assemblies, one of the innovations introduced by the movement in the mental hospitals, became the symbol of the democratization of the asylum; they were considered a very important component of the process of deinstitutionalization, in that they encouraged mental patients to participate in the social life and in important decisions. Although initially modeled on the therapeutic community, they differed in that participants were encouraged to question the basic tenets of institutional psychiatry, including those relating to roles and power, admissions and discharges, medications and privileges, etc. The goal was to get the patients to become more involved, critical, and assertive regarding their own destiny.

It is time to go; we thank Maria, leave the ward, and go outside. On the way to the exit of the hospital, Dr. Domenici shows me the greenhouse, kept by an independent cooperative of patients. Another cooperative cleans the hospital, as well as other public buildings in town. Cooperatives have been used extensively to offer jobs to ex-mental patients, who could not find regular jobs given the shortage of positions for unskilled workers in town, as well as in the whole nation.

The Team Meeting

It is almost 1 p.m. and we have to rush to the S.I.M., the headquarters of the service, to attend the staff meeting. The S.I.M. is conveniently located downtown, in the old city, in a building that houses also other social services.

When we arrive the meeting has already started and the staff are in the middle of a volatile discussion regarding the case of an old woman who lives in a nursing home run by a religious order and was referred to the service a week earlier for a condition of serious manic excitement. The service is currently offering a day program to this woman and has succeeded, so far, in having the nuns of the nursing home provide intensive assistance overnight – this in order to avoid a hospitalization.

The old woman is picked up at the nursing home early in the morning by a worker of the service and brought to the day center for evaluation and treatment. She is currently on medications, dosage is monitored daily because of her age and physical conditions. After that she is in charge of two young female nurses who have been assigned to her; she is taken around on errands, brought to see some relatives, and taken wherever she wants to go. Her requests have always been very reasonable, and she seems to enjoy very much having her wishes met so nicely. She takes her meals at the day center, where a bed is also available for her to sleep in the afternoon.

She has been treated like that for a week and she is slightly improved, but the problem now is that the nuns feel overburdened and have said they will not stand the situation much longer. Now the question is what to do for the nights to come, since the episode is likely to last for a while. The first, obvious, alternative is to admit her to the hospital, i.e., to a medical department of the general hospital, since, there is no psychiatric ward, but this would just displace the problem: The woman would be a burden for the night shifts in the hospital and it is likely that soon the internal medicine colleagues would require that psychiatric nurses be deployed on the night shifts to deal with her. Another alternative would be to have the woman sleep in the bed located in the day center, cared for by a special night shift organized for the occasion. This would avoid the hospitalization, although a psychiatric shift would still be required. This is the final choice, if things do not get better soon.

Then they move to talk of other cases. They are especially worried about a few young, first-break psychotics whom they fear may become chronic. After striving so intently to rescue people from chronicity, they are very sensitive to this risk. The nurses involved seem competent, active, and autonomous.

The social workers then take over, speaking of a number of chronic patients who are housed in the apartments. I get the impression of an extremely complex network of services and interventions that provides first-class practical and social support, as well as professional care, for the chronic mentally ill.

The Sheltered Apartments

At the end of the meeting, Franca, a social worker, takes us to see the sheltered apartments. This is a group of eight apartments located in two adjoining buildings in a residential area of the city; they accommodate 36 patients. Other patients, who are more independent and live on their own, with a low level of supervision, are housed in 10 apartments scattered around the city. Franca explains that there is an agreement between the S.I.M. and the administration of public housing, so that 5% of the apartments are reserved for mental patients at reduced rent.

Upon arrival we meet one of the cleaning women, who has just finished her job. She is part of a cooperative, which has a contract with the S.I.M. for work six hours a day in the apartments. They do the rooms, clean the apartments, fix lunch, iron, mend, etc.; they also supervise the patients and involve them in house activities for the purpose of rehabilitation. There are also two nurses of the S.I.M. in charge of the apartments, who work there practically full-time — one in the morning and one in the afternoon.

We visit all the apartments and meet almost everybody. The patients look, in general, rather seriously disabled. I have the impression that most of them are as ill as those seen in the mental hospital and that it requires all that organization and a lot of professional skill and staff personal involvement to keep them out of the hospital.

Franca introduces us to a middle-aged male patient and explains that this will be a great day for him. In the afternoon they are going together to town to rent a violin. Talking with a relative a few days before, Franca discovered that the patient, Vladimiro, used to play the violin when he was young. She suggested that he try again, that he rent one, take some lessons and, if he does OK, buy one. Vladimiro agreed, and Franca also found a teacher, but now he is full of excuses — he will not make it, he is ashamed in front of others, etc. Franca is extremely supportive and patient with him, but also inflexible: They will go for sure, she says, after the guests have gone: "Next time the doctors come, you will be able to play a serenade in their honor." Vladimiro nods with a dubious smile, just to please Franca, but I bet they will go. She is quite determined, smart, and understands the patients; obviously, they just adore her.

The Sheltered Workshop

Piero, the coordinator of the workshop, a jovial and energetic man in his forties, welcomes us warmly and shows us his creatures, the wooden animals that are manufactured in the workshop. He has designed them all and contrived a production procedure that can be used by these seriously disabled patients. With pride he tells us that he always carries paper and pencil with him to capture momentary inspirations. He used to be a nurse in the hospital, in charge of "ergotherapy" (work therapy). As an effect of deinstitutionalization he was given responsibility to start the workshop; he has been in charge of it for 10 years now, but he is still a nurse. He does not resent that; he likes his job, the patients, and the freedom of creativity. He certainly shows a lot of talent and ingenuity.

The patients are actually members of the workshop, which is, legally speaking, a corporation, and share the profits: 30 million lire (approximately $24,300.) in the past year for 10 full members and five apprentices. This is not much, but all members have disability pensions and either live with their families or receive room and board from the S.I.M. They look very disabled, except for two who do most of the work and help with the others. There is a second nurse to help Piero.

Next door there is a weaving workshop, with even more handicapped patients. The two nurses there have hard time just trying to encourage social interaction, while production seems really unattainable.

We do not have time to visit the second floor, where there is a day center for 10 retarded adolescents. To my surprise I hear that in Arezzo no youngster is hospitalized for mental retardation or permanently admitted to a special institution. All live with their families. This is the result of a comprehensive and integrated system for children and adolescents that has a long-lasting tradition of stressing family involvement and psychosocial components, while minimizing medical aspects. Purposely, there is no child psychiatrist on the staff — only psychologists, social workers, and rehabilitation therapists (20 staff total).

The *Primario*

We then move on to meet the *primario* (head) of the S.I.M., Dr. Paolo Martini. He is in his forties, a person of exquisite manners who inspires respect and confidence at first glance. His staff admire him very much for his humanity, experience, and dedication and regard him as their undisputed leader.

Martini's grandfather was the director of the state mental hospital of Macerata (another city in central Italy); his father was the deputy director of the Arezzo mental hospital and lived with the family on the hospital grounds, as it used to be in those times. Consequently, this third generation doctor learned about psychiatry from an early age. He participated in the deinstitutionalization of Arezzo's psychiatric services right from the beginning, in 1971, and has been the head of the S.I.M. since its opening in 1974.

He likes to speak of the services. In spite of the high standard of community services he is not satisfied; his constant concern is quality of care. He thinks they need to develop more specific rehabilitation programs and techniques and strategies of community intervention for the new cases, especially for young psychotics. They are also presently involved in implementing data collection, for research purposes and in order to have a better system of evaluating the services.

SOME DATA

In Arezzo years of commitment to favoring community care instead of hospitalization are reflected in a rather low rate of admissions. In 1986 there were 77 (general) hospital admissions (72 voluntary, 5 involuntary) in the

Arezzo catchment area (including the city and five small towns, for an overall population of 116,087, with 94,833 aged 15 and above). In the last ten years there has been a substantial decrease in the hospitalization rate (Figure 15.1). Even more striking are data regarding involuntary commitments: The *overall* number of commitments since the 1978 reform is 25, with an annual rate of 2.9 per 100,000 adult population!

Total one-year psychiatric prevalence rate was 1,381 in the calendar year 1986 (1,265 average in the years 1981–1986), slightly higher than those reported by some other Italian psychiatric registers: South Verona (1,218), Portogruaro (712) (Tansella & De Salvia 1986), and Lomest-Pavia (818) (Marinoni et al., 1983). One-year prevalence has increased over the years (898 in 1976; 1,052 in 1980; 1,381 in 1986), probably as an effect of increased comprehensiveness, visibility, and accessibility of the services. The rate of cases "new to the register" was 445 in 1986, also higher than those reported from the aforementioned Italian registers. *No new long-stay patients are reported.*

Total number of interventions in 1986 was 65,990 (see Figure 15.2). As to

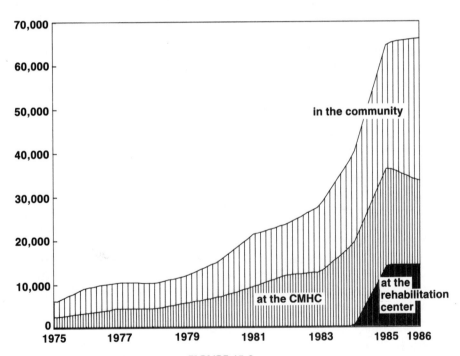

FIGURE 15.2
Arezzo Mental Health Service (1975–86)
Number of Interventions per Year

the site of interventions: 19,044 took place at the S.I.M.; 22,100 were home visits; 2,642 were interventions at the general hospital; 8,104 took place in other social services and institutions (Corlito et al., 1987). Besides the high total number of interventions, the high proportion of interventions in the community is worth mentioning. The impressive number of home visits results from the fact that practically all long-term active patients living in the territory are monitored daily. Arezzo ranked first in home visits in the 1984 C.E.N.S.I.S. national survey.

The staff of the S.I.M. includes 9 psychiatrists, 20 nurses, 4 social workers, 2 psychologists; there are 10 rehabilitation therapists and 3 more nurses working in the sheltered workshop; 38 nurses work in the mental hospital.

IN CONCLUSION

It seems that the present situation continues a long tradition of deinstitutionalization, which keeps Arezzo among the sanctuaries of the Italian psychiatric renewal. The original policy of minimizing medical and institutional aspects of psychological and psychiatric interventions for both children/adolescents and adults has been pursued consistently over the years and has produced impressive results in limiting the number of patients in institutions and the number of admissions to the general hospital. The choice of not having a psychiatric unit is also very attractive, in that it leaves personnel available for other purposes and spurs the workers' ingenuity in finding alternative solutions.

CHAPTER 16

The Gown Meets the Town: The South Verona Community Psychiatric Service

ASSUMING RESPONSIBILITY FOR A TERRITORY

THE WORKERS OF THE INSTITUTE OF PSYCHIATRY of the University of Verona agreed with the spirit of Law 180 from the outset. They offered to assume responsibility for the implementation of the law in one of the districts of Verona. This decision implied tackling the difficulties of community psychiatry and giving up some of the privileges of an academic institution (such as *choosing patients*), while keeping up with university duties (teaching and research).

Italian university psychiatric departments had always been relatively separate from the public mental health system and were regarded as elite facilities having mainly teaching and scientific purposes. They generally treated the acute, less severe cases, on a voluntary basis only. Serious psychotics, long-term patients, chronic recidivists, and all involuntary commitments went to the state hospital. Many of them are still like that; unfortunately, only about half of the 27 university departments are reported to have assumed responsibility for a catchment area, since the psychiatric reform recommended, but did not enforce, their involvement. This situation continues to impede the implementation of the reform, as insufficient numbers of personnel (especially psychiatrists) receive hands-on community training.

There is another reason for the relative isolation of university departments in the recent past: The academic status of psychiatry was neither solidly grounded nor autonomous until very recently. In Italy the divorce of psychiatry and neurology was slow and difficult and occurred much later than in the U.S. The first university psychiatric departments, detached from neurology departments, were not founded until the 1960s. Thus, it was not until the late 1960s that psychiatry became a separate, *albeit still optional*, teaching course in Italian medical schools. The progressive separation of psychiatry and neurology that had begun in the '60s became official university policy in 1976, in conformance with the European Economic Community standards. These standards, issued in 1975, were required for all its members so that the teaching of physicians would be similar throughout Europe. This was felt to be necessary as a quality control measure, since the E.E.C. allows free movement of physicians between member states.

The psychiatric department of the University of Verona, established in 1970, consisted of 36 beds located in the *Policlinico*, the medical center of the School of Medicine, a general hospital of about 1,000 beds total. The activity was in the typical Italian university psychiatric department mode: Admissions either came from a waiting list or were requested by the emergency room of the hospital (the only agency of the province of Verona— 750,000 pop. —offering psychiatric crisis intervention). Therefore, patients admitted were usually either people in an acute crisis or those expecting a "university level" of care (i.e., more "sophisticated" than that offered by standard public services). A number of cases would come from far away.

Patients deemed dangerous to themselves or others were not allowed on the department, but had to be sent, usually involuntarily, to the 1,000-bed state hospital some 10 miles from Verona. Former state hospital patients were admitted, but, given the characteristics of the department (many requests for admission, short length of stay and rapid turnover, restrictions about dangerousness), the serious and chronic ones were almost always referred to the state hospital.

Inpatient care was the primary treatment modality offered. However, over the years, as a result of a policy actively pursued by the team, inpatient care gradually decreased and outpatient care expanded: At the end of 1977, the mean number of occupied beds was less than 15 out of 36 available. This meant discouraging admissions from far away, as the team felt more and more that unless outpatient follow-up was available they could not live up to the expectations of persons who sought this "special" university care.*

Several factors were involved in the development of this new policy. All

---

*The group had already developed the idea that admission to a hospital, however sophisticated the treatment might be, reinforces regression and dependency, so that, all in all, outpatient care (or hospitalization as short as possible and outpatient care) is *always* preferable. If not feasible, it *should* become feasible.

staff members shared an interest in the psychosocial approach and were motivated to improve the quality of care, the effectiveness, and the integration of the service. Several members engaged in training in psychotherapy (especially systemic family therapy); a psychiatrist (one of the authors: LB) spent a year studying and working with the Soteria Project in Palo Alto, California. In addition, there was a strong interest and a commitment to the ideas of deinstitutionalization as they were spreading in Italy in those years. Close contact was maintained with colleagues active in deinstitutionalization and leading representatives of the movement for psychiatric renewal were invited to be faculty members in the residency curriculum. Site visits involving both professionals and nurses were made to those places where deinstitutionalization was progressing.

In 1976, when the region Veneto (equivalent to a state in the U.S.) presented a plan to introduce a new system of psychiatric care based on psychiatric wards in general hospitals, the Verona psychiatric department opposed the plan, in the belief that it would simply add psychiatric beds to those existing in the large state hospital, without taking into account the great need for outpatient and community facilities. Instead, the staff issued a list of alternative recommendations that was sent to administrators, colleagues, and newspapers. In the end it was recommended that multiprofessional teams in charge of *all* psychiatric needs for their territory be established throughout the region. Existing beds were to be used while alternative services were developed. Another recommendation was that no psychiatric wards should be opened until an evaluation of the per capita need for general hospital psychiatric beds was performed *after* the community teams and services had been established.

Because of these recommendations, the plans to open general hospital wards were dropped. The South Verona staff also formally asked the administrators to be assigned a catchment area, but the request was never answered. This action, taken as a resolution of the *whole* group—from the department chairman (A. Balestrieri) to the junior nurses—strengthened the group itself and gave momentum to thinking and acting "alternative," i.e., community-oriented.

In 1976 the staff began making family visits in teams of two or three people to provide on-the-spot crisis intervention in an attempt to avoid hospitalization. Also, crisis intervention at the emergency room was intensified. The psychiatrist on duty was helped by a nurse of the team, who would participate in the assessment and would then insure continuity of care. The door of the ward was kept always open; if very disturbed patients were admitted, efforts were made to minimize limitations to personal freedom by offering extra personal care—one or two workers remaining with such patients for extended periods of time and accompanying them on errands within the hospital, to the bar, etc., sometimes outside — before allowing the door to be locked.

At the beginning colleagues of other departments were not very happy about having mental patients roaming relatively freely in the hospital. Usual stereotypes were voiced: "There are children and impressionable sick patients around" and the like. Every single episode was addressed with tact and firmness and meetings were organized to explain the determination of the psychiatric team to go beyond custody; unions were also successfully involved in supporting these ideas.

> Mario, 44, is a chronic schizophrenic who lives with his elderly father and an elderly uncle. Since home is quite boring and rather depressing, he likes to take long walks all over the city. One of his favorite spots is the railroad station, where he contributes as a false positive (in fact he *does have* a house and a family) to the overall number (very small, though) of the homeless-type guys. He goes there when he needs to get a coffee for free, by asking people in a very polite and captivating way. He is very visible because of an idiosyncratic gait: he walks with his body straight, but leaning backwards at an impossible angle, as if the law of gravity did not apply to him. He is admitted, from time to time, for intervening precipitating factors.
>
> After the opening of the doors he was the very first to venture into the corridors of the hospital and it took only a few minutes for somebody to accompany him back to the unit, asking if he was "one of yours." The answer was yes, and that it was OK if he walked around. The person looked quite puzzled.
>
> People in the hospital got accustomed to him, since he is a very polite person. He then ventured to visit the departments. Nothing happened until he went to the pediatric department, wearing a doctor's overall he had put on upon entering the department following a group of students. He had gone there just because he was visiting *all* the departments, but the colleagues did not like it and built up a case. Suspicion was voiced that he might be a pederast, and a formal complaint was made to the director of the hospital. The detail about the overall increased the suspicions.
>
> A meeting of the professional colleagues, a representative of the nurses, and the director of the hospital was called, to explain that Mario neither had sexual perversions nor was dangerous. It was hard, though, to calm the colleagues down, since these are very resistant stereotypes. The nurse representative, a union activist who had a sincere interest in the movement for psychiatric renewal and had participated to a number of our meetings, was very helpful in supporting our stance. They finally seemed reassured, but nonetheless required that he not go there again. Mario easily agreed to that and refrained from roaming in the departments from then on.
>
> Presently an incident like that is rather unlikely to occur, because the aforementioned stereotypes have *changed* over the years as a simple effect of time and habit.

It is apparent that the South Verona service had begun applying the principles of the psychiatric reform law well before its passage in May 1978.

Hence, when the psychiatric reform passed, the decision to become part of the public system by assuming responsibility for a catchment area was taken unanimously, without hesitation.

Once given responsibility for a geographically defined area, the South Verona Community Psychiatric Service had to provide the full range of psychiatric interventions for the adult population (14 years and above), including involuntary commitments, long-term care, rehabilitation, etc. Because of the known adverse effects of hospitalization, especially as to the risk of chronicity (as it has been extensively reported in the literature, e.g., Test & Stein, 1978c), first priority was to avoid, or at least minimize, hospitalization. A rapid saturation of the 15-bed unit was also feared.

At the time no community programs existed in the territory, so a day program was started and temporarily located on the inpatient unit. The staff was divided into three working teams, each responsible for a subdivision of the territory. This division was made in order to maximize the possibility of continuity of persons involved with a client. Crisis intervention was stressed further, by offering prompt interventions to acute needs.

In 1980, the Community Mental Health Center was founded, which has been operational ever since; it underwent successive changes over the years, as expected, because it is meant to be a flexible tool to meet the needs of the users at any given time (Faccincani et al., 1985). Its inauguration was celebrated with a series of conferences on public mental health held in the community theater, an exhibition on the state hospital at the Mental Health Center, and various meetings with different categories of citizens in order to illustrate the purposes of the new center. The celebration had its climax during a popular festival, in the park next to the Mental Health Center. It was organized in collaboration between the institute, local health authorities, the municipality, and volunteer organizations. Stands of refreshments and handicrafts were set up in the park; during the two days of the festival jugglers and actors took turns performing in the park and repeatedly moved on, in a parade, to the streets. Some 3,000 people participated, and the festival had a vast resonance in the city. The theme of the festival—"overcoming the mental hospital"—was given added significance by a geographical coincidence: The Community Mental Health Center and the park were on the grounds of the former Verona state hospital, an asylum constructed at the turn of the century. The hospital had moved to new buildings in the mid '60s and since then the area, a beautiful land rich in age-old trees, has been used for the medical school, the C.M.H.C., and the park; presently a number of human services and facilities for the elderly are being constructed, thus accomplishing the metamorphosis of the area.

In 1980 two apartments were assigned to the service. However, a project of starting a small community alternative to hospitalization has been hampered by a shortage of nurses; it has been implemented only very recently. The apartments have been used so far to accommodate patients who are in need of temporary housing for whatever reason, but do not need supervision overnight.

THE SOUTH VERONA AREA

Verona is a city of about 260,000 population, located in northeast Italy, halfway between Milan and Venice, in the region called Veneto (capital city: Venice; Figure 16.1). Traditionally an agricultural town, its economy has developed rapidly (manufacturing industry, commerce, and tourism) in the last few years. As to health services, the city is divided into three catchment areas. The South Verona area consists of three suburban districts and three small rural communities in the southern outskirts of the city. Resident population is 75,000; it increased by immigration in the 1950s and 1960s because of industrial development, but has been stable ever since. It is a middle- and working-class neighborhood; medical personnel and students are also represented because of the medical school (established in 1969). Social structure is relatively solid, based on lasting family bonds (even with the extended family); social services are adequate. Some sociodemographic characteristics are listed in Table 16.1.

FIGURE 16.1
Northern Italy

TABLE 16.1
South Verona Sociodemographic Characteristics

Area (in square Km.)	75.75
Population (Dec. 31, 1981)	74,852
Mean population density (pop./sq.Km.)	988.1
Age (% of total population)	
<14 years	18.9
14–64 years	69.9
>65 years	11.2
Employed population by economic sector	
Agriculture	2.6%
Industry	32.9%
Services	64.5%
Rate of unemployment	6.5%*

*Data provided by the Provincial Office of Labor, Verona.

STAFF, FACILITIES AND SERVICE ORGANIZATION

The permanent staff assigned to South Verona includes nine psychiatrists, three psychologists, three social workers, and 24 psychiatric nurses. There are also, at any given time, 13 psychiatric residents (they work full-time and on average stay two years* and four to six medical students in training, who attend the service for four months on a rotation basis, and a variable number of volunteers. Professional staff are also engaged in teaching and research, so, for example, three of the eight psychiatrists do only limited clinical work. Staff members are divided into three multidisciplinary teams, each referring to a subsector of the catchment area (Figure 16.2).

With the exception of 10 nurses who cover the three round-the-clock shifts in the hospital unit, all staff work in both the intramural and the extramural programs. In other words, the *same* personnel staff *all* the programs ("single-staff" module) within and outside of the hospital. Also, the aforementioned nurses of the unit are assigned to the three teams, involved in case discussions during team meetings, and encouraged to do some community work, when possible, according to their shifts.

The South Verona Community Mental Health Service offers the following programs (Zimmermann-Tansella et al., 1985):

*Differently from their American colleagues, residents are not paid. A law to offer residents paid positions was presented to the parliament some time ago, but nothing has been done to date. However, given the excess of doctors in Italy and the shortage of positions, it is unlikely that a regular job can be found for three to five years after getting the medical degree. For the same reason, i.e., the excess of doctors, competition for residencies is fierce; therefore, residents are ready to do anything. Here is an example of the impact of general, social and professional factors on the organization of services and work characteristics.

- *Community Mental Health Center*, open six days a week, from 8 a.m. to 8 p.m. This facility is used in different ways: as a day hospital for chronic patients, as a walk-in center, as a place where staff meet and extramural interventions are planned and coordinated. It is considered the main facility of the service.
- *Psychiatric unit*, an open ward of 15 beds located in the university medical center (about 1,000 beds total).
- *Outpatient department*, which provides consultations, individual and family therapy. No group therapy is presently available, but there have been groups in the past.
- *Home visits and other extramural interventions*; these are made by all staff members in reply to emergency calls and for follow-up purposes and long-term care. The latter have proved very useful to *prevent* relapses of chronic patients and hence reduce the frequency of rehospitalization. Visits to known "high-risk" patients are planned in advance and offered on both a regular and an as-needed basis, so as to provide continuing support and care to our most difficult patients and their families.
- *Psychiatric emergency room*, part of the casualty department of the

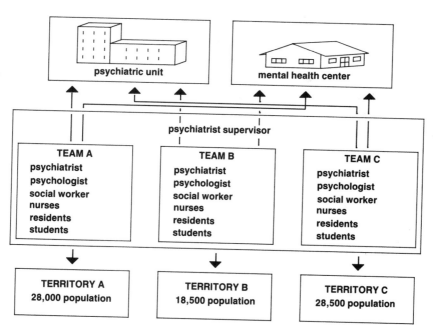

FIGURE 16.2
South Verona Community Psychiatric Service

medical center. During working hours the psychiatrist on duty is usually assisted by a member of the team, who is (or will become) responsible of the patient requiring the emergency intervention; this is done in order to extend the practice of therapeutic continuity to persons to the emergency room.

- *Psychiatric consultation-liaison service*, providing consultations for patients and doctors of other departments of the hospital.
- *Residential facilities.* Two apartments are available for up to six people who do not need supervision overnight. Two other apartments house a therapeutic community; it started on November 1, 1987 with three patients and can accommodate up to eight people. It is for disabled "veterans" who are unable to live independently and who either do not have a family or cannot, for whatever reason, live with their families. Although it is intended as a transitional accommodation, permanent stay is accepted if the patient does not have a more appealing alternative.

Transitional work opportunities are provided by two public sheltered workshops in town and a number of other initiatives run by charitable organizations and self-help groups. Some of these also offer residential accommodations. This is a rapidly expanding sector in Italy, filling the gap of public services with regard to transitional settings. These initiatives are usually supported and controlled by public administrations so that the risk of their becoming profit-oriented and exploitative seems, at least presently, rather low. Patients in need of housing may be temporarily accommodated in hotel rooms, paid for by the U.S.L.

A cooperative, paid for by the municipality, provides supporting persons at home to help the disabled and their families in tasks like cleaning, cooking, shopping, etc. Several South Verona mental patients receive this kind of service. The same cooperative provides job opportunities for those patients whose work incapacity is not too serious, yet serious enough to handicap them in these times of high unemployment rate. A gardening cooperative for more disabled mental patients is on the drawing boards.

PRINCIPLES OF INTERVENTION

The general goals of the South Verona community service are those of community psychiatry at large (Sabshin, 1966; Weston, 1975), i.e., assuming full responsibility of the psychiatric needs of the population in terms of prevention and rehabilitation, as well as treatment. In addition, the service believes its principal responsibility is to the *more disturbed and disturbing* individuals, to whom it attempts to provide care in the least restrictive environment, i.e., with a minimum use of the hospital. This is directly related to the lack of a state hospital backup after the Italian reform; thus, community services are really "alternative" rather than "complementary or additional to mental hospitals"(Tansella & Williams, 1987).

There is a commitment to meet the needs of the users according to the principles detailed in Chapter 3. As already mentioned there in the section on "interpreting the request," symptoms are regarded as messages conveying relevant information about needs that are not being met. Professional work is intended as going beyond a psychological interpretation to recognize and address the underlying needs — *all* the needs.

For example: Tiziana, a 45-year-old widow, who has a child of 17 with severe, multiple handicaps (physical and mental), was admitted several times in the past to the mental hospital for episodes of severe depression. Her way of expressing discomfort is through a very annoying, tenacious complaintfulness. Because of this, and also because of her sticky, total dependency, she tends to alienate others, including mental health workers. This is a basic problem in dealing with her.

At a first level of analysis, one may notice that Tiziana shows a "morbid" need for attention and dependency. In the authors' experience, a perverted expression of needs is *always* a consequence of a chronic, severe frustration of those needs, especially in an institutional setting. One has also to keep in mind the so-called "pathoplastic" effect of institutions: excessive dependency and demands represent a true "transference neurosis" towards the institution or a "reimbursement syndrome."

The authors have found that it is absolutely useless to stick to this level of analysis. All this may sound trivial; however, unfortunately, such patients most often tend to be judged negatively and their needs given a bad connotation, i.e., labeled with negative psychopathological terms — dependent, hysterical, immature, etc. — which on many occasions are used as pseudo-scientific euphemisms to describe patients with unpleasant characteristics.

One has to get control of the team countertransference and identify a second level of needs, where the person's fundamental, existential needs emerge. Tiziana, in the course of her life, was always trying to get the *minimum vital allowance* of affection and support, in addition to more basic needs like food, transportation, and the like, which she needs especially when she is regressed. She has no family to support her and the handicapped child is only a source of guilt. She loses motivation, and does not look after the house. When the degree of mess becomes unbearable, she gets extremely anxious and disorganized.

The intervention consists of accepting her need for regression without being judgmental but, at the same time, without encouraging it either — a difficult task for a psychiatric team, but the only therapeutic one. For instance, Tiziana prefers to come to the center for lunch, just to be with people and also to avoid the bother of preparing her meal. At a first, superficial level of analysis, Tiziana is just lazy and stingy (she does not want to spend money on food). This issue is discussed with her, and an agreement is reached on which day she may come to the center. On the other days she *is helped to fix lunch at her place*, by a worker, who also makes sure that she keeps the house reasonably clean. When she feels better, she has much more initiative and needs neither help nor encouragement. In the authors' opinion, it is always wrong to *push* passive patients; one has to *pull* them or, better yet, *accompany* them to do things.

Most of the time, an effective approach to community work requires that clinical, psychological, and concrete resource issues be equally addressed and integrated.

Mariella, 27, had four admissions in a year for severe depression with suicidal attempts and guilt-related auditory hallucinations (voices accusing her of sexual faults). Symptoms started in coincidence with setting the date of her wedding; instead, she left her fiancé and became delusional about being in love with a soccer game champion.

Family conditions are very bad: The father has been blind and hemiplegic for a long time, since a traffic accident. The mother is clearly schizophrenic and embodies the fears that Mariella may just be at the outset of a similar career. All the relatives share the idea that there is a hereditary disease and that Mariella is doomed.

During her initial stay at the hospital she is very worried that her parents cannot make it without her help, a rather realistic concern given their severe disabilities. The social worker succeeds in getting a woman to work 15 hours a week in the house, paid for by the U.S.L. administration. This has an immediate tranquilizing effect on Mariella. The therapeutic team is then confirmed in its interpretation of the illness as being the only acceptable way for Mariella to get away from an unbearable burden within the family, the only alibi she can use without feeling too guilty.

The depressing characteristics of the family are so evident that it is decided to offer Mariella another "psychiatric" alibi not to reenter the family at discharge: she is accommodated in an apartment of the service together with two other well-compensated female patients with whom she had established a good relationship. The parents are violently opposed to this plan; the team tries to negotiate, but to no avail. Mariella, of course, cannot stand against the family, and eventually goes back home. The proposal to attend a work cooperative three days a week, while apparently acceptable to the parents, is unacceptable to Mariella, who perceives it as too much independence and separation. As a result, she has a relapse.

The team has to come to terms with such strong family bonds and with Mariella's ambivalence and accept, at least for the present time, these needs of *them*. Here the approach cannot be but ecological. The implications that therapeutic interventions have for the whole family, not just the individual patient, must be considered. After a long team discussion, it is decided to make clear to Mariella *and the family* that her dilemma between a drive towards a more autonomous life, which is characteristic of her age, and her problem of conscience of having to care for her seriously disabled parents, is understood and accepted by the team. She will be helped to deal with this problem and provided with all the support she needs to find *her own solution*.

Informed of this resolution, Mariella looks quite relieved. Her clinical condition improves in the following days as does her cooperation with treatment.

The example illustrates the need for combined (clinical, psychological, and social) interventions, as well as the difficulties and mistakes that may ensue when one level of interpretation is overlooked in favor of another.

Since the use of crisis teams reduces hospitalization, as has been extensively documented by systematic research, crisis intervention techniques have been given high priority. Home visits are highly regarded and especially encouraged for this purpose. They are usually made by more than one worker, usually a *team* of two or three, *including a psychiatrist*. This is done because home visits are considered a valid diagnostic and therapeutic tool — an alternative to traditional in-office modalities. In fact, the causes of a problem and possible solutions are often self-evident in the patient's natural social environment.

> Consider Pietro, one of our long-term patients. He had a psychotic episode in his twenties and has lived a very peripheral life ever since. He works only episodically and lives with his parents on a disability pension. However, he has not shown any positive symptoms in the last few years.
>
> One day he reports to his therapist that the neighbors are after him, that they spy and control him all day long. He has been anxious for a while, restless, insomniac, probably worried because of a brief illness of his elderly father, which reminded him of the aging of his parents and the related possibility of remaining alone in the short run.
>
> In the course of the home visit, a curious layout of the house, passed unnoticed before, attracts the attention of the mental health workers. Pietro's family lives on the second floor; the neighbor, who lives on the first, has a window overlooking the staircase that allows him to control the access. In fact, he is at the window when the workers arrive and scrutinizes them thoroughly when they go upstairs; he is still there, checking, when they leave. His watching presence is clearly disturbing, even to an occasional visitor, as the workers are! Probably Pietro's recent anxiety and restlessness had worried him and he is just trying to figure out what is going on with Pietro; or he is just very curious and intrusive. This issue is discussed at length with Pietro; it is even suggested that he blind the window, if necessary! Humor is used extensively, together with a reality orientation in dealing with the problem of a concerned, intrusive neighbor.

Hospitalization may be avoided if prompt home crisis intervention is provided and the team guarantees follow-up visits as needed.

> For example, an urgent request for intervention is made to the service by an angry neighbor, who had a window broken by an old lady living next door. A home visit is made. The arena is a rotten, abandoned farm, out in the country. The angry neighbor had bought a wing, completely remodeled it, of course

investing a considerable amount of money, and just moved in. It did not take long to discover that his hopes of having a quiet spot out in the country clashed with the territorial instinct of the old lady who had lived alone there for years, since the death of her husband. The workers try to talk to her in vain: she comes to the window, but she refuses to open the door; she looks very wild indeed!

Unexpected help comes from a family living in a house nearby (the "good" characters of the story). They have developed, somehow, a trusting relationship with the woman over the years, and she opens the door to them and eventually agrees to see the "doctors." At a closer scrutiny, she looks demented and moderately malnourished.

Since the house is a terrible mess, the workers suggest that a cleaning company be called; the woman agrees so long as it is for free. The U.S.L. administration pays for the cleaning, the house looks much better, she is happy with that, and expresses gratitude to the mental health workers. In this case, a concrete intervention, cleaning the house, resulted in the team's being able to establish contact.

Little by little she gets accustomed to home visits made by the same workers and ends up enjoying their company and their help with housekeeping and, shopping. They bring her food and give suggestions about her diet. Drinking habits are also discussed with her; in addition, the wine dealer nearby is asked not to sell alcohol to her. Eventually she agrees to a physical evaluation by the doctor and lab screening at the hospital. She turns out to be diabetic, so appropriate treatment is negotiated with her, to overcome her distrust towards any medication. Eventually she also agrees to take a tranquilizer to decrease anxiety and facilitate sleep. Although big crises do not occur, she is excited most of the time and shows verbal aggressiveness towards the "bad," intruding neighbor. On one occasion she refuses again to open the door to the workers, and dumps . . . urine on them from the window.

It takes about three months after initial contact to reach a fully reliable degree of cooperation; support and a minimum use of benzodiazepines resolve the symptomatology. Two years later, everything is fine; even the new neighbor is finally accepted and the relationship quite satisfactory. She was never hospitalized, a real asset with a person like her, where a hospitalization, by uprooting her from her usual environment, would have probably precipitated a confusional state.

In the experience of the South Verona group, home visits involving multidisciplinary teams serve also as an effective means to increase group spirit, to prevent burnout, and to train the staff in the development of effective, alternative intervention strategies. However, experience has shown that crisis intervention alone is not enough, especially in the case of chronic recidivists: The service has to focus on *preventing* crises.

For example, research conducted in Portogruaro, another area of the region, where a psychiatric register exists, showed that the great majority of crisis interventions in a catchmented community service are from patients who not only had previous psychiatric contacts (85%) but also had previous admissions (79%) and, generally, repeated admissions in the past (63%).

Simply put, most crisis interventions involve chronic, previously hospitalized patients. Since in a catchmented service most patients are already known to the staff (71% in the research mentioned), these patients may well be followed up and provided long-term, community-based care, which, it is hoped, would prevent the exacerbation of symptoms and the occurrence of a crisis (Pancheri, 1986). This is consistent with what is reported by the Madison, Wisconsin, emergency services.

Long-lasting personal relationships between staff and patients are considered an essential component of treatment and very much encouraged. In addition, there the rational planning of specific treatment modalities is emphasized. Therefore, individual treatment plans are made and regularly revised in team meetings.

There are resocialization activities available at the Mental Health Center—a newspaper group, a tea party group, an art group, a knitting group, an excursion group, etc. These groups involve about 10 veterans who attend the center regularly; they have been rather successful so far, and plans exist to add more groups and develop a more comprehensive day program based on the principles of psychosocial rehabilitation and social skills training. Since the service has always been struggling with shortage of permanent staff (especially nurses) and emergencies rather than with rehabilitation, much is still needed in this field. A vocational rehabilitation program is expected to start in the near future.

Casework, case management and advocacy are everyday routines. The work with families deserves special mention. Since most patients (83%) live with their families, much work is done with them in terms of supportive counseling or family therapy. Some families are seen in formal family sessions, using the one-way screen and based on methods developed by the Milan school (Palazzoli et al., 1978), the so-called systemic family therapy. New cases seem to benefit greatly from this approach, both in terms of symptom reduction and prevention of dependency on hospitalization. In contrast, families with "veterans," i.e., patients with long careers as patients, resist, drop out easily, and look for more traditional approaches (hospitalization, medications; Burti et al., 1984). However, the systemic approach has, overall, proved to be very useful in community work with families: It provides a relational model of interpretation for symptomatic behaviors and family reactions and also clarifies the role of the service and of other contextual components. Most professional members of the staff have training in family therapy and use the model extensively.

For example, Maddalena, a 45-year-old housewife, has had several episodes of manic-depressive psychosis in the past. She comes to the center one day very excited, emotional, and restless. Her therapist talks to her and carefully inquiries about *possible reasons* for her being so excited.

After prolonged inquiry, complicated by her emotional excitement, she recognizes she has become rather worried recently, fearing that her son Luigi, 12, who has just changed school, might already be in trouble with the new teachers because of discipline problems, as had actually happened before. Her husband had met the teachers, but did not say much to her, and she fears that he may be hiding something.

Since we know Maddalena and her family well, we are aware that the son might be in real trouble: He has already incurred serious disciplinary provisions before. We also know, though, that the son is often used by the couple in their marital games: Maddalena often exaggerates the problems she has in controlling Luigi, to attract the attention of her husband, a businessman peripheral to the family, who tries to get involved as little as possible, especially with her.

With this doubt in mind and before taking any resolution, the counselor contacts the husband and invites him to talk. After some resistance, with the excuse that he is very busy, he finally agrees to come. He minimizes the problems of the son. "Maddalena worries too much," he says. The usual game: Maddalena is worried about the son; husband minimizes. The counselor poses more stringent questions, rejecting trite statements about Maddalena being "too emotional." Finally the husband admits the teachers told him that Luigi is doing well: He *did not report this to Maddalena* because "she tends to be too permissive" with the son. A brief fight follows; after it Maddalena is visibly relieved and the crisis is practically over.

What we wish to stress in presenting this case is that the therapist never gave in, but kept trying to frame the symptomatology within the context of that family. This brought out important information that eventually solved the problem and terminated the symptoms.

The following example shows how the systemic model (and techniques) helped to redefine some contextual components related to the team and the treatment setting.

Vilma, 39, married with one daughter of 14, has been seriously depressed for the last six months, in spite of real strenuous efforts on the part of the team. She had started to become depressed about 18 months earlier, when she retired to devote herself completely to her family. Before, being the personal secretary of one of the most prominent university professors, she had a busy and prestigious role and was very much appreciated for her skills, energy, and dedication.

She has been treated with antidepressant medications for a long period, to no avail. She has also been admitted to the inpatient unit several times for a condition of psychomotor blocking and serious anorexia. In addition, she is seen with her family in formal family therapy sessions at regular intervals.

Reasons for the depression look quite obvious. She lost a very satisfactory working role to become a housewife, for which she has little interest and no previous experience. In addition, the family is already accustomed to doing without a housewife.

The interaction with the team and the service is very peculiar: Vilma is somehow manipulative; the team gets very involved with the case; everybody tries very hard to help her, to give and receive suggestions, to change interventions and medications etc. The only result is frustration. Family sessions also are frustrating and seem useless.

Eventually, the team decides to have a session of supervision with the Milan group (Dr. Cecchin and associates) *with the family*. The need of the woman to "take some time to work things out" becomes apparent and is extensively commented upon by the supervisor in the session. Also, the overinvolvement of the team and the consequential poor results become apparent. Having been part of the university, Vilma is perceived as a colleague, hence her "manipulative" attitude and the team's therapeutic overinvolvement.

The effects of the intervention are significant: Team members slow down their therapeutic urgency, stick to one treatment and stay with it. Vilma also seems more relaxed; she has a brief admission and is discharged improved. She then decides to apply to go back to work. Some time later her application is accepted: She is a little anxious, but her mood is back to normal. Team members still wonder what really changed the things: medications, supervision, good luck in that the application was accepted?

STRUCTURE OF THE SERVICE

Ideally, in an organization there should be consistency among goals, technology, and structure (Perrow, 1970). At the South Verona Community Service continuity of care is facilitated by the same staff members' working in both the intramural and extramural programs ("single staff" module). The same persons follow the same patient wherever he/she is treated at any given time. This greatly facilitates the build-up of personal, trusting, often affectionate relationships between staff and patients. Usually, and especially in the case of chronic patients and those at risk of becoming chronic, a core team of two or three workers is assigned to each patient so that at least one is available, in spite of turnover, shifts, vacations, etc. Patients are encouraged to come or call any time they feel they need help, without an appointment or a referral. If a patient shows up, he is likely to find one of his therapists, somebody he knows and trusts already—a real asset in case of excitement and behavior disorganization, when personal relationships are a key resource to solve the crisis.

For instance, in the case of Maddalena, it was essential that the worker knew all her previous history and had a personal close relationship with her. Otherwise her "manic" attitude would mean little to the observer, other than a symptom. As we have repeatedly insisted, we regard symptoms as meaningful expressions of person's world, to be framed and understood within his/her life history. This "contextualization" is greatly facilitated by a close knowledge of the person.

TEAMWORK

All important decisions regarding patients are taken within the team, after extensive discussion. A 15- to-30-minute case-centered meeting takes place every morning. In addition, there are two one-and-one-half-hour team meetings per week; one takes place in the center, while the other takes place in the unit, the latter in order to (1) have more direct information about those patients who are currently admitted, and (2) involve the nurses on duty in the unit, who otherwise have few opportunities to be involved in teamwork. In addition, there is a one-hour single case discussion once a week. Seminars are held on a quasi regular basis.

Minimal hierarchy and authority based on actual experience rather than academic credentials are stressed. Residents in training, who necessarily have only limited experience, work closely with the nurses, who have extended experience in community work, to their mutual advantage. The nurses find it gratifying to "teach the doctors." Residents and nurses are given a great deal of responsibility and initiative; if they have to make an important decision on the spot, such as admitting someone to the unit, they know it will be endorsed by the team. Staff professionals act more as coordinators and facilitators than as supervisors. In especially difficult cases they are ready to back up residents and nurses and to join them in the field. The fact that workers are never left alone, that they can count on reciprocal supervision in the team, as well as minimal hierarchy and empowerment, contributes to prevention of burnout, which is rarely seen in South Verona. Last but not least, although several professionals on the staff have had a formal training in systemic family therapy, teamwork encourages more interdisciplinarity than specialization — systems theory is by no means a credo.

THE TRAINING OF RESIDENTS

Residents in training are assigned cases right from the beginning. This is made possibly by the aforementioned extensive teamwork, both in doing interventions and in the decision-making process. Each resident has a caseload of 8–12 patients whom he follows continuously, across programs, during all his training period. This results in meaningful personal relationships between the residents and the patients and provides the trainee with a *longitudinal* perspective of the cases — a rare feature in residency programs. At the same time, because of the "single-staff" module, rotation through different services is not necessary in order to acquire multiple experiences. Subsequent residency periods partially overlap (by one to three months) to reduce, as much as possible, the adverse effect of the turnover on therapeutic relationships.

MEDICATIONS

As to the use of medications, the usual dosage for an acutely psychotic patient admitted to the hospital unit is 300–400 mg. of chlorpromazine, or the equivalent, per day; 600 mg. per day is an almost absolute upper limit. Psychotic outpatients are usually maintained on a dosage of 100 mg. of chlorpromazine, or equivalent, per day; 40 patients are currently on long-acting depot neuroleptics (fluphenazine decanoate: 5–25 mg. every three weeks; haloperidol decanoate: 25 to 100 mg. every four weeks). The attitude of the staff is one of using the drug with the minimum of side effects at the *lowest* possible dosage. Staff is also in favor of discontinuing neuroleptics after a fair amount of time after the episode in new cases; this does not hold as well for the veterans.

Tricyclic antidepressants are used in the course of an episode of depressive psychosis at a dosage of 75 to 100 mg. of either imipramine or amitriptyline, or equivalent, per day. Maintenance dosage is 50 to 75 mg. per day. They are used in case of neurotic depression only after a trial with benzodiazepines has failed. MAOIs are not used because of their dangerous side effects. Lithium salts are used in manic-depressive psychosis. ECT has been used in three cases in the last five years.

RESEARCH

The group devotes many resources to research. Most of projects are in epidemiology and community care. A psychiatric case register has been operational since 1979 (Tansella et al., 1985). Besides a number of books and publications in international journals, research has already had an important fallout effect, in terms of providing useful knowledge for planning the programs and information for clinical use.

OTHER PSYCHIATRIC AGENCIES IN TOWN

In addition to the South Verona Community Psychiatric Service (CPS), in Verona there are the following mental health agencies:

- The state psychiatric hospital, with 366 long-stay patients, 18 of whom are from South Verona (as of December 31, 1986).
- Three outpatient services for children and adolescents (0–18 years).
- Two private psychiatric hospitals (with a total number of 220 beds). Their referrals come from the Verona province (including South Verona), but also from out of the region. According to our psychiatric register, 61 people from South Verona have been admitted to them in 1986.

- Two psychiatric units and two outpatient services in another general hospital in town, serving the two other territories of the U.S.L., which include part of downtown Verona and a mountainous district for an overall population of 111,000 (service No. 1), and the rest of downtown Verona and a rural district with an overall population of 123,000 (service No. 2). Unlike the South Verona service, these two do not have a community center yet; they use instead part of the ward for day care. There are consultation facilities outside, in the territory, with a psychiatrist and paraprofessionals one or two days a week, two sheltered workshops, and some apartments.

THE SOUTH VERONA PSYCHIATRIC REGISTER

The case register began operating on December 31, 1978, starting with a prevalence count and is directed by Professor M. Tansella, Institute of Psychiatry. Since then all psychiatric contacts made by South Verona residents (with psychiatrists, psychologists, social workers and psychiatric nurses) have been recorded. General practitioners, psychiatrists, and psychologists in private practice do not report data to the register. Basic demographic and clinical data are recorded for each patient, together with the dates and some basic data (referral sources included) of all contacts; special precautions are taken to ensure confidentiality (Baldwin, Leff, & Wing, 1976). For inpatient admissions the diagnosis is recorded according to the I.C.D., 9th revision (World Health Organization, 1978). For outpatient and home visits, emergency contacts, and ward referrals, the diagnosis is coded according to an eleven-fold classification system giving collapsed I.C.D.-9 categories. The diagnoses made by other institutions are reviewed by the senior psychiatrist responsible of the register (M. Tansella), so that they fit into one of the 11 diagnostic groups (Tansella et al., 1985).

PSYCHIATRIC CARE IN SOUTH VERONA: SOME DATA*

The great majority of the South Verona residents requiring some kind of psychiatric intervention (long-stay inpatients of the mental hospital are not included) are assisted by our Community Psychiatric Service. In the years 1983–86, for example, an average 71.0% of the South Verona psychiatric patients were treated by the Community Psychiatric Service only, 4.2% by other institutions as well, and 24.8% only by other institutions* (Figure

---

*The data reported in this section have been extracted from the South Verona Psychiatric Case Register's annual reports (Tansella, Balestrieri & Meneghelli, 1979–1982) as well as from other relevant published papers.

16.3). Drug addicts, who by definition are followed by another service, are excluded. This low utilization of other services occurred despite ready availability of psychiatric beds in the private hospitals and outpatient facilities.

Distributions of various types of care in the years 1979 to 1986 are represented in Table 16.2 and Figures 16.4 and 16.5. Inpatients on one day (one-day prevalence* represent the *rates* per 100,000 adult population, i.e., aged 14 and above) of patients already in the hospital on census day (December 31st of the previous year). Inpatients are divided by length of stay: long-stay patients were defined as those who have been in hospital for one year or longer on census day; short and medium-stay, those who have spent less than one year in hospital at the same date.

Outpatients on one day (one-day prevalence) are defined as those who

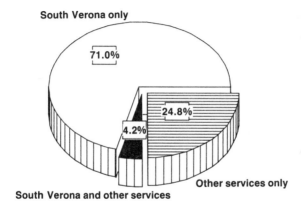

South Verona only

71.0%

24.8%

4.2%

Other services only

South Verona and other services

Data from Tansella, Balestrieri, & Meneghill, 1979–1987.

FIGURE 16.3
South Verona Residents Contacting Psychiatric Services in One Year
(mean 1983–86)

*It must be remembered that in all these cases we are dealing with "reported" prevalence of an illness. By this we intend that only those cases ("index" cases) who have actually contacted the services are actually investigated and appear in the figures. Thus, if a patient, although sick, does not contact a doctor/service reporting data to the register, he will escape the study. "True" prevalence, instead, counts all the cases in a given area, but it requires a time-consuming and costly population study (i.e., going out and examining everybody in the area). Problems of case definition in this type of studies should be mentioned. It is generally thought that most people with serious, visible illnesses, like schizophrenia, will eventually contact a service, while minor, less evident ailments, like neuroses and psychosomatic disorders, tend to remain more secluded. Therefore, the reported prevalence of schizophrenia will come closer to its so-called "true" prevalence, than will that of neurotic and psychosomatic disorders.

TABLE 16.2
Patient Care in South Verona (1979–1986)
(rates × 100,000 pop. 14 years and above)

TYPE OF CONTACT	1979	1980	1981	1982	1983	1984	1985	1986
Inpatients on census day								
Long stay	47.9	57.0	51.7	47.8	42.8	41.9	36.7	35.1
Short and medium stay	40.0	35.5	21.6	19.8	32.9	22.6	27.2	19.1
total	87.9	92.5	73.3	67.6	75.7	64.5	63.9	54.2
Outpatients on census day	145.8	153.4	156.7	130.2	157.9	206.5	185.3	280.6
Patients in contact on census day	233.7	245.9	230.0	197.8	233.6	271.0	249.2	334.8
New episodes in the year	769.0	796.7	723.5	908.2	985.3	976.0	883.5	877.0
Total one-year prevalence	1,002.7	1,042.6	953.5	1,106.0	1,218.9	1,247.0	1,132.7	1,211.8

(Tansella, Balestrieri, & Meneghelli, 1979–1987)

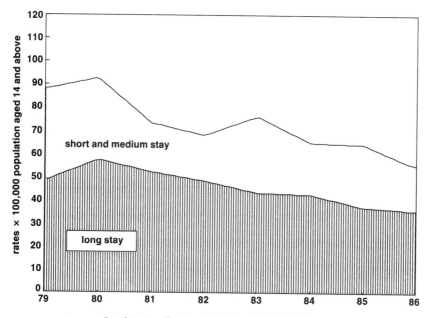

Data from Tansella, Balestrieri & Meneghill, 1979–1987.

FIGURE 16.4
Inpatient Care in South Verona (1979–86)
One-day Prevalence

had a contact on census day plus those with a "current episode" of outpatient care (i.e., those who had an outpatient contact both *before* and *after* the census day with less than three months between visits). One year prevalence is also (one-day prevalence plus new episodes in the year) presented in Table 16.3 and Figure 16.5 (additive graph).

It may be observed in Figure 16.4 that the one-day prevalence of long-stay (one year or more in hospital on census day) inpatients remained unchanged from 1979 to 1982 and has been diminishing since, reflecting the trend of the mental hospital to disappear "by extinction." It is well-known that the mental hospital is the main place where long-stay used to accumulate. It is worthwhile to note that in South Verona, while the closure of the front door of the state mental hospital has stopped the main form of recruitment of potential new long-stay patients, these patients have not become long-stay elsewhere, i.e., either in the general hospital unit or in private hospitals (Balestrieri, Micciolo, & Tansella, 1987). Short- and medium-stay patients show a noticeable decrease in the same period, thus giving an early indication of the shift from hospital to community care.

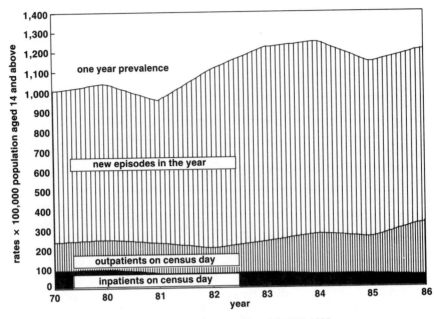

Data from Tansella, Balestrieri & Meneghill, 1979–1987.

FIGURE 16.5
Patient Care in South Verona (1979–86)
One Day and One Year Prevalence

TABLE 16.3
Mean One-year Prevalence by Diagnosis, and Site of Care, South Verona (1979–1986)
(rates × 100,000 pop. 14 years and above)

DIAGNOSIS	OUTPATIENT CARE	INPATIENT CARE	TOTAL	OUTPATIENT CARE / INPATIENT CARE
Schizophrenia and other functional psychoses	65.9	61.6	127.5	1.07
Affective psychoses	28.2	35.2	63.4	0.80
Organic psychoses	21.4	11.8	33.2	1.81
Neuroses and psychosomatic disorders	329.0	89.4	418.4	3.68
Personality disorders	46.4	31.4	77.8	1.48
Alcohol and drug dependence	160.4	55.7	216.2	2.88
Other diagnosis, not known and no psychiatric disorders	134.2	41.2	175.4	3.26
TOTAL	785.5	326.3	1,111.8	2.41

(Tansella, Balestrieri, & Meneghelli, 1979–1987)

The total one-year prevalence remained fairly stable over the years (Figure 16.5). Rates (about 1%) are lower than those reported in other countries (Babigian, 1977; Dupont, 1979; ten Horn, 1980; 1986; Wing & Fryers, 1976; Wing et al., 1967), but similar to those found in other areas in Northern Italy (Tansella et al., 1987; Marinoni et al., 1983).

Table 16.3 and Figure 16.6 report the mean one-year reported prevalence (data cover the period 1979–1986; annual prevalences were averaged), by diagnosis and type of contact. All South Verona subjects who contacted psychiatric services during the calendar year were divided into two groups: those receiving outpatient care only (outpatient care) and those with at least one hospitalization during the year (inpatient care).

Schizophrenia and affective psychosis are the most represented diagnoses among patients admitted in the year. Neuroses and psychosomatic disorders are the most represented diagnoses among patients never admitted in the year, i.e., patients treated only in the community. However, it should be noted that a substantial proportion of subjects with a diagnosis of psychosis having psychiatric contacts during the year are treated without admission to

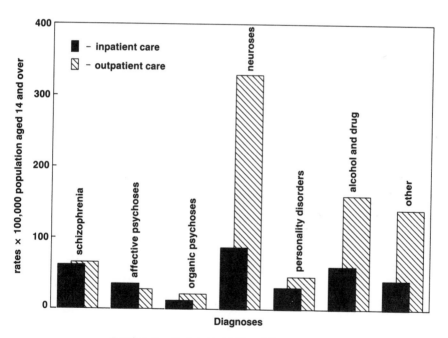

Data from Tansella, Balestrieri & Meneghill, 1979–1987.

FIGURE 16.6
Mean One-year Prevalence Rates by Diagnosis, South Verona (1979–86)

the hospital. In the years 1979–1986 the ratio of patients receiving outpatient treatment only to patients admitted to the hospital during the year (outpatient care/inpatient care), is 2.41; i.e., people treated as outpatients *only* are more than twice as many as those admitted at least once in the year. These data confirm the community orientation of our approach.

Table 16.4 and Figure 16.7 show data on inpatient care in South Verona one year before (1977) and eight years after (1979–1986) the psychiatric reform. The number of admissions to the state hospital dropped to zero in 1982, in compliance with the law. The total number of admissions to inpatient facilities decreased by 14%, (while the total number of hospital days and mean number of occupied beds decreased by 45%). These figures refer to *all* inpatient beds in Verona, including private ones. However, the most impressive feature regards compulsory admissions, which in the years after the reform (1979–1986) varied between 1/3 to 1/10 of those recorded before the reform (Figure 16.8).

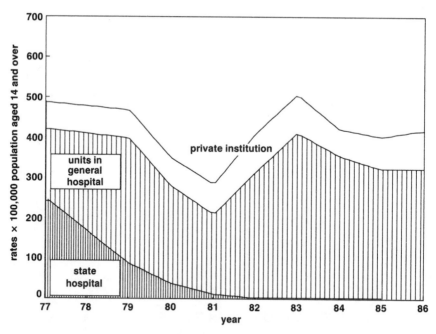

Data from Tansella, Balestrieri & Meneghill, 1979–1987.

FIGURE 16.7
Admissions of South Verona Residents
Before (1977) and After (1979–86) the Psychiatric Reform

TABLE 16.4

Admissions of South Verona Residents before (1977) and after (1979–86) the Psychiatric Reform

(rates × 100,000 pop. aged 14 and over)

TYPE OF CONTACT	1977	1979	1980	1981	1982	1983	1984	1985	1986
Admissions									
—compulsory*	54.6	7.9	9.8	10.0	13.2	18.1	4.8	8.0	14.4
—To state mental hospital (voluntary only)	194.2	85.9	35.4	8.3	0	0	0	0	0
—To psychiatric units in general hospital (voluntary only)	172.0	303.6	232.1	188.4	298.3	391.5	348.4	311.5	306.1
Total public care	420.8	397.4	277.3	206.7	311.5	409.6	353.2	319.5	320.5
Private care	66.8	71.9	70.8	70.0	95.6	97.1	66.1	79.9	97.3
All admissions	487.6	469.3	348.1	276.7	407.1	506.7	419.3	399.4	417.8
Mean No. of occupied beds per day	103.9	92.9	85.4	70.7	66.7	68.1	63.5	56.6	56.4

*Compulsory admissions were to the state mental hospital before the reform; to the units in general hospitals, after the reform.
(Tansella, Balestrieri, & Meneghelli, 1979–1987)

289

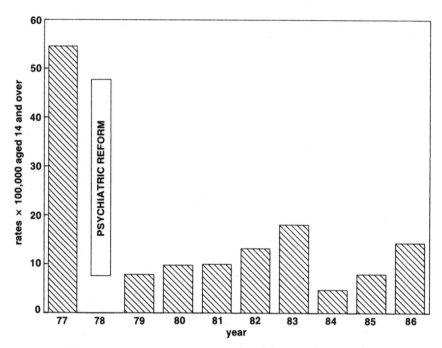

Data from Tansella, Balestrieri & Meneghill, 1979–1987.

FIGURE 16.8
Compulsory Admissions of South Verona Residents
Before (1977) and After (1979–86) the Psychiatric Reform

Chronic Patients

As to chronic patients, the number of new long-stay inpatients, those who were not long-stay on December 31, 1979, but became long-stay afterwards, was investigated (Tansella, in press a). In addition, the number of new long-term users of community services (i.e., patients without intermissions between two subsequent contacts—including short hospitalizations— longer than 90 days in the year—a definition after Sturt, Wykes, & Creer, 1982) was determined. This definition of long-term users is rather inclusive, as it includes persons who had only sporadic contacts with the service, so long as they were not more than three months apart.

The study did not reveal any accumulation of *new long-stay* patients in the period 1980–1985 (Figure 16.9). These results are in contrast with those reported in other countries (Häfner & Klug, 1982; Wykes & Wing, 1982). The study revealed instead a consistently increasing number of new long-term patients. However, in terms of outcome, there seem to be important differences between the long-stay and the long-term status. A follow-up study was performed on two cohorts of chronic patients: 25 long-stay and 29 long-term patients (Balestrieri et al., 1987). The two cohorts were comparable as to diagnostic category and sociodemographic characteristics. At two-year follow-up 22 (88%) of the long-stay patients were still long-stay and the remaining three had died. In contrast, only 13 (45%) of the long-term patients were still long-term (Figure 16.10); three had died, one had become long-stay, five were still followed, but not as intensively to quality them as long-term, and seven were out of care.

The authors draw the conclusion that, unlike the mental hospital, community services do not foster a rigid pattern of "chronic" dependency on the institution. What happened to those patients was that after an acute episode, during which they were closely followed by the services (and this qualified them for "long-term" users), they recovered or improved and had fewer contacts. In other words, community services would have more flexible patterns of care, with seemingly lower chronicity-inducing effects.

In addition, *none* of the *first-ever* patients contacting the South Verona

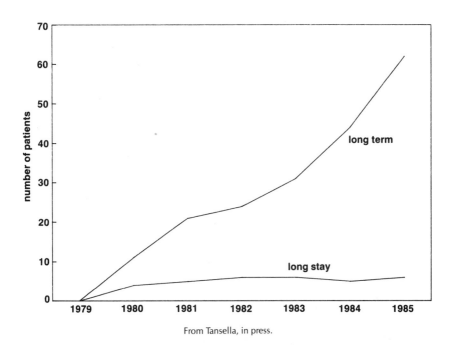

From Tansella, in press.

FIGURE 16.9
Number of New Chronic Patients
South Verona (1979–1985)

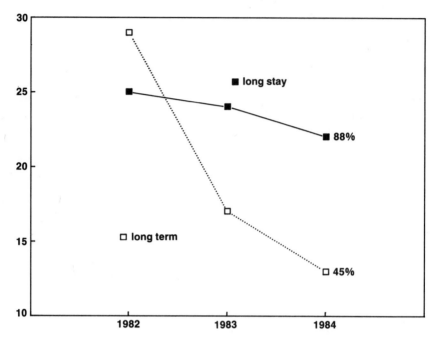

From Balestrieri, Micciolo, & Tansella, 1987.

FIGURE 16.10
Outcome of New Chronic Patients,
South Verona, 2 Year Follow-up

community service since 1978 has become a long-stay inpatient, neither in the South Verona hospital unit nor in the private hospitals (which they can access easily if they wish), let alone in the state hospital, where admission is prohibited by law.

In conclusion, these data seem to show that in the past eight years the South Verona community psychiatric service has faced *all* the problems presented by psychiatric patients living in the territory, without the backup of the traditional state hospital. The stopping of all admissions (including readmissions) to the state hospital did not overload community services, nor did it bring about a shift to the private care system. Moreover, with the exception of a temporary increase in admissions to the South Verona inpatient unit in 1982–1983, probably a transient effect of the stopping of readmissions to the state hospital (effective January 1, 1982) and also of a number of unrelated reasons (Zimmermann-Tansella et al., 1985), total annual admissions have shown a decreasing trend. In other words, not only has the revolving-door phenomenon *not* been observed, but also the overall number of admissions has decreased. This might be conservatively interpreted as an effect of the implementation and continuing improvement of alternative community services. In sum, data seem to confirm the expectation that a comprehensive, community-based psychiatric service providing both crisis intervention and continuity of care in the community can effectively reduce the need for hospitalization of psychiatric patients, including the most serious ones, who traditionally spent long periods of their lives in closed institutions. The reduction in hospital use occurred without having a community residential alternative to hospitalization available! As to outcome, quality of life, and client satisfaction, positive observations have been made and encouraging feedback has been provided by the users. However, studies investigating these areas are still in progress and results are not yet available.

REASONS FOR THE RESULTS

The reform, of course, accounts most for the results. It provided the legal, administrative, and motivational components for a new way of practicing psychiatry. The blocking of admissions to the state hospital forced the service to find alternative ways to deal with the presenting problems and stimulated the workers' ingenuity. This is, somehow, an issue too often overlooked. Individual problem-solving, based on knowledge, but also on experience and ingenuity, is a basic ingredient in psychiatry. Set ways of doing things are good for dispatching large numbers of people, treated as if they were all alike (or at least divided into few, gross categories; see, for instance, Wilson's description, Chap. 4, p. 33), as happens in institutions. Formalized procedures do not allow the treatment of a particular individual in his own existential context.

As to the staff, the initial group is still there and constitutes a strong nucleus, which has taken in newcomers over the years and grown progressively more comfortable working together while maintaining its initial ideals and tradition. The unfortunate experience of other teams, where a rapid turnover is the rule, confirms the importance of this point. Some turnover seems to be an advantage, as long as a subgroup remains stable over time. This is true of the residents, who turn over every two years. They bring new energy and enthusiasm, ask questions, and pose due criticism with the eyes of the outsider. This process actually enhances the functioning of the whole system.

The interest in family therapy, shared by most team members from the early days, resulted in an extremely valuable tool to work in the community. It seems that, especially in times of change, using all that the social background offers is a basic ingredient for obtaining good results. In another area, let alone another country, completely different strategies should be used, in order to take advantage of different natural support systems. A community service has to rely so heavily on existing resources that their kind and availability determine strategies and interventions to be used.

MAJOR PROBLEMS

Principal problems derive from the still partial development of the whole system. The still unaccomplished reallocation of resources from the *manicomio* to the Verona U.S.L., as happens in the whole nation (see the sections on implementation and data) is responsible for a shortage of both personnel and funds (Figures 16.11, 16.12, 16.13). Of the 33 nurses planned for the South Verona Psychiatric Service, only 24 have been assigned. Therefore, in order to have enough nurses working in the territory, shifts on the inpatient unit are understaffed. In addition, the sheltered apartment, which can house up to eight disabled people in a setting alternative to the hospital, has only now started after long delays. All this has gone against the plan to ask for the discharge of two or three patients from our territory who are still in the state hospital. They do not have families and are fairly disabled, but might be successfully rehabilitated and resettled if provided with a residential facility and enough support and supervision in the community. Some admissions to the ward might be avoided as well, once the sheltered alternative is fully operational.

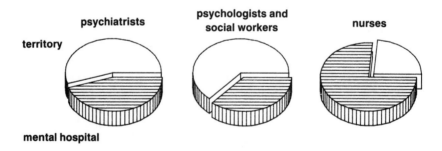

Mental hospital: 366 patients

Territory: 310,000 population (2,575 patients)

Data provided by the Dept. of Mental Health, USL 25.

FIGURE 16.11
Mental Health Services of Verona
Distribution of Personnel (1986)

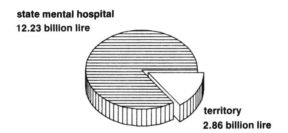

state mental hospital
12.23 billion lire

territory
2.86 billion lire

State mental hospital: 366 patients
Territory: 310,000 population (2,575 patients)

Data provided by the Dept. of Mental Health, USL 25.

FIGURE 16.12
Mental Health Services of Verona
Annual Costs (1986)

Another problem regards the lack of specific services for some categories of patients, such as alcoholics, who therefore have to come to psychiatric services and constitute a significant burden. They were traditionally admitted to the state hospitals, where they represented a respectable percentage of the whole population (up to 20% in those areas where alcoholism is more diffuse, such as northeastern Italy). More appropriate services were not developed until recently; even Alcoholics Anonymous and other self-help

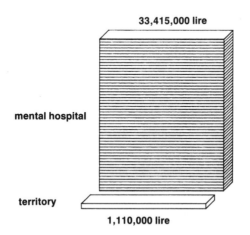

33,415,000 lire

mental hospital

territory

1,110,000 lire

FIGURE 16.13
Mental Health Services of Verona
Annual Costs per Patient (1986)

organizations started only in the past few years, probably under the pressure of the problems becoming more apparent because of the blocking of admissions to state hospitals.

Other problems are somehow related to the structure and the organization of the service. Having the same people following patients in different settings is more demanding and, probably, time-consuming and stressful than dividing up areas of responsibility and working separately. The lack of a sharp division of roles and tasks, while greatly improving coordination and consistency of interventions, exposes staff to possible confusion and undesired reciprocal overlapping and interferences. Manipulative patients know how to contact different staff members and eventually get what they want. However, this system and the related close teamwork and permanent supervision are excellent for the prevention of burnout.

The philosophy of intervention, i.e., focusing especially on the phenomenological and relational components, raises the risk of possibly neglecting clinical aspects, like diagnosing and monitoring physical ailments and medication. We are well aware of this possibility and watch for it.

A CASE HISTORY

Cesare, 47, has been paranoid schizophrenic since he was 20. He had his first episode while working as a military policeman on a isolated island near Sicily. He did not want to enter the army, but his father, a despotic person, ordered him to. He spent 15 years in the state hospital and was discharged when his father, who had always opposed his discharge, died. This happened before the psychiatric reform. He went to live with his elderly mother; the two were assigned an apartment in a popular housing program located in South Verona.

The case was referred to the South Verona C.P.S. by the neighbors, who perceived Cesare as a nuisance and a threat because of his fighting with his mother, making noise in the night and acting bizarre. There were a number of concurrent precipitating factors: Firstly, it was the transition time after the reform and Cesare, who did not like psychiatric consultations and medications, availed himself of delays in referrals for discontinuing both. Secondly, after so many years of hospitalization, Cesare adjusted poorly to the outside world; in addition, he and his mother were not accustomed to living together and had to work many issues through—hence the fights. Thirdly, the housing program had concentrated many problematic families in the same buildings at the same time: The level of reciprocal tolerance was inversely proportional to that of the problems.

During a home visit Cesare was found very excited; he looked somehow menacing in his attitude, but the doctors who had followed him in the hospital in the past assured the workers that he had never been dangerous. This relieved the workers and allowed more freedom of maneuvering. Other symptoms were delusions of grandeur: He would speak a lot of his contacts with statesmen, to whom he wrote frequently. Cesare refused categorically to come to the service, but agreed to see the workers at home. He would not take any sort of medication.

Two sets of interventions were then made: One consisted in visiting Cesare on a regular basis, doing problem-solving, especially in relation to the mother, and accompanying him on his errands, which he liked very much. The intended goal was to gain his trust without intimidating him with excessive pressures. The other consisted in meeting with the neighbors, listening to their complaints, reassuring them as to their fears, removing stereotypes and educating them with regard to mental illness, even helping them with *their* problems, which they had in abundance!

This work continued for about three months. Unfortunately, the excitement did not decrease and there were repeated fights with the mother. Disagreement had to do with money—she complained that he spent too much on "unnecessary" items like cigarettes, newspapers, books, etc. He also had a fight with somebody in the street, and was beaten up. This made him more paranoid: He bought a knife, which he kept ostensively secured to his wrist. The author (L.B.) negotiated with him about the knife and finally bought it from him; but he went on to buy another one. At that point, we resolved to commit him. He did not oppose at all; yet he showed a very compliant attitude. A thorough explanation about the reasons why the workers had to commit him, in spite of their aversion to restrictive provisions, was given. He looked sincerely surprised when told that everybody was afraid of him! During a two-week stay (on the second week he agreed to remain voluntarily) he was put on medication, with a satisfactory reduction of the excitement. He was discharged on a depot neuroleptic, given our low expectations for his compliance. He did not like it, but he agreed under the pressure of the workers.

Relationships with neighbors improved and, little by little, disagreements with the mother were negotiated, although never completely solved. He also helped at home and, when the mother could not move because of a varicose ulceration at her ankle, he showed unsuspected skills and availability. He did housework, went shopping, took the mother to see her doctor. The mother never recovered fully; instead her circulatory problems worsened and she started to show signs of dementia. Interestingly, there was a period, before we were certain about this, that we were very puzzled and uncertain either to believe her or Cesare. She was always complaining that he had stolen her money. He really was very patient with her. Since her disability was worsening, a woman neighbor was paid by the U.S.L. to help with housework. This caring of the service for their needs deeply reinforced the therapeutic relationship— probably he realized then that we *did care* for him and the mother.

When W.H.O. officers made a site visit, they were brought on a home visit to Cesare. He was great—made an impeccable report on the conditions of mental patients before and after the law and also made very positive comments on the South Verona C.P.S., which he had never voiced before. Indirectly we learned he really liked us. He felt very gratified having been chosen and his delusions decreased: He had "really" been contacted by W.H.O. officers!

It was in that period that he decided, against our advice, to make a trip to Sicily, to see the places where he had lived and had "gone crazy." In spite of our worries, the trip was uneventful; he came back happier and more grounded. Somehow it seemed that revisiting the real places where his life had changed so dramatically had a beneficial effect on him.

Unfortunately, his mother had to be hospitalized in a nursing home for the worsening of her dementia and physical conditions. The neighbor took care of him, but he was very worried, fearing that mother might die. We could not blame him: We were even *more* worried, with the idea he had to live on his own! But, against all the odds, he did fairly well alone. A precaution was taken: an electric stove was installed in place of the gas one, to *prevent* any possible danger (probably unlikely), but especially to reassure the neighbors, worried from the time *the mother* had left the gas open.

When mother died, Cesare did quite well. Then we were afraid he would spend the little savings the mother had left him. Team members agreed to help him with the bureaucracy of the inheritance if he promised to deposit the money in a bank and not to use it for current expenses. He agreed and kept the promise.

There was another serious crisis in the building when his neighbor, a young and attractive woman, mother of four children, who was kind of a Dulcinea in Cesare's delusions, in spite of the rumors following her numerous affairs, was stabbed to death by her jealous lover. Cesare was shocked, but overcame it.

More recently, he was also able to negotiate with the woman who does housework for him: She wanted a raise in salary, but the administration refused. Cesare discussed with her and supplemented the difference.

In conclusion, how is Cesare doing presently, eight years after his first contact with us? He still speaks of his delusions from time to time and is maintained on medications (12.5 to 25 mg. of fluphenazine decanoate every three to four weeks), but he lives at home with a minimal supervision, knows how to administer his disability pension, and has a number of meaningful relationships with relatives and acquaintances. He is able to interact appropriately, reads newspapers and books and, all in all, seems relatively satisfied with his life. He probably could benefit from the psychosocial rehabilitation program at the C.M.H.C., but at least so far has refused to attend. He might agree in the future.

American Ventures

The three programs described in Part IV are not representative of community mental health in the U.S. They were selected because of their high quality reputations. They also share another characteristic — the leaders of each are known to us, making them easily and openly accessible. The visits had no money attached. We were not looking at them from the perspective of either a granting or a regulatory agency. The two-day discussions were frank, open, and honest. A draft of our description was circulated to each program's staff for comment. All comments received in response were woven into the body of the report.

We attempted to look at the programs systematically by addressing the same questions to each (see CMHC questionnaire, Appendix G). As may be seen from the questionnaire's content, we believe that sociodemographics are highly relevant contextual factors that can limit or enhance a program's effectiveness. Morrisania (see Chapter 19) is continually waging an uphill fight against its severely limiting context. Both other sites have actually been able to work effectively to reduce programmatic constraints by finding new funding sources, developing their own housing, etc.

After the visit each program was rated on 11 variables listed in section II, Overall Program Ratings (e.g., staff quality and morale, preservation of client power, normalization, etc.). It is of some interest that the Morrisania program won the ratings race; yet, in some ways, such as lack of comprehensiveness and control over access, it really cannot be compared with the Boulder and Madison programs. As noted in the description, Morrisania is presented in part as a contrast *to the other two: It is in a megalopolis, deals with an urban area in which minorities are the majority, and has a coherent overarching theoretical framework that guides its practice. The other two communities are actually larger than Morrisania's catchment area but they have much less poverty and few minority group members. Basically, because of the nature of its South Bronx context, the Morrisania program is an island of refuge in a storm-tossed sea. The seas in Boulder and Madison are quite calm by comparison.*

CHAPTER 17

A Community of Options: Boulder County, Colorado

OVERVIEW AND BACKGROUND

BOULDER, COLORADO, IS A COLLEGE TOWN NESTLED against a steeply rising range of mountains on the eastern slopes of the Rockies. The University of Colorado, with about 30,000 students, is the town's largest single employer. There are, in addition, a number of high tech companies employing substantial numbers of persons in the area. Major sections of the county are occupied with farms and ranches. It is basically a young, growing, prosperous, yuppie-oriented town. To some it remains a hippie haven; it also has the Naropa Institute, a large Buddhist learning center. There are many artisans working in and around the town. The downtown has been revitalized by a mall and the restoration of the Boulderado, an 1890s style gold rush hotel.

Boulder, with 90,000, and Longmont, with 50,000, are the largest population centers in Boulder County. The remaining 60,000 persons are scattered throughout the county in small towns and on ranches and farms. Boulder is a young (more than 90% less than 64 years old), white community (7.9% minorities). Median family income is $30,200 per annum for a family of four. The unemployment rate in the spring of 1987 was 6.1%, up somewhat from the previous spring due to layoffs by a substantial employer that year. On any given day there are between 60 and 80 homeless in Boulder County. Roughly 17% of the populace of Boulder County are below the poverty line and 16% of those with an annual income of $15,000 or greater have no health insurance; 33% of those with a annual income of less than $15,000 have no health insurance.

The Boulder County Mental Health Center has an annual budget of nearly five million dollars. It has 125 fulltime equivalent staff (250 total employees), plus a large number of volunteers. Roughly 28% of the staff is devoted to administration. The non-M.D. full- and part-time staff include 60 psychologists, 38 M.S.W.'s, 10 nurses, and 33 other counselors. They have 3.4 full-time equivalent physicians, with additional time bought by contract for evening, weekend, and special program coverage. Three of the four adult psychiatrists working at the center have been there for at least 10 years. In 1986, the center had 120,000 total contacts of all kinds, including 44,000 individual therapy contacts, almost 22,000 group therapy contacts, 18,700 partial care contacts, and about 5400 case management contacts. The 24-hour-a-day emergency psychiatric service had over 6,000 contacts (20% seen face to face) in 1986; more than 50% were new to the center.

The center's costs are divided as per Figure 17.1. With the exception of inpatient care and partial hospitalization, the costs very closely parallel the rate of contacts with the center (see Figure 17.2). Inpatient costs were 19%

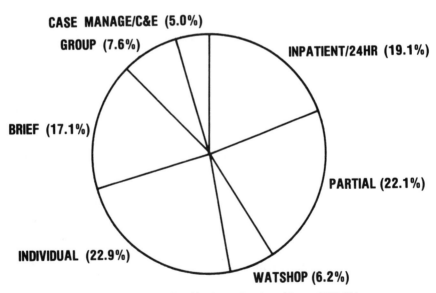

(Mental Health Center of Boulder County, Inc. Annual Report, 1985–86.)

FIGURE 17.1
MHCBC Fiscal Year Costs
(FY '85–'86)

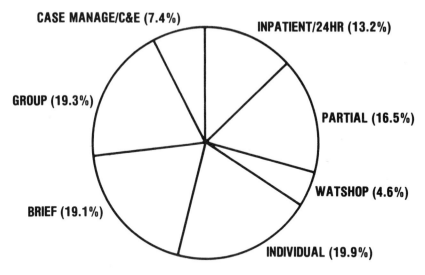

(Mental Health Center of Boulder County, Inc. Annual Report, 1985–86.)

FIGURE 17.2
MHCBC Fiscal Year Contacts
(FY '85–'86)

of the budget but represented only 13% of the contacts. Partial care cost 22% of the budget and represented only 16½% of contacts. Figure 17.3 shows the center's sources of revenue for 1986. The portion called Client Paid (42%) includes mostly Medicaid reimbursement. In 1986, Medicaid generated just over 1.1 million dollars in revenue for the program. Directly assessed client fees generated about $250,000 and other third-party insurance generated just over $200,000 in revenue.

ADMINISTRATIVE PHILOSOPHY

Phoebe Norton, an M.S.W., has been executive director of the Mental Health Center of Boulder County for six years. She provides strong administrative leadership by seeing her role *as helping the board define its mission and priorities*. She does not see her job as defining how the mission will be carried out; rather, she sees herself as providing space and helping to find the resources for professionals to do what works best to accomplish the mission she and her board have defined.

In collaboration with the center's board of directors, she identified three areas of programmatic priorities:

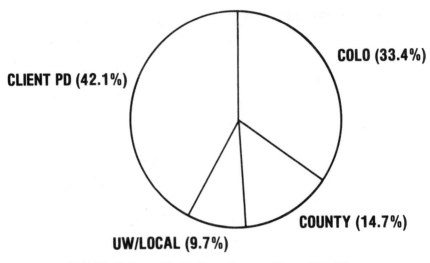

(Mental Health Center of Boulder County, Inc. Annual Report, 1985–86.)

FIGURE 17.3
Sources of Revenue
1986

1. Within the limits of public resources they will provide easily accessible services to those who don't have any private sector services available to them. Specially targeted are persons with major mental illness.
2. Emergency services are central to the function of the center. They should be well advertised, rapidly accessible services available to persons who don't make or keep the usual mental health type appointments.
3. Child and adolescents at risk for out-of-home placement must receive a high priority for services focused on maintaining them at home, in foster care, or in group homes. Placement in intensive residential care (i.e., hospital or residential treatment centers) within or outside of the county should be avoided if at all possible. Early intervention to support the families of origin of high-risk children should be the first intervention of choice.

As may be seen in what follows, the program is actively, and mostly successfully, pursuing these program goals. The extract material was taken from a program description written by Dr. Richard Warner, the medical director of the Boulder County Mental Health Program.

THE BOULDER TREATMENT SYSTEM

The Mental Health Center of Boulder County is a comprehensive community mental health center which offers a full range of psychiatric services to the 210,000 residents of the mixed urban and rural region of Boulder County, Colorado.

The center sees about 4,000 clients each year; about 2,000 cases are active at any one time and about 350 of these suffer from functional psychoses.

Philosophy regarding most severely disturbed and disturbing clients: In the face of growing problems it has become apparent that community care for psychotic patients demands a range of support services far greater than was generally appreciated in the early decades of the deinstitutional era. Effective community support requires that the mental health agency: adopt total responsibility for the severely disabled client's welfare, including helping the patient acquire such material resources as food, shelter, clothing and medical care; aggressively pursue clients' interests — insuring that other social agencies fulfill their obligations, for example, or actively searching for patients who drop out of treatment; provide a range of supportive services which can be tailored to fit each patient's needs and which will continue as long as needed; educate the patient to live and work in the community; and provide support to family, friends, and community members.

The community support system of the Mental Health Center of Boulder County has been built on the premise that no psychotic patients should remain in degrading and nontherapeutic environments. In Boulder County the mental health center places no physically healthy functional psychotics in nursing homes. The administrators of the center have actively discouraged local nursing home operators from opening wards for chronically ill psychiatric patients, arguing that nursing homes cannot provide an adequate quality of care and environment for such patients. In Boulder County there are no boarding homes housing the mentally ill (though there is a cheap hotel clients have used on occasion), and when patients are located living on the streets or in an emergency shelter efforts are made to accommodate them in one of the residential facilities described below.

INTENSIVE RESIDENTIAL TREATMENT

Cedar House is a large house for 15 psychiatric patients in a residential and business district of the city of Boulder. It functions principally as an alternative to a psychiatric hospital and in part as a halfway house. Like a psychiatric hospital it offers all the usual diagnostic and treatment services but, costing less than a third as much as private hospital treatment, it is feasible for patients to remain in residence for quite long periods of time if necessary. Usually admitted with some kind of an acute psychiatric problem (most often an acute psychotic relapse), a client may stay anywhere from a day to a year or longer; the average period is three to four weeks.

About 25 patients a month are admitted, one-third of whom will be committed, at least for the initial 72 hours. Thirty percent of the clients are new; the rest are regulars. Since the establishment of the mobile Community Support team in 1984, the number of long-term system veterans admitted to Cedar House has dropped from two-thirds of the admissions to one-third. These admissions have been replaced by persons carrying mostly psychotic depressive diagnoses.

Unlike a psychiatric hospital, Cedar House is noncoercive. No patient can be strapped down, locked in, or medicated unwillingly. Staff must encourage patients to comply voluntarily with treatment requirements and house rules. The people who cannot be managed are those who repeatedly walk away or run away and those who are violent. Since the alternative for patients who are unable to stay at Cedar House is hospital treatment, *which virtually none prefer*,* the large majority of residents accept the necessary restrictions. Very few patients (about 10%, usually assaultive or runners) need to be transferred to hospital. In practice, most clients with schizophrenia or psychotic depression can be treated at Cedar House through all phases of their illness, and many patients with acute mania can also be managed successfully. There is little doubt that a large number of the people treated in this residential facility would be subject to coercive measures, such as restraints or seclusion, if they were admitted to a hospital where such approaches are available and routinely used. The avoidance of coercion is considered to be the first step in the important process of maintaining the psychotic patient's status and self-esteem.

To the same end, the environment is deliberately styled to be similar to that of a middle-class home, not a hospital. The floors are carpeted, a fire burns in the hearth, a cat curls up in the most comfortable chair, shelves of books are available, residents and visitors come and go fairly freely, staff and patients interact casually, eat together and are encouraged to treat one another with mutual respect. The goal is to allow therapists and clients alike to retain their dignity and humanity and to foster cooperation.

In line with this emphasis, each resident is intimately involved in running the household. He or she is responsible for specific tasks which are assigned and supervised by one of the residents. These cooperative living arrangements reduce treatment costs, increase the residents' sense of belonging, and can be useful training for marginally functional people. A full-scale, therapeutic community style of patient government has not been established. In view of the relatively brief length of patient stay and the necessity for staff and administration to exercise close control over patient admission and discharge (in order to make room for new acute admissions at all times), patient government is not considered workable. The ethos of the community, however, calls for residents routinely to be concerned with the care of others.

Residential treatment of this intensity requires a staffing pattern similar to that of a hospital. A mental health worker and a nurse are on duty at all times. At night, one of the two is awake and the other sleeps. On weekdays, two experienced therapists work with the patients. A psychiatrist is present for three hours a day, a social worker directs the program, and a secretarial assis-

*Emphasis by LRM, LB

tant manages the office work and the purchasing of household supplies. The treatment setting calls for staff who are tolerant and empathic, and it brings out their capacity independently to find inventive solutions to difficult problems.

There is no commonly used form of psychiatric treatment or diagnostic measure which cannot be provided for residents of this treatment facility (except for electroconvulsive therapy). Patients with acute or chronic organic brain disorders, for example, can be evaluated using the laboratories and diagnostic equipment of local hospitals. Consulting physicians provide treatment for medical problems.

An essential step in the treatment of people entering Cedar House is the evaluation of the patient's social system. What has happened to bring the patient in for treatment at this particular time? What are his or her financial circumstances, living arrangements and work situation? Have there been recent changes? Are there family tensions? From the answers to such questions as these, a plan may be made which will hopefully diminish the chances of relapse after the patient leaves residential treatment.

The period of residential treatment also allows the opportunity to spend time observing the patient's illness, selecting a suitable drug when necessary, monitoring and adjusting the dosage to minimize side effects and evaluating the benefits. A distinct advantage of the more leisurely pace of this residential treatment program compared with brief hospitalization is that it allows an opportunity for selected psychotic patients to be treated without drugs.

A determined trial of treatment without antipsychotic drugs (often several weeks' or months' duration) is made with certain patients. Appropriate cases include psychotics with good prognostic features, patients who have previously functioned quite well without the use of drugs, and those who are in their first psychotic episode. Other candidates for neuroleptic-free treatment are patients who have failed to respond positively to antipsychotic drugs, those with relatively mild psychoses who steadfastly refuse drug treatment, and some who have developed tardive dyskinesia. The benzodiazepines have proved extremely valuable as an alternative to the antipsychotic drugs in many cases and as an adjunct in others. In the short run, the minor tranquilizers are generally more effective than the neuroleptics in calming agitated patients and they often markedly reduce psychotic symptoms. Tolerance to the antipsychotic action of these drugs does develop in due course, so their value is mainly during the first hours and days after an admission to the acute treatment setting.

Cedar House is a relatively expensive program (about $110 per day). The required level of staffing imposes high fixed costs which cannot be reduced without seriously altering the nature of the program. Such costs would not be justifiable for an agency with a small catchment area (much below 200,000 persons). With the fixed costs of Cedar House, as available funding decreases, cuts have to be made instead in outpatient services and other parts of the community support system, with consequent deterioration in continuity of care. In these circumstances the risk is of creating a new type of revolving door patient — one who repeatedly reenters the residential community facility.

By comparison with an intensive community treatment program such as Stein and Test's in Madison, Wisconsin (see Chapter 18), Cedar House is more institutional. By treating patients a stage further removed from their usual surroundings it may be somewhat more like a hospital in stigmatizing and dehumanizing its clientele. On the other hand, programs which are more deeply immersed in the community rely more heavily upon drug treatment for their success, often using rapid tranquilization for the treatment of acute episodes of illness. Periods of hospitalization have to be brief; psychotic behavior must be efficiently brought under control if the patient is to remain in the community. The Cedar House intensive residential program allows treatment decisions, including decisions on the use of medications, to be taken at a more measured pace and it offers the possibility of drug-free treatment in selected cases.

Additional Information, Based on a Visit by LRM

Although clearly not a hospital, Cedar House sees itself as a psychiatric inpatient unit. The morning report is like that found in hospitals, discussion is focused principally on the patient's diagnosis, nurses are generally in charge, and there is an explicit focus on things medical. Neuroleptic and antidepressant drug blood levels are routinely obtained. Nurses must hand out all medications. A fair amount of time and energy is expended on getting collateral and record-based information about clients, with less reliance on information elicited from the clients themselves.

Admissions come mostly from the Center's Crisis Service. The Community Support Team and outpatient MHC therapists may admit without going through the Crisis Service. All clients are seen by the Cedar House psychiatrist (usually Dr. Warner) within 24 hours. Cedar House staff do not usually follow clients after discharge; they either return to their therapist/case managers or are hooked up with the MHC outpatient department. Insufficient supported, supervised housing creates impediments to discharge.

The in-house program has varied considerably but there are daily community meetings (9:30–10:15 a.m.) and two mandatory afternoon groups per week (art, living skills, music, calisthenics, peer socialization, or group therapy). There is a nightly "chore group" from 7:00 to 7:30. The TV is kept off until chores are finished. Suspension from the house or restriction to the house or bedroom is used for behavioral control.

Individual client attention is available during the daytime hours from a nurse, two therapists, and a residential treatment coordinator. In general, these sessions are focused on assessment of goals attained and establishment of new goals (i.e., planning) with the clients. There is not a great deal of formal, individual, in-office psychotherapy as such. Outside therapists are urged to remain involved and invited to meetings. The Longmont team (Cedar House is in Boulder but is used as an alternative by nearby Longmont and the rest of the community as well) sends someone weekly to coordinate care of their patients.

Meals at Cedar House are mostly a staff responsibility. Breakfast and lunch are set out by a mental health worker, who is helped by a client at lunch. There is a cook five days a week to prepare dinner. Staff do it the other two days. Clients do setup and cleanup. It is said that meal preparation is used as a test of functioning, but it is not clear exactly how this works in practice.

In order to address issues of continuity of care across two different geographical sites (Boulder and Longmont) and three types of inpatient facility (Cedar House, psychiatric wards in general hospitals and Fort Logan, the state hospital), liaison persons from each meet on a weekly basis to iron out difficulties and ease access between the various facilities and programs.

As a residential alternative to psychiatric hospitalization, Cedar House is larger than most and more medical than most. Because of these two factors alone, the nature of relationships there tend to be rather more hierarchical than horizontal. While informal peer-oriented contacts are certainly possible, the house's day program is clearly hospital like, with outside experts being brought in to run the groups.

On the other hand, Cedar House's ability to let patients stay a long time and its willingness to take committed patients and to treat without drugs are very unusual and, in our minds, excellent features. Also, the fact that it handles the vast majority of patients in this system who would otherwise be hospitalized makes it a *critical*, rather than an add-on, element of the system. Since the other two options—short stays in private psychiatric wards (usually not in Boulder) or long ones in the state hospital (also not in Boulder)—are generally much less appealing to patients, especially those who have experienced them (as most have), Cedar House has been, over time, a potent force in the formation of antihospitalization attitudes among clients and staff alike. There is very little pro-hospital sentiment anywhere in the system. The MHC psychiatrists are on salary (supplemented by covering weekends), so there is no advantage to them to use a hospital bed. Because three of them have been there for 10 years or so, they are quite comfortable with the use of Cedar House. In the same vein, because Cedar House has been in existence for 10 years, staff throughout the system are quite accustomed to its being the primary site of intensive residential care. For us, it is the most innovative and creative piece of the Boulder system.

MOBILE COMMUNITY SUPPORT TEAM

Until 1984, outpatient care for Boulder County psychotic clients was provided by the center's outpatient teams in the city of Boulder and in the town of Longmont. Caseloads on these teams are about 30 clients for each therapist. In order to improve services to the most severely disturbed psychotics and to decrease the revolving door phenomenon, a new team offering intensive community care was established in 1984. Therapists on this Community Support Team (modeled after Madison's mobile community team) have small caseloads of around 15 clients. The team is responsible for 75 of the most difficult-to-treat patients (50 diagnosed as schizophrenic, 25 as manic-depressive) out of a total of 350 psychotics being treated by the center's teams. Patients assigned to the program are those who tend to relapse frequently and who appear to be most in need of the special services provided by the team. These services include: a day care program; therapist contact several times a week when needed; help with money management; home visiting; emergency intervention; daily monitoring of medication; and placement in one of the center's supervised apartments or in the halfway house.

The team operates out of a large, old fraternity house. Since it is separate from the center's main outpatient offices, the patients may use the building fairly freely as a drop-in facility.

Establishing a team with a special mission and assigning to it staff with a particular interest in treating psychotic patients have eased many of the staffing problems commonly encountered in treating this population of patients. Staff on this team have had little difficulty in abandoning the traditional 50-minute therapy session and in developing flexible and innovative responses to their client's crises. Team members provide support for one another in working with very demanding clients, and they are able to establish reasonable goals for progress in treatment, which are substantially different from the expectations of outpatient therapists on teams treating less disturbed patients. On the other hand, the creation of a new team has multiplied the number of inter-team disputes. The same patient, for example, may be treated at different times by the center's emergency service, by the jail outreach program, by Cedar House, and by the Community Support Team. Even small differences in philosophy become magnified by such an arrangement, and concerns about the use of scarce treatment resources are pushed to the foreground. Despite the need for a significant initial investment of administrative effort to work out such problems, the team has clearly improved the center's ability to care for its most difficult clients.

Additional Information

The team has five staff plus 18 hours a week of psychiatrist time. Thirty-five of the clients are on daily monitoring of medications and 35 are on money management. Generally, receiving their daily allowance is paired with taking medication. The meds and money transactions constitute a substantial segment of the day program offered (i.e., 10–12 a.m. daily), although on most days there is an additional group activity (cooking, art, yoga, outdoors). An additional 13 clients are on injectable neuroleptics.

In their role as case managers, team members make about 150 in-residence visits per month. This team also controls access to, and is responsible for, the center's supervised housing program.

The team's effectiveness has recently been documented in an evaluation by Moira Powers, Ph.D., who found that since the C.S.P.'s team inception (three years ago) its clients' days in hospital have been halved (from 6.6 to 3.3 days per month) and their readmissions have decreased by 28%.

It seems that, while this team is still evolving its modus operandi, this aggressive outreach has decreased readmission rates substantially. The ethics of pairing money and meds still troubles this observer. Targeted and low-dose regimes are not often discussed *as such*, although they are used to some extent in practice.

SUPERVISED APARTMENTS

An important function of the Community Support Team is to manage the center's long-established system of supervised and rent-subsidized housing. The unemployed psychotic, unless living with his or her family, is likely to live in a seedy low-rent room, a boarding home, or nursing home. Many, having fallen ill early in life, have little experience of independent living. Some have poor judgment and lack the capacity to manage a household. For such people supervised housing is a necessity.

Many agencies have demonstrated that cooperative apartments work well for chronically ill patients who are leaving hospitals after several years of residence but until recently such group homes have less commonly been proved viable for younger psychotic patients who have not spent years in an institution. These patients, generally more volatile, subject to relapse and likely to abuse drugs and alcohol, require a more intensive level of supervision. In the Boulder supervised living program, staff members hold house meetings for residents at least once a week in their apartments, in addition to providing other outpatient services. The therapist often has to give a good deal of assistance with budgeting and in many cases actually manages the patient's money. Help with household management often involves sorting out problems with "crashers" or disputes over household chores.

More than 40 center patients live in supervised apartments in Boulder County. For many psychotics, living alone is the best arrangement, since the stresses of cooperative living may provoke relapse; others find loneliness to be a major problem. Supervised apartments in Boulder range in size from one person (five such) to eight-person households. At some of the larger houses a university student is hired to live in (rent free) and to provide a little supervision in the evenings. These larger houses can accommodate clients who have more limited capacity for independent living. By supplying increasing amounts of staff support on the premises, it has been possible to develop a range of community living arrangements up to the level of the traditional, staffed halfway house ("980"), for clients with progressively lower levels of functioning.

In high-rent Boulder, some form of rent subsidy is necessary for clients, who must often exist on limited Social Security income. Such financial assistance is available through the federal Department of Housing and Urban Development, either as direct rent subsidies or as grants to mental health agencies to build or buy new accommodations. Interested members of the public have also provided houses at reduced rent for mental health center clients. In most instances, the center operates as a tenant, subleasing the house or apartment to the patients.

Additional Information

Because of rent subsidies clients pay only $40–$110 per month plus utilities. In both the apartments and group home (980), clients don't really eat together, although at 980 two meals are shopped for and prepared by staff and clients. In general, we believe that apartment mates with long institutional histories are the ones usually reluctant to share food and meals because of having been taken care of in hospitals and having learned there to be afraid of theft. However, Boulder clients, with little institutionalism, still exhibit this "institutionalized" characteristic.

JAIL SERVICE

In the U.S. many psychotics end up in local jails. To mitigate this problem it has become increasingly important for mental health agencies to supply outreach services to jails in their catchment areas. In Boulder, the jail outreach program, in operation for many years, consists of a well-trained mental health professional visiting the jail twice a week, accompanied once a week by a psychiatrist. On other days, the center's emergency service responds to urgent calls to evaluate inmates. The principal objective of the service is to arrange proper treatment for all seriously mentally ill inmates, which usually involves the transfer of psychotic patients to an appropriate treatment setting. This goal requires the development of working relationships with jail staff, judges, defense lawyers, and the district attorney's office. Occasionally, the judge or district attorney will not allow the release of a mentally ill person because the crime is too serious; in these cases, placement in the forensic unit of the state mental hospital is recommended. Sometimes the defense attorney opposes such a transfer and more complex negotiations ensue. In fact, the criminal justice system sets up very few serious obstacles to the evaluation, treatment and disposition of jail inmates; the main problems arise within the mental health system itself. Two important issues are, "Which psychotics should be released from jail?" and "Where do they go when hospital beds and other treatment resources are in short supply?"

Many mental health professionals feel that jail is good for certain psychotic patients. Sometimes it is argued that the "structure" of the correctional institution is reassuring to the patient, or that everyone, regardless of mental illness, must learn the consequences of his or her actions. Other professionals will point out that many psychotics who enter jail do *not* learn from the experience; that they cycle through repeatedly for the same offenses, sometimes merely to gain shelter; and that the crimes of psychotic jail inmates are often a product of poor judgment or poverty which flow from their illness. Correctional staff will report, moreover, that very many psychotic inmates do *not* respond to the institutional structure; they are so resistant, in fact, to the usual controls that they spend their entire period of incarceration locked into solitary confinement in order to protect themselves and others from abuse and exploitation.

Most professionals would agree that an acutely psychotic and agitated person should be transferred from jail to a treatment setting; most would also agree that a psychotic whose symptoms are under good control and whose crime was completely unrelated to his or her illness need not be released. In between these clearcut cases there is much room for philosophical disagreement. How should we respond, for example, to the client whose crime is a product of his psychosis but who chooses to refuse treatment to control his illness? A solution which usually meets with general approval is for the client to answer to his charges and to be obliged to accept psychiatric treatment as a condition of bond, suspended sentencing, or probation. An overall consensus may never be reached within the agency on the philosophy of individual responsibility in mental illness, however hard one strives for a uniform attitude. In the final instance, the administrators of the agency must formulate a jail policy if the community support system is to work efficiently and if good relations with the criminal justice system are to be preserved.

Agency administrators will also feel it necessary to be involved in jail policy because of the impact on the use of treatment resources. Often the psychotics who spend most time in jail are those who have proved particularly difficult to treat in community programs. The number of psychotics in the jail can be an indicator of a shortage of hospital beds or residential placements relative to the number of psychotics in the community. To respond to the needs of the local jail is to be confronted with the adequacy of the entire community support program.

The Boulder jail was a "model" one when built. Its 220 inmate spaces are now insufficient and a new one is under construction. Colorado law requires 24-hour nurse coverage in jails; hence, nurses provide the initial screening for the Mental Health Center personnel who evaluate clients in the jail. They are also able to do the ongoing care (medication) in the jail.

HOSPITAL BEDS

Paradoxically, one of the most crucial elements in a community support system is the psychiatric hospital. However comprehensive the community programs may be, there will remain a handful of patients who cannot be cared for outside of the hospital. A few patients consistently refuse treatment and will always walk away from an open-door establishment; a few become violent and fail to respond to the usual forms of treatment, representing a danger to mental health staff and members of the public. Some psychotics exacerbate their condition by constant using of hallucinogens or alcohol or by inhaling volatile solvents. When even the most well-supervised community placements fail, these patients are likely to end up in jail or on the street; moreover, the effort to help them will have put an immense strain on the community support system. Many hours of work will have been put into makeshift treatment plans which have little hope of success.

Recognizing that the severely restricted access to state hospital beds was creating major problems of this type, in 1983 the administrators of the Boulder County program and other Colorado mental health centers negotiated with the State Division of Mental Health to allocate state hospital beds to each county on an equitable basis. The resulting arrangement has proved highly beneficial. County mental health centers now work closely with the state hospital to use their limited number of beds to best effect. The number of psychotics in the Boulder County jail has been drastically reduced. At any time the number of adult patients of Boulder County in state or private hospitals is around 15 to 20. About 10 of these patients will be long-term inpatients who will be in the hospital for over a year. The remainder are medium- and short-stay patients, staying from a few days to a few months. Clearly, the number of psychotics who need long-term hospital care are few — less than 3% of the 350 or so functionally psychotic patients enrolled at the Boulder County Mental Health Center — but it is of prime importance for the community that this level of care be available.

Additional Information

Boulder County is allotted 15 beds in the Fort Logan MHC, to which they admitted 85 patients in 1986. Fort Logan is located in nearby Denver. It is one of Colorado's two "state" hospitals. These beds are paid for by the state; hence there is no incentive for Boulder not to use them. About 10 of them basically do not turn over (i.e., these patients are in for over a year); these are the Boulder County truly long-stay patients. The other five beds are filled with patients who usually stay less than three months. Fort Logan was originally designed as a model to replace that of traditional state hospitals: It was focused on active treatment and short stays. In its heyday it was widely viewed as the state hospital of the future. Now it is functioning much more like the state hospital of old, the asylum of last resort.

Boulder also admits patients to psychiatric wards in general hospitals. In 1986 there were 152 such admissions for a total of 2,278 days (average stay of 15 days). These beds cost over $500 a day, are mostly in general hospitals in Denver (35 miles away), and are paid for by Medicaid or by a $28,000 fund the MHC sets aside to pay for such care when no other alternative is available.

Regarding involuntary treatment, there were just over 300 72-hour holds in Boulder in 1986, 225 instituted by the police. Of these, 74 went on to be committed. On any given day Boulder has 25 patients on commitments.

Comment: Ten truly long-stay patients is a modest, and perhaps minimal, number. One must wonder, though, what would happen if the state began to charge Boulder for care at Fort Logan, while at the same time making 50% or more of the cost of the 15 beds available to them for local programs.

VOCATIONAL SERVICES

Reflecting a belief that the provision of a working role is often of central importance in the development of self-esteem and higher functioning in psychotic patients (Warner, 1985), vocational programs have been heavily emphasized in the Boulder County Support System. During times of high unemployment and economic recession, however, it is not possible to meet client needs in full. The center's sheltered workshop obtains work from private industry, and in hard times such contracts are difficult to find. Consequently, the number of clients employed in the workshop fluctuates between 35 and 50, the waiting list for placement usually being several weeks long. While the mental health center can subsidize the business income of the sheltered workshop to a certain extent, it is impractical to increase the subsidies too far.

A little less than one-half of the Sheltered Workshop's income is from the center subsidy. The total cost of the program is $50 per day per client. "The result of this pressure is a tendency to keep the more productive patients on the workshop rolls and to screen out the lower functioning clients." Clients are paid by the piece at the level they would earn in private industry at their own level of productivity. In practice they will earn anywhere from 95¢ to $5 an hour.

For several years the center operated a transitional employment program (TEP) through which higher-functioning clients were placed in jobs in private industry under close professional supervision. Some of these jobs were on the production line of a furniture factory; others involved office work. Job training was done by the mental health center's program supervisor, and if the client-employee was unable to work one day, the center insured that someone else turned up to work, even if the supervisor had to do it himself or herself.

This program was recently terminated because the State Department of Vocational Rehabilitation demanded a three-month limit on TEP's. Center staff see this as their unwillingness to accept the possibility of failure. The state vocational rehabilitation department is seen as good for planning, testing, and getting clients training but as not very effective in direct work-seeking. The Center for People with Disabilities in Boulder is less bureaucratic, faster, teaches applicants skills directly, and looks for appropriate work placements for them according to staff.

With the limitations imposed by the labor market, economic conditions and restricted vocational services, other options for clients must be found. Many of the lower-functioning patients are referred to the day care program; higher-functioning clients are encouraged to find volunteer jobs in local libraries, hospitals and other public agencies.

Comment: Boulder does not have either a Fountain House model psychosocial rehabilitation center or an ex-client-run program with a vocational focus. It's not clear whether changing the current sheltered workshop format to a membership-oriented club would provide more, and wider range of, vocational opportunities. Supported, community-based, work opportunities are not plentiful. The training component in vocational rehabilitation does not seem to be well addressed by the present arrangement.

CRISIS TEAM (EMERGENCY PSYCHIATRIC SERVICES)

The Crisis Team is staffed by masters in psychology or social workers. Because of the nature of the Boulder community and the availability of volunteers who will then be looking for regular jobs, the Crisis Team is able to train volunteers for one year before they become eligible to work on it. The team works in three shifts with two or three people on a shift, for a total staff of 15. It is possible for a person to wait as long as 30 minutes for a call to get through to them. There is a roughly two-hour wait between the time of the call and when someone can be seen.

Seventy-five percent of the calls are from the concerned person himself and 20–30% of clientele are unknown walk-ins. They average 600–700 calls a month and roughly 20% are seen face to face. They routinely see anyone who is thought to be a danger to himself or others, as well as all psychotics and children. In addition to self-referred clients there are police referrals and emergency referrals from the community hospital.

After business hours the crisis team operates out of offices in a private psychiatric hospital. The on-call backup psychiatrist is always called about any involuntarily detained people, about admissions to hospital or residential care, or with any questions regarding medication, medical problems, or difficulty with diagnosis. The team can refer as necessary to hospital, jail, the alcoholism treatment center, battered women's shelter, juvenile detention, or nursing homes. If residential care is not necessary, the team can refer clients to the adult outpatient services. Because of a two-to-three-week wait to be seen there, a crisis group and an assessment group have been started to bridge the time gap between referral and intake. This is an in-office-only crisis intervention team.

THE RAPE CRISIS TEAM

Boulder has a nationally known Rape Crisis Team that began as a purely voluntary organization. In the last year, it has obtained funds to enable it to have a fulltime coordinator and administrative assistant. They use more than 50 volunteers in its program for rape victims, advocating for them, educating the public regarding rape, providing ongoing support groups, and offering public self-defense classes.

CHILD, ADOLESCENT AND FAMILY SERVICES OF BOULDER COUNTY

This service has a clinical director of its own with stature within the hierarchy equivalent to that of clinical director of adult services. She heads both the Boulder and Longmont Child and Adolescent Services. Including support staff and contract employees, the outpatient team has roughly seven fulltime equivalent positions. The outpatient team provides regular individual and family counseling services to clients at the mental health center and, in addition, consults with the schools of the Boulder valley. Extensive consultation and assessment services in Headstart programs and with social services, youth programs, the child protection agency, juvenile probation, and other agencies are also available. There are day treatment programs in elementary schools in Boulder and Longmont and day treatment for adolescents in Longmont.

The Adolescent Day and Residential Treatment Program was begun in 1984 as a result of combining Medicaid with the special state Senate Bill 26 monies. This program is the combined effort of the mental health center, the school system, and the social services department of Boulder County. Basically it provides an intensive specialized educational program with a number of therapeutic components for roughly 20 adolescents. The program is focused on adolescents between 12 and 16 who are in special education, are handicapped academically or emotionally, and for whom hospital or other residential treatment has been utilized or is being seriously considered. The program has 24 staff, including staff of the eight-bed residential facility. The day program staff is comprised of three fulltime teachers, three fulltime therapists, three fulltime teacher assistants, and six residential counselors, plus a director of the program. The extended day program (after school) has a fulltime director and two counselors. The special educational program is very intensive, with a teacher and teacher assistant in each of three classrooms. The adolescents are taught the curriculum of the appropriate grade from the Boulder County system. The extended day program covers the three hours after school. It is focused on prevocational skills, leisure time skills, and socialization in the context of a positive group experience. There are also fulltime summer and jobs programs.

Family involvement is required, and there is generally one family therapy session a week for each of the children. There are twice-weekly groups for the adolescents and two or three individual sessions per week per child. In addition, there is an evening parent group. The school and residential program has four hours of child-psychiatrist time. Some 80% of the children in the program are on probation and roughly 60% leave the program successfully. This program, along with other adolescent programs, have cut the use of out-of-county placement from 100 a year to 25!

The last program under the umbrella of the Child, Adolescent and Family Services is the Community Infant Project. This project is in its third year of serving high-risk parents and their infants. The focus is on early intervention through parenting skills training and help with attachment problems to ensure the optimal development of infants and young children up to three years of age. The families are selected because the child is thought to be at risk for abuse. In 1986, 61 families received ongoing treatment from the team. The team does on the order of 170 home visits per month. Ergo, each family in treatment will be seen a couple times a month at home and several more times in the center.

ADULT OUTPATIENT SERVICES

There is a two-person geriatric team which goes out to private homes and nursing homes where geriatric clients are living to provide services. They make on the order of 30 home visits per month.

The Boulder Adult Outpatient Clinic has four and a half fulltime equivalents plus support staff. It operates on a sliding scale fee basis between $3 and $60. There are very few patients with third-party coverage. Most of those with any sort of insurance are seen by private practitioners in the city. On its rolls the team has roughly 100 veterans of the system who need case management rather than psychotherapy. In addition, there are about 200 clients in psychotherapy. The adult outpatient team is not completely happy with the role of case manager.

Someone who shows up for therapy goes through a three-step process, beginning with the acquisition of face sheet information by an administrative person, who then finds an appointment time with a clinician. The intake slots are limited, so there can be a substantial wait before the patient is evaluated. At the intake a mental status, treatment goals, and treatment plan are formulated. Ordinarily clients are seen once a week in what one might call psychodynamic, eclectic, but short-term, psychotherapy. All the therapists are under weekly clinical supervision with the team leader, Kirk Hartman, M.S.W. Most family therapy is done by the child and adolescent family service, but the adult service does do couple work. All clinicians are asked to do at least one group. There is a time-limited women's group, a mixed adult group to sharpen interpersonal skills, a crisis group, an aftercare group, a borderlines' group, and *nine* batterers' groups. There is, in addition, a weekly prolixin group with a nurse, and an assessment group for people who are in the process of moving between various services. There is a similarly constituted but smaller adult outpatient team in Longmont.

The Colorado abuser situation is a little different from that in most states, since any time the police find that abuse has occurred they are required to book the man and take him to jail. There he will be remanded to treatment as a condition of bond. The batterer is then placed in a 24-week group that uses a text called *Learning to Live without Violence* (Sonkin & Durphy, 1985). Group leaders try to teach a number of anger control techniques, such as early recognition of signs of anger, timeouts, and avoidance of violence perpetuation.

Costs of the various treatments are: the individual therapy, $51 an hour; group at $18; case management, $21 a visit; and brief therapy (that is, a less than 30-minute session), $36.

THE OUTPATIENT DRUG ABUSE TEAMS
IN BOULDER AND LONGMONT

The center received special drug abuse money and bought seven staff plus eight hours per week of psychiatric time with it. The team has 250 cases open at any one time and sees a total of 600 cases in a course of a year. This is basically a psychodynamically oriented counseling program with detoxification done either in the hospital or at Cedar House. There are substantial drug abuse problems in Boulder, in part because of the college but also because of its being a "hippie" center.

ALCOHOLISM SERVICES

In the Colorado system, the public health department is responsible for alcohol treatment services. Alcoholics who are polydrug abusers or who are psychotic are referred to the mental health center; otherwise the alcoholism recovery center provides inpatient detoxification and an outpatient clinic. Antabuse monitoring and AA are also used.

AMI

The Alliance for the Mentally Ill (AMI) has members on the center's board. Twice a year the Alliance cosponsors a course with center staff on major mental illness, inviting the mentally ill, their relatives, and the public. The Alliance helped in the development of the supervised apartment program and generally is in very close relationship with the mental health center. There is a small, newly formed manic-depressive group.

VOLUNTEERS

There are volunteers on the Rape Crisis Team (more than 50), the Community Support Team, Cedar House, and Friendship Club (a Mental Health Center program). Volunteers are also used in a Maitri style program in which they provide a social network or in one case live one-to-one with a seriously disturbed person. It is possible to find these 150 volunteers because of the presence of the university and Naropa Institute in Boulder.

MISCELLANEOUS INFORMATION

The center has a great deal of continuing education for its staff—advanced psychopharmacology, short-term therapies, etc. In the last five years they've used ECT one time.

PROGRAM COMMENTS

The Boulder County Mental Health Program is large, diverse, and highly specialized and differentiated in its functioning. The degree of specialization of functioning seems to be driven in large part by the kinds of money that are available to support various staff activities. For example, except for the way the money was obtained, they would not have started the Adult Outpatient Drug Abuse Program as a separate entity, but rather would have included it under Adult Outpatient Services. The program literally has something for anyone who might need services. They have identified two areas where they feel deficient: the client mutual help area, and supervised living arrangements. They need about 10 more apartment spaces and another, more intensively staffed group home or halfway house arrangement for 10 long-term, low-functioning clients in the community. Some would come out of Fort Logan, several are Cedar House frequent users, and others are just not doing well in the present living arrangements.

Our comments with regard to the existing programs follow:

1. *Crisis intervention services:* These are readily available by telephone and apparently it is possible to be seen relatively quickly. However, the team members never leave their offices to do in-residence crisis intervention, although they do go to the jail and general hospital emergency rooms. By not doing so, they probably have a hospitalization or alternative to hospitalization rate which is higher than it needs to be.

2. *Continuity:* It is very difficult to come into this system and experience any continuity of persons. The crisis intervention team does

not follow people and it serves only as a first contact point. Following this contact a client could be referred to any one of a number of specialized services or to some kind of residential care where he would not see the same persons at all. So, a customer can be seen by the crisis team, be sent to Cedar House, and go from there to the Adult Outpatient Clinic for follow-up treatment and case management. This would require the client to deal with three completely different staffs, probably a less than ideal situation for seriously disturbed persons.

3. *Responsibility:* The system is responsible for everyone who comes to it. The only "back doors" are to Fort Logan for 15 very difficult-to-manage patients and to various adolescent treatment centers for 25 adolescents who can't be taken care of within the county's existing resources.

4. *Medication:* The team is rather thoughtful, innovative, and concerned about tardive dyskinesia. For example: They will use benzodiazepines to control psychotic behavior acutely; they will attempt to treat either newly identified psychotics or psychotics who have not responded to neuroleptics without neuroleptics; they will switch from lithium to tegretol rather rapidly if the person is nonresponsive to lithium; they believe in as low-dose a regime as possible for psychotic clients who are on the mobile community support teams roster. This is basically a thoughtful, responsible medication policy by physicians who have larger roles in the system than mere prescription writing. The policy evolved because they have three psychiatrists who have been there for 10 years or more, are used to working together, and are of a basically one mind about the question of how drug therapy should be approached. In addition, they provide themselves with ongoing educational activities about newer notions of drug (and other) treatment. Although they are not *consciously* using "targeted" or "low-dose" strategies, they do so in practice.

5. *Family orientation:* Although not all the clinicians have a family and/or social network focus, the Child, Adolescent and Family Services clearly is staffed with very competent family-oriented persons. The Adolescent Treatment Program with its school and residence is clearly quite family-focused. The Community Support Program team provides a lot of family support and counseling.

6. *Leaving the system:* Not much is said about the possibility of leaving the system and going out on your own, but one has the feeling that the overall laissez-faire atmosphere of the town and the Mental Health Center is probably conducive to people's being able to leave if they wish.

7. *Rewards:* There is no system of rewards for more face-to-face contact and better outcome.

8. *Hierarchy:* The hierarchy in the Boulder program is modest. Under the executive director (Phoebe Norton) are a medical director (Dr. Warner) and two clinical directors — one for adult and one for child and family services. Each small specialized program seemed to be left pretty much on its own to develop its own modus operandi.

9. *Theoretical orientation:* There is no clearly identifiable umbrella theoretical orientation. It seemed as though the Adult Outpatient Clinic had (like most) been psychoanalytic/psychodynamically oriented and was now gradually moving more into time-limited and group techniques. The physicians are very well integrated into the program but do not dominate it in an ongoing way. My sense was that most folks there were basically pragmatists who wanted to do whatever worked best. Serious ideological commitments were hard to identify.

CHAPTER 18

An Integrated System: Dane County, Wisconsin

OVERVIEW AND BACKGROUND

THE INFORMATION INCLUDED HERE IS derived from two full days of interviews with service unit managers (e.g., Emergency Services) and key administrators. Relevant written materials (see references) were also reviewed.

Literature from the Wisconsin Department of Health and Social Services provides a basic description of the county and of the Dane County Mental Health Program.

> Dane County, in southern Wisconsin, has a population of approximately 336,000 (190,000 in Madison) and is notable for its state government and state university activities. There is little heavy industry in the county, and there is considerable agricultural activity (mainly dairying). Dane County's per capita income is well above the state average ($25,000 for a family of four), and unemployment is usually low (4.8%). Less than 5% of the county's population is minority. There are only a handful of homeless persons. All employed persons have health insurance coverage—hence it is estimated that less than 10% of the population has no coverage of any type. Dane County, and Madison in particular, have traditions of progressive social services programs, funded in part through county taxes.
>
> Madison has a very large labor pool of talented, trained people, and there are experts of all kinds to provide specialized services. New programs routinely emerge in the community, and there is a full roster of traditional suppliers of human services in the public, private and voluntary sectors. Major institutions and services are relatively open to innovation and change. In sum, the environment is relatively flexible and the services array is very diverse.

Leaders of organizations, public and voluntary, relate to each other through task forces and committees on which they serve, as well as through consultation and joint programming at the client level. Madison is small enough so that human service professionals can interact easily across organizational lines.

Community values as expressed in the Madison area media are strongly identified with the desirability of amenity-oriented programs, including the provision of services for groups traditionally unserved.

Responsibility for assessing needs, planning programs, arranging for services, and coordinating provision of care for persons with chronic mental illness, as well as other disability areas, rests with the nine-member Dane County Unified Services Board appointed by the county executive. There are five citizens at large and four members of the County Board of Supervisors on it. The Unified Board allocates state funding received by Dane County for human services, county dollars and monies from voluntary sources to contract services providers in order to offer the service delivery system needed.

The Dane County Mental Health Center, Inc., is a private, nonprofit corporation that was founded in 1948 as a child guidance clinic. The Center contracts with the Dane County Community Support and Health Services Department (formerly the Unified Services Board), the United Way of Dane County, and other public and private funding sources to provide services to Dane County citizens. These services include outpatient psychotherapy, alcohol and drug counseling, medication reviews, outreach services, court evaluations, emergency services, hospital screening and evaluation, information and referral, alcohol assessments and the training of mental health professionals. The Center's community support programs furnish recreational, consultative and continuous follow-up treatment to individuals with long-standing emotional difficulties who need assistance in making adjustments to community living. The overall DCMHC staff is quite large (150 people) with programs and staff distributed among three downtown locations and one near-downtown location. (1985, pp. 93–95)

ADMINISTRATION

The information about administration is derived from two hours with David LeCount (the Dane County Mental Health coordinator), from written material he provided, and from various documents describing the Dane County Mental Health Center and its operations. The total mental health budget for Dane County was $6.6 million in 1986. The current arrangement providing state funding for county programs via a unified services board is the result of a decision by the state mental health department more than 10 years ago to phase down hospitals and serve only as a funding, accounting, and regulatory agency. Of the mental health program's funding 79.7% is state and county money. These revenue sources are outlined in Figure 18.1. Figure 18.2 outlines how the mental health money is spent. The 19% spent on day services/treatment (roughly $1.25 million) is inflated approximately $500,000 by what is spent on 19 long-term beds at Badger Prairie Health

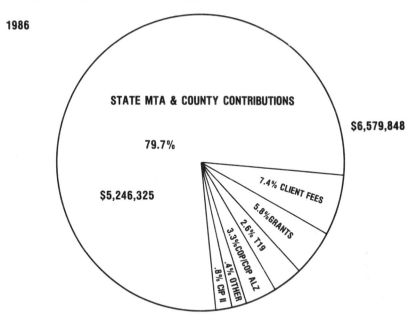

1986

STATE MTA & COUNTY CONTRIBUTIONS

79.7%

$6,579,848

$5,246,325

7.4% CLIENT FEES

5.8% GRANTS

2.6% T19

3.3% COP/COP ALZ

.4% OTHER

.8% CIP II

(Dane County Unified Service Board, Annual Report, 1986)

FIGURE 18.1
Mental Health Revenues

Care Center (a skilled nursing facility). In turn, the 9.2% spent on inpatient care does not include this hospital-like residential care cost. LeCount has been the contract monitor for years. Most of the 25 contracts are renewed annually although occasionally programs are rebid and money may be re-aligned among programs as part of the annual budget process. Both Le-Count and Paul Meyer, head of the Unified Services Board, provide stable leadership that consistently supports community maintenance as a viable option for the severely mentally ill. We were very impressed with LeCount's ability to move between administrative/fiscal responsibilities and individual case assessments.

Five problem areas were identified by the administrators:

1. Patients on general assistance in Dane County are assigned to a health maintenance organization (roughly 60% of the population of Madison participates in HMO's). This has created a problem within the system because persons on medical assistance can, by virtue of the HMO's freedom-of-physician choice provision, get into a hospi-

1986

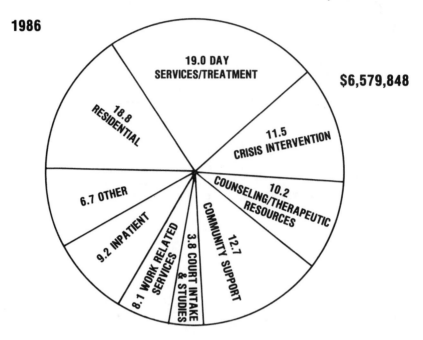

(Dane County Unified Service Board, Annual Report, 1986)

FIGURE 18.2
Mental Health Expenditures

tal without going through the crisis team. This is the only group of patients that can circumvent their gate-keeping function.

2. The Unified Services Board feels there is a front door pressure problem. They want to develop more spaces in various kinds of intensive residential care settings.

3. They feel they must do more to maintain children and adolescents in the community. At the present time the county has 12 adolescents in Mendota State Hospital and another 90 placed out of the county by the county's Department of Social Services for children and youth. Because of the town's reliance on HMO's, adolescent inpatient units have not been developed. Hence they feel they must create programs that will provide alternatives to inpatient care for children and adolescents.

4. Because Dane County is relatively rich in services, clients frequently have relationships with many agencies. In these instances, defining who will be the primary case manager has created problems. A

tracking system is being developed to provide data that will help the system deal more effectively with this issue.

5. They lack sufficient respite care and crisis beds to take care of the clients in their 300-bed community residential program. They are about to begin a program with three beds in foster homes for respite care, one per home, and one bed in each of two foster homes for crisis care. The respite care bed is paid for at the rate of $700 a month and the crisis beds at $900 per month. At the present time they intend to pay for them only if used.

In 1985, the mental health system served 2,300 clients and an additional 500 persons labeled chronically mentally ill (there are probably about 1200 chronically mentally ill in the county). The vast majority (79%) were unmarried, of whom 23% were divorced or separated, and 55% never married. One-quarter of the clients live alone and another 26% live in households with nonfamily members.

The typical client seen in 1985 was a young adult in the age range of 19 to 44 who comprised 80% of the clients served over the course of the year. The vast majority of clients seen were males (68.5%) who entered the system primarily through court referrals for a range of problems, most of which were related to substance abuse. While 94% of the clients seen were White, Blacks (3.6%), and Hispanics (1.4%) were much more likely to be served than Whites in relation to their overall numbers in the population.

Compared to the population of Dane County as a whole, clients tend to be relatively undereducated, with 29.5% fewer having completed high school (83.7% in Dane County vs. 54.2% of Center clients) and 20% fewer having completed college (30.9% in Dane County vs. 14.9% of Center clients). Indeed, it is those persons who are "school dropouts," either at the high school or college level, who have the highest rates of entry into the service system. Moreover, 27.8% of the clients seen in 1985 were unemployed, reflecting an unemployment rate 8.4 times greater than that found in the population of Dane County as a whole. Finally, a comparison of incomes of the client population with the county as a whole reveals the devastating impact of deficits in education and jobs on financial and other material resources available to persons who seek help. The median income of persons living in family households ($8,604) is $14,420 less than the median income of persons in this group in Dane County; the median income of persons living in nonfamily households ($4,997) is $903 less than the median income of persons in this group in Dane County. Fifty-three percent of clients have annual incomes of less than $6000 and another 21% earn between $6,000 and $12,000. The MHC has 115 total F.T.E.'s split among 131 total employees. There are 2.2 F.T.E. psychiatrists, 2.2 F.T.E. psychiatric residents and 1.5 F.T.E. Ph.D. clinical psychologists. Twenty staff are involved only in administration. This count does not include the Support Network, residential or employment program staff. (Mental Health Center of Dane County, Inc., 1985)

INPATIENT SERVICES

The Dane County program is basically antihospitalization. They have access to acute inpatient beds in five places: the University Hospital, psychiatric wards in three general hospitals, and the Mendota Mental Health Institute. *All* of the costs ($405,000 in 1986) of these beds are billed to the county program, which later recovers whatever the state collects — about $150,000 in 1986. The average length of stay was 21 days at Mendota (3,800 total days) and eight days in community hospitals (430 total days). Sixty patients were admitted to psychiatric wards in general hospitals, all voluntarily. One hundred twenty-one patients were admitted to Mendota Mental Health Institute (the renamed state hospital), 99 of whom were involuntary. Although there were 99 involuntary admissions to the Mendota Mental Health Institute in 1986, there were only 17 patients committed. Thus, although initially involuntarily placed in Mendota, at the 72-hour probable cause hearing or the day 14 commitment hearing, the patient had already been converted to voluntary status or was out of the hospital.

The Badger Prairie 19-bed contract is for skilled nursing home level of care and hence counted (by the *authors*) as inpatient. These beds seem to be used as long-stay state hospital beds are elsewhere. Patients are usually admitted there from either Mendota State Hospital or one of the local short-term private hospitals. The average length of stay at Badger Prairie is a little over seven months. Thirty-one clients were served there in 1986.

Inpatient care is the intervention of last resort. This is well demonstrated in Figure 18.3, showing inpatient days, 1976–86. When someone is hospitalized, the crisis team immediately goes to the hospital to evaluate the client. Team members then work with the doctor to get the client out as quickly as possible. They are motivated by both belief system (least restrictive alternative) and money; the size of the outpatient treatment budget is reduced if too much money is spent on inpatient care.

The Dane County program has always been reluctant to develop intensive nonhospital residential services, such as Soteria or Crossing Place. The current attempt to create crisis beds in foster homes appears to be the first move away from that position. However, rather than putting together a good-sized unit of six to eight beds, the administrators have decided to go with the Polak and Kirby (1976) model of surrogate parents, with one bed in each of two foster homes. They made this decision — that is, not to start a six-to-eight-bed alternative to hospitalization — because they judged the surrogate parent model to be more normalizing and cheaper and because they have only a handful of clients who are potential candidates for such beds (i.e., in need of hospital-level intensity of care but without Medicaid coverage to pay for it). Also, they have had success using a single 48-hour crisis bed in the hospital across the street from the MHC.

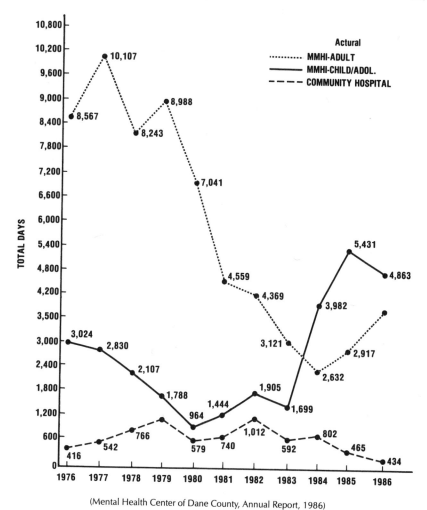

(Mental Health Center of Dane County, Annual Report, 1986)

FIGURE 18.3
Inpatient Days (1976–1986)

MOBILE COMMUNITY TEAM (MCT)

Madison's Mobile Community Team is widely recognized as innovative and has been emulated in a number of sites in the U.S. and Australia. Here are the summary characteristics of this part of Dane County's community support program:

The Mobile Community Treatment Program of Dane County (MCT) was founded in 1980 as part of the Dane County Mental Health Center (DCMHC). Patterned on the successful Program for Assertive Community Treatment (PACT), MCT uses a team approach in case management, and actively involves clients with the many other services and providers in the Madison, Wisconsin area. Mobile Community Treatment (MCT) is designed to provide a support system for severely disabled psychiatric clients in the community. The basic philosophy of the program is to help clients learn the skills required to cope and to problem solve by working side by side with the client in situations that he or she finds most difficult. The focus throughout treatment is on action rather than talk, and building on client strengths rather than dwelling on weaknesses. The main goals of MCT are to reduce the frequency and duration of psychiatric hospitalizations and to increase self-esteem and independence.

MCT helps people develop daily living skills such as shopping, taking the bus, budgeting, and structuring time. MCT helps its clients find apartments, apply for jobs, or join groups in the community. It plans social and recreational activities for clients as well. MCT tries to link clients with available community resources, and to advocate for clients whenever necessary.

Madison, as the state capitol and the site of the largest University of Wisconsin campus, has a rich and dense network of organizations providing assistance to the mentally ill. Coordination among services is especially important in the urbanized setting. The variety of services available makes it possible for the CSP to develop service plans especially tailored to individual client needs. (Wisconsin Department of Health and Social Services, 1985, p. 92)

A new version of Dr. Test's Program for Assertive Community Treatment (PACT) program (Stein & Test, 1978a,b; 1985) is in operation independent of, and in addition to, the MCT. This research program is focused on intensively treating clients with relatively little system experience, as a means of preventing chronicity. In its random assignment design the Mobile Community Team serves as the control condition for the PACT program. The two programs are clinically similar, with the exception that the PACT program takes only newly identified clients between the ages of 18 and 30. These two programs cost $833,000, or 12.7% of the budget. The PACT program served 108 clients in 1986 and the MCT served 245. The clientele of the MCT are principally multiply hospitalized, committed patients (including outpatients) with schizophrenia and major affective disorders. They receive an average of 44 hours service per year per client at a cost of $56 an hour. The team attempts to avoid borderline patients if at all possible. The average age of the clientele is 35 and about half of the *active* 125 clients on the MCT roles are also on some type of guardianship—mostly to ensure medication compliance. About 100 patients receive daily medication at the mental health center. Eighty of these 100 patients have their medication paired with receipt of their daily financial allowance. One fulltime person does a budget with each client. The client's expenses are determined and the remaining money divided into 30 daily allowances and given to him after he takes his medication. The team has arranged a voucher system with a local supermarket for clients who spend their food allowances on nonfood items. The team has daily contact with roughly 75% of the clients.

The MCT delivers medications to roughly 10 people in the community on a daily basis, and there are a handful of people with whom they have twice-daily contacts. At any given moment they have five or six people who are not doing well. They usually have several clients on the 19-bed long-stay locked ward at the Badger Prairie Nursing Home. In general, MCT clients are not involved in psychosocial rehabilitation (the Support Network) because they can't function well enough. The Mobile Community Team is open from 8:00 a.m. to 10:30 p.m., the crisis team covers after that. They have 13 staff members: Four are registered nurses, plus an RN who directs the program; the others are community support specialists.

The MCT runs four groups: a two-hour Wednesday evening recreational group with Goodwill at the Madison Community Center; a free VCR movie showing on Friday evenings; an open group for two hours on Saturday afternoon to do something in the community; and a Sunday brunch group at Hardee's on State Street (the main thoroughfare). They also have optional movement groups and they try to teach kitchen skills with an occupational therapist. The kitchen group is a bit of a problem, as the staff of the Mental Health Center doesn't like to be in the kitchen when the MCT clients are there. Interestingly, only two or three MCT clients live with their families and only 25 or 30 have families that are interested. Ten to 12 live in group homes but most live on their own or in the Center's supported housing.

About 10% of the Mobile Community Team's clients have tardive dyskinesia. The team psychiatrists, who see each client every four to six weeks, are not presently using a targeted drug strategy. Rather, they attempt to keep doses as low as possible. Each client is given individual instructions about the drugs they are taking, and these are repeated several times. They do not, however, have formal classes on side effects of drugs. The average MCT patient on injectable prolixin will receive between 15 and 20 mg biweekly, but the range is from .3 to 62.7 per week. About one-fourth of MCT clients are given injectable medication.

Further descriptive material about the MCT:

> The preferred type of case management does not, in the eyes of MCT, necessarily require professional staffing. From the beginning, the staffing philosophy of MCT has been that experience and personality, not formal training, were central to choosing staff, and that anyone, including paraprofessionals, who would empathize with clients and be willing to do the less desirable work would be a good staffer to employ. Highly trained staff without a special awareness of client needs are avoided since they might quickly become bored,

or begin to substitute therapy for practical services. "Down-to-earth" combined with experience is more valuable than advanced theoretical training in providing the services MCT stresses.

Since MCT works with clients who are among those with the greatest risk for hospitalization in the county, many of whom have had extensive hospitalization, it does not expect that many clients will ever be able to function in the community without extensive support services. This is not a preparation or rehabilitation program, getting clients ready to make it on their own. This is more of a maintenance program, which recognizes that some clients will stabilize or change enough to move into another less intense program, but that many will remain for years with need for the intensity and range of services MCT can access. This thinking follows the approach validated by PACT. In initial efforts to discover treatment strategies, PACT thought of itself as preparing clients to live independently after a period of protection and skills development. It quickly became evident that the types of clients being accepted were unlikely to maintain community life without extensive support, that the problems of meeting basic needs were beyond the resources of clients.

With these assumptions, MCT is reluctant to allow clients to drop out of the program or for services to clients to lapse (since in the view of program staff the cessation of services is likely to lead to hospitalization). Costly and, perhaps, dysfunctional hospitalization can be averted if staff can be "gate keepers" and it is MCT's policy to work assertively to keep clients in the program. If clients do not keep appointments, do not appear for groups customarily attended, or do not follow medications regimens, MCT staff will seek out the client and make serious efforts to keep the client involved. Letting services lapse because of oversight or letting clients be lost because they are tired of being involved is quite unacceptable to the program.

Admissions: There is basically a two-step admission process for MCT. A person needing services is first discussed by a DCMHC Intake Committee, on which the MCT manager serves. If MCT is thought to be the appropriate unit for providing service, then the potential client's file or record is reviewed by MCT staff. The staff reviews the case against MCT criteria for intake, and considers the staff's ability to provide needed services. These criteria are shaped to place particular emphasis on hospitalization history, diagnostic records, and whether or not there are any other supports in place.

Since with MCT's team approach all staff are involved in delivering services to all clients, there is an effort to involve the whole team in intake decisions.

The program tries to take the most difficult cases, and to pass the less difficult ones along to other programs in the community which can mobilize fewer resources. MCT clients are described by staff as, for the most part, people who have extreme difficulty with all facets of community living.

People living in Dane County but outside Madison pose problems MCT has not been able to solve. The time costs of transportation are such that the program cannot implement its mobile and intensive support model for those who live outside the city. Therefore, rural populations remain essentially unserved. Clients who live in rural Dane County are at times encouraged to move to Madison so MCT can provide more services.

Morale of MCT staff: Morale in MCT has been very good over time, with staff confident of their ability to solve client needs problems. Expansion of budget, clients, and staff are perceived by program staffers to be signs of program success and acceptance. Morale is pinched a bit by concern for fiscal matters (all are aware of the nine days of enforced closure in 1982), but concern is relatively modest. Most staff people think the program is well enough established that it will certainly continue at its present level. Morale is also boosted by the numerous visitors from across the nation, many from community support programs. Although these visitors come to MCT more as a result of the visibility of the psychiatrist associated with DCMHC (Dr. Leonard Stein) and MCT than because of MCT's having a national reputation, the visits are flattering and serve to raise morale.

Morale is kept high through the conscious efforts of the manager, who has a warm, confident style of interaction with staff. As well, events and ceremonies like birthday parties evidence and support high morale.

Sources of job satisfaction: The main sources of satisfaction MCT staff mention are keeping people out of the hospital and doing work that is socially useful and desirable. Other things mentioned by staff were that salaries and fringe benefits were quite good, they learned about themselves through their work, and they enjoyed the varied, flexible aspects of the work environment. Liking the clients was mentioned by several staff people. Some clients got better, and others "did well" by staying out of the hospital and in the community. "These aren't just your ordinary upper-middle-class people in their suburban style houses," one person said. "I get a kick out of them, and how different they are." These reactions to clients are quite unlike the literature on staff burnout.

Essential services offered in 1983 by MCT:
- Case management and interagency coordination to assist clients to use helping systems;
- Case finding, locate clients: Reach out to inform them of available services;
- Services to help MCT clients meet basic human needs: Food, clothing, income assistance, medical services, and subsistence;
- Mental health care and treatment services, including inpatient care, medications and counseling;
- Crisis service for 24-hour, quick response to needs for assistance;
- Comprehensive psychosocial rehabilitation services including day treatment, training in activities of daily living, social and recreational activities, and vocational-work related activities such as sheltered employment opportunities;
- Housing and housing assistance to provide a range of rehabilitative and supportive housing options;
- Backup support, assistance, consultation, and education for families of clients;
- Assist clients to use natural support systems;
- Provide a grievance procedure and establish mechanisms to protect client rights.

(Wisconsin Department of Health and Social Services, 1985)

The program is, by design, comprehensive. It can provide directly or arrange everything any client might need. It is proactive, intrusive, and controlling.

CRISIS INTERVENTION/EMERGENCY SERVICE

In our view this service is the linchpin of the Dane County program. It is open 24 hours a day, seven days a week. The emergency telephone service, with a staff of six, handles about 1500 phone calls a month. The crisis staff of nine has 20 face-to-face contacts per day and 160 new face-to-face contacts a month. Over 2900 individuals were served in 1985. The service staff are able to follow patients for from a few days to several months (averaging just over seven hours per client at $30 an hour) until they are stabilized (about 300 cases a year). Roughly 60% of their clientele comes from the Dane County "chronic" population. Two-thirds of the patients are repeaters.

Goals — The goals of the Emergency Services are:
A. To enhance the well-being of persons in emotional crises and return them to a functional level of response as rapidly as possible.
B. To take advantage of the emotional crisis period to help such persons make changes in their life situation which enable them to function at a more satisfactory level than prior to the crisis.
C. To prevent hospitalization, its stigma and expense through the formulation of alternative treatment plans and the assertive implementation of such plans.
The treatment philosophy within the Emergency Services can be summarized in the following statements:
A. Immediate availability of mental health professionals for intervention in mental health emergencies is essential and will facilitate the speed of the helping process.
B. Close attention to the needs of referral sources is essential in achieving and maintaining their involvement and cooperation in the resolution of the helping process.
C. The development and maintenance of a social support system and short-term intense treatment plan are essential in preventing the hospitalization of persons experiencing mental health emergencies.
D. Outpatient treatment, when adequately structured, will result in a "better" recovery from a mental health emergency than will inpatient treatment.
E. Careful monitoring and case management are necessary to ensure persons in crisis receive the attention needed and do not "fall through the cracks" of the service system.
(Emergency Services Program Description, Madison, WI, 1987)

It is Madison police policy to consult with the crisis staff about all police-generated involuntary admissions. All mental health center patients must also be evaluated by the crisis team if hospitalization is being considered. The crisis team acts as the inpatient gate keeper by controlling the purse strings. Only the team can authorize payment for inpatient beds. Hence, the team is able, in practice, to withhold payment for a patient admitted to a hospital via a private physician if it seems the admission was inappropriate (see the guidelines outlined in Table 18.1).

The crisis team is staffed by nine master's level social workers, each with a minimum of five years' experience, several part-time psychiatrists, several mental health technicians, and three nurses. Watching them in action, we were tremendously impressed with their innovativeness, thoughtfulness, and hard-headedness around the use of hospital. Roughly 40% of their contacts are outside of the Mental Health Center (where the service is located physically), mostly in emergency rooms of local hospitals. They do roughly one home visit a day, preferably with two staff or one staff and a police officer. Since the crisis system was put in place, the inpatient bed utilization has been reduced from roughly 10,000 bed days a year in 1977 to just under 4,000 bed days in 1986 (see Figure 18.3). Bed days used via the 19-bed

TABLE 18.1
Guidelines:
Authorization for Dane County Unified Services Board (USB)
Funding of Voluntary Hospitalizations

The Crisis Intervention Service (CIS) staff of the Dane County Mental Health Center Emergency Services serve as agents of the USB in authorizing the expenditure of USB funds for voluntary, acute psychiatric inpatient hospital admissions of an emergency nature. *All* of the following criteria must be satisfied for funding to be authorized.

1. Individual is a resident of Dane County.
2. Individual is willing to sign a voluntary admission form or a "passive" voluntary admission is appropriate.
3. Use of alcohol is not primary in the behavior necessitating hospitalization.
4. Individual is behaving or threating to behave dangerously by:
   A. Being a threat to physical safety of others

   OR

   B. Being a threat to physical safety of self or being gravely disabled so that significant physical harm will result if not hospitalized.
5. Individual is displaying symptoms of a significant mental illness.
6. Other alternative outpatient treatment modes have been fully investigated and judged insufficient to meet client's clinical needs.
7. Hospitalization is judged an effective treatment for the disorder.

A decision by the CIS staff to deny USB funding for inpatient psychiatric treatment may be appealed to the USB Mental Health Coordinator. Upon receiving an appeal, the USB Mental Health Coordinator will schedule a clinical case review meeting involving CIS staff, USB staff and the person(s) requesting the decision review. This review meeting will be held as soon as practically possible.

contract with the Badger Prairie skilled nursing facility are not included in this count. In 1986, there were 181 admissions to various hospitals, 99 of whom (all involuntary) were hospitalized at the Mendota Mental Health Institute. The county has no long-term patients in the state hospital (Mendota) because these beds are to be used, by state law, only for acute care. In addition to the usual crisis intervention service, this group provides two rather unusual services: (1) A group for survivors of suicide who are themselves disturbed by it, and (2) a pre-crisis intervention service for the families with a chronically mentally ill offspring who is decompensating or for whom the family, for some other reason, is no longer able to provide care. The focus of the pre-crisis service is on how to bring the client/offspring into the system so he or she can be stabilized before a serious crisis evolves.

THE SUPPORT NETWORK

This program is in the third of its transformations, the latest being a fairly traditional Fountain House model psychosocial rehabilitation center. Its first incarnation was as a pure staff consensus clubhouse/day treatment program started by an occupational therapist. There was an attempt to change the program to a Fountain House model, but this attempt is described as having failed because procedures could not be changed unless the entire staff agreed and the program was driven too much by staff interest. Its second form was as a psychoanalytically oriented traditional day hospital program with lots of individual and group therapy. The director was a psychoanalyst who believed strongly in the value of individual therapy and didn't pay much attention to the overall milieu. Its present form began when the current director took over two years ago and committed the program to becoming a "true" Fountain House model (see Chapter 9, pp. 151–64). This change was accompanied by a 80% staff turnover over 18 months and a petition from some of the members objecting to the changeover. Basically these members wanted to continue to have the individual psychotherapy model of the previous director.

As presently constituted, the program is somewhat unusual as a Fountain House model in that there are direct psychiatric services provided on site. The clubhouse psychiatrist sees roughly 100 of the 200 members. He runs two medication groups per week with a nurse in attendance. Each of these groups averages an attendance of 15 to 20 members. The program uses a "primary nurse" model so that members see their assigned nurse first before seeing the doctor. Often time with the doctor is then not necessary. The three nurses also do units like the rest of the staff. It is quite unusual for a Fountain House model program to have nurses, acting as nurses, in the clubhouse. The director has addressed this issue in a paper (Backes, Cohen, Gundlach, Myers, Propst, Rawls, & Hennings, 1987). Basically Backes believes, and we agree, that unless the medication function becomes a unit, with full member participation like the other units in the clubhouse, it will skew the program in an inappropriate ("patienthood") direction. The psychiatric residents from the University of Wisconsin who rotate through the Mental Health Center also spend time at the Support Network; however, they don't perform medical functions there, but rather operate as unit workers.

Other than the medication issue, the program is a fairly typical Fountain House model, with the usual unit structures, meetings, transitional employment, etc. There are daily unit meetings and a weekly program meeting, all with members present. All meetings are open to member participation, as are other functions such as hiring committees and intake. Staff fairly clearly run the meetings, and the show in general, with the help of a few of the very high functioning members. There is an evening and weekend social program operating 365 days a year, and they operate 24 supervised apartment units.

In 1986 the Support Network served 262 clients for an average of 196 hours each at a cost of about $12 an hour. On any given day they have between 75 and 90 clients in the program, up from 50 before the changeover. They have five transitional employment placements (TEP's), with plans for expansion. In addition to the Support Network, there are three other vocationally oriented programs: Madison Opportunity Center, Goodwill Industries, and Chrysalis. Between the three programs there are 52 clients involved in transitional employment. Transitional employment lasts an average of four months. In 1986 these three programs served a total of 350 Mental Health Center clients. Just over 8% of the county mental health budget is spent on work-related services. The county is moving now toward a more community-based supported work model (versus a sheltered workshop one), so that more clients will have community-based work opportunities.

There is another day program (Off the Square) in Madison run by the YMCA of Metropolitan Madison, Inc. It is located just off of State Street and has a reputation for being a drop-in spot for the homeless and other persons with no real attachments. We did not visit this drop-in center, but we were told that it provides a place with less structure and fewer demands than the Support Network. It seems well suited to clients who want a place to go and belong but cannot stand the level of demand and stimulation at the Support Network.

ADULT SERVICES

Mobile Outreach to Seniors Team

The Mental Health Center's Mobile Outreach to Seniors Team (M.O.S.T.) is a mobile community-based and interdisciplinary team provid-

ing direct and indirect mental health services to community-based Dane
County residents, age 55 or older, and their families/support systems. The
central purpose of M.O.S.T. is to promote the physical, social, and emotional well-being of older people by making mental health services more
accessible and acceptable, and thereby reducing the risk of deterioration and
unnecessary institutionalization. The professional diversity of the M.O.S.T.
staff (4.05 F.T.E.'s), including two clinical specialists, four nurse clinicians
and a geropsychiatrist (.10 F.T.E.), enables a comprehensive approach to
care. Nurse clinicians are utilized primarily in rural areas, as they are more
acceptable to older folks than regular mental health workers and they are
especially adept at conducting comprehensive assessments.

Services are community-based and provided primarily through a collaborative relationship with 10 or 15 senior centers in Dane County. Team members, each assigned to serve in specific areas of the county, provide ongoing
monthly consultation to the outreach staff at the local senior center and
generally act as that area's resource person regarding mental health and
aging issues. The M.O.S.T. staff provides direct and indirect support services to older people in their natural settings. Services are available Monday
through Friday, 8 a.m. to 5 p.m., with 24-hour crisis backup to respond to
emergencies. The team provides assertive case management, including: case-
findings of the hard-to-reach, comprehensive assessments, highly individualized and often interagency care planning and coordination, direct intervention and advocacy, and information and referral. The team concentrates
on the provision of mental health services and attempts to collaborate with
other providers to carry out other related services, including case management when feasible. This enables the M.O.S.T. team to focus its efforts and
serve greater numbers of older people. Similarly, the geropsychiatrist expands his capacity by acting as a consultant to the older person's primary
physician rather than following each person indefinitely.

The team also engages in prevention through presentations to the general
public and to groups of older people on topics of aging, mental health,
caregiving, sobriety, etc. Through these prevention and intervention measures, the M.O.S.T. team has been successful in maintaining 96% of its
clients in their natural settings (it served 151 older clients in 1986–87).

Through the continuation of these prevention and intervention measures
by the M.O.S.T. staff, it is anticipated that many older Dane County residents will be enabled to live more independent and enriched lives, maintaining or regaining abilities, thereby reducing the risk of deterioration and
unnecessary institutionalization. It is also anticipated that other providers
and the links in the service system will be strengthened by the direct and
indirect services of M.O.S.T.

One of M.O.S.T.'s important system initiatives have been the peer counseling program that was developed in 1983 in response to state and local

requests. Dane County's peer counseling program (Elder Friends) is a state-promoted initiative designed to link the aging and mental health networks in expanding mental health services to older people through the use of trained, older persons. In Dane County, the program is funded by the Commission on Aging, with the M.O.S.T. program collaborating with the commission on aging and the local technical college to provide the initial 40 hours of peer counselor training. The M.O.S.T. staff also provides bimonthly consultation to the peer counselors at the local centers.

The need for mental health services through the peer counseling concept is based on older persons' reluctance to seek mental health services through traditional systems. Rural persons tend to be especially receptive to this program. Of the 36 active peer counselors, the vast majority is providing services in the rural areas. It is an important component of the mental health delivery system, particularly in rural areas, where professional services remain extremely limited and often unacceptable. Peer counselors are used to help other seniors who are experiencing bereavement, loneliness or other emotional conditions by means of individual weekly or biweekly visits or telephone contacts.

M.O.S.T. is a three-year demonstration project, funded largely by NIMH, but also by USB and Co. Office of Aging. It was created by expanding a small but highly successful community outreach team for the elderly composed of two part-time staff (.60 social worker and .50 nurse). M.O.S.T. is in its second year of operation.

Jail Services

Another adult services function is outreach and intervention in jail, to which one fulltime equivalent is assigned. At any one time there will be roughly 20 people in the jail with mental health problems. They are treated with brief psychotherapy and drugs; if they are psychotic, they are transferred to the Mendota Mental Health Institute for treatment for one to two months. One or two clients a month require transfer. The jail holds 400.

Psychotherapy

Three fulltime equivalents, all with master's degrees in social work, counseling, or psychology, offer psychotherapy under the Adult Services umbrella. They do about 85% individual therapy and have an average of 401 days treatment time, up from 200 days four years ago. Psychotherapy is not a high priority item at the center or for county funding agencies. There is usually a waiting list of 40–50 persons, or about one month. It is acknowledged that this service is having a hard time defining exactly who it should be treating. In the past these therapists saw indigent neurotics. Now 15–20%

of their clients are so-called chronically mentally ill. This reflects the significant shift in clientele to more seriously ill persons, e.g., severe borderlines, severely depressed individuals, abuse and incest victims/perpetrators. Many of these clients have multiple problems and need of case management and access to a variety of services in addition to psychotherapy. Roughly 90% of clients are seen for no fee at all. The demand for this service has gone up, and the increased treatment time is attributed to the clients' being more difficult now. The psychotherapy team saw 771 clients in 1985 for a total of 8,135 psychotherapy hours, at a unit cost of $47.50 an hour.

CHILD, ADOLESCENT, AND FAMILY SERVICES

Regarding services for children and families, Dane County is in a state of flux. As is characteristic of the center, there are several individual projects focused on specific patient groups.

1. *Directing Energies for Life Transitions Through Adolescence (DEL-TA).* This group assesses and treats families referred by the Department of Social Services in which the adolescent is being considered for out-of-home placement. They do roughly equal proportions of in-home and in-office family therapy. They also run both parent and adolescent groups. This is a new project, begun in August of 1986. Basically, the staff members see only families sent to them by court order. At the time of our visit, they had treated only ten families, but in none of those instances was it necessary to take the child out of the home. The project has two fulltime equivalent positions.
2. *Substance Abuse:* The adolescent unit also does its own drug and alcohol abuse treatment (rather than having it done as part of the other drug and alcohol abuse unit). They have one fulltime equivalent for this work. They use adolescent and family groups.
3. *The Teen Depression Project:* 350 ninth graders were screened and 26 were thought to be clinically depressed. They were encouraged to seek treatment. The staff members do assertive case management to alert unseeing parents to their child's problem. Treatment (mostly individual and family) is done either at the Mental Health Center or by referral to private practitioners if money is available. Staff also run support groups at the schools and try to see to it that the system is working for the kids.
4. *Black and Others Outreach Support Team (Boost):* This is a new project focused on minorities. It is an outreach program from local community churches that attempts to intervene with children six to

twelve years old referred by the schools as being at risk for getting into trouble. The two fulltime staff are used to try to divert blacks from the criminal justice system into the mental health system. This new project is really just getting off the ground.

Finally they do traditional child therapy with multiproblem children, with 1.75 fulltime equivalents devoted to it. They also have a small program for dually diagnosed children (mentally retarded and mentally ill), with 13 clients.

LIVING ARRANGEMENTS PROGRAM

Dane County has 298 slots in a variety of more or less structured settings. Almost 19% of the county budget is spent on housing. There are seven group homes with a total capacity of 66; there are 50 spaces in adult family homes; there are 150 slots in what they call special living arrangements, basically apartment placements with case management. There is one boarding home with four spaces and 24 slots in congregate apartments associated with the Support Network and Goodwill Industries. Finally, they have the new programs of three respite beds and two crisis beds in adult family homes. They served a total of almost 400 clients in 1986 in these programs. When we asked about them, it was said that they were all transitional; however, it seemed quite clear that transitional meant that clients could leave if they wanted to but there were no clear limits on length of stay. The stated goal is to prepare people for more independent living. The most intensively staffed residences (group homes) take mostly persons coming directly out of inpatient care, including Badger Prairie. It is rather unusual (for the authors) that many of the mobile team clients, the most disturbed and disturbing at the center, live in their own separate individual apartments, not in supported housing arrangements.

THE DRUG AND ALCOHOL TREATMENT UNIT

This is a fairly unusual drug and alcohol unit, as they do not follow the "standard" disease and total abstinence model of drug and alcohol treatment. They get about 1,100 referrals a year. One-third drop out almost immediately. They spend about 20 hours per client, and just about every client gets a combination of group and individual treatment that costs about $700 per client treatment episode. They do little family work because most of the clients are not in families. The program is not a prepackaged one but rather focused, in general, on getting clients to take responsibility, control, and power over their lives. They do not use urine tests and do not force people to take Antabuse. The groups are focused on support, the notion of *wanting* to be dry, and on setting weekly goals for each individual. They run groups of eight weekly sessions with a two-month follow-up. They want clients to become aware of how much they drink, to help them manage stress better, and to enhance self-control via goal-setting. In the goal-setting they do not demand total abstinence but instead encourage progressive decrease in consumption. The unit does not require involvement with Alcoholics Anonymous and in fact sometimes sees Alcoholics Anonymous as a problem because AA is so against the use of any drugs by these clients. This AA stance presents special problems to the large number of substance-abusing psychotics on neuroleptics.

Detoxification is done in hospital or in drug and alcohol halfway houses in town.

INVOLUNTARY COMMITMENT

The state of Wisconsin has two statutes that allow commitment to treatment. The regular mental health commitment law, Chapter 51, is a fairly usual one in that the person must be dangerous and mentally ill. It also contains a "least restrictive alternative" clause. The police, three persons, or an institution may obtain detention orders. A probable cause hearing is held within 72 hours. If there is cause to be detained at 72 hours, a commitment hearing must be held within 14 days of admission. Of the 153 probable cause hearings held in 1984, only 17 went on to commitment. Commitment lasts for six months and is renewable (not usually done). Commitment means an individual is committed to the county's Community Support and Health Services Department for both in- and outpatient services. In a typical month, March 1987, a total of eight persons was committed.

The other commitment proceeding is called Adult Protective Services/ Placement, Chapters 880 and 55 of the state code, generally referred to as "guardianship." The process begins when a person is determined incompetent and a guardian appointed (Chapter 880). Then protective services (Chapter 55) come into play; anything from medication to placement on a locked ward can be ordered as necessary. This is intended as a means of being sure that chronically ill, geriatric, and developmentally disabled clients get some form of attention. These clients are generally those seen as "untreatable." It is rather difficult to unravel numbers given for these adult protective services placements, but basically being in protective service means that one must receive a community-based service as designated by the court. The guardian, usually a family member or a community worker, oversees the implementation of the court-ordered services, especially compliance with medication. Chapter 55 placements and services are reviewed annually and a small percentage of them brought back to court to change the arrangement. The Adult Protective Services and Placement assessments are done in a separate unit by two fulltime psychologists.

Wisconsin provides for several levels of guardianship. Some patients are on limited guardianship focused on being sure they are medication compliant. This is justified because the clients are judged as being incompetent when *off* medication. Other patients are on more extensive guardianships in terms of which areas of their lives are controlled. At any one time 19 clients are on total guardianship in the county-contracted unit in Badger Prairie Nursing home. Most of them will eventually return to the community.

In addition to the Chapter 55 assessments, this unit does 350 court ordered evaluations of juveniles a year. All juveniles being considered for out-of-home placement must have a court ordered psychological evaluation.

ALLIANCE FOR THE MENTALLY ILL (AMI)

The national organization of the alliance (NAMI) was formed at a meeting in Madison in 1979. The local chapter is pleased with the Dane County program. Its major leadership figure, Mrs. Beverly Young, says that as long as Paul Meyer heads the board, AMI will have no complaints. The local chapter is very active lobbying with the state legislation to identify and protect CSP funds and expand reimbursement for case managers.

This chapter, as led by Mrs. Young, does not agree with several of the overall national NAMI goals. In contrast to the national organization, the Madison parents do not see medications and easier commitment as long-term solutions to their problems.

COMMENTS ON THE DANE COUNTY SYSTEM

This very broad array of highly differentiated services is expanding and evolving, especially in the areas of aging and child and adolescence. It prides itself on spending roughly 85% of its budget on the chronically mentally ill. The system is certainly delivering a great deal of service (average annual expenditure of $4,400 per client) to a traditionally underserved group. This is done at the expense of more traditional psychotherapeutic services and heretofore probably also at the expense of the old and young. The two county level bosses, Meyer and LeCount, are both very impressive persons. Meyer has a very good grasp of the programs, their strengths and weaknesses, and the political realities with which he had to deal. LeCount has an extraordinary grasp of each of 25 different agencies with whom he contracts. In addition to that, he is quite amazing in having a very good view of what is going on with individual clients.

The leadership at the Dane County Mental Health Center is comprised principally of Drs. Len Stein and Ron Diamond, Robert Mohelnitzy and Gail Marker. Stein, Diamond and Mohelnitzy have been there for many years, and Marker joined them two and one-half years ago. Dr. Stein has recently withdrawn to some extent, as he has other responsibilities with the Robert Wood Johnson Foundation.

During our visit we asked Stein to comment and identify the elements of the program that were most crucial to its success. He listed four critical elements:

1. *Philosophy:* The sickest persons should get the most public resources. Psychosis is a lifelong problem so the mental health system should support people in life, not prepare them for it.
2. *Service array:* The breadth, comprehensiveness and timeliness of the interventions (e.g., everywhere, at any time) make them effective.
3. *Fiscal incentives:* Community care is rewarded; hospital care is not.
4. *Leadership:* The long-term presence of the leadership team (of which he is the most visible and widely known individual) ensures continuity.

The major overall problem we see concerns the level of paternalism and the "doing to" activity it generates throughout the program. It is almost impossible to not be treated and followed. Given the state's commitment and the protective services laws, it seems very hard to escape the mind police. The strongest part of the program, to us, is in some ways not its best-known part; that is, we see Emergency Services as the portion of the program that should be receiving greater recognition. The Mobile Community Team (derived from the PACT model) gets most of the attention now. However, it seems to us that in the long run the emergency/crisis intervention team is really the most important link in the system. We got the distinct feeling that the morale of the Mobile Community Team was not as good as it once had been, as the team has begun to reach its limits and is having to resort to all kinds of social control to make clients behave. Because of this, team members no longer feel the need to be the creative and innovative problem solvers they once were. The emergency service workers, in contrast, were very alive and lively, and we really thought they approached their problems in a most professional but innovative and creative way.

Another relatively untalked about strength of the program is the number of supervised living arrangements available to clients. Even though they have 300 spaces, they still have an 85-person waiting list.

Because of the highly differentiated, project-oriented nature of both the funding mechanisms and the way the center has chosen to grow, it is almost impossible to have continuity of persons. It is possible for a client to remain with the crisis team through a crisis, but if additional treatment is needed he or she will be passed immediately to one of several highly differentiated teams.

Interestingly, we could not identify a prevalent guiding theoretical orientation (e.g., psychoanalytic, behavioral). Rather, each of the projects and teams seems to have developed its own. The crisis team focuses on social networks, but we were less impressed with the amount of attention given to families and social networks by the rest of the program. Medication is clearly seen as the mainstay of the treatment of psychotic individuals. Getting any serious psychological attention for such a person appeared to be quite difficult. In this system it seems you can be case managed to death, but no one is likely to sit down and spend a concentrated period of time discussing your experiences, thoughts, feelings, and reactions. The attitude and orientation of the program (if not a philosophy) are clearly pragmatic, down-to-earth, problem-solving, and anti-institutional — which may account for what we noted in the preceding sentence.

Because of its relatively differentiated and specialized quality, the program is able to be relatively nonhierarchical. There are, of course, the bosses at the county level and bosses in the Mental Health Center. However, our sense was that each of the individual programs operates as a relatively small, independent, family-sized unit. This minimally hierarchical arrangement seems to contribute to positive staff morale, as staff feel like they have both the responsibility and the power to make on-the-spot clinical decisions. We were impressed by the adult Alcohol and Drug Abuse program because of its nontraditional approach. Given the overall (lack of) success rates of more traditional programs, nontraditional ones deserve to be implemented and studied.

The major overriding problem for this system, as we see it, is an outgrowth of the program's paternalistic view of the clientele on whom 85% of its resources are spent. For example, the we-them distinction is clearly made by program staff with regard to the chronic psychotic client. This was pretty clearly stated when we were told that the Mental Health Center staff didn't like to be in the kitchen when the Mobile Community Team's clients were there, as they were just too unpleasant. This attitude, when combined with the center's very close relationship with the local chapter of the Alliance for the Mentally Ill, may make it difficult for clients to preserve or gain any power. There is a client-run program (the Lighthouse) in Madison but it is very small, has no office, and basically meets from 7 to 9 p.m. on Friday night. We did not, in our meetings with people at the Mental Health Center, find anyone, with the exception of the director of the Support Network, who showed much investment in client-run programs or was seriously concerned with ways to preserve and enhance client power. This may just reflect lack of information on our part.

It's a something-for-everyone caring system, but at the same time a dependency-inducing one. It's a good system but one from which it is hard to escape. It is a safety and certainty oriented system within which it's hard to take chances. All of this tends to induce "veteran" (chronic) status. It's probably as good as what we've got in the U.S. because of its administrative thoughtfulness, stability, and strong leadership. However, its emphasis on conformity, compliance, and control makes us anxious about its chronicity inducing and maintaining capabilities.

CHAPTER 19

Working Against the Odds: Morrisania Mental Health Services, South Bronx, New York

INTRODUCTION AND BACKGROUND

THIS CASE STUDY IS ABOUT A VERY SPECIAL SOCIAL CONTEXT. It is about a program that struggles daily with America's most distressing social realities — unemployment, poverty, racism, homelessness, violence, substance abuse, teenage pregnancy, crime and family disruption — all resulting in multigenerational demoralization. It is the description of a mental health program located in one of America's worst urban disaster areas — the South Bronx.

The program's ten-year-old building faces the abandoned, decaying Morrisania Hospital, with its rock-broken windows. The four-block walk from the "L" on the Grand Concourse reminds one of a scene from an end-of-civilization science fiction movie. Former President Carter highlighted the plight of the South Bronx, but little construction or rehabilitation of buildings has taken place since then. The still extant small shops are triple locked and barred. Disillusionment, frustration, and hopelessness are almost palpable. At 9 o'clock in the morning, many of the men we passed were already intoxicated — why not, what else is there to do? An affluent society's garbage dump. Is it *possible* to be mentally healthy living in such a context? Can a mental health program be anything but a cruel sop tossed out amidst the rubble to give the *illusion* of addressing the problem? Would its budget be better spent as direct grants to families?

The Morrisania mental health program is a 9 a.m. to 5 p.m., five-day-a-week operation consisting of a day hospital and outpatient adult and children services. It is located in the Morrisania Family Care Center, the other half of which is occupied by an outpatient medical clinic.*

Donald B. Brown, M.D.†, and Myrtle Parnell, M.S.W., both long-term veterans of the Morrisania program, describe the area as follows:

> In the ten years preceding the establishment of the Morrisania mental health program, the Southwest Bronx community had undergone drastic changes. It had been a well-established homogeneous middle-class Jewish family neighborhood centered on the broad and elegant boulevard known as the Grand Concourse. This community, however, was experiencing tensions on its fringes from the in-migration of poor, transient Puerto Ricans and Blacks. The more affluent families began to move to less stressed neighborhoods in nearby suburbs, thus beginning a process of "white flight."
>
> Greatly accelerating this flight was the opening of Coop City, a housing complex with its own schools and services. It was a new middle-class enclave for 60,000 people in a well-protected section of the Bronx which was well-insulated from the encroachment of urban blight by its remoteness and inaccessibility by public transportation. Having been subsidized by the state to be affordable to middle-class families, the complex allowed the remaining middle income families of the Morrisania area to move out en masse, leaving behind a neighborhood bereft of effective leadership, social cohesion and political clout.
>
> Unfortunately, the City did not take a "systems view" of the city-wide housing problem. It did not stop to wonder what the effect of the creation of an opportunity for many thousands of middle-class people to suddenly leave their old neighborhoods for "the better life" would be on threatened neighborhoods.
>
> Moving into the area were large numbers of poor Blacks and Puerto Ricans, attracted by good housing stock that was vastly superior to what they had left behind. Many of these new people were working poor and many were on Welfare. They could not afford the kind of rents the buildings had previously maintained. The housing stock rapidly deteriorated. An epidemic of arson was partially fueled by landlords who turned to insurance companies for their profits. Vacant lots containing piles of the unsightly rubble of burned out buildings became this area's most striking feature. The family-oriented shopping and services that the area had previously known left. Drugs, violence and crime became omnipresent. Community cohesion and political power had not developed, at least in part, due to the transient nature of the population.

---

*The center's 120,000-person catchment area lies in the southwest Bronx between the Grand Concourse and the Harlem River. Yankee Stadium is a famous and popular landmark.
†Dr. Brown, who collaborated on this chapter, is Director of Mental Health Services, Morrisania Neighborhood Family Care Center.

A typical case in our clinic is a single parent, mother of several children, living in a deteriorated building that has no locks on the entrance door and where the mailboxes are regularly violated. The apartment door may have several locks attesting to the degree of concern about intruders. There may be one or more abandoned buildings on the block.

The presenting problem may be the mother's "nervousness," depression or disorganized behavior, or one of the children misbehaving in school. The mother regrets that she dropped out of school and wants her children to do better.

The family subsists on Welfare assistance, food stamps and Medicaid, has a two-party rent check (requiring the signatures of both the tenant and the landlord) because of previous non-payment.

The children are likely to be kept indoors after school because drugs and violence are so prevalent in the neighborhood. Many of our families have been the victims of burglaries, muggings, physical and sexual abuse, murder and/or have been touched by crime through family or social network connections.

There is usually a strong kinship network that includes friends and fathers of the children, which is essential to the family's survival. Resources, social and financial, are not the exclusive possessions of an individual or family. It is understood that in times of crisis "what's mine is yours." This system of reciprocal obligation is a major survival mechanism among the poor.

The religions may be different from those of the middle-class. The poor prefer the Pentecostal Church, Espiritismo or Santaria. Ministers, sisters of the church and faith healers are the natural helpers in time of emotional or spiritual crisis.

Our patients know that, at best, they are not valued and, at worst, they are seen by the larger society as burdens, lazy, dumb and worthless. Their existence is one of vulnerability to the violence in the streets. Life is a series of crises held together by their relationships with, and the resourcefulness of, their family, friends, and religion. (Brown & Parnell, in press)

Some indicators of the urban disorganization in the Morrisania catchment area are:

1. In 1982, 45% of persons there received public assistance.
2. Out-of-wedlock births increased 107% (1970–78), versus 13% city-wide (New York City Human Resources Administration, 1983). More than 20% of these infants are born to teenagers.
3. Fifty-five percent of the households earn less than $10,000 a year. A total of 71.8% of families are in the three lowest poverty categories.
4. The Morrisania area is educationally deprived as well. For persons over 18, only 29.5% are high school graduates and 2.2% graduated from college.
5. Violent death (homicide and suicide) and alcoholic cirrhosis of the liver are the third and fourth leading causes of death.

THE MORRISANIA PROGRAM

The clinic's annual budget is financed by a three million dollar contract for psychiatric services between the New York City Health and Hospitals Corporation (HHC) and the city's mental health department. The city then bills Medicaid to recover what it can. Roughly 75% of the clients seen in the clinic have either Medicaid or Medicare coverage. The clinic has 7.5 fulltime equivalent psychiatrists, 4 psychologists, and 3.5 R.N.'s on its staff. In addition, there are 27 other fulltime equivalent positions held by social workers, occupational therapists, and psychotherapists. This does not include staff from the child development section,* nor does it include administrative staff shared with the medical portion of the clinic occupying the same building. The outpatient department had a total of 1,450 active clients in 1987. There were, including sessions with children, 18,000 face-to-face contacts. The day hospital served 146 clients in 1986. Dr. Brown, program director since 1976, writes (in press):

> In late 1976, the aging Morrisania City Hospital in the southwest Bronx was closed and moved to new facilities five miles north. The outpatient services for the hospital had been located across the street in the new Morrisania Neighborhood Family Care Center for two years. Primary care and specialty medical services continued to be situated there as a freestanding facility of the New York City Health and Hospitals Corporation.
>
> At the time the hospital closed, construction of a new wing to the N.F.C.C., the Mental Health Annex, was completed. It was funded by some of the very last federal monies appropriated for the construction of buildings as part of the original federal Community Mental Health Center's Act.
>
> As is common in the public hospital system in New York City, our program was set up with an affiliation contract with Montefiore Medical Center (part of the Albert Einstein College of Medicine). This allowed our program to be a training site for medical students and residents. Our staff psychiatrists and psychologists were eligible to become faculty in the medical school.

While the affiliation with the Albert Einstein College of Medicine provides an "academic" aura for the program, it also results in a fragmentation in staffing—the medical staff are Montefiore employees; the nonmedical staff and center administrator are employees of the City's Health and Hospital Corporation—thus creating two lines of authority.

Dr. Brown (in press), continues:

> Our Treatment Model:
> Making our clinical services relevant and useful to the poor community we were to serve was our primary goal in developing and running this new pro-

---

*Part of New York's mental retardation service system.

gram. Our patients would need validation of their strengths and coping abilities and not a clinical stance which focused on pathology and deficiency. The services needed to involve the natural support networks of our patients as well as be coordinated with other health and human service providers.

1. Systems Clinical Theory:
We believed that upon making a shift from the traditional individual clinical approach to one which encompassed the organization of the social world around the distressed individual or family, our therapeutic effectiveness would be enhanced in a number of ways:
First, we would become more attentive to cultural values and the norms of our patients and the communities in which they lived.
Second, many options for intervention would open beyond solely offering help to the individual. These would include working with natural support systems as well as other institutions important in the patient's life. Clinicians would work as a systems brokers.
Third, our clinical approach would easily become problem oriented and pragmatic—emphasizing the present rather than the past. Systems clinical theory would provide an excellent basis for understanding and treating the crises of the poor and vulnerable mentally ill in terms of relevant changes in the immediate context of the life of individuals and families.
An additional benefit was that systems theory would remove, or shift to a larger social view, the stigmatizing effect of labeling the problem as belonging solely to the identified patient. Blame would be decreased. Our focus would be shifted toward the view of maximizing strengths and coping abilities in a particular context.

2. Structure of the Services:
We designed our services to be brief (six to eight weeks) and crisis oriented and to be well integrated with longer term treatments. We wanted to be able to respond immediately, recognizing that much of the stress for which people seek help actually involves survival issues. We wanted to be sure we never had a waiting list.
Our charts were organized to include a time line and a genogram modified to show non-family members (important caretakers, Godparents and friends) as well as other agencies involved. The genogram structures information so that existing supports could be assessed for the patient and his/her family, along with the potential for therapeutic interventions.
We recognized at the outset of our program that our ideal of systematically making home visits as part of crisis treatment—and even offering ongoing family therapy in the home—would not be feasible. That idea involved too radical a departure from the established administrative structures and requirements in the N.F.C.C. and we did not pursue it.

3. Staffing:
Sixteen of the 34 staff originally hired were Black or Hispanic. Of the 13 highest trained professionals (the supervising nurses, doctors, psychologists and supervising social workers), ten were from the majority white, Anglo-American culture, while only two were Black and one was Hispanic. The importance of this early racial and cultural imbalance of the staff was to become clear in subsequent phases of the program's development.

4. Staff Supports and Training:

Systems theory teaches (and common sense tells us) that the characteristics of the interpersonal context in which psychiatric service delivery takes place will affect the nature of the service that is delivered. Thus, to the extent that we could succeed in providing staff with an effective support system, opportunities for their personal development, and for learning new skills, we expected that they could have a much better chance of achieving similar goals with their patients.

5. Supervision:

Clinical supervision of staff was set up according to a model derived from systems theory of the supervisor as consultant helping to increase competency and promote growth in the treatment social system, just as the therapist intervenes with similar goals in the social system of the identified patient and/or family. Thus, wherever possible, supervision was live. It was conducted as a practical, live consultation built into the actual service delivery. Supervisors worked using the one-way mirror or sat in with the primary therapist to help untangle some complications in a case or to help in evaluating and developing a treatment plan.

6. Teams:

To maximize mutual support and sharing of skills, services were delivered by interdisciplinary teams consisting of approximately six to ten members (including trainees of various disciplines). Team leaders ran weekly team meetings that facilitated open interchange among staff regarding work-related problems as well as collaboration and mutual learning about cases by staff of different disciplines and cultural backgrounds.

Case conferences were held regularly. Everyone on a treatment team typically had a chance to observe and comment upon a live case as it was being supervised. In being observed, all clinicians (including the supervisors) were forced to confront issues of trust and fears of exposure in ways which are similar to what patients experience in any therapy situation. Once that trust is established, there develops a sense of support which increases the possibilities for both staff and patients to take risks and try new behaviors.

From the outset, our program had insufficient representation of Black and Hispanic professionals and supervisors. Our Hispanic paraprofessional staff struggled with an extra burden of having a large number of complex cases involving critical survival issues. This was due to their patients' inability to successfully negotiate in English such systems as Welfare, hospitals or the schools, or to handle a conflict with a landlord. These staff members were most intensely affected by the crisis of overwork.

Out of the strong feelings aroused by issues relating to race and ethnicity and feelings of exploitation, a Minority Coalition was formed during our second year. This group was interdisciplinary and included all levels of staff from paraprofessionals to psychiatrists. The Coalition directly met with me (the Program Director) to deal with the issues of hiring of more minority professional staff and improving the support of paraprofessionals by working towards giving each one a minority supervisor.

Coalition members became very involved in helping to successfully recruit new minority staff and worked to develop enriched staff training about cultural issues. In addition, the Coalition helped to bring the entire program to a new level of awareness and open discussion about issues of race and ethnicity in both our relationships with one another and with our patients. For example, I learned from my Black and Hispanic colleagues that as a White man trying to avoid what I believed to be further "oppression of minorities" some of my liberal permissive and egalitarian attitudes ran counter to the need for the effective executive authority, clear hierarchy and structure essential for the program's health and survival at this stage of its development.

ADMINISTRATION

This section is based on interviews with Donald Brown and Steven Goldstein (the Ph.D. chief psychologist who has been with the program since its inception) and Elsie Maldonado (now social work administrator of the facility, she started in the program as a psychiatric social worker in 1976).

The clinic suffers from a long history of fragmentation. The facility's life began split; the mental health side of the clinic was and still is affiliated with Montefiore Hospital, while the physical health side of the clinic was affiliated with a nearby Catholic hospital (it now has no affiliation). There is also a split in responsibility for dealing with the so-called chronically mentally ill. A majority of these patients, roughly 500 or so, many from Morrisania's catchment area, are followed in a continuing care clinic run by Bronx Psychiatric Center (the state hospital). Morrisania handles an additional 250 "veterans," some of whom live outside the catchment area. A few Morrisania patients attend the day center at the state hospital and are getting other services at Morrisania.

The center's particular administrative arrangement gives rise to further problems. For instance, facilities of the Health and Hospitals Corporation, designed to provide acute hospital care, lack the administrative support needed to develop community-based nonmedical programs, such as residences. In addition, when the community support concept was originally floated and given state and federal money, Morrisania was not able to apply. This has been changing in recent years, in that the HHC can now run Community Support Programs, of which Morrisania's homeless program is now one. However, this situation has meant that until recently they haven't been able to deal with the most common problem of their clientele—the lack of decent, affordable housing.

At the present time the staff is racially quite well balanced: Four of seven and a half psychiatrists are minority. All of the program's units are administered by minority professionals. In addition, the line staff is more than half minority, mostly Hispanic. The program finds it increasingly difficult to hire trained minority individuals because it pays less well than nearby voluntary hospitals. In addition, the pool of minority applicants is smaller since the decline in tuition aid under the Reagan administration. For example, at New

York University there are only four Blacks and two Hispanics in a class of 144 social work students.

The housing problem threatens to overwhelm clients and staff alike. With upward revisions in early 1988 the New York City welfare housing allowance is $290 for a mother with two children. Apartments in the area, when available, rent for about $400 per month. Section eight housing subsidy and public housing waiting lists are years long. A seniors rental preference program also has a long waiting list. The SSI system is a bit more generous, providing $376 a month plus food stamps and Medicaid. In contrast to city and state welfare it does not require frequent face-to-face contacts for continuation. Eviction is a very common and devastating event. There are 4,000 per year in the Bronx alone. Entire families must frequently rely on shelters or double up in occupied apartments for periods of time.

The question may legitimately be asked: How has the program continued to exist and do its job and keep staff for as long as it has? Although occasionally ambitious professionals come to Morrisania for a year or two of training and then move on, many of the staff with whom we met had been there for seven or more years. The reasons are well captured by Ms. Maldonado (social work) and Mrs. Rosetta Jenkins, chief of nursing programs:

> *Ms. Maldonado:* "I'm a Puerto Rican raised in the Bronx where I saw that the institutions were not serving the poor and minorities. My commitment to the work is an idealistic one. In the '60s and early '70s change and innovation were possible but now there are fewer resources and more bureaucratization. Despair is now much more common among the clients. Families have been depleted of economic and interpersonal resources. The stresses of crowding, poverty and lack of personal security contribute to family conflict and violence. They just can't take care of their sicker members because they are too stressed themselves. This helps explain why so many of our patients use the Franklin Avenue shelter as a second bedroom to the family home."

> *Mrs. Jenkins:* "I believe and a lot of people agree with me that this is the very best place around. It's because of the family and systems philosophy of operation. It involves a lot of encouragement to do family work with a lot of collegial support and supervision available. The people who have been here for a long time are the old guard—we're sustaining a cause and carrying out a mission. The program's greatest virtue is the respect and dignity with which clients are treated. For them, this is a very unusual experience."

At one point, Mrs. Jenkins left Morrisania and went to work at another hospital's psychiatry program. She quite vividly contrasts the two programs' approaches:

> "The other program is one of stagnation, sameness, homeostasis and chronicity. For example, the day hospital schedule at Morrisania is changed at

least twice a year while the other one is never changed. Their only motivation is financial. At Morrisania minorities are all in key leadership positions with the exception of the directorship. At the other program only whites are in charge.

"Our own racial difficulties were addressed when the Minority Coalition became the watchdog of hiring. We were able to confront the myth of 'the happy family without differences.' In fact, forcing respect for cultural *differences* (as they did) actually muted racial issues in the program and led to an overall improved understanding of the patients."

Dr. Goldstein cited five factors as crucial to their survival:

1. They are really trying to serve.
2. There is substantial training available for everyone in family therapy and other forms of treatment.
3. They have an experimental attitude toward and encourage the application of new therapies.
4. There is less hierarchy than in most places because they use a family and systems model rather than a medical one. The egalitarianism that stems from the model is reinforced by the experience and skill of the operators themselves, which mutes professional/nonprofessional differences.
5. The generally positive expectations at all levels create an ambiance that invites people to do well.

HOSPITALIZATION

The Morrisania program hospitalizes only clients (90 a year, 35 committed) who are already on their rolls. New clients who look like they will need hospitalization are sent directly to one of three public hospitals in the Bronx (all outside the catchment area). Psychiatric inpatient beds in the Bronx are always scarce. Because of this, hospitalizing someone is a time-consuming and difficult process. There are a total of 315 acute adult and 530 long-stay psychiatric inpatient beds in the Bronx (population 1.1 million). This is a ratio of 27 acute public beds per 100,000 population, as compared with 36 per 100,000 in New York City as a whole. This number of beds must be seen in the context of the Bronx: There are *no* mobile emergency services available, *no* residential alternatives to hospitalization, only 413 community residential beds, and a serious overall housing shortage. Hence, it is a situation in which hospital beds are in great demand.

Since the late '70s there has been an increasing number of admissions and a steady decline in the length of stay in the municipal hospitals' acute inpatient units in the Bronx. For example, Bronx Municipal Hospital Center's length of stay went from 27.7 days in 1979 to less than 14 days in 1987. The acute beds are serving as a rapidly revolving door. The center attempted to liaison with hospitals where their patients were admitted but soon found that it was a useless expenditure of staff time. Hospital staff were just too overwhelmed by admission and discharge pressures to deal with individual referral sources.

DAY HOSPITAL

The day hospital administrator is a Hispanic nurse who joined the program when she took it over in September 1986. In July 1987, she was joined by a white psychiatrist. The day hospital has 40 places and an average length of stay of about nine months. Eighty percent of the clients live with their families. The clients come from three sources:

1. Emergency rooms send patients who have decompensated but are not sick enough to require hospitalization.
2. The Morrisania outpatient clinic refers patients who are decompensating and need intensive care to avoid hospitalization.
3. State hospital inpatients are sent if they need further treatment and structure after discharge.

Most patients are schizophrenic; almost all are on neuroleptics. Basically, the criterion for admitting people to the day hospital is that they are sufficiently motivated about treatment to regularly get to the program or that their family or social network can assure their attendance. Staff have no problem with taking acutely psychotic clients. They will take active drug takers who can commit to a detoxification program and/or drug or alcohol ancillary programs like NA and AA. They try not to admit actively suicidal or homicidal people.

The treatment program is composed of three phases: Newly admitted clients are assigned to the lunch group (three to seven patients) that plans, shops, cooks, and serves lunch to the entire hospital. Upon graduation from the lunch group (usually three to six weeks), patients go to a goal-setting group and then to a predischarge group. Members of the predischarge group are focused primarily on what they need to have in place before they can leave the program. Woven in with these groups is a range of other activities: crafts, recreation, computer and other work-oriented skill groups. Once a week therapy groups are held in both English and Spanish. There are also weekly women's, nonverbal, movement, drama, and music groups in English and Spanish. The initial assessment is quite family and ecosystem oriented. In all cases, family members are urged to participate in multifamily psychoeducation sessions and/or once weekly family therapy. The program operates with 10 F.T.E.'s.

OUTPATIENT DEPARTMENT

Brown and Parnell (in press) write:

> The outpatient service structure was designed to fit our systems theory concept that requests for help arise at a time of failed adaptation and crisis. The first goal of clinical interventions was to help individuals and families attain a new level of adaptation. Some patients would not be expected to return for months or years until another crisis exceeded their problem-solving capacity. Others would continue for supportive and/or growth oriented psychotherapies, while still others benefited sufficiently from the brief intervention to go on with their lives without further help.
>
> Continuity of patient care was achieved by organizing staff schedules for the outpatient department (O.P.D.) so as to allow each clinician time to see their crisis/walk-in patients for follow-up appointments. Interventions were made in the very first meeting. More thorough evaluations were made over subsequent visits. The possibilities of change were assessed by seeing how the patient (and family) responded to immediate efforts at change rather than through prolonged assessment interviews.
>
> During the first interview, not only was the mental and medical (when indicated) state of the individual patient assessed and individual crisis treatment initiated, but information was gathered about family members and significant others in the patient's social field. The problems presented by our patients were varied, requiring at times medical/psychiatric assessment and intervention, social system, family/individual assessment and interventions by a therapist and/or advocacy and support by the paraprofessional.
>
> In establishing our program with a systems clinical theory working culture, we were putting into operation new ideas about minorities and the poor. We were clear among ourselves that poverty itself is not a mental illness. We, therefore, assumed that our patients have strengths and organized our assessments to elicit the positives and coping abilities in individuals, families and social systems, rather than the pathology.
>
> We assumed also that patients knew what they needed and our job was to help them with the problems presented. Our goal was to help resolve the crisis and return the person/family to regain their previous level of functioning as quickly as possible. It was often possible to achieve this goal by intervening in the social system and advocating for the patient.
>
> Our purpose is to teach the patient about the particular system and how it works, so that s/he can eventually manage independently. Instead of escorting the patient ourselves, we may identify some person in the client's network who has the skills and availability to help the patient. For the clinician, resolving these issues is a very tedious and protracted task, requiring numerous calls and extreme frustration as the policies and procedures in other agencies, as well as the assigned worker, who changes so frequently.
>
> Patients who first came alone were told that the possibilities for help would be increased if all relevant people involved came in for an assessment as part of

a group meeting. Patients too frightened or ashamed to discuss their problems with anyone else were given the private help they requested, and the involvement of others was later encouraged.

Dr. Brown (in press) continues:

> Group treatment for over 150 patients-a-year in 15 different groups is an important ongoing feature of our program. Our "menu" of groups includes activity, socialization, parenting skills, and insight oriented "personal growth" groups, to name a few. We have not yet achieved the hoped-for goals of seeding the development of self-help groups for our patients. Some groups are formed to meet a specific need in providing social supports. One such group consists of middle-aged Hispanic women who have recently migrated to New York City. This group, led by two middle-aged Spanish-speaking social workers, one a WASP (White Anglo-Saxon Protestant), the other a Puerto Rican who has lived in New York for over 30 years, addresses issues of acculturation and adaptation to life in New York, through direct example and open discussion.
>
> New treatment modalities continue to be developed. One psychiatrist has become certified as an acupuncturist and offers this service four days a day to selected patients. A small group of clinicians have been learning stress reduction techniques and hypnosis. They have been applying this in their clinical work as well as training other staff in its use.

The outpatient department is run jointly by a black Ph.D. clinical psychologist and a Hispanic woman psychiatrist. It operates with 5.5. M.D. and 14 non-M.D. F.T.E.'s. In order to control patient flow more effectively, several changes have been instituted; there is no longer a separate crisis team and all new patients are seen in three or four brief treatment and evaluative sessions prior to a diagnosis and disposition meeting. Those who don't complete the series (about 50%) are dropped from the rolls. Psychotherapy, when offered, is usually individual (70%), focused on specific problems, time-limited, and whenever possible conducted by the evaluator. The staff work in three-person teams — one evaluator with a social worker and psychiatric supervisor. Currently outpatient staff carry 40–50 cases, except for the psychiatrists, who act as supervisors and consequently carry fewer individual patients (about 20). They are required to have 25 face-to-face contacts and 17½ hours of contact time each week. Outpatient clinicians are generalists; they do whatever is needed with every client, hence serving as designated case managers. This is not a term, or set of functions, about which one hears much talk in this setting. Recently a person has been hired to be exclusively responsible for keeping a roster of concrete available resources, that is, apartments, SSI, etc. There is also a renewed emphasis on use of groups. The 250 chronically mentally ill clients on their roster are seen usually on a monthly basis. Sixty are on injectable neuroleptics. Cecily Dell (a Ph.D. psychologist), a seven-year veteran outpatient therapist, describes her work as follows:

"We operate on 'dental model' — treat the cavity and ask people to come back when they have another. The solutions we have to offer are limited because we can't address the source of stress — the social and economic conditions. If we find someone with a developmental crisis we can be quite helpful. When my old clients call I'll see them again as frequently as needed to get them through the crisis. I have difficulty deciding exactly who should be logged into the clinic because if a person isn't registered you don't get credit for a visit against the required 25 contacts. However, registering all members of a family is time-consuming and duplicative. At the moment the city requires that those persons who don't have some form of insurance pay $7 per visit per family member. This is almost impossible for our families. For this fee to be waived I have to fill out a special form at specified intervals. So, it becomes a problem of my motivation and time. I spend about one-quarter of my time in the child program. I see about 20 to 25% of my clients on a strictly family basis. I see one-third of my clients weekly, one-third bimonthly, and one-third monthly. The weeklies are child clients and borderlines. Bimonthlies are bipolars who are generally functioning OK. Roughly one-quarter of my clients have had multiple hospitalizations. Our problem is that our family orientation clashes with the individual one of the rest of the system. The extra paperwork sorely tests my motivation to see families. Home visits are something that I'd like to do, but they are just too dangerous and too expensive. I have to take another person with me, it must be a male, and I have no car — so it becomes a real production. In spite of that, I do about one a month."

Everyone with whom we spoke had some concerns about his or her work. For example, one felt that groups are not used enough. Another felt the groups that are conducted are not properly organized. However, there was absolute agreement that they liked working at Morrisania. There was general agreement that is enjoyable because of the attitude toward innovation, the solidarity among the staff, and the amount of supervision and teaching available.

CHILD PROGRAM

This 4.5 F.T.E. program headed by a Chilean woman child psychiatrist started three years ago. The staff members now see 20 walk-in cases a month and have about 250 active cases at any given time. Referrals are equally split between schools and families. Eighty-five percent come from single-parent families, one-third are preschool age children, and another third are adolescents. They are treating 20 children with attention disorders with stimulants. Their principal clinical focus is problem-oriented immediate family intervention (60% receive only family therapy). About half the kids are also evaluated at school or at home. Learning-disabled children can be evaluated by either Morrisania's child development center or the schools.

The child clinic runs a variety of groups: parenting skills; parents with preschool age children; an evening group for working parents; and two regular therapy groups for kids, one latency age and the other adolescent. They use a consultant to make clinical decisions about the duration of groups and whether they will be open or closed. Drug-abusing adolescents are referred out to specialized programs. As elsewhere in the center, morale is good. To give therapists a sense of not having to face a difficult situation alone, problem cases are treated with live supervision behind a one-way mirror.

The service chief trained in a psychoanalytic child program in Manhattan but decided that for child work a family and community orientation would be more helpful than an analytic play therapy one. Her experience at Morrisania has confirmed her notion that at least with their clientele change is easier to produce from the outside in (behavior) than from inside out (insight).

HOMELESS PROGRAM – FRANKLIN AVE. MEN'S SHELTER IN SOUTH BRONX

Background: The homeless program grew out of Dr. Brown's involvement in the training of Albert Einstein psychiatric residents. In 1984–85 three residents began to visit shelters as part of their training in community psychiatry. In 1985 the three residents were granted approval of a proposal to form small groups of homeless men and move them together into apartments (à la Fairweather et al., 1969). The Community Support grant was awarded to Montefiore Hospital. No sooner had the grant been given than the hospital's insurers asked that an additional $250,000 premium be paid before they would assume liability for this program. A protracted series of negotiations between Montefiore and the City Department of Mental Health ensued. It was finally decided that the HHC would accept the program and it would be transferred to the Morrisania Neighborhood Family Care Center (MNFCC), with Dr. Brown as the director. However, during these negotiations (November '86 to October '87), the program's contract was frozen, making any changes in staff and purchasing impossible. This led to a loss of staff, demoralization – the usual consequences of such prolonged administrative haggling. As of November 1, 1987 the center will administer the grant.

2. *Description of the shelter:* New York City's current policy with regard to homelessness is to convert large underutilized buildings into shelters. Most are located in socially disorganized areas of the city where little community resistance is anticipated. The Franklin Avenue Armory barrack-type shelter is located in a particularly dilapidated section of the South Bronx. Four hundred and fifty of its 650 men are crowded into the Armory's large gym-like ground floor.

3. *The population:* The men are between 20 and 35 years old; 56% black and 41% hispanic; 12% have reported previous psychiatric hospitalizations; 41% have been treated for substance abuse; 75–80% are currently abusing some substance; and 62% have been arrested and 22% convicted of a felony. Violence is common. Interestingly, 25% of the shelter users are *employed*, usually in entry-level jobs.

Because of the Bronx's housing shortage, the shelter functions as a second bedroom for 500 men from families in the surrounding community. Those with families within walking distance frequently go home during the day to eat, wash, and change their clothes and then return to the shelter to sleep.

The shelter has a staff of 150. Some staff are former homeless persons. Many have the same social problems and personal habits as the shelter inhabitants. The staff is focused on custodial and maintenance activities. Drug dealing is said to go on across staff and client lines.

4. *The mental health program:* The staff consists of one social worker, one case manager, one psychiatrist, and one program director in the daytime and two evening fulltime caseworkers. The original grant proposed forming groups of chronically mentally ill men within the facility to then be moved out as a group, as in the Fairweather model, into homes or apartments in the community. However, it soon became clear that there were two major problems with the plan: (1) There are only 413 community residence beds for mentally ill persons (estimated need: 1,500) in the entire Bronx. (2) Almost all the community placements *required* clients to be on medication. Shelters are known to attract persons adverse to taking psychopharmacologic agents. Although program staff discuss the role of medications with clients and encourage them to get them for specific indications, they do not prescribe them directly because they do not want to be seen as "controllers." They instead refer to a city clinic.

Their experience is that the nonpsychotic homeless man is often seen as a rather disturbed and disturbing individual because of his demoralization, depression, low frustration tolerance, frequent display of anger, and inability to follow through. Thus, even though these are *not* long-term psychiatric institution ex-inmates, they still have many of the qualities associated with institutionalism.

Because of the abovementioned problems, the program has been refocused on two groups of shelter residents: (1) newly admitted persons, and (2) persons in crisis. The crisis portion of the program is meant to serve the 12% of the population that is chronically mentally ill. Interventions involve intensive case management, attempting to link clients with various services, to help them form a network in the shelter with other men in similar situations, and whenever possible to negotiate a reunion with families. The staff encourage these men to play an active role in finding others in the shelter they believe could benefit from the program.

The first-timer portion of the program grew out of the workers' concern about the settling in they observed after two or three months at the shelter. In the six months prior to our visit the shelter had an average of two new first-timers a day.

The program served 172 shelter residents during its first year and helped 78 men move out into either temporary or permanent living arrangements, most (43 of the 78) into substance abuse rehabilitation programs. Located on the third floor of the armory, the program operates without appointments, has an open door, and gives free access to its phone as an incentive for involvement. The program is seen by its participants as a basically friendly place. Many of the men come up and spend time socializing. So, in addition to the more precisely defined functions, it operates a evening drop-in center.

Regarding the future of the program, Dr. Mullins (the program psychiatrist) believes that:

1. They need to find, renovate, and operate their own single room occupancy hotel (it should be noted here that there were 60% fewer SRO rooms available in New York City in 1980 than in 1973). They want to return to the single room occupancy model, with all of its problems, because they believe these men can best survive in a situation where they can control the amount of social contact they have.
2. Program staff need to do more home visiting and use a psychoeducational approach with the families to facilitate reintegration.
3. They need to expand their efforts for dealing with the systems that impinge on them. They are finding that their agency liaison is now easier and things happen much more quickly because they have developed personal relationships within the relevant agencies.

It is notable that the city has decided that its homeless problem is best addressed by renovated permanent shelters. In the South Bronx there is a plethora of abandoned apartment buildings that could be rehabilitated to become public housing. The city seems not to understand that it costs $20,000 a year per person in barracks arrangements and up to $300,000 a year per family in the hotels being used to house homeless families! City policy has also managed to break up couples by not allowing any unmarried persons who have lived together to be housed in their family program. The crowded first floor of the Armory, a sea of cots, seems a place devoted to dehumanized warehousing—a not very appealing long-term solution.

COMMENTARY

The Morrisania program is a lesson in the power of ideology to sustain effort in the face of seemingly insurmountable odds. Staff struggle daily to transform the machinations of an unfriendly system into a positive influence on the lives of a multiproblem clientele. They continue to struggle both because of the consistency of the philosophy and because of the attention devoted to staff morale. It seems to have been very effective in preventing staff burnout. They have evolved a coherent systemic model within a fragmented, disjointed system. Elements we consider vital to effective program functioning — mobile crisis intervention, intensive residential care, and transitional and permanent supported housing — are totally absent. They have limited control over the entry and exit gates and their efforts vis-à-vis the larger system are mostly ineffective.

While most public mental health clients are poor and have multiple problems, the Morrisania catchment area contains a much larger number of such persons (as compared with Madison and Boulder) because of the pervasiveness of the poverty and lack of community resources. This difference can perhaps be best understood by comparing the numbers of families with incomes of less than $10,000 in each of the three areas: Boulder, Colorado, 14%; Madison, Wisconsin, 25%; South Bronx, 55%. Despite all the programmatic and bureaucratic deficiencies, of all the programs we've seen, this one most nearly approximates what we would consider to be an effective clinical approach to a community mental health clientele. The following summary and conclusion from an article by Brown and Parnell (in press) state very well how closely their principles are to those we've described elsewhere in this volume:

> Emphasize Mutual Support and Networking: In dealing with the special stressors of working with the poor and mentally ill, it has been important to have a working environment in which our staff can share information and emotional support. Likewise, we have worked hard to develop an administrative style which provides a model for respecting difference, while cooperating and resolving conflicts. Frequent parties, mutual sharing of ethnic foods and maintaining team cohesiveness have made work in this domestic war zone not only bearable, but exciting. Administrators who don't understand the special issues of dealing with our patient population have become uncomfortable with this different approach and pressure continues to be exerted, which threatens the spirit of sharing and teamwork. This requires constant sharing of information and "advocacy work" on our own behalf.
>
> Recognize Strengths, Normalize the Problems: The stresses we experience are a "normal" aspect of delivering human services to the poor in public institutions. What we do achieve, often against great odds, needs special recognition and praise. Our sense of helplessness and demoralization is mitigated when we learn that others are in the same situation and have found ways to cope.

Encourage Growth and Change: Patients, families, staff, programs, communities and the entire service system each have their own cycles of development, crisis and adaptation. A spirit of encouraging learning, growth, innovation and change, keeps us moving forward in trying new clinical interventions redesigning aspects of the program, or teaching/advocating for our needs with other service providers, administrators, or politicians.

Morrisania is the only one of the three American programs that is serving substantial numbers of homeless persons. Unfortunately, a basically sound approach to the problem may be foundering because of bureaucratic problems and poor city planning. Given what we saw in the South Bronx, we wonder whether government wants to do anything serious about the homelessness problem. In an area with literally hundreds of empty buildings available for renovation, and where housing is the most obvious and pressing need, it boggles the mind that shelters are the principal solution. No one seems to be focused on developing and providing permanent, affordable, decent housing to all of the citizens of the South Bronx — some of whom are currently homeless, some of whom are mentally ill, some of whom are just plain poor folks trying to survive.

The problems within the center's setting are ones that are extraordinarily difficult to address, mostly because they are often ones generated in the bureaucracy that controls the setting but is unresponsive to the center's change efforts. Worse yet, it's not just one outside bureaucracy but *several*. Within the center itself, there are some racial problems, principally the result of a *bureaucratic* inability to let experience and competence count as much as degrees in the promotion ladder. This greatly affects the paraprofessionals who have been with Morrisania for quite some time, are now well trained family and system clinicians, but who cannot get management positions because they don't have proper credentials in the city's personnel system. As a result they feel, justifiably, exploited. Again, it's a *system* problem. Fortunately, some paraprofessionals have been able to take advantage of the program's special support for them to get credentials (i.e., special schedules have been arranged so that they can attend school while working). Maintaining balance in the Center's multiracial staff is an ongoing concern. However, because Morrisania is a ship full of persons trying to hang on and get through a storm together this issue is really secondary.

In terms of the 11 program variables we identified as important in the evaluation of the programs, this program is very high on staff quality, continuity, staff morale, normalization, contextualization, flexibility, leadership, teamness, respect for clients and demedicalization. It is not quite so high on preservation of client power and the consultative, "being with" facilitative attitude we'd like to see. However, we must acknowledge that it's hard to preserve client power that doesn't exist. It's not surprising that they have no consumer groups at the moment. Parents and consumers are so busy trying to survive that they have no time to organize and obtain power for themselves vis-à-vis the mental health system.

This program is being documented in the literature (Brown, in press; Brown & Parnell, in press; Goldstein, 1986; Goldstein & Dyche, 1983; Simon, 1986). We hope this publicity will help it become more widely known so that its clinical model can be applied in other, perhaps more salubrious, settings.

Ingredients of Success

CHAPTER 20

What We Have Learned from All This

Based on our experience with a large number of community programs, careful study of the Italian reform and in-depth analysis of the three Italian and three American programs described in the previous section, we have identified a number of common elements that contribute in varying degrees to programmatic success.

STRONG LEADERSHIP

Successful programs usually have strong, dedicated, committed, consistent leadership. This is true of all six programs we have presented. To be a major force behind a transformation in an entire nation's mental health program may, however, require the charisma of a Basaglia. Nevertheless, fine local programs can be led by trusted, highly involved persons with sufficient power to make things happen. For programs to continue to grow and evolve, consistency of leadership over time seems necessary. Common sense tells us that it is easier to pass the baton of noncharismatic leaders; Italy's experience with Basaglia's loss is certainly a testimony to this phenomenon. The vacuum he left when he died in 1980 has never really been completely filled. Without its strong leader the Democratic Psychiatry movement found it difficult to press for more rapid implementation of Law 180.

Stable leadership in a setting that allows experiential validation of new clinical practices also serves an important training and dissemination function. Basaglia's original group in Gorizia drew students from all over Italy. A cadre of community mental health workers was trained in a paradigm that represented a dramatic change from previous practice. They subsequently went out to work in other parts of the country. By the time the law was actually changed in 1978, Gorizia and Trieste-like community programs were already in place in a number of Italian cities. The positive clinical role models provided by the leadership in the programs we've described are very important to both recruiting and training students. In turn, students provide them with new energy and enthusiasm and take what they learn to implement in new settings.

PROFESSIONAL SUPPORT GROUPS

Transforming a system from a hospital to a community orientation is personally risky. Leaders who propose this change are out of step with existing realities and hence viewed as deviant. Basaglia, for example, was still defending himself in court when he died. The suit was one that had been filed six years earlier. One important lesson we can learn from Basaglia relates to his foresight in forming the alternative psychiatric society, Democratic Psychiatry, in Italy. This society provided a sense of belonging, a place where professionals who held similar views could share them and where a new consensus could be evolved. This view was dramatically different from the existing one but difficult to define as deviant, since the group evolved an alternative consensus representing many mental health professionals. Although dominated by psychiatrists, the Society for Democratic Psychiatry was ecumenical in its membership. This professional proletarianization provided a living model for the way Basaglia believed mental health structures should be reorganized. That is, they should be nonhierarchical insofar as possible, be democratic in terms of the power residing in developing consensus, and be competence-based rather than degree-based in terms of task assignments. The programs we describe generally operate in this way as well — small, collegial teams with decision-making power.

Democratic Psychiatry served as a magnet drawing mental health professionals from all disciplines. Most especially it provided a format for expression to students committed to human rights reform. These high energy recruits provided the fuel that powered Democratic Psychiatry's engine. This is still true of the Italian programs presented. Student volunteers are very important in the Boulder County program. Dane County's reputation draws students and visitors from many countries. Morrisania's recruiting ability is due to its application of a consistent theoretical model and an unusual context. Although they're not volunteers, its trainees are surely high energy recruits.

A CONSENSUS THAT CHANGE IS NEEDED

It is notable that if there was ever a popular consensus in the U.S. that the mental health system needed reform it was in the Kennedy era. A wide array of professional and lay groups (36 in all) came together to produce the 1961 Report of the Joint Commission on Mental Health. There is some disagreement about whether President Kennedy proposed his 1963 bill to please his sister Eunice Shriver or whether he had in fact read the Joint Commission's report and taken on its cause. Dr. Jack Ewalt (Chairman of the Joint Commission) maintains it was the latter, but the former explanation is most prevalent in the present-day mythology. It is likely that both versions are true to some extent. There was, it seems, a modest consensus in the early '60s that dramatic changes in the U.S. mental health system were needed. The consensus did not evolve until nearly a decade later in Italy.

In Italy the strategy used to gain popular support for the plight of the mental patient in the *manicomio* was to pair it with that of the exploited factory worker. Hence, the labor unions (mostly leftwing) became major sources of popular blue-collar support for the work of Democratic Psychiatry.

In the U.S. "popular" support came mostly from professionals and mental health laymen's advocacy groups like the Mental Health Association. The rhetoric in this country really seemed to have been humanistic: We should not treat members of a free, open, democratic society in a way that may imprison them against their wills for long periods of time and deprives them of their civil liberties.

In the U.S., attention to the "cause" of the mental patient seems to have been diverted to the war in Viet Nam. When the country found it could not support both guns and butter and as guns consumed more and more of the federal budget, the initial dream of 2,000 CMHC's covering the entire U.S. was scaled back.

In Italy it would appear that, although a consensus for change still exists, it has been tempered economically by the end of Italy's "miraculous" economic development post World War II and socially by the paralysis that followed by Aldo Moro's assassination.

After perhaps a decade of relative quiescence a new popular consensus for change seems to be evolving in the U.S. The major new player in this game is the National Alliance for the Mentally Ill (NAMI) (also see Chapter 8). Formed only in 1979, this group's influence has grown by leaps and bounds. Its members lobby effectively in Congress, browbeat television programs that misrepresent images of mental patients, and have been actively involved in a major restructuring of the NIMH that resulted in their achieving a number of their goals. They are an ever vigilant group looking for ways to get better care for, improve the image of, and destigmatize their offspring.

A second new player in the newly redeveloping consensus for change is former mental patient self-help movement. Although not as well organized, moneyed and powerful as NAMI, these groups have begun to develop their own alternative mental health programs. They have been effective in initiating change through class action suits against various state mental health systems about hospital conditions, patient rights, involuntary administration of psychotropic medications, and lack of treatment in least restrictive environments. By the mere fact of their having been filed, these suits have caused changes in behavior within state mental health systems.

If these two new teams (clients and parents) don't get stalemated in a serious adversarial posture, they may well be able to press for the contextual conditions necessary to implement widely the types of effective community-based programs described in this book. The individual programs described have developed supportive local networks to varying extents. Genoa and Morrisania are both operating in political and economic contexts that are not always supportive. They seem to survive through internal networking and consensus-building.

A STABLE, PREDICTABLE SOURCE OF FINANCIAL SUPPORT

Law 180 was passed in Italy in May 1978. A comprehensive national health insurance scheme combining features of the British and Scandinavian schemes was passed by the Italian parliament in December 1978. The plan provided for countrywide catchment-area-based health services utilizing general practitioners as the first line of service. The plan is paid for by a payroll tax and the money is distributed more or less on a capita basis to each region (equivalent to states in the U.S.). Hence, support for community-based psychiatry was made available. Within regions and catchment areas competition among the medical specialties for funds has been keen and has sometimes led to inequities. Also, Italian economic problems result in the National Health Service constantly being buffeted by spending and personnel freezes. What is important, however, is that the National Health Service is here to stay and mental health will receive a reasonably predictable share of the financial pie. Programs will expand and contract but their survival should not be threatened.

The situation is more complex and difficult in the United States. Support for CMHC's went through several permutations. Basically, CMHC's received eight-year staffing grants that required increasing levels of local matching funds. It rapidly became important for CMHC's to develop their local resources to meet the match. While the ways in which this was done varied widely, the result was almost always a patchwork of local monies from a variety of sources. State funds, the traditional support for public mental health care, were often withheld or given only grudgingly because of the early federal decision to bypass the states in funding the CMHC's.

Interestingly, this need to develop local resources contributed to the legitimate criticism of the CMHC's as not serving the most seriously disturbed and disturbing persons. That is, *financial needs* encouraged CMHC's to treat middle-class neurotic patients who had health insurance.

In 1981, when federal CMHC money was converted into block grants to states, each center became beholden to the state for its share of federal support. In fact, as was the case in Washington, DC, when federal staffing grants ran out, a number of jurisdictions closed CMHC's or merged them into existing programs at reduced funding levels. In a sense, the declining eight-year federal staffing grant support contained the seeds of destruction of the program designers intentions. They had banked on state and local support to take over when the federal support ran out. Predictably, this did not always occur. Hence, uncertainty over its eventual survival was built into every federally funded CMHC.

Exemplary U.S. programs we have described (especially Boulder and Dane counties) survived by serving the perceived needs of their communities, by the successfully lobbying at local and state levels for money, and by having enough political power from boards, legislators, etc., to be a force with which to be reckoned. In addition, their state leadership (whence support comes) has been generally enlightened.

Today, the two biggest obstacles to the widespread development of adequate community-based care in the U.S. are: (1) the absence of a reliable, predictable source of support, such as national health insurance; and (2) the presence of far too many hospital beds that eat up a disproportionate share of resources. Italy is still spending a lot on its state hospitals. However, since new patients can't be admitted, they will eventually disappear. Unfortunately, this policy of non-institutionalization does not look like it's going to make the transatlantic voyage. For the most part, America seems to have tacitly agreed to continued production of new "veterans." So far as we know, no state has yet proposed closing all of its mental hospitals to admissions. This is so despite the availability of cost-effective alternatives (e.g., mobile crisis intervention and intensive residential alternatives).

Other obstacles to community program development in the U.S. are: (1) It's out of fashion; (2) appropriate training programs are lacking; and (3) divisive professional territoriality with CMHC programs persists. The training issue is also a problem in Italy, but the other two basically don't exist. Community mental health is mandated by law, so it can't be out of fashion. In Italy there are such high rates of unemployment, even among doctors, that most people are just happy to have a job; unlike doctoral-level professionals in the U.S., they don't need to control the program to feel useful.

Based on this analysis, what kinds of changes are needed in the American system to make the type of community mental health system we espouse widely available?

First, and most critically, a system of capitation-payment-based national health insurance is needed. Such a system would pay for *what* is delivered, not where. It would provide a reliable source of funding for a true community smorgasbord of programs and facilities.

Second, a guaranteed annual income or some other form of nondependency-inducing and -perpetuating welfare is needed. It should provide enough money so recipients can live, not merely struggle to exist. Poverty, because of the endless stress it engenders, is a major contributing cause of *prolonged* mental illness (Warner, 1985).

Third, the relevant professional disciplines must provide in-vivo experiential training in community mental health. As part of this, stable community and academic program leadership should be rewarded. Sufficient numbers of role models are needed to assure a continual supply of appropriately trained new professionals.

Fourth, a policy of non-institutionalization should be implemented by blocking admissions to *all* large psychiatric institutions. As buildings are emptied they should be demolished or *immediately* converted to some other use, such as nursing homes for the elderly long-stay patients already in them. They should not be targeted as terminal care centers for AIDS patients. They have never been good places in which to be crazy and are certainly not good places in which to die in a dignified manner. *Anticipated* savings should be transferred to community programs on a $0.50 on the dollar basis.

Leadership, money, and non-institutional contexts are critical to the development of effective community mental health programs.

CHAPTER 21

Contextual Confusions and Some Recommended Remedies

WHAT IS COMMUNITY MENTAL HEALTH ANYWAY? For us it is the delivery of prompt, adequate, and consistent answers to the real social, psychological, and medical needs of a defined population. It is the provision of a wide enough array of services, programs and facilities so that everyone sent for or seeking help can find options relevant to his or her needs in the smorgasbord offered. It is a system organized for and by the customers.

Community mental health in the United States has had a checkered, on again, off again, career. It was in vogue from the mid-18th century until the civil war era. It flickered a bit in the early 20th century but was basically dormant until the appearance of the Joint Commission's report in 1961 and the CMHC legislation of 1963 that flowed from it. In the '60s it grew like topsy as a consequence of federal support, only to flatten out and then decline in the '80s. In the late '70s it spawned a child (C.S.P.) that seems to have provided a conceptualization to rejuvenate community programs. Meanwhile, the "old" CMHC program got its politics straightened out by the Reagan administration — no more were the "feds" going to dictate where, and for what, their support for mental health would be spent within individual states.

Community mental health is *public* mental health. The American two-tier health care system has not yet invented private community mental health for seriously disturbed and disturbing persons. If there were health insurance money available, it is likely that it would soon be available. Many

Italians believe that everything in life is politics; public mental health is politics with poverty, racism, sexism, marginalization, stigmatization, and social control thrown in for good measure. Community workers are faced constantly with the effects of society's ills. Their clients are usually powerless, unorganized, demoralized and dependent. The somewhat paradoxical definition of "mental health" as a quasi "medical" undertaking frequently confuses staff. Is "mental illness" for real or is it a metaphor of convenience — one that legitimizes attention to what are really social problems with psychological sequelae? Have we just reframed social ills as medical problems so someone might pay to have them addressed? Following the mental illness model with its defect in the individual assumptions, staff are constantly confronted with the fact that the political system impinges negatively on their clients. Confusion mounts — if so and so has this genetically determined chemical imbalance that's produced his disease, why is it his disease seems always to get worse when he can't find housing or loses his woman friend? Even the *presumed magical* drugs can't prevent his getting worse under these conditions.

Physicians imbued with too much power are asked (in some instances required) to be agents of social control. They hospitalize and "treat" patients against their wills. Yet physicians are ill trained to be controllers; they've been led to believe they're healers who will be voluntarily sought out for their ministrations. In community work real choices for clients and staff are limited by what the community (however defined) wants done. Just trying to get a clear picture of who wants to do what to whom can be very confusing. Throw in the contradictions of systems versus individual defect theories and the social problem versus medical disease issue and you've got potential for a real mess. So it goes daily in community mental health work; it's messy. The private practice voluntary model does not usually apply. Unfortunately, that's how almost everyone's been trained, so it's applied anyway and doesn't work. Who is to blame? Why the clients, of course, because they're "unmotivated" or "chronic"! Unfortunately, they are not often powerful enough to resist these blame attributions. Program directors and staff are relieved while clients acquire yet another unneeded failure experience to go with all their others.

Given the confusing, demoralizing, and often degrading state of many public mental health programs, it's not surprising that staff may forget their manners in interactions with the users. To do so is to contribute personally to an already unpleasant state of affairs. In talking to users, especially public mental health ones, it's vital to be respectful, truly attentive, and nonjudgmentally understanding — in short, to treat them with dignity. The golden rule must apply to these interactions, in order to establish a reciprocal relationship that may provide an opportunity for staff to be helpful in an ongoing way. Without such a relationship, especially one that's focused on addressing real client problems and needs, helping becomes coercive manipulation of objects. Proper relationships provide support, sustain effort, and facilitate change.

The helping process, even if begun under auspicious circumstances, has a number of potential pitfalls. Basically, overenthusiastic intrusion into all aspects of clients' lives will leave them expectant, dependent, and ultimately disillusioned when this month's savior proves to be no more reliable than last's. Hence, we strongly recommend that staff be encouraged to "be with" and "do with" clients, while expecting them to learn better how to help themselves. Staff may also suffer disappointment at their clients' perceived failures. Their burnouts will likely be attributed to their clients' lack of motivation or "chronicity." These problems can be minimized by having staff working in small teams and being sure clients are actively involved in, and exercise control over, the helping process. Staff must always remember that clients' lives are theirs to live, not the staff's. With this in mind, power and status issues must be acknowledged and discussed. Staff should do only as much as needed, and asked for, in the helping process. The process should pay constant attention to the principles of contextualization, normalization and preservation of power described in this volume.

Working in community mental health programs is often regarded as second-class citizenship because the pay is low, the clientele notoriously difficult, the setting's reputation tarnished, and the working conditions usually unpleasant. This is true because the resources needed to make community mental health into a first-class operation are being spent on inpatient care. Most workers know that in order to be more effective their programs need more resources. They are not likely to be the benefactors of some wonderful governmental largesse. So, what to do? Follow the Willie Sutton model: "Willie, why do you keep robbing banks?" "'Cuz, that's where the money is." Ergo, mental health money must be gotten out of hospitals, particularly large ones. Until this happens community programs will get only leftovers. This does not mean that clients should be forced out of institutions. Rather, large institutions (state hospitals) should not be allowed to admit anyone. In a few years they'll disappear by attrition. We know how to operate effective community programs that use only a few beds in places called hospitals.

Magical relief of pain and suffering is an almost universal human wish. As the source of fulfilling this wish, pills have replaced religion in many parts of our society. The pain and suffering experienced by community mental health clients are all too real and must be addressed. Are pills the best way to deal with their problems? In some situations yes, they may be, at least temporarily. In other situations they may do more harm than good, especially if used for a long time. We seem to have become accustomed to using pills too frequently, often without attending to their long-range costs — especially tardive dyskinesia. These need to be subtracted from the benefits accrued in the short run. Because psychotropic drugs are the sole purview of powerful, unquestioned physicians, nonphysicians tend to overlook or disregard what's going on with medications in clients they otherwise know very well. Good information about the use, abuse, and toxic potential of the various classes of psychotropic drugs must be made available and used by clients and staff. Lack of such information is irresponsible and dangerous.

In order to design a well functioning community system there needs to be a coherence and coordination of administrative and clinical principles, staff attitudes and values, and types of programs and facilities offered. Actually the distinction drawn between administrative and clinical issues, on the one hand, and staff values and attitudes, on the other, is arbitrary; they should be all of a piece. Perhaps the differences between them are better understood as different organizational levels within an overall open system. For example, without a defined catchment area within which the program controls the gates, it will not be possible to plan how much crisis intervention or how many residential alternative, day program, and housing spaces will be needed. Without this information it is not possible to know how many staff members with the correct attitudes, values, practices, and relevant training should be hired. Elements of a system are by definition interdependent; changing one part is inevitably reflected throughout it. We believe that it is possible to plan and implement effective community mental health programs only if all the elements are attended to; piecemeal planning is fruitless.

Services and facilities provided by programs should comprise a widely varied array; we use the word "smorgasbord" frequently to help visualize this notion. The array will have three major subdivisions: outpatient, residential, and day and evening programs.

The outpatient service, especially through its provision of in-residence crisis intervention and resolution, should be the linchpin in the system. Multiperson groupings (e.g., families, networks, problem-focused groups) should be the preferred modus operandi. A variety of brief, focused, psychosocial interventions should be readily available for particular problems. However, the thoughtful application of newly developed or researched approaches should also be encouraged. Case management functions should be provided by the *team* responsible for each client so that someone is available who knows, and has a relationship with the client, at all times.

Residential programs, especially the intensively staffed ones (e.g., hospital wards and alternatives), are the system's most expensive single element. Hence, their use should be carefully monitored and controlled. However, barring compelling reasons against doing so, every newly identified functional psychotic deserves one or more trials of drug-free psychosocial treatment, usually in a residential alternative to hospitalization. Drug-free treatment trials may require many days of residential care. We recommend use of this expensive resource for this purpose because of the long-term savings that will accrue to the system if disability can be prevented or minimized. Halfway houses should be available to facilitate transition to supported permanent housing. The housing staff is to be flexibly available to families, group homes, apartments, single room occupancy hotels, etc., on an as-needed basis.

Homelessness is mostly an economic problem. Its long-term solution *awaits* serious governmental attention and intervention. Meanwhile, the current bandaid solution — shelters — is creating another problem — shelter institutionalism. Interestingly, it appears that these nocturnal pseudo-voluntary almshouses are no less "total" in their deleterious effects on persons than large involuntary mental hospitals.

Day and evening programs are necessary in part because many public mental health clients can't, or won't work. Those who can't work should be repeatedly offered opportunities to try again. Unfortunately, until a workable incentive system is developed, it will be impossible to motivate those who won't work. Even though it might break the poverty-dependence cycle, giving up the security of a welfare dole for an entry-level job that consigns them to membership in the working poor is not a worthwhile trade-off for most mental health clients.

Good community mental health staff are raised, not trained. It's very hard to train adults to do no harm, follow the golden rule, and treat people with respect and dignity if they don't already embody these key values and attitudes. There are guidelines for selecting staff from among groups of candidates; however, it's not a very scientific process. If new staff do the job as it's described and convey the necessary values and attitudes, the program will reinforce and expand whatever they bring to it. Of course, staff who have special technical training in a variety of areas, e.g., research, psychopharmacology, family therapy, are needed. Their work should be organized so that they remain firmly embedded as team members while using their special expertise. If staff work is organized in nonhierarchical, supportive family-like teams that accomplish goals, risk of "burnout" is reduced. If it does occur it can be dealt with in a variety of ways, principally focused on the remoralizing effects of being successful.

The Italian mental health reform of 1978 addressed the issue of *preventing* institutionalization in a radical way. It decreed the phasing down of state mental hospitals by prohibiting admissions to them. However, it did not prescribe the rapid discharge of existing patients, thus avoiding the risks related to mass deinstitutionalization. Admissions, if necessary, have to take place in small units (no more than 15 beds) located in general hospitals. Catchmented, community-based mental health services have to provide all interventions for the psychiatric needs of a given population (50,000 to 200,000 population) *without the backup of the state hospital.*

A number of studies has shown the successful implementation of the reform in different settings. Negative reports have also been published, and pessimistic opinions on the applicability of such an innovative reform on a national basis have been expressed.

However, a nationwide survey (CENSIS, 1985) has shown that a fairly comprehensive network of services has been developed in all of Italy since the reform. Community mental health centers have opened in 675 of 698 catchment areas (versus 750 out of 2,000 in the U.S.). Inpatient units in general hospitals have been developed in all regions. Although the bed rate (5.4 per 100,000 population) is still lower than the one planned, and is unevenly distributed among regions, these units do not seem to be overburdened by their caseloads. As a consequence of stopping admissions, the number of inpatients of state mental hospitals decreased from 60,000 in 1977 to less than 30,000 in 1984. Most importantly, the lack of state hospital backup has precipitated neither an increase in short-term admissions to the general hospital units nor a shift to private hospitals.

Six model programs (three Italian and three American) have been presented. They encompass a wide variety of political, social, economic and demographic conditions. Their philosophies, principles, and practices comprise a widely varied array. Each is unique, yet certain commonalities, such as stable leadership, can be identified.

We have had a great deal to say about the central importance of *context* to effective community work—client context, staff working context, organizational context, administrative context, community context, political context, etc. In Italy a context developed at each level that allowed for a dramatic change in the way mental health services would be delivered. A seemingly radical notion was legislated into standard practice for an entire country. For a variety of reasons America's 1963 attempt at reforming its mental health system has had only limited success. Yet, a great deal of useful experience was acquired in the process. What we've presented is a selected amalgamation of the Italian and American experiences with community mental health. We believe that the open system psychosocial intervention model we propose can be implemented in most locales if it is properly adapted to fit local conditions and if attention is directed to contextual constraints. Even without a *system* of capitation payment based health care (as is true in the U.S.), what we propose will cost no more than is presently being spent on public mental health—*if* a policy of non-institutionalization is put in place.

It need not be a national policy to work; states, counties, and cities could develop quality community programs with savings derived from reduction in use of hospital-based care.

It had been our intention to provide practical, commonsense, flexible, good enough administrative and clinical guidelines to allow the development and implementation of effective psychosocially oriented community mental health systems in a wide variety of locales. Only their thoughtful application over time, in many contexts, will tell us whether or not we have been successful.

Appendices

APPENDIX A

Medications for Mental Illness and Other Mental Disorders

ANYONE CAN DEVELOP a mental disorder—you, a family member, a friend, or the fellow down the block. Some disorders are mild, while others are serious and long-lasting. These conditions can be helped. One way—an important way—is with psychotherapeutic drugs. Compared to other types of treatment, these medications are relative newcomers in the fight against mental illness. It was only about 30 years ago that the first one, chlorpromazine, was introduced. But considering the short time they've been around, psychotherapeutic drugs have made dramatic changes in the treatment of mental disorders. People who, years ago, might have spent their entire lives in mental hospitals because of crippling mental illness may now only go in for brief treatment, or might receive all their treatment at an outpatient clinic.

Psychotherapeutic drugs also may make other kinds of treatment more effective. Someone who is too depressed to talk, for instance, can't get much benefit from psychotherapy or counseling, but often, taking medication will improve symptoms so that the person can respond better.

SYMPTOM RELIEF, NOT CURE

Just as aspirin can reduce a fever without clearing up the infection that causes it, psychotherapeutic drugs act by controlling symptoms. Like most drugs used in medicine, they correct or compensate for some malfunction in

Information from DHHS Publication No. (ADM)87-1509 Alcohol, Drug Abuse, and Mental Health Administration. Printed 1987.

the body. Psychotherapeutic drugs do not *cure* mental illness, but they do lessen its burden. These medications can help a person get on with life despite some continuing mental pain and difficulty coping with problems. For example, drugs like chlorpromazine can turn off the "voices" heard by some people with schizophrenia and help them to perceive reality as others do. And antidepressant drugs can lift the dark, heavy moods of depression.

How long someone must take a psychotherapeutic drug depends on the disorder. Many depressed and anxious people may need medication for a single period—perhaps for several months—and then never have to take it again. For some conditions, such as schizophrenia or manic-depressive illness, medication may have to be taken indefinitely or, perhaps, intermittently.

Like any medication, psychotherapeutic drugs do not produce the same effect in everyone. Some people may respond better to one drug than another. Some may need larger doses than others do. Some experience annoying side effects, while others do not. Age, sex, body size, body chemistry, habits, and diet are some of the factors that can influence a drug's effect.

QUESTIONS FOR YOUR DOCTOR

To increase the likelihood that a medication will work well, patients and their families must actively participate with the doctor prescribing the drug. They must tell the doctor about the patient's past medical history, other drugs being taken, anticipated life changes—such as planning to have a baby—and, after some experience with a drug, whether it is causing side effects. When a drug is prescribed, the patient or family member should ask the following questions recommended by the U.S. Food and Drug Administration and other groups:

- What is the name of the drug, and what is it supposed to do?
- How and when do I take it, and when do I stop taking it?
- What foods, drinks, drugs, or activities should I avoid while taking the drug?
- What are the side effects, and what should I do if they occur?
- Is there any written information available about the drug?

In this booklet, medications are described by their generic (general) names and in italics by their trade names (brand names used by drug companies). They are divided into four large categories based on the symptoms for which they are primarily used—antipsychotic, antimanic, antidepressant, and antianxiety drugs. Some are used for more than one purpose; antidepressants, for example, have been found helpful for treating some anxiety disorders.

An index at the end of the booklet gives the trade name of the most common prescribed drugs and notes the section that contains information about each type of drug. Another index lists the generic name of the drug and tells which section to refer to for information.

ANTIPSYCHOTIC DRUGS

A person who is psychotic is out of touch with reality. He may "hear voices" or have strange and untrue ideas (for example, thinking he is the President of the United States, a religious leader, or a movie star).* He may get excited or angry for no apparent reason, or spend a lot of time off by himself, or in bed, sleeping during the day and staying awake at night. He may neglect his appearance, not bathing or changing his clothes, and may become difficult to communicate with — saying things that make no sense, or barely talking at all.

These kinds of behaviors are symptoms of psychotic illness, the principal form of which is schizophrenia. All of them may not be present when someone is psychotic, but some of them always are. Antipsychotic drugs, as their name suggests, act against these symptoms. These drugs cannot "cure" the illness, but they can take away many of the symptoms or make them milder. In some cases, they can shorten the course of the illness as well.

There are a number of antipsychotic drugs available. They all work; the main differences are in the potency — that is, the dose (amount) prescribed to produce therapeutic effects — and the side effects. Some people might think that the higher the dose of medication, the more serious the illness, but this is not always true.

A doctor will consider several factors when prescribing an antipsychotic drug, besides how "ill" someone is. These include the patient's age, body weight, and type of drug. John A., a 6-foot, 180-pound, 25-year-old, might be taking three times as much medication as Mary B., a 5-foot, 105-pound, 65-year-old, but they may both be equally ill. Past history is important, too. If a person took a particular medication before and it worked, the doctor is likely to prescribe the same drug again. Some less potent drugs, like chlorpromazine (*Thorazine*), are always prescribed in higher numbers of milligrams than others of high potency, like haloperidol (*Haldol*).

A person has to take a large amount of a "high-dose" antipsychotic drug (such as chlorpromazine) to get the same effect as a small amount of a "low-dose" drug (such as haloperidol). Why don't doctors just prescribe "low-dose" drugs? The main reason is the difference in side effects (actions of the drug other than the one intended for the illness). These drugs vary in their side effects, and some people have more trouble with certain side effects

*"He" is used here to refer to both men and women.

than others. A side effect may sometimes be desirable. For instance, the sedative effect of some antipsychotic drugs is useful for patients who have trouble sleeping or who become agitated during the day.

Unlike some prescription drugs, which must be taken several times during the day, antipsychotic medications can usually be taken just once a day. Thus, patients can reduce daytime side effects by taking the medications once, before bed. Another feature of some of these drugs is their availability in forms that can be injected once or twice a month, thus assuring that the patient complies with the doctor's orders.

Most side effects of antipsychotic drugs are mild. Many common ones disappear after the first few weeks of treatment. These include drowsiness, rapid heartbeat, and dizziness or faintness when changing position.

Some people gain weight while taking antipsychotic drugs and may have to change their diet to control their weight. Other side effects which may be caused by some antipsychotic drugs include decrease in sexual ability or interest, problems with menstrual periods, sunburn, or skin rashes. If a side effect is especially troublesome, it should be discussed with the doctor, who may prescribe a different drug, change dosage level or pattern, or prescribe an additional medication to control the side effects.

Movement difficulties may occur with some antipsychotic drugs. These include muscle spasms (of the neck, eye, back, or other muscles), agitation, restlessness, pacing, difficulty concentrating, or a general slowing-down of movement and speech and a shuffling walk. Some of these side effects look a lot like symptoms of psychotic illness, but aren't. If they appear or continue when someone is taking an antipsychotic drug, notify the doctor, who can prescribe a specific medication to control the side effects.

Just as people vary in their responses to antipsychotic drugs, they also vary in their speed of improvement. Some symptoms diminish in days, while others take weeks or months. In many cases, improvement is seen over a period of several weeks. For many patients, substantial improvement is seen by the sixth week of treatment (although this is not true in every case). If someone does not seem to be improving, a different type of medication may be tried. Drug treatment for a psychotic illness can continue for up to several months, sometimes even longer. When the patient is totally or largely symptom-free for a period of time, the dose of the drug may gradually be lowered. If the symptoms do not return, the drug may be tapered off and discontinued.

Even if a person is feeling well, or at least better, he should not just stop taking the medication. Suddenly stopping an antipsychotic drug may cause a withdrawal reaction which could include nightmares, sleep disturbances, stomach cramps, and diarrhea. Tapering off medication while continuing to see the doctor is important.

Some people may need to take medication for an extended period of time, or even indefinitely, to remain symptom-free. These people usually have chronic (long-term, continuous) schizophrenic disorders, or have a history of many schizophrenic episodes, where the likelihood of becoming ill again is high. In these cases, medication may be continued in as low a dose as possible to still control symptoms. This type of treatment, called maintenance treatment, prevents relapse in many people and removes or reduces symptoms for others.

While maintenance treatment is helpful for many people, a drawback for some is the possibility of long-term side effects, particularly a condition called tardive dyskinesia. This condition is characterized by involuntary movements of the lips, tongue, and jaw — and, sometimes, of the hands and feet. The disorder may range from mild to severe. For some people, it cannot be reversed, while others recover partially or completely. Tardive dyskinesia is seen most often after long-term treatment with antipsychotic drugs and is more common in elderly women. There is no way to determine whether someone will develop the disorder, and if it develops, whether the patient will recover. At present, there is no effective treatment. The possible risks of long-term treatment with antipsychotic drugs must be weighed against the benefits in each individual case by patient, family, and doctor.

Clinical researchers are investigating two new types of long-term treatment designed to provide the advantages of medication while reducing the risks of tardive dyskinesia and other possible side effects. A "low-dosage" approach uses far lower maintenance doses of antipsychotic drugs than have generally been employed, while an "intermittent dose" treatment involves stopping the drug when the patient is symptom-free and beginning it again only when symptoms reappear. Both approaches are promising and will continue to be explored.

Antipsychotic drugs can have unwanted effects when taken with other medications. Therefore, the doctor should be told about all drugs being taken, including over-the-counter preparations, and the extent of the use of alcohol. Some antipsychotic drugs interfere with the action of antihypertensive drugs (taken for high blood pressure), anticonvulsants (taken for epilepsy), and drugs used for Parkinson's disease. Some antipsychotic drugs add to the effects of alcohol and other central nervous system depressants, such as antihistamines, antidepressants, barbiturates, some sleeping and pain medications, and narcotics.

ANTIMANIC DRUGS

Manic-depressive illness (bipolar disorder) is characterized by mood swings: severe highs (mania) and lows (depression). Patients may have several episodes of mania and only one of depression — or just the opposite.

Sometimes, these mood swings follow each other very closely (within hours or days), but they may also be separated by months or years.

When someone is in a manic "high," he is overactive, overtalkative, and has a great deal of energy. He will switch quickly from one topic to another, as if he cannot get his thoughts out fast enough; his attention span is often short, and he can easily be distracted. Sometimes, the "high" person is irritable or angry and has false or inflated ideas about his position or importance in the world. He may be very elated, full of grand schemes which might range from business deals to romantic involvements. He may engage in wild spending sprees. Often, he shows poor judgment in these ventures.

Depression will show in a "low" mood, lack of energy, changes in eating and sleeping patterns, feelings of hopelessness, helplessness, and guilt, and sometimes thoughts of suicide.

These "highs" and "lows" may vary in intensity and severity. The drug used most often to combat a manic "high" is lithium. It is unusual to find mania without a subsequent or preceding period of depression. Lithium evens out mood swings in both directions, so that it is used not just for acute manic attacks, or flare-ups of the illness, but also as an ongoing treatment for bipolar disorder.

Lithium will diminish severe manic symptoms in about 5 to 14 days, but it may be anywhere from days to several months until the condition is fully controlled. Antipsychotic drugs are sometimes used in the first several days of treatment to control manic symptoms until the lithium begins to take effect.

Someone may have one episode of bipolar disorder and never have another, or be free of illness for several years. However, for those who have more than one episode, continuing (maintenance) treatment on lithium is usually given serious consideration.

Some people respond well to maintenance treatment and have no further episodes. Others have moderate mood swings that lessen as treatment continues and may disappear entirely. Some people may continue to have episodes that are diminished in frequency and severity. Some manic-depressive patients may not be helped at all. Who will respond in what way cannot be determined beforehand. Providing there are no physical conditions which present problems, and there are no serious adverse reactions, lithium can continue to be taken indefinitely.

Regular blood tests are an important part of treatment with lithium. These tests measure the amount of the drug in the body. If too little is taken, the drug will not be effective. If too much is taken, it may be toxic (poisonous). The range between an effective dose and a toxic one is small. Blood tests are given often at the beginning of treatment, to determine the best lithium level for the patient, and less often as treatment goes on. How much lithium needs to be taken may vary over time, depending on how ill a person is, his body chemistry, and his physical condition.

Anything that lowers the level of sodium (table salt is sodium chloride) in the body may cause a lithium buildup and lead to toxicity. Reduced salt intake, heavy sweating, fever, vomiting, or diarrhea may do this. An unusual amount of exercise or a switch to a low-salt diet are examples. It's important to be aware of conditions that lower sodium and to share this information with the doctor. The lithium dose may have to be adjusted.

Signs of lithium toxicity may include nausea, vomiting, drowsiness, and mental dullness, slurred speech, confusion, dizziness, muscle twitching, abnormal muscle movement, and blurred vision. A serious lithium overdose can be life-threatening.

When a person first takes lithium, he may experience side effects, such as drowsiness, weakness, nausea, vomiting, tiredness, hand tremor, or increased thirst and urination. These usually disappear or subside quickly, but hand tremor may persist. Weight gain may also occur. Diet will help, but crash diets should be avoided because they may affect the lithium level. Drinking low-calorie or no-calorie beverages will help keep weight down. Kidney changes, accompanied by increased thirst and urination may develop during treatment. These conditions and the thyroid problems that may occur are generally reversible and treatable.

Because of possible complications, lithium may either not be recommended or may be given with caution when a person has existing thyroid, kidney, or heart disorders, epilepsy, or brain damage. Women of childbearing age should be aware that lithium can cause deformities in babies born to women taking lithium. Special caution should be taken during the first 3 months of pregnancy.

Lithium, when combined with certain other drugs, can have unwanted effects. Some diuretics (drugs that remove water from the body) increase the level of lithium and can cause toxicity. Other diuretics, like coffee and tea, can lower the level of lithium. Problems may occur when lithium is combined with hydroxyzine (*Atarax, Vistaril*), antipsychotic drugs, or methyldopa (*Aldomet* and others). *Someone who is taking lithium should tell all the doctors he sees about all other medications he is taking.*

With regular monitoring, lithium is a safe and effective drug that enables many people, who otherwise would suffer from incapacitating mood swings, to lead normal lives.

Not all patients with symptoms of mania benefit from lithium. Some have been found to respond to another type of medication, the anticonvulsant drugs (which are usually used to treat epilepsy). Carbamazepine is the anticonvulsant that has been most widely used. Manic-depressive patients who cycle rapidly—that is, they change from mania to depression and back again over the course of hours or days, rather than months—seem to respond particularly well to carbamazepine.

Early side effects, although generally mild, include drowsiness, dizziness, ataxia, confusion, disturbed vision, perceptual distortions, memory impairment, and nausea. They are usually transient and often respond to temporary dosage reduction. More serious are the skin rashes that can occur in 15 to 20 percent of patients. These rashes are sometimes severe enough to require discontinuation of the drug. However, neither carbamazepine nor any other anticonvulsants have been approved by the Food and Drug Administration for manic-depressive illness. These drugs must undergo further study and testing before they merit FDA approval and general use.

ANTIDEPRESSANT DRUGS

The kind of depression that can benefit from drug treatment is more than just "the blues" or the "downs" of everyday life. It's a condition that's prolonged, lasting 2 weeks or more, and it interferes in a marked way with a person's ability to carry on daily tasks and to enjoy activities that previously brought pleasure.

The depressed person will seem sad or "down." He may have trouble eating and lose weight (although some people eat more and gain weight when depressed). He may sleep too much or too little, have difficulty going to sleep, sleep restlessly, or awaken very early in the morning. He may speak of feeling guilty, worthless, or hopeless. He may complain that his thinking is slowed down. He may lack energy, feeling "everything's too much," or he might be agitated and jumpy. A person who is depressed may cry. He may think and talk about killing himself and may even make a suicide attempt. Some people who are depressed have psychotic symptoms, such as delusions (false ideas) that are related to their depression. For instance, a psychotically depressed person might imagine that he is already dead, or "in hell," being punished.

Not everyone who is depressed has all these symptoms, but everyone who is depressed has at least some of them. A depression can vary in intensity from severe to moderate to mild.

Antidepressant drugs are used most widely for serious depressions, but they can also be helpful for some milder depressions. These drugs take away or reduce the symptoms of depression, and help the depressed person return to normal life and functioning. They are not "uppers" or stimulants—they can't make someone feel any better than he usually does, but they can help a person to feel as good as he did before he became depressed.

Antidepressant drugs are also used for disorders characterized principally by anxiety. They can block the symptoms of panic, including rapid heart-beat, terror, dizziness, chest pains, nausea, and breathing problems. They can also be used to treat some phobias.

When someone is taking antidepressant drugs, improvement will not generally begin to show immediately. With most of these drugs, it will take from 1 to 3 weeks before changes begin to occur. Some symptoms diminish early in treatment; others, later. For instance, a person's energy level or sleeping or eating patterns may improve before his depressed mood lifts. If there is little or no change in symptoms after 3 to 6 weeks, a different drug may be tried. Some people will respond better to one drug than another. Since there is no way of determining which drug will be effective before-hand, the doctor may have to prescribe first one drug, then another, until an effective one is found. Treatment is continued for a minimum of several months and may last up to a year or more.

While some people have one episode of depression and then never have another or remain symptom-free for years, others have more frequent epi-sodes or very long-lasting depressions that may go on for years. Some people find that their depressions become more frequent and severe as they get older. For these people, continuing (maintenance) treatment with antide-pressant drugs can be an effective way of reducing the frequency and severi-ty of depressions. Those that are commonly used have no known long-term side effects and may be continued indefinitely. The dose of the drug may be lowered if side effects become troublesome.

Lithium can also be used in maintenance treatment of repeated depres-sions where there is evidence of a manic or maniclike episode in the past.

There are a number of antidepressant drugs available. They differ in their side effects and, to some extent, in their level of effectiveness. Tricyclic antidepressants (named for their chemical structure) are considered more effective for treatment of depression than monoamine oxidase inhibitors (MAOIs), but MAOIs are often helpful in so-called "atypical" depressions, where there are symptoms like overeating, oversleeping, anxiety, panic at-tacks, and phobias. Newer antidepressants (including tetracyclics, unicy-clics, and others) still must pass the test of time and further scientific studies.

Dosage of antidepressant drugs is variable, depending on the type of drug, the person's body chemistry, age, and, sometimes, body weight.

Doses are generally started low — and raised gradually over time until the desired effect is reached without the appearance of troublesome side effects.

There are a number of possible side effects with tricyclic antidepressants that vary, depending on the drug. For example, amitriptyline (*Amitril, Elavil, Amitid,* and *Endep*) tends to make people very drowsy and sleepy, while protriptyline (*Vivactil*) hardly does this at all. Because of this kind of variation in side effects, one antidepressant might be highly desirable for one person and not recommended for another. Most tricyclics complicate some specific heart problems. Other side effects with tricyclics may include blurred vision, dry mouth, constipation, dizziness when changing position, increased sweating, difficulty urinating, changes in sexual desire, decrease in sexual ability, weight gain, muscle twitches, fatigue, and weakness. Not all these drugs produce all side effects, and not everybody gets them. Some will disappear quickly, while others may remain for the length of treatment. Some side effects are similar to symptoms of depression (for instance, fatigue and constipation). For this reason, the patient or family should discuss all symptoms with the doctor, who may change the medication or dosage.

MAOIs may cause some side effects similar to tricyclics. Dizziness when changing position and rapid heartbeat are common. MAOIs also react with certain foods, alcoholic beverages, and other drugs (such as aged cheeses, Chianti and other red wines, and over-the-counter cold preparations) to cause severe high blood pressure, headaches, seizures, and stroke. For this reason, people taking MAOIs *must* stay away from restricted foods, drinks, and medications.

An overdose of antidepressants is serious and potentially lethal. It requires immediate medical attention. These drugs should be taken only in the amount prescribed and should be kept in a secure place away from children.

Symptoms of a tricyclic overdose develop within an hour and may start with rapid heartbeat, dilated pupils, flushed face, and agitation, and progress to confusion, loss of consciousness, seizures, heart irregularities, cardiorespiratory collapse, and death. Reactions caused by mixing MAOIs with aged cheeses and other restricted foods often do not appear for several hours. Signs may include raised blood pressure, headache, nausea, vomiting, rapid heartbeat, possible confusion, psychotic symptoms, and coma.

When taking antidepressant drugs, it is important to tell all doctors being seen (not just the one who is treating the depression) about all medications being used, including over-the-counter preparations, and alcohol, if it is used regularly. Antidepressants interact with a large number of drugs and other substances; these interactions may change the effect of the antidepressant or cause unwanted reactions. Tricyclics may interact with thyroid hormone, antihypertensive drugs, oral contraceptives, some blood coagulants, some sleeping medications, antipsychotic drugs, diuretics, antihistamines, aspirin, bicarbonate of soda, vitamin C, alcohol, and tobacco.

MAOIs also have negative interactions with a large number of drugs and other substances. The more common include local anesthetics, over-the-counter cold and allergy preparations, amphetamines, antihistamines, insulin, narcotics, antiparkinsonian drugs, alcohol, and monosodium glutamate (MSG).

When used with proper care, following doctors' instructions, antidepressants are extremely useful drugs that can reverse the misery of a depression and help a person feel like himself again.

ANTIANXIETY DRUGS

Everyone experiences anxiety at one time or another—"butterflies in the stomach" before giving a speech or sweaty palms during a job interview are common symptoms. Other symptoms of anxiety include irritability, uneasiness, jumpiness, feelings of apprehension, rapid or irregular heartbeat, stomach ache, nausea, faintness, and breathing problems.

Anxiety is often manageable and mild. But sometimes it can present serious problems. A high level or prolonged state of anxiety can be very incapacitating, making the activities of daily life difficult or impossible.

Phobias, which are persistent, irrational fears and are characterized by avoidance of certain objects, places, and things, sometimes accompany anxiety. A panic attack is a severe form of anxiety that occurs suddenly and is marked by intense fear, breathlessness, pounding heart, and feelings that one may die.

Antianxiety drugs calm and relax the anxious person and remove the troubling symptoms. There are a number of antianxiety drugs currently available. The preferred drugs for most anxiety disorders are the benzodiazepines. Antidepressant drugs are also very effective for panic attacks and some phobias and are often prescribed for these conditions. Recently, antidepressants have also been used for more generalized forms of anxiety, especially when accompanied by depression.

The most commonly used benzodiazepines are chlordiazepoxide (*Librium, Librax, Libritabs*, and others) and diazepam (*Valium*). Benzodiazepines are relatively fast-acting drugs. Most will begin to take effect within hours, some in even less time. These effects are long lasting, so that often the benzodiazepines can be taken only two or three times a day. Dosage of the drug is generally started at a low level and gradually raised until symptoms are diminished or removed. The dosage will vary a great deal depending on the symptoms and the individual's body chemistry. Benzodiazepines have few side effects. Drowsiness and loss of coordination are most common. Fatigue and mental slowing or confusion can also occur. These effects make it dangerous to drive or operate some machinery when taking benzodiazepines—especially when the patient is just beginning treatment. Other side effects are rare.

Benzodiazepines combined with other drugs can present a problem, notably when taken together with commonly used substances such as alcohol. Following the doctor's instructions is important. The doctor should be informed of all other drugs the patient is taking, including over-the-counter medications (those available without a prescription). Benzodiazepines increase central nervous system depression when combined with alcohol, anesthetics, antihistamines, sedatives, muscle relaxants, and some prescription pain medications. Particular benzodiazepines may influence the action of some anticonvulsant and cardiac drugs. Benzodiazepines have also been associated with abnormalities in babies born to mothers who were taking these drugs.

With benzodiazepines, there is a potential for the development of tolerance and dependence as well as the possibility of abuse and withdrawal reactions. For this reason, the drugs are generally prescribed for brief periods of time (days or weeks), and sometimes intermittently, for stressful situations or anxiety attacks. For the same reason, ongoing or continuous treatment with benzodiazepines is not recommended for most people. A very small number of patients may, however, need long-term treatment.

Consult with the doctor before discontinuing a benzodiazepine. A withdrawal reaction may occur if the drug is abruptly stopped. Thus, after benzodiazepines are taken for an extended period, the dosage is gradually tapered off before being completely stopped. Symptoms may include anxiety, shakiness, headache, dizziness, sleeplessness, loss of appetite, and, in more severe cases, fever, seizures, and psychosis. A withdrawal reaction may be mistaken for a return of the anxiety, since many of the symptoms are similar.

Except for alprazolam (*Xanax*), an overdose of benzodiazepines is almost never life-threatening, but taken together with alcohol or other drugs, it may lead to serious and possibly life-threatening complications.

Although benzodiazepines or tricyclic antidepressants are the preferred drugs for most anxiety disorders, occasionally, for specific reasons, one of the following drugs may be prescribed: antipsychotic drugs; antihistamines (such as *Atarax, Vistaril,* and others); barbiturates such as phenobarbital; propanediols such as meprobamate (*Equanil*); and propanolol (*Inderal, Inderide*).

INDEX OF DRUGS

To find the section of the text that describes the drug you or a friend or family member is taking, find either the generic (chemical) name and look it up on the first list, or the trade name and look it up on the second list. If you do not find the name of the drug on the label, ask your doctor or pharmacist for it. (Note: some drugs, such as amitriptyline and chlordiazepoxide, are marketed under numerous trade names, not all of which can be mentioned in a brief list such as this. If your drug's trade name does not appear in this list, look it up by its generic name or ask your doctor or pharmacist for more information.)

Alphabetical Listing of Medications by Generic Name

GENERIC NAME	TRADE NAME	TYPE OF DRUG
acetophenazine	Tindal	antipsychotic
alprazolam	Xanax	antianxiety
amitriptyline	Amitid	antidepressant
	Amitril	
	Elavil	
	Endep	
amoxapine	Asendin	antidepressant
butaperazine	Repoise	antipsychotic
carbamazepine	Tegretol	antimanic
carphenazine	Proketazine	antipsychotic
chlordiazepoxide	Librax	antianxiety
	Libritabs	
	Librium	
chlorpromazine	Thorazine	antipsychotic
chlorprothixene	Taractan	antipsychotic
clorazepate	Azene	antianxiety
	Tranxene	
desipramine	Norpramin	antidepressant
	Pertofrane	
dextroamphetamine	Dexedrine	stimulant
diazepam	Valium	antianxiety
doxepin	Adapin	antianxiety
	Sinequan	
fluphenazine	Permitil	antipsychotic
	Prolixin	
haloperidol	Haldol	antipsychotic
halazepam	Paxipam	antianxiety
imipramine	Imavate	antidepressant
	Janimine	
	Presamine	
	Tofranil	
isocarboxazid	Marplan	antidepressant
lithium carbonate	Eskalith	antimanic
	Lithane	
	Lithobid	
lithium citrate	Cibalith-S	antimanic
lorazepam	Ativan	antianxiety
loxapine	Daxolin	antipsychotic
	Loxitane	
maprotiline	Ludiomil	antidepressant
mesoridazine	Serentil	antipsychotic
methylphenidate	Ritalin	stimulant
molindone	Lidone	antipsychotic
	Moban	
nortriptyline	Aventyl	antipsychotic
	Pamelor	
oxazepam	Serax	antianxiety
perphenazine	Trilafon	antipsychotic
phenelzine	Nardil	antidepressant
piperacetazine	Quide	antipsychotic
prazepam	Centrax	antianxiety
	Vestran	
prochlorperazine	Compazine	antipsychotic

protriptyline	Vivactil	antidepressant
thioridazine	Mellaril	antipsychotic
thiothixene	Navane	antipsychotic
tranylcypromine	Parnate	antidepressant
trazodone	Desyrel	antidepressant
trifluoperazine	Stelazine	antipsychotic
triflupromazine	Vesprin	antipsychotic

Alphabetical Listing of Medications by Trade Name

TRADE NAME	GENERIC NAME	TYPE OF DRUG
Adapin	doxepin	antidepressant
Amitid	amitriptyline	antidepressant
Amitril	amitriptyline	antidepressant
Asendin	amoxapine	antidepressant
Ativan	lorazepam	antianxiety
Aventyl	nortriptyline	antidepressant
Azene	clorazepate	antianxiety
Centrax	prazepam	antianxiety
Cibalith-S	lithium citrate	antimanic
Compazine	prochlorperazine	antipsychotic
Daxolin	loxapine	antipsychotic
Desyrel	trazodone	antidepressant
Dexedrine	dextroamphetamine	stimulant
Elavil	amitriptyline	antidepressant
Endep	amitriptyline	antidepressant
Eskalith	lithium carbonate	antimanic
Haldol	haloperidol	antipsychotic
Imavate	imipramine	antidepressant
Janimine	imipramine	antidepressant
Librax	chlordiazepoxide	antianxiety
Libritabs	chlordiazepoxide	antianxiety
Librium	chlordiazepoxide	antianxiety
Lidone	molindone	antipsychotic
Lithane	lithium carbonate	antimanic
Lithobid	lithium carbonate	antimanic
Loxitane	loxapine	antipsychotic
Ludiomil	maprotiline	antidepressant
Marplan	isocarboxazid	antidepressant
Mellaril	thioridazine	antipsychotic
Moban	molindone	antipsychotic
Nardil	phenelzine	antidepressant
Navane	thiothixene	antipsychotic
Norpramin	desipramine	antidepressant
Pamelor	nortriptyline	antidepressant
Parnate	tranylcypromine	antidepressant
Paxipam	halazepam	antianxiety
Permitil	fluphenazine	antipsychotic
Pertofrane	desipramine	antidepressant
Presamine	imipramine	antidepressant
Proketazine	carphenazine	antipsychotic
Prolixin	fluphenazine	antipsychotic
Quide	piperacetazine	antipsychotic
Repoise	butaperazine	antipsychotic

Ritalin	methylphenidate	stimulant
Serax	oxazepam	antianxiety
Serentil	mesoridazine	antipsychotic
Sinequan	doxepin	antidepressant
Stelazine	trifluoperazine	antipsychotic
Taractan	chlorprothixene	antipsychotic
Tegretol	carbamazepine	antimanic
Thorazine	chlorpromazine	antipsychotic
Tindal	acetophenazine	antipsychotic
Tofranil	imipramine	antidepressant
Tranxene	clorazepate	antianxiety
Trilafon	perphenazine	antipsychotic
Valium	diazepam	antianxiety
Vesprin	trifluopromazine	antipsychotic
Vestran	prazepam	antianxiety
Vivactil	protriptyline	antidepressant
Xanax	alprazolam	antianxiety

APPENDIX B

Summary of Boulder's Consumer Grant Proposal to the Robert Wood Johnson Foundation, January 1988

PROPOSAL ABSTRACT

MENTALLY ILL CONSUMERS in Boulder County were asked to identify needs not being met by the Mental Health Center's continuum of community support services that the consumers themselves might help to meet. Repeatedly, the clients talked about their feelings of isolation, uselessness, boredom and the concommitant high incidence of substance abuse among mentally ill adults in Boulder County.

Although the Mental Health Center of Boulder County, Inc. has an extensive continuum of services for chronically mentally ill adults, there continues to be a great need for low cost alternatives and supplements to professional intervention and treatment. Mentally ill adults who function well when they are not experiencing acute episodes of illness, represent a tremendous untapped resource. This proposal is designed to develop the unused skills of mentally ill adults, to empower them to help themselves and others, to give them opportunities for paid and volunteer employment, and to promote the consumer movement in our region and beyond.

This request is for $306,384 from the Robert Wood Johnson Foundation to be used over a three year period to establish two consumer-governed Resource, Information and Support Centers for over 300 chronically mentally ill adults in Boulder County. These Centers will be located in large houses in the cities of Boulder and Longmont and will be staffed by professional managers and mentally ill adults who have received specialized training in case management and group leadership.

The Centers will include a computerized information desk; a peer counseling and telephone hot-line program; drop-in capacity; structured activities; simple shared meals; case aide support and advocacy for securing resources; specialized on-site services such as health screening, dental aid, and legal aid; and other programs designed by the consumers.

Membership will be open to any resident of Boulder County but is primarily intended for those who have a history of major mental illness. A professional manager and a professional assistant will be hired for each Center by that Center's Consumer Governing Council. This model is unique in that it leaves the power with the mentally ill consumers, while giving them the help of professional staff so that they are not overwhelmed or victimized. Ongoing funding will be provided by Medicaid for specific therapeutic services, by member contributions for food and supplies, and by community donations.

APPENDIX C

Law No. 36:
Provisions on Public
and Private Mental Hospitals

ARTICLE 1: "People affected by mental illness *have to* be guarded and treated in mental hospitals when they are dangerous to themselves or others or of public scandal and are not, and cannot, be guarded and treated elsewhere."

Based on this provision, a court could permit treatment in a private house, and in that case the patient and the doctor would have to assume all the obligations imposed by the regulation.

Article 2: Admission "is requested by the relatives or the guardian and may be requested by anybody else in the interest of patients and society."

"It is temporarily authorized by the police magistrate, on the basis of a medical certificate, . . . and finally by the court . . . on the basis of a report of the superintendent of the hospital, after a period of evaluation that cannot exceed one month. All mental hospitals have to have a distinct and separate room to house patients admitted on a temporary basis."

"In case of emergency the local police authority may order a temporary admission, on the basis of a medical certificate, but a report has to be made to the district attorney within three days, passing the document mentioned . . . "

Modalities for discharge are regulated by article 3: "Discharge from the mental hospital of recovered patients is ordered by the court after the petition either of the superintendent of the hospital, or of the persons mentioned in the first paragraph of the preceding article [i.e. relatives, guardian, any interested party] or the Provincial Deputation . . . "

" . . . The superintendent of the hospital may order a trial discharge when the patient achieves a substantial improvement and will immediately notify the district attorney and the police authority."

Article 4 reads: "The superintendent has full authority in medical matters and a role of supervisor in administrative affairs as to the care of patients and is responsible of the state of the hospital and of the implementation of this law within the limits of his attributions. He also has disciplinary power within the limits of the following article."

"The superintendent will participate, with a consultative vote, in the sessions of the Provincial Deputation or of administrative Committees and Councils, when technical medical matters are discussed."

Article 5 reads: "Special regulations of each mental hospital have to include mixed medical and administrative dispositions, as those regarding the appointment of technical medical personnel, the number of nurses in proportion to the number of the patients, working and free hours, disciplinary provisions to be attributed to the competence either of the superintendent or of the administration, and other related provisions . . . "

Article 6 deals with the attribution of expenses; however, except for transportation expenses and some special cases, such as foreign citizens and convicted patients, remits the matter to the common norms.

Articles 7 through 11 pertain to minor issues, like inspections, controversies and the like.

Motion by the Assembly of the Members of the Italian Psychiatric Association, Approved March 1975

THE 32ND NATIONAL CONGRESS of the Italian Psychiatric Association (S.I.P.), held in Bologna March 19–23, 1975, after extensive debate on the present operational state of psychiatry in the country, on legislative initiatives presented or under discussion in front of the Parliament, on cultural and ideological differences that emerged over years of dialectic probing and discussing, also in the light of recent dramatic events in locales that only nominally may be defined as psychiatric, *approves* the content of the recommendation of the executive board of June 18, 1972, outlining the program for a psychiatric care modality open to the inalienable needs of a changing social reality.

It considers necessary to reaffirm some basic statements, in order to sensitize public opinion, social and political forces, and all authorities concerned:

1. rejection of separate laws for psychiatric care that would continue discrimination against the mental patient and the mental health worker and would perpetuate the asylum;
2. incorporation of psychiatry within the laws governing general health care;
3. abolishing of the 1904 law;
4. abolishing of forensic mental hospitals;
5. abolishing of the state mental hospital and relocation of the hospital-based therapeutic function to the general hospital;

6. integration and decentralization of psychiatric intervention in the community, intended as the field of action and management of all social and health services, where the mental health team will provide prevention, treatment and rehabilitation, under the control and management of the local administration, according to the principle of therapeutic continuity, thus avoiding the dichotomy between the intramural (hospital) and extramural (community) intervention. This community-based operational model should be implemented whenever the general hospital changes from being an autonomous body to being part of the Local Unit of Social and Health Services;

7. a commitment to a different education and training process for medical and paramedical personnel, that today is detached from reality and still characterized by a plethora of irrelevant notions, insensitive to the global needs of the patient, who should be regarded as a citizen and a laborer, part of a cultural, social and political reality.

APPENDIX E

Law No. 180: Voluntary and Compulsory Health Treatments, May, 1978

The House of Deputies and the Senate
of the republic passed:
THE PRESIDENT OF THE REPUBLIC
promulgates
the following law:

ARTICLE 1: VOLUNTARY AND COMPULSORY HEALTH SURVEY AND TREATMENT

HEALTH ASSESSMENT (diagnosis) and treatment are voluntary.

In the cases mentioned in this law and in those cases explicitly foreseen by State laws, the Health Authority can order compulsory health survey and treatment with respect for the person's dignity and the civil and political rights guaranteed by the Constitution, including, in as much as possible, the right to freely choose the physician and the health care center.

Compulsory health survey and treatment at the expense of the State, public bodies or institutions, are carried out by public territorial health care centers and, when hospitalization is needed, in public or state-subsidized hospital facilities.

From: Schefer-Hughes & Lovell, 1987, pp. 292–298.

During the compulsory health treatment, those who are under treatment have the right to communicate with any person they think right.

Compulsory health survey and treatment mentioned in the previous paragraphs, must be associated with initiatives that will assure the consent and participation of the patient.

Compulsory health survey and treatment are ordered by a Mayor proceeding, in his capacity of local Health Authority, on a justified proposal made by a physician.

ARTICLE 2: COMPULSORY HEALTH SURVEY AND TREATMENT FOR MENTAL DISORDER

The measures mentioned in paragraph 2 of Article 1, can be taken against those persons suffering from mental disorder.

In the cases mentioned in the previous paragraph, the proposal for compulsory health treatment can envisage hospitalization care only if mental disturbances are such as to require urgent therapeutic intervention, if these interventions are not accepted by the patient, and if there are not the conditions and the circumstances for taking immediate and timely health care measures outside the hospital.

The measure implementing compulsory health treatment in hospitalization conditions must be preceded by the ratification of the proposal mentioned in the last paragraph of Article 1, made by a public health service physician, and must be justified in accordance with the previous paragraph.

ARTICLE 3: PROCEDURE RELATIVE TO COMPULSORY HEALTH SURVEY AND TREATMENT IN HOSPITALIZATION CONDITIONS FOR MENTAL DISORDER

The measure, mentioned in Article 2, by which the Mayor imposes compulsory health treatment in hospitalization conditions, supplemented with the justified proposal of a physician — as mentioned in the last paragraph of Article 1 — and with the conformation — as mentioned in the last paragraph of Article 2 — must be notified by a communal Messenger within 48 hours from the admission into the health center, to the tutelary judge of the same district of the communal administration.

The tutelary judge within the following 48 hours, after having made inquiries and ordered the necessary controls, issues a justified decree for the confirmation or nonconfirmation of the measure, and communicates it to the Mayor. In case of nonconfirmation, the Mayor orders the cessation of the compulsory health treatment in hospitalization conditions.

If the measure mentioned in the first paragraph of this article, is taken by the Mayor of a communal administration different from the patient's place of residence, the Mayor of the patient's domicile must be informed. If the measure mentioned in the first paragraph of this article is taken against aliens or stateless persons, the Prefect must inform the Home Office and the competent Consulates.

Should compulsory health treatment exceed 7 days or should it be further prolonged, the physician responsible for the mental health service, as mentioned in Article 6, must in due time send a justified proposal indicating the further assumable duration of the treatment itself to the Mayor who has ordered the hospitalization of the patient; and the Mayor must inform the tutelary judge, with the formalities and for the accomplishments mentioned in paragraph 1 and 2 of this Article.

The physician mentioned in the previous paragraph is obliged to inform the Mayor (either the patient is discharged or remains in the hospital) of the cessation of the conditions which require compulsory health treatment; moreover he is obliged to communicate the eventual impossibility to carry on the treatment itself. The Mayor within 48 hours from the receipt of the communication of the physician, must inform the tutelary judge.

If necessary, the tutelary judge takes the required urgent measures to preserve and administer the patient's properties.

Omission of the communications mentioned in paragraph 1, 4 and 5 of this article causes the cessation of all effects of the measure, and is considered and "omission of office deeds crime," unless there is sufficient evidence for a more serious crime.

ARTICLE 4: PUBLICATION AND MODIFICATION OF COMPULSORY HEALTH TREATMENT MEASURE

Anyone can make a request to the Mayor for the revocation or modification of the measure enforcing or prolonging compulsory health treatment.

The Mayor decides within 10 days on the request of revocation or modification. Revocation or modification measures are put into force with the same procedure as for modified or revoked measures.

ARTICLE 5: JURISDICTIONAL PROTECTION

Anyone who undergoes the compulsory health treatment and anyone who has interest in it, can appeal against the measure ratified by the tutelary judge, to the Court of his jurisdiction.

Within 30 days, beginning from the expiry of the period of time as mentioned in the second paragraph of Article 3, the Mayor can appeal against the nonratification of the measure enforcing the compulsory health treatment.

In the trial held in a court of law, the parties can stand without defence counsels and can be represented by a person in possession of a mandate written at the foot of the appeal or in a separate document. The appeal can be sent to the Court by means of registered letter with a receipt notice.

The president of the Court fixes the hearing of the parties with a decree written at the foot of the appeal which is notified to the parties and to the Public Prosecutor by the Registrar.

The president of the Court, after having received the measure enforcing the compulsory health treatment and after having heard the Public Prosecutor can suspend the treatment itself even before the hearing.

The president of the Court decides on the request of suspension within 10 days.

The Court after having heard the Public Prosecutor decides in the counsel room on the basis of information and evidence requested by the Court or by the parties.

The appeals and the following proceedings are stamp-duty free. The decision of the Court is not subject to registration.

ARTICLE 6: PROCEDURES RELATIVE TO COMPULSORY HEALTH SURVEY AND TREATMENT IN HOSPITALIZATION CONDITIONS FOR MENTAL DISORDER

Prevention, care, and rehabilitation relative to mental illness are usually carried out by mental health service centers outside the hospital.

From the coming into force of this law, mental health treatments which require hospitalization and which are at the expense of the State or public bodies and institutions are carried out in the mental care centers mentioned in the following paragraphs, except for what is specified in Article 8.

The regions and autonomous provincial administrations of Trento and Bolzano*—taking also into account the territorial ambits foreseen in paragraph 2 and 3 of Article 25 of the Decree of the President of the Republic N. 616 of July 24, 1977—single out the general hospitals in which appropriate mental health centers for diagnosis and care must be created within 60 days from the coming into force of this law.

The centers mentioned in paragraphs 2 and 3 of this article—which are regulated in accordance with the Decree of the President of the Republic No. 128 of March 28, 1969, concerning compulsory special centers in the general hospitals and which must not have more than 15 beds—with the purpose of guaranteeing the continuity of the health service for the protection of mental health, are linked to the other mental health service centers of the territo-

---

*The provinces of Trento and Bolzano have a different statute from that of other Italian regions; therefore they are mentioned separately.

ry, as far as staff and functions are concerned, in a departmental organization.

The regions and the autonomous provincial administrations of Trento and Bolzano single out the private medical establishments which have the prescribed requirements necessary for voluntary and compulsory health treatments in the hospital context.

As to health service needs, the provincial administrations can draw up conventions with the establishments mentioned in the previous paragraph in accordance with the following Article 7.

ARTICLE 7: TRANSFERENCE TO REGIONAL ADMINISTRATIONS OF THE FUNCTIONS RELATIVE TO MENTAL HOSPITAL SERVICES

Beginning from the coming into force of this law, the administrative functions — until now carried out by provincial administrations — concerning mental health service in hospitalization conditions, are transferred to both ordinary and special statute regional administrations, for the territories under their jurisdiction. The autonomous provincial administrations of Trento and Bolzano maintain their present competence.

Hospital health service — regulated under Articles 12 and 13 of the Decree N. 264 of July 8, 1974, afterwards modified and transformed in Law N. 386 of August 17, 1974 — includes hospitalization for mental disorders. The present regulations concerning the competence of the expenditures are in force until December 31, 1978.

Beginning from the coming into force of this law, the regional administrations exercise the functions which they accomplish for the other hospitals, for mental hospitals as well.

Until the date of coming into force of the National Health Service Reform, and at any rate not further than January 1, 1979, the provincial administrations continue to perform the administrative functions relative to the management of the mental hospitals, and any other function relative to mental health and hygiene centers.

The regions and the autonomous provincial administrations of Trento and Bolzano plan and coordinate the organization of mental health and hygiene centers with the other health service facilities of the territory, and carry out the gradual removal of the mental hospitals and the different utilization of the existing facilities. These initiatives cannot involve higher expenses in the provincial administration budgets.

At any rate it is forbidden to build new mental hospitals, to use the existing ones as specialized mental departments of general hospitals, to create mental departments or units in general hospitals, and to use for this purpose neurological or neuropsychiatric departments or units.

The prohibitions—mentioned in Article 6 of the Decree N. 946 of December 29, 1977, afterwards modified and transformed in Law N. 43 of February 27, 1978—are applied to mental hospitals which depend upon provincial administrations or other public bodies, or upon public welfare and charity institutions.

Personnel of public mental hospitals and mental health service centers outside the hospital are employable in mental diagnosis and care centers of general hospitals as mentioned in Article 6.

The relationships between provincial administrations, hospital administrations, and other health care and in-patient facilities are regulated by appropriate conventions, in compliance with a standard scheme, which must be approved, within 30 days from the coming into force of this law, by means of a Decree of the Ministry of Health agreed by the regional administrations and the Italian provincial administration association and after having heard, as far as personnel problems are concerned, the most representative trade unions.

The standard scheme of Convention shall also regulate the staff and functions liaisons, mentioned in paragraph 4 of Article 6, the financial relations between provincial administration and in-patients facilities and the employment, also by command, of the personnel mentioned in paragraph 8 of this article.

From January 1, 1979, during the negotiations for the renewal of the labour agreement, between the agreement, regulations will be set out for the gradual equalization between the salary and economic regulations of the personnel of public mental hospitals and mental health and hygiene service centers and the salary and economic regulations of the corresponding categories of the personnel of general hospitals.

ARTICLE 8: PATIENTS ALREADY ADMITTED IN MENTAL HOSPITALS

The rules of this law are also applied to patients already admitted in mental hospitals at the time of the coming into force of this law.

The head physician responsible for the unit, within 90 days from the coming into force of this law (with single justified reports), communicates the names of the patients who, in his opinion need to continue the compulsory health treatment in the same in-patient facility, and indicates the assumable duration of the treatment itself to the Mayor of the respective places of residence. The head physician responsible for the unit is also bound to accomplish the duties mentioned in paragraph 5 of Article 3.

The mayor applies the measure of compulsory health treatment in hospitalization conditions in accordance with the regulations mentioned in the last paragraph of Article 2 and notifies it to the tutelary judge with the formalities and for the accomplishments mentioned in Article 3.

Omission of the communications mentioned in the previous paragraphs causes the cessation of all effects of the measure and is considered an "omission of office deeds crime," unless there is sufficient evidence for a more serious crime.

Taking into account paragraph 5 of Article 7 and in temporary derogation from what is established in paragraph 2 of Article 6, only those who had been admitted before the coming into force of this law and that need mental health treatment in hospitalization conditions can be admitted in the present mental hospitals, provided that they request it.

Comparison between U.S. and Italian Professional and Paraprofessional Mental Health Workers

THE ONLY PROFESSIONAL ROLE where there are similarities between Italy and America is that of the psychiatrist. However, in spite of his/her undisputed prominence in the Italian system, he has, we believe, a lower status, and certainly a lower income than his American colleague. In Italy there is an enormous surplus of M.D.s: one physician to 240 inhabitants. Unemployed doctors are available for underpaid and low prestige jobs.

Psychologists arrived relatively late on the scene: they still are trying to trace the boundaries of their competence, especially with regard to psychiatrists.

Social workers can hardly be compared to their American colleagues. They have a four-year curriculum that only in recent years was assimilated to the university level. Their main task is dealing with job and welfare issues. Officially, they are not allowed to do therapy.

Nurses: The term is used generically to include the *inservienti* (they correspond to aides); the *infermiere unico (professionale)* (which means "unified (professional)" — he/she practically corresponds to the American nurse) and the *caposala* (a registered nurse). The *inservienti* take a three-month course on general notions of higiene; the *infermiere unico* (professionale) takes a three-year course on medical disciplines. His/her training has to comply with European Community standards. Although some regions have specialized courses in psychiatry, they are not recognized officially. The *caposala* takes an extra year of training. He/she is in charge of a department or service and has special organizational tasks. Note that no category of nurses has a college level education.

According to these official roles and task assignments, the system appears pyramidal and very vertical. However, where an effective multidisciplinary team work is implemented, differences and hierarchy are currently blurred, tasks assigned according to effective competence instead of formal roles, and initiative extensively delegated.

Community Mental Health Program Questionnaire

I. Program Descriptors

A. Sociodemographic

1. Population of catchment area
2. Average family income
3. Number below poverty line
4. Percent of population with third party payment
5. Unemployment rate
6. Number homeless
7. Number minority

B. Administrative

1. Program development history
2. Total number of staff:
    M.D.'s (% FMG's)
    Ph.D.'s
    S.W.'s
    Tech's
    Volunteers
    Other (OT's, Art Therapists, etc.)
3. Total budget

*Loren R. Mosher, M.D., 1/28/87

4. Funding sources and amounts
5. Client funding - #SSI, SSDI, AFDC, state & local welfare
6. Decentralization
7. Total number clients on active rolls
8. Number admissions to hospital/year/stay
9. Number commitments/year/stay
10. Alternative to hospitalization—spaces, number of admissions, cost, stay
11. Number O.P.D. visits
12. Number home visits
13. Transitional living (#) admissions, cost, stay

$^1/_2$, $^3/_4$ way

14. Permanent living

    a. Group home   —supervised
               cost   —unsupervised (or prn)
    b. Apartments   —supervised
               cost   —unsupervised (or prn)

15. Case management (number clients)
16. Psychosocial rehabilitation (number clients)
17. Self-help
18. Use of community resources
19. Jail
20. N.A.M.I.
21. Specialized Programs

    Kids
    Drugs
    Geriatric
    Abuse

22. Voc. rehabilitation, H.U.D.
23. Relationship with state

C. Clinical

1. 24 hour crisis intervention
2. Team concept
3. Responsibility
4. Continuity of persons
5. Medication

    role ascribed
    prescribing practice, dosage

6. Family

    —involvement
    —treatment

—attitudes
—in home crisis intervention
7. Morale—maintainence techniques
8. Social networks
9. Escape from system
10. Contact Rewards
11. Theoretical orientation
12. Hierarchy

II. Overall Program Ratings

1. Staff quality

poor   excellent
1   10

2. Staff morale

1   10

3. Preservation of client power

1   10

4. Normalization

1   10

5. Contextualization

1   10

6. Flexibility

1   10

7. Leadership

1   10

8. Teamness

1   10

9. Respect for clients

1   10

10. Consultative, being with, facilitative attitude

1   10

11. Demedicalization

1   10

References

A network for caring: The community support program of the National Institute of Mental Health (1982). U.S. Department of Health and Human Services, National Institute of Mental Health, DHHS Pub. No. (ADM) 81-1063.

Amministrazione Provinciale di Arezzo (Ed.) (1974). I Tetti Rossi. Dal Manicomio alla Società. Firenze: Mazzottà.

Anthony, W. A., & Blanch, A. (1987). Supported employment for persons who are psychiatrically disabled: A historical and conceptual perspective. *Psychosocial Rehabilitation Journal, 11*, 5-23.

Anthony, W. A., Buell, G. J., Sharrett, S., & Althoff, M. E. (1972). Efficacy of psychiatric rehabilitation. *Psychological Bulletin, 78*, 447-456.

Anthony, W. A., & Dion, G. (1986). *Psychiatric rehabilitation: A rehabilitation research review*. Washington, DC: National Rehabilitation Information Center.

Arce, A. A., & Vergare, M. J. (1985a). Psychiatrists and interprofessional role conflicts in community mental health centers. In *Community mental health centers and psychiatrists*. Edited by the Joint Steering Committee of the American Psychiatric Association and the National Council of Community Mental Health Centers. Washington, DC and Rockville, MD.

Arce, A., & Vergare, M. (1985b). An overview of community residences as alternatives to hospitalization. *Psychiatric Clinics of North America, 8*, 423-436.

Babigian, H. M. (1977). The impact of community mental health centers on the utilization of services. *Archives of General Psychiatry, 34*, 385-394.

Bachrach, L. L. (1976). *Deinstitutionalization: An analytical review and sociological perspective*. Washington, DC: U.S. Government Printing Office.

Backes, R., Cohen, J., Gundlach, E., Myers, T., Propst, R., Rawls, A., & Hennings, B. (1987). *Medical services in the Fountain House model*. Presented at the Fourth Annual Fountain House Seminar, Seattle, WA.

Bacigalupi, M., Crepet, P., & Levato, C. (1982). Psichiatria a Roma. Ipotesi e proposte per l'use di strumenti epidemiologici in una realtà in trasformazione. In D. De Salvia, & P. Crepet (Eds.), *Psichiatria senza manicomio. Epidemiologia critica della riforma*. Milano: Feltrinelli.

419

Baldwin, J. A., Leff, J., & Wing, J. K. (1976). Confidentiality of psychiatric data in medical information systems. *British Journal of Psychiatry, 128*, 417–427.

Balestrieri, M., Micciolo, R., & Tansella, M. (1987). Long-stay and long-term psychiatric patients in one area with a community-based system of care. A register follow-up study. *International Journal of Social Psychiatry, 33*, 251–262.

Barton, R. (1959). *Institutional neurosis*. Bristol: Wright.

Barton, W., & Sanborn, C. J. (Eds.) (1977). *An assessment of the community mental health movement*. Lexington, MA: D. C. Heath.

Basaglia, F. (Ed.) (1968). *L'istituzione negata*. Torino: Einaudi.

Basaglia, F. (Ed.) (1973). *Che cos'e'la psichiatria?* Torino: Einaudi.

Basaglia, F. (1985). What is psychiatry? In R. F. Mollica (Ed.), The unfinished revolution in Italian psychiatry: An international perspective. *International Journal of Mental Health, 14*, 42–51.

Basaglia, F., & Ongaro-Basaglia, F. (1971). *La maggioranz deviante*. Torino: Einaudi.

Basaglia, F., & Ongaro-Basaglia, F. (Eds.) (1975). *Crimini di pace. Ricerche sugli intellettuali e sui tecnici come addetti all'oppressione*. Torino: Einaudi.

Battle, C. J. (1981). The iatrogenic disease called burnout. *Journal of American Medical Women's Association, 36*, 357–359.

Beard, J. H., Malamud, T. J., & Rossman, E. (1978). Psychiatric rehabilitation and long-term rehospitalization rates: The findings of two research studies. *Schizophrenia Bulletin, 4*, 622–636.

Beard, J. H., Propst, R., & Malamud, T. J. (1982). The Fountain House model of psychiatric rehabilitation. *Psychosocial Rehabilitation Journal, 5*, 47–53.

Beck, A. T., Rush, A. J., Shaw, B., & Emery, G. (1979). *Cognitive therapy of depression*. New York: Guilford.

Beers, C. W. (1939). *A mind that found itself*. New York: Doubleday.

Beigel, A., & Levenson, A. I. (Eds.) (1972). *The community mental health center*. New York: Basic Books.

Beiser, M., Shore, J. H., Peters, R., & Tatum, E. (1985). Does community care for the mentally ill make a difference? A tale of two cities. *American Journal of Psychiatry, 142*, 1047–1052.

Bellack, A. S., Turner, S. M., Hersen, M., & Luber, R. F. (1984). An examination of social skills training for chronic schizophrenic patients. *Hospital and Community Psychiatry, 35*, 1023–1028.

Bellak, L. (Ed.) (1964). *Handbook of Community Psychiatry and Community Mental Health*. New York: Grune & Stratton.

Bellak, L. (Ed.) (1974). *A concise handbook of community psychiatry and community mental health*. New York: Grune & Stratton.

Bennett, D. H. (1985). The changing pattern of mental health care in Trieste. In R. F. Mollica (Ed.). The unfinished revolution in Italian psychiatry: An international perspective. *International Journal of Mental Health, 14*, 70–92.

Bennett, D. H., & Wing, K. K. (1963). Sheltered workshops for the psychiatrically handicapped. In H. Freeman, & J. Farndale (Eds.). *Trends in the mental health services*. London: Pergamon.

Bertelsen, K., & Harris, M. R. (1973). Citizen participation in the development of a community mental health center. *Hospital and Community Psychiatry, 24*, 553–556.

Bianchi, L. (1925). *Eugenica, igiene mentale e profilassi delle malattie nervose e mentali*. Napoli: Idelson.

Black, B. J. (1970). *Principles of industrial therapy for the mentally ill*. New York: Grune & Stratton.

Bleuler, M. (1975). Personal communication.

Bleuler, M. (1968). A 23-year longitudinal study of 208 schizophrenics and impressions in regard to the nature of schizophrenia. In D. Rosenthal, & S. S. Kety (Eds.), *The transmission of Schizophrenia*. Oxford: Pergamon Press.

Bockoven, J. S. (1963). *Moral treatment in American psychiatry*. New York: Springer.

Bolman, W. (1972). Community control of the community mental health center: II. Case Examples. *American Journal of Psychiatry, 129*, 181–186.

Bond, G. R., Witheridge, T. F., Setze, P. J., & Dincin, J. (1985). Preventing rehospitalization of clients in a psychosocial rehabilitation program. *Hospital and Community Psychiatry, 36*, 993–995.

Bordin, E. S. (1979). The generalizability of the psychoanalytic concept of the working alliance. *Psychotherapy, 16*, 252–260.

Borland, J. J. (1981). Burnout among workers and administrators. *Health and Social Work, 6*, 73–78.

Braun, P. B., Kochansky, G., Shapiro, R., Greenberg, S., Gudeman, J. E., Johnson, S., & Shore, M. F. (1981). Overview: Deinstitutionalization of psychiatric patients: A critical review of outcome studies. *American Journal of Psychiatry, 138*, 736–749.

Brown, D. B. (in press). Putting systems theory into service: The evolution of the Morrisania family care center community mental health program. In A. Menfi (Ed.). *Family therapy training and career development in the public sector*. New York: Brunner/Mazel.

Brown, D., & Parnell, M. (in press). Mental health services for the urban poor: A systems approach. In M. P. Mirkin (Ed.), *The social & political contexts of family therapy*. New York: Gardner Press.

Brown, G. W. (1981). Life events, psychiatric disorder and physical illness. *Journal of Psychosomatic Research, 25*, 461–473.

Brown, G. W., & Birley, J. (1968). Crises and life changes and the onset of schizophrenia. *Journal of Health and Social Behavior, 9*, 203–214.

Brown, G. W., & Harris, T. O. (1978). *The Social Origins of Depression*. London: Tavistock Publications.

Budson, R. D. (1978). *The psychiatric halfway house*. Pittsburgh, PA: University of Pittsburgh Press.

Budson, R. D., Meehan, J., & Barclay, E. (Eds.). (1974). *Developing a community residence for the mentally ill*. Boston: Commonwealth of Massachusetts.

Burti, L., & Mosher, L. R. (1986). Training psychiatrists in the community: A report of the Italian experience. *American Journal of Psychiatry, 143*, 1580–1584.

Burti, L., Faccincani, C., Mignolli, G., Siani, R., Siciliani, O., & Zimmermann-Tansella, Ch. (1984). Terapia sistemica e servizio territoriale: un addio allo specchio? In L. Boscolo, & G. Cecchin (Eds.), *Atti del IV Convegno Annuale del Centro Milanese di Terapia della Famiglia*. Milano: Centro Milanese di Terapia Familiare.

Burti, L., Garzotto, N., Siciliani, O., Zimmerman-Tansella, Ch., & Tansella, M. (1986). South Verona's psychiatric service: An integrated system of community care. *Hospital and Community Psychiatry, 37*, 809–813.

Calderaro, N. (1987). Personal communication.

Calvaruso, C., Frisanco, R., & Izzo, S. (Eds.). (1982). *Indagine Censis-Ciseff sulla attuazione della riforma psichiatrica e sul destino dei dimessi dagli O.P.* Roma: Edizioni Paoline.

Canosa, R. (1979). *Storia del manicomio in Italia dall 'unita ad oggi*. Milano: Feltrinelli.

Canton, G., & Santonastaso, P. (1984). Psychological distress and life events in neurotic patients. *Psychopathology, 17*, 144–148.

Caplan, G. (1974). *Support systems and community mental health*. New York: Behavioral Publications.

Caplan, G., & Caplan, R. B. (1967). Development of community psychiatry concepts. In A. M. Freedman, & H. I. Kaplan (Eds.), *Comprehensive textbook of psychiatry) (1st ed.)*. Baltimore: Williams & Wilkins.

Caplan, G., & Killilea, M. (Eds.). (1976). *Support systems and mutual help: Multidisciplinary exploration*. New York: Grune & Stratton.

Carling, P. (1984). *Developing family foster care programs in mental health: A resource guide*. Washington, DC: U.S. Department of Health and Human Services.

Carpenter, M. D. (1978). Residential placement for the chronic psychiatric patient: A review and evaluation of the literature. *Schizophrenia Bulletin, 4*, 384–398.

Carpenter, W. T., & Heinrichs, D. W. (1983). Early intervention, time-limited, target pharmacotherapy of schizophrenia. *Schizophrenia Bulletin, 9*, 533-542.

Carpenter, W. T., Heinrichs, D. W., & Hanlon, T. E. (1987). A comparative trial of pharmacologic strategies in schizophrenia. *American Journal of Psychiatry, 144*, 1466-1470.

Carpenter, W., Heinrichs, D., Hanlon, T., Kirkpatrick, B., & Summerfeld, A. (in press). An experimental study of targeted drug treatment in schizophrenia. *Journal of Schizophrenia Research*.

Cauce, A. M. (1986). Special networks and social competence: Exploring the effects of early adolescent friendships. *American Journal of Community Psychology, 14*, 607-628.

Cecere, F. (1985). Dal manicomio al territorio. *ISIS News, 6*, 2-5.

Centro Studi Investimenti Sociali (CENSIS) (1984). *Le politiche psichiatriche regionali nel doporiforma e lo stato attuale dei servizi*. Roma: CENSIS.

Centro Studi Investimenti Sociali (CENSIS) (1985). *L'attuazione della riforma psichiatrica nel quadro delle politiche regionali e dell'offerta quantitativa e qualitativa dei servizi: Liguria*, Mimeo. Roma: CENSIS.

Centro Studi Ministero della Sanita (1977). *L'assistenza Psichiatrica Ospedaliera ed Extraospedaliera. Rapporto no. 14*. Roma.

CHAMP, c/o Macro Systems, Silver Spring, MD.

Chamberlain, J. (1978). *On our own: Patient-controlled alternatives to the mental health system*. New York: McGraw-Hill.

Chien, C., & Cole, J. O. (1973). Landlord-supervised cooperative apartments: A new modality for community-based treatment. *American Journal of Psychiatry, 130*, 156-159.

Chouinard, G., Bradwejn, J., Jones, B. D., & Ross-Chouinard, A. (1984). Withdrawal symptoms after long-term treatment with low-potency neuroleptics. *Journal of Clinical Psychiatry, 45*, 500-502.

Ciompi, L. (1980). Catamnestic long-term study of the course of life and aging of schizophrenics. *Schizophrenia Bulletin, 6*, 606-618.

Clark, G. H., & Vaccaro, J. V. (1987). Burnout among CMHC psychiatrists and the struggle to survive. *Hospital and Community Psychiatry, 38*, 843-847.

Cobb, S. (1976). Social support as a moderator of life stress. *Psychosomatic Medicine, 38*, 300-314.

Cohen, S., & Syme, S. L. (Eds.). (1985). *Social support and health*. Orlando: Academic Press.

Cohen, C. I., Teresi, J., & Holmes, D. (1985). Social networks and adaptation. *Gerontologist, 25*, 197-304.

Corlito, G., Martini, P., Domenici, F., Cesari, G. P., & Petrillo, M. (1987). *A community alternative to psychiatric hospitalization*. Paper presented at the 6th Mediterranean Congress of Social Psychiatry. Zagreb, Yugoslavia, October 1-4.

Coulton, C. J., Fitch, V., & Holland, T. P. (1985). A typology of social environments in community care homes. *Hospital and Community Psychiatry, 36*, 373-377.

Cournos, F. (1987). The impact of environmental factors on outcome in residential programs. *Hospital and Community Psychiatry, 38*, 848-852.

Day, R., Nielsen, J. A., Korten, A., Ernberg, G., Dube, K. C., Gebhart, J., Jablensky, A., Leon, C., Marsella, A., Olatawura, M., Sartorius, N., Stromgren, E., Takahashi, R., Wig, N., & Wynne, L. C. (1987). Stressful life events preceding the acute onset of schizophrenia: A cross-national study from the World Health Organization. *Culture, Medicine and Psychiatry, 11*, 123-205.

Davis, J. M. (1980). Antipsychotic drugs. In H. Kaplan, A. M. Freedman, & B. J. Sadock (Eds.), *Comprehensive Textbook of Psychiatry, Volume 3*. Baltimore: Williams & Wilkins.

Davis, T., & Specht, P. (1978). Citizen participation in community mental-health programs: A study in intergroup conflict and cooperation. *Group and Organization Studies, 3*, 456-466.

Dean, A., & Lin, D. (1977). The stress buffering role of social support. *Journal of Nervous and Mental Disease, 166*, 7-15.

Debernardi, A. (1980). Suicidi e legge 180. *Epidemiologia e Prevenzione, 3-4*, 57-58.

De Salvia, D. (1983). Lo sviluppo dell'assistenza psichiatrica in Italia. Uno studio valutativo. *Prospettive Sociali e Sanitarie, 14-15*, 22-28.

De Salvia, D. (1984). Elementi di statistica ed epidemiologia sull'applicazione della 180. *Fogli di Informazione, 106*, 1-22.

De Salvia D. (1985). Teoria e utilizzazione dei sistemi informativi. In M. Tansella (Ed.). *L'approccio epidemiologico in psichiatria*. Milano: Boringhieri.

De Salvia, D., & Crepet, P. (Eds.). (1982). *Psichiatria Senza Manicomio. Epidemiologia Critica della Riforma*. Milano: Feltrinelli.

Deutsch, A. (1948). *Shame of the states*. New York: Arno Press.

Dincin, J., & Witheridge, T. F. (1982). Psychiatric rehabilitation as a deterrent to recidivism. *Hospital and Community Psychiatry, 33*, 645–650.

Dohrenwend, B. P. (1975). Sociocultural and sociopsychological factors in the genesis of mental disorders. *Journal of Health and Social Behavior, 16*, 365–392.

Dohrenwend, B. P., & Egri, G. (1981). Recent stressful life events and episodes of schizophrenia. *Schizophrenia Bulletin, 7*, 12–23.

Dupont, A. (1979). Psychiatric case registers. In H. Haefner (Ed.), *Estimating needs for mental health care*. Berlin: Springer Verlag.

Emener, W. G. (1979). Professional burnout: Rehabilitation's hidden handicap. *Journal of Rehabilitation, 45*, 55–58.

Ewalt, J. R. (1987). Personal communication.

Faccincani, C., Burti, L., Garzotto, N., Mignolli, G., & Tansella, M. (1985). Organizational aspects of community care. The South-Verona mental health center. *New Trends in Experimental and Clinical Psychiatry, 1*, 201–216.

Fairweather, G. W., Sanders, D., Cressler, D., & Maynard, H. (1969). *Community life for the mentally ill: An alternative to institutional care*. Chicago: Aldine.

Falloon, I. R. H., Boyd, J. L., McGill, C. W., Razani, J., Moss, H. B., & Gilderman, A. M. (1982). Family management in the prevention of exacerbations of schizophrenia. *New England Journal of Medicine, 306*, 1437–1440.

Fenton, W. S., Mosher, L. R., & Matthews, S. M. (1981). Diagnosis of schizophrenia: A critical review of current diagnostic systems. *Schizophrenia Bulletin, 7*, 452–476.

Fenton, W. S., Leaf, P. J., Moran, N. L., & Tischler, G. L. (1984). Trends in psychiatric practice, 1965–1980. *American Journal of Psychiatry, 141*, 346–351.

Ferrannini, L. (1987). Personal communication.

Foley, H. A., & Sharfstein, S. S. (1983). *Madness and government: Who cares for the mentally ill?* Washington, DC: American Psychiatric Press.

Fountain House. (1985). Summary of Transitional Employment Results, Memorandum 279, 10 December.

Frank, J. D. (1971). Therapeutic factors in psychotherapy. *American Journal of Psychotherapy, 25*, 350–361.

Frank, J. D. (1973). *Persuasion and healing: A comparative study of psychotherapy*. Baltimore: Johns Hopkins University Press.

Frank, L. R. (1986). The policies and practices of American psychiatry are oppressive. *Hospital and Community Psychiatry, 137*, 497–501.

Freudenberger, H. J. (1980). *Burnout*. New York: Anchor Press.

Freudenberger, H. J. (1986). The issues of staff burnout in therapeutic communities. *Journal of Psychoactive Drugs, 18*, 247–251.

Frieswyk, S. H., Colson, D. B., & Allen, J. G. (1984). Conceptualizing the therapeutic alliance from a psychoanalytic perspective. *Psychotherapy, 21*, 460–464.

Fromm-Reichmann, F. (1948). Notes on the development of treatment of schizophrenics by psychoanalytic psychotherapy. *Psychiatry, 11*, 263–273.

Frisanco, R. (1987). L'indagine Censis-Ministero della sanità sull'attuazione della riforma psichiatrica. In M. G. Giannichedda & F. Ongaro-Basaglia (Eds.), *Psichiatria, tossicodiapendenza, perizia. Richerche su forme di tutela, diritti e modelli di servizio*. Milano: Franco Angeli.

Galzigna, M., & Terzian, H. (1980). *L'Archivio della Follia*. Padova: Marsilio Editori.

Gardos, G., Cole, J. O., & Torey, D. (1978). *Withdrawal syndromes associated with antipsychotic drugs. American Journal of Psychiatry, 135*, 1321–1324.

Giacanelli, F. (1975). Appunti per una storia della psichiatria in Italia. In K. Dorner, *Il Borghese e il Folle*. Roma-Bari: Laterza.

Glasscote, R. M., Cumming, E., Rutman, I., Sussex, J. N., & Glassman, S. M. (1971).

Rehabilitating the mentally ill in the community. Washington, DC: Joint Information Service of the American Psychiatric Association and the National Association for Mental Health.

Glasscote, R. M., Kraft, A. M., Glassman, S. M., & Jepson, W. W. (1969). *Partial hospitalization for the mentally ill: A study of programs and problems.* Washington, DC: Joint Information Service and National Association for Mental Health.

Goldberg, D. P., & Huxley, P. (1980). *Mental illness in the community: The pathway to psychiatric care.* London: Tavistock.

Goldman, H. H., & Morrissey, J. P. (1985). The alchemy of mental health policy: Homelessness and the fourth cycle of reform. *American Journal of Public Health, 75,* 727–731.

Goldman, H. H., Adams, N. H., & Taube, C. A. (1983). Deinstitutionalization: The data demythologized. *Hospital and Community Psychiatry, 34,* 129–134.

Goldmeier, J. (1977). Community residential facilities for former mental patients: A review. *Psychosocial Rehabilitation Journal, 1,* 1–45.

Goldmeier, J., Shore, M. F., & Mannino, F. V. (1977). Cooperative apartments: New programs in community mental health. *Health and Social Work, 2,* 119–140.

Goldstein, S. (1986). Bye bye Brady bunch. *The Family Therapy Networker.* January–February, 31–32/76–78.

Goldstein, S. J., & Dyche, L. (1983). Family therapy of the schizophrenic poor. In W. R. McFarlane (Ed.), *Forces from outside the family.* New York: Guilford.

Golomb, S. L., & Kocsis, A. (1988). *The halfway house: On the road to independence.* New York: Brunner/Mazel.

Gomes-Schwartz, B. (1978). Effective ingredients in psychotherapy: Prediction of outcome from process variables. *Journal of Consulting and Clinical Psychology, 46,* 1023–1035.

Gottlieb, B. H. (1985). Social networks and social support: An overview of research, practice and policy implications. *Health Education Quarterly, 12,* 5–22.

Gottlieb, N. H., & Green, L. W. (1984). Life events, social network, life-style and health: An analysis of the 1979 National Survey of Personal Health Practices and Consequences. *Health Education Quarterly, 11,* 91–105.

Gove, S. (1978). The effect of social support in moderating the health consequences of unemployment. *Journal of Health and Social Behavior, 19,* 157–165.

Gramsci, A. (1955). *Quaderni del carcere: Gli Intellettuali e l'organizzazione della cultura.* Torino: Einaudi.

Greenblatt, M., Becerra, R. M., & Serafetinides, E. A. (1982). Social networks and mental health: An overview. *American Journal of Psychiatry, 139,* 977–984.

Grob, G. (1973). *Mental institutions in America, social policy to 1875.* New York: Free Press of Clencoe.

Grob, G. (1983). *Mental illness and American society, 1875–1940.* Princeton: Princeton University Press.

Gruenberg, E. M., & Huxley, J. (1970). Mental health services can be organized to prevent chronic disability. *Community Mental Health Journal, 6,* 431–436.

Gruenberg, E. M., Snow, H. B., & Bennett, C. L. (1969). Preventing the social breakdown syndrome. In F. C. Redlich, *Social Psychiatry.* Baltimore: Williams & Wilkins.

Grunebaum, H. (1986). On harmful therapy. *American Journal of Psychotherapy, 60,* 165–176.

Gunderson, J. G. (1978). Defining the therapeutic processes in psychiatric milieus. *Psychiatry, 41,* 327–335.

Gunderson, J., Will, O. A., & Mosher, L. R. (Eds.). (1983). *Principles and practice of milieu therapy.* New York: Jason Aronson.

Gunderson, J. G., Frank, A. F., Katz, H. M., Vannicelli, M. L., Frosch, J. P., & Knapp, P. H. (1984). Effects of psychotherapy on schizophrenia: II. Comparative outcome of two forms of treatment. *Schizophrenia Bulletin, 10,* 564–598.

Gutstein, S. E., Rudd, D., Graham, C., & Rayha, L. (in press). Systemic crisis intervention as a response to adolescent crisis: An outcome study. *Family Process.*

Häfner, H., & Klug, J. (1982). The impact of an expanding community mental health service on patterns of bed usage: Evaluation of a four-year period of implementation. *Psychological Medicine, 12*, 177–190.

Hammer, M. (1981). Social supports, social networks and schizophrenia. *Schizophrenia Bulletin, 7*, 45–57.

Hammer, M. (1983). 'Core' and 'extended' social networks in relation to health and illness. *Social Science and Medicine, 17*, 405–411.

Harding, C. M., Brooks, G. W., Ashikaga, T., Strauss, J. S., & Breier, A. (1987a). The Vermont longitudinal study of persons with severe mental illness, I: Methodology, study sample and overall status 32 years later. *American Journal of Psychiatry, 144*, 718–726.

Harding, C. M., Brooks, G. W., Ashikaga, T., Strauss, J. S., & Breier, A. (1987b). The Vermont longitudinal study of persons with severe mental illness, II: Long-term outcome of subjects who retrospectively met DSM-III criteria for schizophrenia. *American Journal of Psychiatry, 144*, 727–735.

Hartley, D., & Strupp, H. H. (1983). Therapeutic alliance: A contribution to outcome in brief psychotherapy. In J. Masling (Ed.), *Empirical studies of psychoanalytic theory*. Hillsdale, NJ: Earlbaum Press.

Hatfield, A. (1984). *Coping with mental illness in the family*. NAMI.

Hatfield, A. (1985). *Consumer guide to mental health services*. NAMI.

Hays, R. B., & Oxley, D. (1986). Social network development and functioning during a life transition. *Journal of Personality and Social Psychology, 50*, 305–313.

Heptinstall, D. (1984). Psichiatria democratica: Italy's revolution in caring for the mentally ill. *Community Care, 1*, 17–19.

Herz, M. I., Endicott, J., Spitzer, R., & Mesnikoff, A. (1971). Day versus inpatient hospitalization: A controlled study. *American Journal of Psychiatry, 127*, 1371–1382.

Hirsch, B. J., & Rapkin, B. B. (1986). Social networks and adult social identities: Profiles and correlates of support and rejection. *American Journal of Community Psychology, 51*, 395–412.

Hirschfeld, R. M., Matthews, S. M., Mosher, L. R., & Menn, A. Z. (1977). Being with madness: Personality characteristics of three treatment staffs. *Hospital and Community Psychiatry, 28*, 267–273.

Hodgman, E., & Stein, E. (1966). Cooperative apartment. *Community Mental Health Journal, 2*, 347–352.

Hogarty, G. E., Anderson, C. M., Reiss, D. J., Kornblith, S. J., Greenwald, D. P., Javna, C. D., & Madonia, M. J. (1986). Family psychoeducation, social skills training and maintainence chemotherapy in the aftercare treatment of schizophrenia. *Archives of General Psychiatry, 43*, 633–642.

Hogarty, G. E., Schooler, N. R., Ulrich, R., Mussare, F., Ferro, P., & Herron, E. (1979). Fluphenazine and social therapy in aftercare of schizophrenic patients. Relapse analyses of a two-year controlled study of fluphenazine decanoate and fluphenazine hydrochloride. *Archives of General Psychiatry, 36*, 1283–1294.

Horowitz, M., & Marmar, C. (1985). The therapeutic alliance with difficult patients. *Psychiatry Update, 4*, APA Press.

Horvath, A. O., & Greenberg, L. (1986). The development of the working alliance inventory. In L. Greenberg, & W. Pinsof (Eds.), *The psychotherapeutic process: A research handbook*. New York: Guilford.

Hoult, J. (1986). The community care of the acutely mentally ill. *British Journal of Psychiatry, 149*, 137–144.

Hoult, J., & Reynolds, I. (1984). Schizophrenia: A comparative trial of community oriented and hospital oriented psychiatric care. *Acta Psychiatrica Scandinavica, 69*, 359–372.

Hoult, J., Rosen, A., & Reynolds, I. (1984). Community orientated treatment compared to psychiatric hospital orientated treatment. *Social Science and Medicine, 11*, 1005–1010.

Huber, G., Gross, G., Schuttler, T., & Linz, M. (1980). Longitudinal studies of schizophrenic patients. *Schizophrenia Bulletin, 6*, 592–605.

Imber-Black, E., Roberts, J., & Whiting, R. J. (Eds.). (1988). *Rituals in families and family therapy*. New York: W. W. Norton.

Istituto Centrale di Statistica (ISTAT). *Annuario statistico Italiano, 1964-1987 edns*. Roma: ISTAT.

Istituto Centrale di Statistica (ISTAT) (1986). *I conti degli Italiani. Compendio della vita economica nazionale*. Roma: ISTAT.

Jablensky, A., & Henderson, J. (1983). Report on a visit to the South-Verona community psychiatric service. *WHO Assignment Report*. Copenhagen and Geneve: WHO.

Jansen, E. (1970). The role of the halfway house in community mental health programs in the United Kingdom and America. *American Journal of Psychiatry, 126*, 1498-1504.

Jerrell, J. M., & Larsen, J. K. (1983). Trends in outcome indicators in sample community mental health centers: 1976-1982. National Institute of Mental Health, Technical Report 83-9.

Jervis, G. (1975). *Manuale critico di psichiatria*. Milano: Feltrinelli.

Joint Commission on Mental Illness and Health (1961). *Action for mental health: Final report of the Joint Commission on Mental Illness and Health 1961*. New York: Basic Books.

Jones, K., & Poletti, A. (1985). Understanding the Italian experience. *British Journal of Psychiatry, 146*, 341-347.

Jones, K., & Poletti, A. (1986). The 'Italian experience' reconsidered. *British Journal of Psychiatry, 148*, 144-150.

Kane, J. M. (1983). Low dose medication strategies in the maintenance treatment of schizophrenia. *Schizophrenia Bulletin, 9*, 528-532.

Kane, J. M. (1984). *Drug maintenance strategies in schizophrenia*. American Psychiatric Press: Washington, DC.

Kane, J. M. (1987). Treatment of schizophrenia. *Schizophrenia Bulletin, 13*, 133-156.

Kane, J. M., Rifkin, A., Woerner, M. Reardon, G., Sarantakos, S., Schiebel, D., & Ramos-Lorenzi, J. (1983). Low dose neuroleptic treatment. *Archives of General Psychiatry, 40*, 893-896.

Kane, J. M., Woerner, M., Weinhold, P., Wagner, J., Kinon, B., & Borenstein, M. (1984). Incidence of tardive dyskinesia: Five year data from a prospective study. *Psychopharmacology Bulletin, 20*, 382-386.

Kanter, J. (1984). *Coping strategies for relatives of the mentally ill*. NAMI.

Kaplan, B., Cassel, J., & Gore, S. (1977). Social support and health. *Medical Care, 15*, 47-58.

Kasius, R. V. (1966). The social breakdown syndrome in a cohort of long-stay patients in the Dutchess county unit, 1960-63. In E. M. Gruenberg (Ed.), *Evaluating the effectiveness of community mental health services*. New York: Mental Health Materials Center.

Kendall, R. E. (1974). The stability of psychiatric diagnosis. *British Journal of Psychiatry, 124*, 352-356.

Kiesler, C. A. (1982a). Mental hospitals and alternative care: Noninstitutionalization as potential public policy for mental patients. *American Psychologist, 37*, 349-360.

Kiesler, C. A. (1982b). Public and professional myths about mental hospitalization: An empirical reassessment of policy-related beliefs. *American Psychologist, 37*, 1323-1339.

Klerman, G., Weissman, M., Rounsaville, B., & Chevron, E. (1984). *Interpersonal psychotherapy of depression*. New York: Basic Books.

Klorman, R., Strauss, J., & Kokes, R. (1977). Premorbid adjustment in schizophrenia: Concepts, measures, and implications. Part III. The relationship of demographic and diagnostic factors to measures of premorbid adjustment in schizophrenia. *Schizophrenia Bulletin, 3*, 214-225.

Knesper, D. J., & Carlson, B. W. (1981). An analysis of the movement to private psychiatric practice. *Archives of General Psychiatry, 38*, 943-949.

Kramer, M., & Pollack, E. S. (1958). Problems in the interaction of trends in the population movement of the public mental hospitals. *American Journal of Public Health, 48*, 1003-1019.

Kresky-Wolff, M., Matthews, S., Kalibat, F., & Mosher, L. (1984). Crossing Place: A residential model for crisis intervention. *Hospital and Community Psychiatry, 35*, 72-74.

Kresky, M., Maeda, E. M., & Rothwell, N. D. (1976). The apartment program: A community living option for halfway house residents. *Hospital and Community Psychiatry, 27*, 153-154.

Kutchins, H., & Kirk, S. (1986). The reliability of DSM-III: A critical review. *Social Work Research Abstracts, 22*, 3–11.

Lacey, R. (1984). Where have all the patients gone? *Guardian*, July 4.

Laing, R. D. (1967). *The politics of experience*. New York: Ballantine.

Lamb, H. R. (1979). Roots of neglect of the long-term mentally ill. *Psychiatry, 42*, 201–207.

Lamb, H. R. (Ed.) (1984). *The homeless mentally ill*. Washington, DC: American Psychiatric Association.

Lamb, H. R., & Lamb, D. M. (1984). A nonhospital alternative to acute hospitalization. *Hospital and Community Psychiatry, 35*, 728–730.

Landy, D., & Greenblatt, M. (1965). *Halfway houses*. Washington DC: U.S. Department of Health, Education and Welfare, Vocational Rehabilitation Administration.

Langsley, D. G. (1980). Community psychiatry. In H. I. Kaplan, A. M. Freedman, & B. J. Sadock (Eds.), *Comprehensive textbook of psychiatry, III*. Baltimore: Williams & Wilkins.

Langsley, D. G. (1985). Community Psychiatry. In H. I. Kaplan, & B. J. Sadock (Eds.), *Comprehensive textbook of psychiatry, IV*. Baltimore: Williams & Wilkins.

Langsley, D. G., & Kaplan, D. M. (1968). *The treatment of families in crisis*. New York: Grune & Stratton.

Langsley, D. G., Pittman III, F. S., & Swank, G. F. (1969). Family crisis in schizophrenics and other mental patients. *Journal of Nervous and Mental Disease, 149*, 270–276.

Langsley, D. G., Berlin, I. N., & Yarvis, R. M. (1981). *Handbook of community mental health*. Garden City, New York: Medical Examination Publishing Co.

Lazare, A., & Eisenthal, S. (1979). A negotiated approach to the clinical encounter, chapter 1. In A. Lazare (Ed.), *Outpatient psychiatry, diagnosis and treatment*. Baltimore: Williams & Wilkins.

Lazare, A., Eisenthal, S., & Frank, A. (1979). A negotiated approach to the clinical encounter, chapter 2. In A. Lazare (Ed.), *Outpatient psychiatry, diagnosis, and treatment*. Baltimore: Williams & Wilkins.

Leff, J., & Vaughn, C. (1980). The interaction of life events and relatives expressed emotion in schizophrenia and depressive neurosis. *British Journal of Psychiatry, 136*, 146–153.

Leff, J., & Vaughn, C. (1987). Expressed emotion. *Hospital and Community Psychiatry, 38*, 1117–1118.

Leff, J., Kuipers, L., Berkowitz, E., Vries, R., & Sturgeon, D. (1982). A controlled trial of social intervention in the families of schizophrenic patients. *British Journal of Psychiatry, 141*, 121–134.

Levine, I. S. (1984). Homelessness: Its implications for mental health policy and practice. *Psychosocial Rehabilitation Journal, 8*, 6–16.

Levine, I. S., Lezak, A. D., & Goldman, H. H. (1986). Community support systems for the homeless mentally ill. In E. Bassuk (Ed.), *The mental health needs of homeless persons*. San Francisco: Jossey-Bass.

Lin, N., Simcone, R., Ensel, W., & Kuo, W. (1979). Social support stressful life events and illness: A model and empirical test. *Journal of Health and Social Behavior, 20*, 108–119.

Lowenstein, L. F. (1981). Residential care and halfway houses in the treatment of emotionally disturbed adolescents: The solution to the problem of over and under protection. *Community Home Schools Gazette, 74*, 350–354.

Luborsky, L., McLellan, A. T., Woody, G. E., O'Brien, C. P., & Auerbach, A. (1985). Therapist success and its determinants. *Archives of General Psychiatry, 42*, 602–614.

Luchons, D. J., Freed, W. J., & Wyatt, R. J. (1980). The role of cholinergic supersensitivity in the medical symptoms associated with withdrawal and anti psychotic drugs. *American Journal of Psychiatry, 137*, 1395–1398.

Madness Network News, Journal of the Psychiatric Inmate Liberation Movement (no longer published). Back issues available from MNN, 2054 University Avenue, Room 405. Berkeley, CA, 94704.

Maj, M. (1985). Brief history of Italian psychiatric legislation from 1904 to the 1978 reform act. *Acta Psychiatrica Scandinavica, suppl. 316*, 15–25.

Malamud, T. J. (1985). *Evaluation of clubhouse model — Community-based psychiatric rehabilitation*. Washington, DC: National Institute of Handicapped Research, Office of Special

Education and Rehabilitative Services, U.S. Department of Education.

Mannino, F. V., Ott, S., & Shore, M. F. (1977). Community residential facilities for former mental patients: An annotated bibliography. *Psychosocial Rehabilitation Journal, 1*, 1–43.

Maranesi, T., & Piazza, A. (1986). Dopo la 180 i dati della prima indagine sull'assistenza psichiatrica in Italia. La verità è dolce. *Scienza Esperienza, 9*, 17–21.

Marder, S. R., Van Putten, T., Mintz, J., Lebell, M., McKenzie, J., & May, P. R. A. (1987). Low and conventional dose maintenance therapy with fluphenazine decanoate. *Archives of General Psychiatry, 44*, 518–522.

Marinoni, A., Torre, E., Allegri, G., & Comelli, M. (1983). Lomest psychiatric case register: The statistical context required for planning. *Acta Psychiatrica Scandinavica, suppl. 67*, 109–117.

Martini, P., Cecchini, M., Corlito, G., D'Arco, A., & Nascimbeni, P. (1985). A model of a single comprehensive mental health service for a catchment area: A community alternative to hospitalization. *Acta Psychiatrica Scandinavica, 316*, 95–120.

Marziali, E. (1984). Three viewpoints on the therapeutic alliance: similarities, differences, and associations with psychotherapy outcome. *Journal of Nervous and Mental Disease, 172*, 417–423.

Marziali, E., Marmar, C., Krupnick, J. (1981). Therapeutic alliance scales: Development and relationship to psychotherapy outcome. *American Journal of Psychiatry, 138*, 361–364.

Maslach, C., & Jackson, S. E. (1979). Burned-out cops and their families. *Psychology Today, 12*, 59–62.

Matthews, S. M., Roper, M. T., Mosher, L. R., & Menn, A. Z. (1979). A non-neuroleptic treatment for schizophrenia: Analysis of the two-year postdischarge risk of relapse. *Schizophrenia Bulletin, 5*, 322–333.

Mayer-Gross, W. (1920). Uber die Stellungnahme zur Abgelaufenen akuten Psychose. *Zectung Gesselahaft Neurologie Psychiatrie, 60*, 160–212.

McGlashan, T. H., Levy, S. T., & Carpenter, W. T. (1975). Integration and sealing over: Clinically distinct recovery styles from schizophrenia. *Archives of General Psychiatry, 32*, 1269–1272.

McNair, D. M., & Fisher, S. (1978). Separating anxiety from depression. In M. A. Lipton, A. D. DiMascio, & R. F. Killiam (Eds.), *Pharmacology: A generation of progress*. New York: Raven Press.

Meddars, N. M., & Colman, A. D. (1985). The assisted independent living program: A new model for community care. *Psychiatric Annals, 15*, 667–672.

Mental Health Center of Dane County, Inc. (1985). *Annual report*.

Mental Health Center of Boulder County, Inc. (1985–86). *Annual report*.

Mignolli, G. (1987). *Sintomatologia psichiatrica, social performance e pattern di utilizzazione dei servizi. Follow-up a sette anni dei pazienti di Verona Sud con diagnosi di psicosi schizofrenica*. Unpublished doctoral dissertation, University of Verona, Italy.

Miller, J. (1983). Psychiatry as a tool of repression. *Science for the People*, March–April.

Minkoff, K., & Stern, R. (1985). Paradoxes faced by residents being trained in the psychosocial treatment of people with chronic schizophrenia. *Hospital and Community Psychiatry, 36*, 859–864.

Misiti, R., Debernardi, A., Garbaldo, C., & Guarnieri, M. (1981). *La riforma psichiatrica: Prima fase di attuazione*. Roma: Il Pensiero Scientifico.

Mitchell, R. E. (1982). Social networks and psychiatric clients: The personal and environmental context. *American Journal of Community Psychology, 10*, 387–401.

Mollica, R. F. (1985). From Antonio Gramsci to Franco Basaglia: The theory and practice of the Italian psychiatric reform. In R. F. Mollica (Ed.), The unfinished revolution in Italian psychiatry: An International perspective. *International Journal of Mental Health, 14*, 22–41.

Moos, R. H. (1974). *Evaluating treatment environments: A social ecological approach*. New York: John Wiley.

Moos, R. (1975). *Evaluating correctional and community settings*. New York: John Wiley.

Morgan, R., Luborsky, L., Crits-Christoph, P., Curtis, H., & Solomon, J. (1982). Predicting the outcomes of psychotherapy by the Penn Helping Alliance Rating Method. *Archives of General Psychiatry, 39*, 397–402.

Mosher, L. R. (1977). Societal barriers to learning: The community psychiatry example. In G. Serban (Ed.), *A critical appraisal of community psychiatry*. New York: John Wiley.

Mosher, L. R. (1978). Can diagnosis be non-pejorative? In L. C. Wynne, R. L. Cromwell, & S. Mattysse (Eds.), *The Nature of Schizophrenia*. New York: John Wiley.

Mosher, L. R. (1982). Italy's revolutionary mental health law: An assessment. *American Journal of Psychiatry, 139*, 199–203.

Mosher, L. R. (1983a). Radical deinstitutionalization: The Italian experience. *International Journal of Mental Health, 11*, 129–136.

Mosher, L. R. (1983b). Recent developments in the care, treatment, and rehabilitation of the chronic mentally ill in Italy. *Hospital and Community Psychiatry, 34*, 947–950.

Mosher, L. R. (1983c). Alternatives to psychiatric hospitalization: Why has research failed to be translated into practice? *New England Journal of Medicine, 309*, 1479–1480.

Mosher, L. R. (1986). The current status of the community support program: A personal assessment. *Psychosocial Rehabilitation Journal, 9*, 3–14.

Mosher, L. R. (in press). Community residential treatment: Alternatives to hospitalization. In A. Bellack (Ed.), *A clinical guide for the treatment of schizophrenia*. New York: Plenum Press.

Mosher, L. R., & Gunderson, J. G. (1979). Group, family, milieu and community support system treatment for schizophrenia. In L. Bellack (Ed.), *Disorders of the Schizophrenic Syndrome*. New York: Grune & Stratton.

Mosher, L. R., Kresky-Wolff, M., Matthews, S., & Menn, A. (1986). Milieu therapy in the 1980's: A comparison of two residential alternatives to hospitalization. *Bulletin of the Menninger Clinic, 50*, 257–268.

Mosher, L. R., & Menn, A. Z. (1977). Lowered barriers in the community: The Soteria model. In L. A. Stein, & M. A. Test (Eds.), *Alternatives to mental hospital treatment*. New York: Plenum Press.

Mosher, L. R., & Menn, A. Z. (1978). Community residential treatment for schizophrenia: Two-year follow-up. *Hospital and Community Psychiatry, 29*, 715–723.

Mosher, L., & Menn, A. (1979). Soteria: An alternative to hospitalization for schizophrenia. In H. R. Lamb (Ed.), *New directions for mental health services — Alternatives to acute hospitalization, 1*. San Francisco: Jossey-Bass.

Mosher, L. R., & Menn, A. (1983). Scientific evidence and system change: The Soteria experience. In H. Stierlin, L. Wynne, & M. Wirsching (Eds.), *Psychosocial interventions in schizophrenia*. Heidelberg: Springer-Verlag.

Mosher, L. R., Menn, A. Z., & Matthews, S. M. (1975). Evaluation of a home-based treatment for schizophrenia. *American Journal of Orthopsychiatry, 45*, 455–467.

Mosher, L. R., Vallone, R., & Menn, A. (1988). The Soteria project: new outcome data. Presented at "New Trends in Schizophrenia" International Conference. Bologna, Italy.

Mosher, L. R., Reifman, A., & Menn, A. (1973). Characteristics of nonprofessionals serving as primary therapists for acute schizophrenics. *Hospital and Community Psychiatry, 24*, 391–396.

Murphy, H. B. M., Engelsmann, F., & Tcheng-Laroche, F. (1976). The influence of foster home care on psychiatric patients. *Archives of General Psychiatry, 33*, 179–183.

Murphy, G. E., Simons, A. D., Wetzel, R. D., & Lustman, P. J. (1984). Cognitive therapy and pharmacotherapy: Singly and together in the treatment of depression. *Archives of General Psychiatry, 41*, 33–41.

National Institute of Mental Health, ADAMHA, DHHS (1987). Toward a model plan for a comprehensive community-based mental health system.

Niskanen, P., & Achte, K. A. (1972). *Course and prognosis of schizophrenic psychoses in Helsinki: A comparative study of first admissions in 1950, 1960, and 1965*. Monographs from the Psychiatric Clinic of the Helsinki University Central Hospital, No. 4.

New York City Human Resources Administration (1983). Report on the Borough of the Bronx. Mimeo.

Newton, P. (1973). Social structure and process in psychotherapy. A sociopsychological analysis of transference, resistance and change. *International Journal of Psychiatry, 11*, 480–526.

Ongaro-Basaglia F., and 10 co-sponsors (1987). Disegno di Legge: Provvedimenti per la programmazione, l'attuazione e il finanziamento dei servizi di salute mentale ad integrazione ed attuazione di quanto disposto dagli articoli f33, 34, 35 e 64 della legge 23 dicembre 1978, n. 833. *Atti Parlamentari, Senato della Repubblica, 2312*, 1–14.

Orndoff, C. R. (1975). Transitional housing. In J. Zusman, & E. F. Bertsch (Eds.), *The future role of the state hospital*. Lexington, MA: D. C. Heath.

Palazzoli, M. Selvini, Boscolo, L., Cecchin, G., & Prata, G. (1977). Family rituals: A powerful tool in family therapy. *Family Process, 16*, 445–453.

Palazzoli, M. Selvini, Boscolo, L., Cecchin, G., & Prata, G. (1978). *Paradox and counterparadox*. New York: Aronson.

Palazzoli, M. Selvini, Boscolo, L., Cecchin, G., & Prata, G. (1980). Hypothesizing-circularity-neutrality: Three guidelines for the conductor of the session. *Family Process, 19*, 3–12.

Pancheri, A. (1986). *L'urgenza psichiatrica nel dopo-riforma. Analisi degli interventi di crisi nel dipartimento di psichiatria di Portogruaro*. Unpublished doctoral dissertation, University of Verona, Italy.

Parks, S. H., & Pilisuk, M. (1984). Personal support systems of former mental patients residing in board-and-care facilities. *Journal of Community Psychology, 12*, 230–244.

Pasamanick, B., Scarpitti, F., & Dinitz, S. (1967). *Schizophrenics in the community. An experimental study in the prevention of hospitalization*. New York: Appleton-Century-Crofts.

Paul, G. L. (1969). The chronic mental patient: Current status-future directions. *Psychological Bulletin, 71*, 81–94.

Paul, G. L. (1978). The implementation of effective treatment programs for chronic mental patients: Obstacles and recommendations. In J. A. Talbott (Ed.), *The chronic mental patient*. Washington, DC: American Psychiatric Association.

Paul, G. L., & Lentz, R. J. (1977). *Psychosocial treatment of chronic mental patients: Milieu vs. social-learning programs*. Cambridge: Harvard University Press.

Paykel, E. S. (1978). Contribution of life events to the causation of psychiatric illness. *Psychological Medicine, 8*, 245–253.

Perrow, C. (1970). *Organizational analysis: A sociological view*. London: Tavistock Publications.

Perry, J. W. (1962). Reconstitutive process in the psychopathology of the self. *Annals of the New York Academy of Sciences, 96*, 853–876.

Phillips, L. (1966). Social competence, the process-reactive distinction and the nature of mental disorder. *Proceedings of American Psychopathology Association, 54*, 471–481.

Phoenix rising, ex-mental patient Newsletter, Box 7251, Sta. A, Toronto, Canada, Ontario, M5W 1X9.

Pilisuk, M., & Froland, C. (1978). Kinship, social networks, social support and health. *Social Science and Medicine, 12*, 273–280.

Pines, A., & Maslach, C. (1978). Characteristics of staff burnout in mental health settings. *Hospital and Community Psychiatry, 29*, 233–237.

Polak, P. R., & Kirby, M. W. (1976). A model to replace psychiatric hospitals. *Journal of Nervous and Mental Disease, 162*, 13–22.

Polak, P., Kirby, M., & Dietchman, W. (1979). Treating acutely psychiatric patients in private homes. In H. R. Lamb (Ed.), *New directions for mental health services—Alternatives to acute hospitalization, 1*. San Francisco: Jossey-Bass.

Potasnik, H., & Nelson, G. (1984). Stress and social support: The burden experienced by the family of a mentally ill person. *American Journal of Community Psychology, 12*, 589–607.

Pratt, M. W., Luszcz, M. A., & Brown, M. E. (1980). Measuring dimensions of the quality of care in small community settings. *American Journal of Mental Deficiency, 85*, 188–194.

Prien, R., Kupfer, D., Mansky, P., Small, J., Tuason, V., Voss, C., & Johnson, W. (1984). Drug therapy in the prevention of recurrences in unipolar and bipolar affective disorders. *Archives of General Psychiatry, 41*, 1096–1104.

Purnell, T. L., Sachson, S. M., & Wallace, E. C. (1982). A quarterway house program for hospitalized chronic patients. *Hospital and Community Psychiatry, 33*, 941–942.

Rabkin, J. G., & Struening, E. L. (1976). Life events, stress and disease. *Science, 194*, 1413–1420.

Ramon, S. (1982). The Italian job. *Social Work Today, 14*, 5.

Randolph, F., Lanx, R., & Carling, P. G. (1988). *In search of housing: Creative approaches to financing integrated housing.* Burlington, VT: The Center for Change.

Rappaport, M., Goldman, H., Thorton, P., Moltzen, S., Stegner, B., Hall, K., Gurevitz, H., & Attkisson, C. C. (1987). A method for comparing two systems of acute 24-hour psychiatric care. *Hospital and Community Psychiatry, 38*, 1091–1095.

Rausch, H. L., & Rausch, C. L. (1968). *The halfway house movement: A search for sanity.* New York: Appleton-Century-Crofts.

Report on Bronx Community District #4, New York City Human Resources Adminstration, 1983.

Reynolds, I., & Hoult, J. E. (1984). The relatives of the mentally ill: A comparative trial of community-oriented and hospital-oriented psychiatric care. *Journal of Nervous and Mental Disease, 172*, 480–489.

Rifkin, A., Quitkin, F., Rabiner, C., & Klein, D. F. (1977). Fluphenazine decoanoate, fluphenazine hydrocholoride given orally, and placebo in remitted schizophrenics. I. Relapse rates after one year. *Archives of General Psychiatry, 34*, 43–47.

Rogers, C. R. (1957). The necessary and sufficient conditions of therapeutic personality change. *Journal of Consultative Clinical Psychology, 51*, 557–564.

Rose, S. M. (1985). *Advocacy and empowerment: Mental health care in the community.* Boston: Routledge and Kegan Paul.

Rosen, B., Klein, D., & Gittelman-Klein, R. (1971). The prediction of rehospitalization: The relationship between age of first psychiatric treatment contact, marital status and premorbid asocial adjustment. *Journal of Nervous and Mental Disease, 152*, 17–22.

Rothman, D. (1971). *The discovery of the asylum: Social order and disorder in the new republic.* Boston: Little, Brown.

Rothman, D. (1980). *Conscience and convenience: The asylum and its alternatives in progressive America.* Boston: Little, Brown.

Rothman, D. J., & Rothman, S. M. (1984). *The Willowbrook wars: Decade of struggle for social justice.* New York: Harper & Row.

Rothwell, N. D., & Doniger, J. M. (1966). *The psychiatric halfway house: A case study.* Springfield: Charles C. Thomas.

Rueveni, J. (1977). Family network intervention: Mobilizing support for families in crisis. *International Journal of Family Counseling, 5*, 77–83.

Sabshin, M. (1966). Theoretical models in community and social psychiatry. In L. M. Roberts, S. L. Halleck, & M. B. Loeb (Eds.), *Community psychiatry.* Madison, WI: University of Wisconsin Press.

Schaffer, N. D. (1982). Multidimensional measures of therapist behavior as predictors of outcome. *Psychological Bulletin, 92*, 670–681.

Schaffer, N. D. (1983a). Methodological issues of measuring the skillfullness of therapeutic techniques. *Psychotherapy Theory, Research and Practice, 20*, 486–493.

Schaffer, N. D. (1983b). The utility of measuring the skillfullness of therapeutic techniques. *Psychotherapy Theory, Research and Practice, 20*, 330–336.

Scheper-Hughes, N., & Lovell, A. M. (Eds.). (1987). *Psychiatry inside out. Selected writings of Franco Basaglia.* New York: Columbia University Press.

Schittar, L. (1968). L'ideologia della comunità terapeutica. In F. Basaglia (Ed.), *L'Istituzione Negata.* Torino: Einaudi.

Schoenfeld, P., Halvey, J., Hemley-van der Velden, E., & Ruhf, L. (1986). Long-Term Outcome of Network Therapy. *Hospital and Community Psychiatry, 37*, 373–376.

Schumacher, E. F. (1973). *Small is Beautiful.* New York: Harper & Row.

Schwartz, C., & Myers, J. K. (1977). Life events and schizophrenia: parts I and II. *Archives of General Psychiatry, 34*, 1238–1248.

Segal, S. P., Baumohl, J., & Moyles, E. W. (1980). Neighborhood types and community reaction to the mentally ill: A paradox of intensity. *Journal of Health and Social Behavior, 21*, 345–359.

Semrad, E. V. (1966). Long-term therapy of schizophrenia: Formulation of the clinical approach. In G. L. Wilson (Ed.), *Psychoneurosis and schizophrenia*. Philadelphia: Lippincott.

Semrad, E. V., & Zaslow, S. L. (1964). Assisting psychotic patients to recompensate. *Mental Hospital, July*, 361–366.

Serban, G. (Ed.). (1977). *New trends of psychiatry in the community*. Cambridge: Ballinger.

Simon, R. (1986). Across the Great Divide. *The Family Therapy Networker*, January–February, 21–30/74.

Sinnett, E. R., & Sachson, A. D. (1970). *Transitional facilities in the rehabilitation of the emotionally disturbed*. Lawrence: University Press of Kansas.

Slavich, A. (1987). Personal communication.

Solomon, P., & Davis, J. M. (1984). Community attitudes toward residential facilities for psychiatric patients. *Psychosocial Rehabilitation Journal, 8*, 38–41.

Sonkin, D. S., & Durphy, M. (1985). *Learning to live without violence: A handbook for men*. San Francisco: Volcano Press.

Soskis, D. A., & Bowers, M. B. (1969). The schizophrenic experience: A follow-up study of attitude and post hospital adjustment. *Journal of Nervous and Mental Disease, 149*, 443–449.

Soteria (1972). A Manual. Unpublished manuscript, Soteria staff.

Spivak, M. (1974). A conceptual framework for structuring the housing of psychiatric patients in the community. *Community Mental Health Journal, 10*, 345–350.

Srole, L., Langner, T. S., Michael, S. T., Opler, M. K., & Rennie, T. A. C. (1962). *Mental health in the metropolis: The midtown manhattan study*. New York: McGraw-Hill.

Stein, L. I. & Test, M. A. (1978a). An alternative to mental hospital treatment. In L. I. Stein & M. A. Test (Eds.), *Alternatives to mental hospital treatment*. New York: Plenum Press.

Stein, L. I., & Test, M. A. (Eds.). (1978b). *Alternatives to mental hospital treatment*. New York: Plenum Press.

Stein, L. I., & Test, M. A. (Eds.). (1985). *Training in the community living model—a decade of experience. New Directions for Mental Health Services, no. 26*. San Francisco: Jossey-Bass.

Steinberg, H. R., & Durrell, J. (1968). A stressful social situation as a precipitant of schizophrenic symptoms: An epidemiological study. *British Journal of Psychiatry, 114*, 1097–1105.

Stern, R., & Minkoff, K. (1979). Paradoxes in programming for chronic patients in a community clinic. *Hospital and Community Psychiatry, 30*, 613–617.

Straw, R. B. (1982). *Meta-analysis of deinstitutionalization*. (Doctoral dissertation). Ann Arbor, MI: Northwestern University.

Stroul, B. A. (1986). *Models of community support services: Approaches to helping persons with long-term mental illness*. National Institute of Mental Health, Community Support Program.

Stroul, B. A. (1987). *Crisis residential services in a community support system*. Report prepared for National Institute of Mental Health Community Support Program.

Struening, E. L. (1986). *A study of residents of the New York City shelter system: Report to the New York City Department of Mental Health, Mental Retardation, and Alcoholism Services*. New York, New York State Psychiatric Institute, Epidemiology of Mental Disorders Research Department.

Strupp, H. H. (1973). On the basic ingredients of psychotherapy. *Journal of Consulting and Clinical Psychology, 41*, 1–8.

Strupp, H. H., Hadley, S. W., & Gomes-Schwartz, B. (1977). *Psychotherapy for better or worse: The problem of negative effects*. New York: Jason Aronson.

Sturt, E., Wykes, T., & Creer, C. (1982). Demographic, social and clinical characteristics of the sample. In J. K. Wing (Ed.), *Long-term community care: Experience in a London borough*. Psychological Medicine Monograph Supplement 2, 5–14.

Sullivan, H. S. (1931). The modified psychoanalytic treatment of schizophrenia. *American Journal of Psychiatry, 11*, 519–540.

Sullivan, H. S. (1970). *The psychiatric interview*. New York: W. W. Norton.

Susser, E., & Struening, E. L. (1987). *First time users of the New York City shelter system: Report to the New York City Department of Mental Health, Mental Retardation, and Alcoholism Services*. New York, New York Psychiatric Institute, Epidemiology of Mental Disorders Research Department.

Tansella, M. (in press a). L'uso di un sistema informativo locale per il monitoraggio dei servizi di salute mentale e la ricerca epidemiologica. *Rivista Sperimentale di Freniatria III*, 688–705.

Tansella, M. (in press b). Evaluating community psychiatric services. In P. Williams, G. Wilkinson, & K. Rawnsley (Eds.), *The scope of epidemiological psychiatry*. London: Tavistock Publications.

Tansella, M., Balestrieri, M., & Meneghelli, G. (1979–1987). *Statistics from the South-Verona psychiatric case register*. Cattedra e Servizio di Psicologia Medica Istituto di Psichiatria. Unpublished annual reports, Universit di Verona, Italy.

Tansella, M., & De Salvia, D. (1986). Case registers in comprehensive community psychiatric service areas in Italy. In G. H. M. M. ten Horn, R. Giel, W. H. Gulbinat, & J. H. Henderson (Eds.), *Psychiatric case registers in public health. A worldwide inventory. 1960–1985*. Amsterdam: Elsevier.

Tansella, M., De Salvia, D., & Williams, P. (1987). The Italian psychiatric reform: Some quantitative evidence. *Social Psychiatry, 22*, 37–48.

Tansella, M., Faccincani, C., Mignolli, G., Balestrieri, M., & Zimmermann-Tansella, Ch. (1985). Il registro psichiatrico di Verona-Sud. Epidemiologia per la valutazione dei nuovi servizi territoriali. In M. Tansella (Ed.), *L'approccio Epidemiologico in Psichiatria*. Milano: Boringhieri.

Tansella, M., & Siciliani, O. (1979). I primi sei mesi di applicazione della legge di riforma dell'assistenza psichiatrica nel consorzio Verona-Sud. *Fogli d'Informazione, 59-60-61*, 442–448.

Tansella, M., & Williams, P. (1987). The Italian experience and its implications. *Psychological Medicine, 17*, 283–289.

Task Force on Community Mental Health Program Components (May, 1975). *Developing community mental health programs: A resource manual*. Boston: United Community Planning Corporation and Massachusetts Department of Mental Health.

ten Horn, G. H. M. M. (1980). Register study: A small cohort of multiple service users from a geographically delimited area. *Acta Psychiatrica Scandinavica Suppl. 285*. Copenhagen: Munksgaard, 305–314.

ten Horn, G. H. M. M., Giel, R., Gulbinat, W., & Henderson, J. (Eds.). (1986). *Psychiatric case registers 1960-1985*. Amsterdam: Elsevier.

Test, M. A., & Stein, L. I. (1978a). Community treatment of the chronic patient: Research overview. *Schizophrenia Bulletin, 4*, 350–364.

Test, M. A., & Stein, L. I. (1978b). Training in community living: Research design and results. In L. I. Stein & M. A. Test (Eds.), *Alternatives to mental hospital treatment*. New York: Plenum Press.

Test, M., & Stein, L. I. (1978c). The clinical rationale for community treatment: A review of the literature. In L. I. Stein, & M. A. Test (Eds.), *Alternatives to mental hospital treatment*. New York: Plenum Press.

Torre, E., & Marinoni, A. (1985). Register studies: Data from four areas in Northern Italy. *Acta Psychiatrica Scandinavica, Suppl., 316*, 87–94.

Torrey, E. F. (1983). *Surviving schizophrenia: A family manual*. New York: Harper & Row.

Torrey, E. F., & Wolfe, S. (1986). *Care of the seriously mentally ill: A rating of state programs*. Washington, DC: Public Citizen Health Research Group.

Turner, J. C., & TenHoor, W. J. (1978). The NIMH community support program: Pilot approach to a needed social reform. *Schizophrenia Bulletin, 4*, 319–348.

Vandenbos, G. R., & Karon, B. P. (1971). Pathogenesis: A new therapist personality dimension related to therapeutic effectiveness. *Journal Personality Assessment, 35*, 252–260.

Vaughn, C., Snyder, K., Jones, S., Freeman, M., & Falloon, I. (1984). Family factors in schizophrenic relapse. *Archives of General Psychiatry, 41*, 1169–1177.

Verga, A. (1852). Prefazione, In Gazzetta Medical Italiana-Lombarda-Appendice Psichiatrica, No. 33t.

Verga, A. (1897). *Studi Anatomica sul Cranio e sull'Encefalo, Psicologici e Freniatrici. Vol. 2.* Milano: Manini-Wijet.

Wadsworth, W. V., Wells, B. W. P., & Scott, R. F. (1962). The organization of a sheltered workshop. *Journal of Mental Science, 108*, 780–785.

Walsh, M. (1985). *Schizophrenia: Straight talk for families and friends.* San Francisco: Warner Books.

Wansbrough, N., & Miles, A. (1968). *Industrial therapy in psychiatric hospitals.* London: Kings Fund.

Warner, R. (1985). *Recovery from schizophrenia: Psychiatry and the Political Economy.* Boston: Routledge and Kegan Paul.

Washburn, S., Vannicelli, M., Longabaugh, R., & Scheff, B. J. (1976). A controlled comparison of psychiatric day treatment and inpatient hospitalization. *Journal of Consulting and Clinical Psychology, 44*, 665–678.

Watkins, C. E. (1983). Burnout in counselling practice. Some potential professional and personal hazards of becoming a counselor. *Personnel and Guidance Journal, 61*, 304–308.

Weinman, B., Kleiner, R., Yu, J. H., & Tillson, V. A. (1974). Social treatment of the chronic psychotic patient in the community. *Journal of Community Psychology, 2*, 358–365.

Weisman, G. (1985a). Crisis houses and lodges: Residential treatment of acutely disturbed chronic patients. *Psychiatric Annals, 15*, 642–644, 647.

Weisman, G. (1985b). Crisis-oriented residential treatment as an alternative to hospitalization. *Hospital and Community Psychiatry, 36*, 1302–1305.

Wendt, R. J., Mosher, L. R., Matthews, S. M., & Menn, A. Z. (1983). Comparison of two treatment environments for schizophrenia. In J. G. Gunderson, O. A. Will, & L. R. Mosher (Eds.), *Principles and practices of milieu therapy.* New York: Jason Aronson.

Weston, W. D. (1975). Development of community psychiatry concepts. In A. M. Freedman, H. I. Kaplan, & B. J. Sadock (Eds.), *Comprehensive textbook of psychiatry – II.* Baltimore: William & Wilkins.

Wilder, J., Levin, G., & Zwerling, I. (1966). A two-year follow-up evaluation of acute psychiatric patients treated in a day hospital. *American Journal of Psychiatry, 122*, 1095–1101.

Williams, P., De Salvia, D., & Tansella, M. (1986). Suicide, psychiatric reform, and the provision of psychiatric services in Italy. *Social Psychiatry, 21*, 89–95.

Wilson, H. S. (1983). Usual Hospital Treatment in the USA's Community Mental Health System. International Journal of Nursing Studies, 20, 75–82.

Wing, J. K., & Brown, G. W. (1970). *Institutionalism and schizophrenia: A comparative study of three mental hospitals 1960–1968.* Cambridge: Cambridge University Press.

Wing, J. K., & Fryers, T. (1976). *Psychiatric services in Camberwell and Salford: Statistics from the Camberwell and Salford psychiatric registers 1964–74.* MRC Social Psychiatry Unit, Institute of Psychiatry, London, and Department of Community Medicine, University of Manchester.

Wing, L., Wing, J. K., Hailey, A., Bahn, A. K., Smith, H. E., & Baldwin, J. A. (1967). The use of psychiatric services in three urban areas: An international case register study. *Social Psychiatry, 2*, 158–167.

Wisconsin Department of Health and Social Services, Division of Community Services, Department of Mental Health (1985). Human resources utilization in community support programs: Case studies of three Wisconsin Programs.

Wolfensberger, W. (1970). The principle of normalization and its implications to psychiatric services. *American Journal of Psychiatry, 127*, 291–297.

Wolfensberger, W. (1972). *The principle of normalization in human services.* Toronto: National Institute on Mental Retardation.

Wolfensberger, W. (1979). The case against the use of the term "disability". *Rehabilitation Literature, 40*, 309.

Wolfensberger, W. (1983). Social role valorization: A proposed new term for the principle of normalization. *Mental Retardation, 21*, 234–239.

World Health Organization (1978). Mental disorders: Glossary and guide to their classification in accordance with the Ninth Revision of the International Classification of Diseases. Geneva: World Health Organization.

Wykes, T., & Wing, J. K. (1982). A ward in a house: Accommodation for "new" long-stay patients. *Acta Psychiatrica Scandinavica, 65*, 315–330.

Wynne, L. C., McDaniel, S. H., & Weber, T. T. (Eds.). (1986). *Systems consultation: A new perspective for family therapy.* New York: Guilford Press.

Zimmermann-Tansella, Ch., Burti, L., Faccincani, C., Garzotto, N., Siciliani, O., & Tansella, M. (1985). Bringing into action the psychiatric reform in South-Verona. A five year experience. *Acta Psychiatrica Scandinavica, Suppl. 316*, 71–86.

Zinman, S. (1986). Self-help: The wave of the future. *Hospital and Community Psychiatry, 37*, 213.

Zinman, S., Harp, H., & Budd, T. (Eds.). (1987). *Reaching across: Mental health clients helping each other*, California Network of Mental Health Clients.

Zusman, J., & Lamb, H. R. (1977). In defense of community mental health. *American Journal of Psychiatry, 134*, 887–890.

Zwelling, S. (1985). *Quest for a cure.* Williamsburg, VA: The Colonial Williamsburg Foundation.

Zwerling, I., & Wilder, J. F. (1964). An evaluation of the applicability of the day hospital in treatment of acutely disturbed patients. *Israel Annals of Psychiatry, 2*, 162–185.

Index